T0238418

Design Issues for Service Delivery Platforms

Martin Bergaus

Design Issues for Service Delivery Platforms

Incorporate User Experience:
A Grounded Theory Study of
Individual User Needs

With a Preface by Prof. Dr. Reinhold Behringer

 Springer Vieweg

Dr. Martin Bergaus
Leeds, UK

Leeds, Leeds Beckett University, PhD Thesis, 2013

ISBN 978-3-658-10540-2   ISBN 978-3-658-10541-9 (eBook)
DOI 10.1007/978-3-658-10541-9

Library of Congress Control Number: 2015942923

Springer Vieweg
© Springer Fachmedien Wiesbaden 2015

Printed on acid-free paper

Springer Vieweg is a brand of Springer Fachmedien Wiesbaden
Springer Fachmedien Wiesbaden is part of Springer Science+Business Media
(www.springer.com)

Preface

Service delivery platforms (SDPs) play an important role in the evolving ubiquitous online mobile connectivity. Data rates and available bandwidth have increased dramatically with the introduction of new generation mobile networks (4G) and are set to increase further with new developments of 5G networks. This enables new mobile services such as video on demand and cloud-based services such as Software as a Service (SaaS). However, mobile bandwidth will always been limited at any single network node, due to physical limitations of wireless connectivity of simultaneous connections. Therefore, measures need to be taken to ensure efficient use of the available bandwidth.

The SPICE project (Service Platform for Innovative Communication Environment), funded by the European Commission in the Framework Programme 6 during 2006-2008, has addressed several of the issues of such SDPs and has contributed to technological improvements of service platform functionality and security. But this has been done mainly from a technology and engineering perspective. What has not been sufficiently investigated were issues related to users and stakeholders of such SDPs.

This book addresses this gap by investigating the user needs related to SDPs. The author has investigated the user requirements of those stakeholders from developers to end users and has developed guidelines for the development of future SDPs. These guidelines have been validated through scientific methods in real-world scenarios, where significant improvements in usability could be observed. Therefore, this book is a MUST-READ for system architects and software developers who are designing and implementing new SDPs. The content of this book will help improving the usability of future SDPs.

Leeds, Reinhold Behringer
Professor of Creative Technology
Leeds Beckett University

Dedication

I would like to dedicate this dissertation to my family and friends, in gratitude to their collective efforts in providing me with invaluable advice, encouragement and wisdom, whilst allowing me space for my own explorations.

I particularly dedicate this thesis to my parents, who have given me all their love, support and understanding. Without them I could not have accomplished the following. Their knowledge of the value of education is truly beyond my comprehension and I am a lucky beneficiary.

Moreover, I dedicate this work to my deceased best friends Johannes Beiglböck and Harald Hörl, who inspired me with their energy and friendship, and who helped me to learn about life and the knowledge how to live a good one. In memory of the comfort and advice they gave me in the past, whenever I needed them.

Vienna, Martin Bergaus

Acknowledgement

The author is thankful to his colleagues for their input and responses to certain ideas, presented in this thesis. I would like to thank the many people who provided support and encouragement throughout the undertaking of this conceptual work.

Firstly, I would like to thank my supervisors Reinhold Behringer and Andrea Gorra and my director of studies Colin Pattinson, for their excellent guidance and support during the research project, and for the opportunity I have had to carry this work out at the Faculty of Arts, Environment and Technology. Thank you very much.

Furthermore, my thanks go to Peter Baumgartner, Erwin Bratengeyer and Johann Götschl in particular, for the initiation of the research program at the Danube University in Krems (Austria), for the many constructive discussions, and for their support. Thanks a lot.

Particular thanks go to Alexander Seewald and Antony Bryant for their contribution of additional information and suggestions, as well as for their readiness to discuss research-related topics, quality evaluation and problems that arose during this study. Thank you very much.

Additionally, I would like say "thank you" to my colleague and friend Bernd Stottok for the extremely helpful discussions we had during the entire research procedure, as well as for his readiness to discuss topics and challenges arising during this investigation.

Last but not least, my friends Petra Bacher, Julius Eiweck and Monika Andergassen, who have shared their caring thoughts with me throughout my research over the last years. Also to my friends Nina Fieber, Susanna Wing, Paul Talbot, and Maria Lambrakis, who checked my work in terms of content and linguistics and supported me with their feedback. Many thanks.

Vienna, Martin Bergaus

Acknowledgement

The author of the MBA thesis/document...

Table of Contents

Table of Figures

Table of Tables

Table of Memos

Index of Abbreviations and Glossary of Terms

Abbreviation	Explanation
1G	First generation of wireless telephone technology; an analogue telecommunication standard using analogue radio signals.
2G	Second generation of wireless telephone technology; a digital telecommunication standard using digital radio signals; Global System for Mobile Communications (GSM) standard, with introduced data services.
2.5G	Second generation of enhanced wireless telephone technology; enables high speed data transfer over upgraded existing 2G networks; High-Speed Circuit Switched Data (HSCSD), General Packet Radio Service (GPRS) or Code Division Multiple Access (CDMA) technology.
3G	Third generation of wireless telephone technology; IMT-2000 family – a generation of standards for mobile telecommunications services, that must allow the simultaneous use of speech and data services; provide peak data rates of at least 200 kbit/s according to IMT-2000 specification; for example mobile internet access, video calls and mobile TV; W-CDMA technology.
3GPP	3rd Generation Partnership Project, worldwide cooperation of standard setting bodies, for the standardising of UMTS (Universal Mobile Telecommunication System) and GSM (Global System for Mobile Communications) technology.
4G	Fourth generation of wireless telephone technology; includes all-IP packet-switched networks, mobile broadband access, and multi-carrier transmission; mobile Worldwide Interoperability for Microwave Access (WiMAX) and Long-Term Evolution (LTE).
AAA	Authentication, Authorisation, Accounting, network service for recognising users, awarding access rights and charging features.
AD-HOC ROUTING	Term for the radio networks, which connect several terminals to an interconnected network, which can be configured by a mobile ad-hoc network. Special routing procedures provide for the fact, that the existing ad-hoc network continuously adapts itself if nodes (end devices) move, appear or fall out.

API	Application Programme Interface is a specification, intended to be used as an interface, by software components to communicate with each other. An API includes different specifications for routines, data structures, object classes and variables.
AMBIENT INTELLIGENCE	Highly specified sensors for radio networks and mini computers in used applications and services. These objects around communication ability serve to enhance people's everyday lives. A sensor in the office ascertains when the temperature is too high (air-conditioning is switched on), or too low (heating is switched on).
AUC	Authentication Centre is a function to authenticate each Subscriber Identity Module (SIM) that attempts to connect to the GSM core network when the mobile phone is switched on.
B3G	Beyond 3rd Generation, is the fourth generation (4G) of cell phone mobile communications standards; provides mobile ultra-broadband internet access; conceivable applications include amended mobile web access, IT telephony, gaming services, high-definition mobile TV, video conferencing and 3D television.
BLUETOOTH	An open wireless technology standard, which facilitates the exchange of data over short distances, from wired and mobile devices, creating personal area networks with high levels of security.
BSC	Base Station Controller is part of a traditional cellular telephone network that is responsible for handling traffic and signalling between a mobile phone and the network switching subsystem.
BSS	Business Support Systems; support business processes within a company; used to manage contract relations with customers easier, suppliers and partners as well as the management of products and resources.
BTS	Base Transceiver Station is a piece of equipment that facilitates wireless communication between user end devices and a network.
CAMEL	Customised Applications for Mobile Network Enhanced Logic, a standard for mobile communication networks, initiated by the European Institute for Telecommunication norms, expanded service offers in UMTS.
CDM	Code Division Multiplexing is a channel access method used by various radio communication technologies (see also CDMA2000).

CDMA2000	Mobile technology standard developed in the mid 1990s; is the competitor of UMTS. This is not represented in Europe, but in America (the USA, South America), parts of Asia (Japan, Korea) and also parts of Africa. CDMA2000 standard also based on the CDMA procedure (Code Division Multiple Access), but not compatible with it.
CELLULAR IP	This is a network protocol standard, makes routing functionality available for mobile participants in IP networks.
CIT	Critical Incident Technique is a procedure that was developed originally as an observation method to uncover critical incidents concerning situative conditions and involved or following reactions. Besides this, there are data from observations to uncover relevant or critical incidents.
CLOUD COMPUTING	Cloud Computing allows suppliers to provide computer performance, storage space and software licences for abstracted, highly scalable and administered IT infrastructure. This will enable users in the future, whether private or commercial, to operate anywhere from low-performance, low-storage-capacity machines, providing they have a reliable internet connection.
CONTEXT AWARENESS	Software technology concept; can change its structure, functionality and behaviour to adapt itself to different situations according to the end device being used. Context-Awareness uses information to tune the behaviour to it. Nowadays context adaptation has to be discussed, as a key requirement for future mobile and ubiquitous systems.
DCSM	Distributed Communication Sphere: communication working field in SPICE.
DIAMETER	Diameter is an authentication, authorisation and accounting protocol, for the authentication of communication partners on a network. The diameter protocol is defined in the RFC 3588, and fulfils the requirements of the AAA transport profile "Authentication, Authorisation, Accounting", from RFC 3539. Diameter is used in the IP Multimedia Subsystem.
DHCP	Dynamic Host Configuration Protocol is a network protocol that is used, to configure network devices for communicating within IP networks: A DHCP client acquires an IP address, a default route and one or more DNS server addresses from a DHCP server. This information is used for configuring its host. The host is able to communicate on the internet.

DNS	Domain Name Server is a hierarchical distributed naming system for computers, services, or any resource connected to the Internet, or a private network.
DSP	Digital Signal Processing is the manipulation of an information signal in order to modify it mathematically in a certain way; it is characterised by the representation of discrete time and discrete frequency.
EDGE	Enhanced Data Rates for GSM Evolution; further development of GPRS or HSCSD, developed to increase data transfer rates by means of new modulation procedures; in comparison to GSM (GMSK), EDGE uses 8-phase Shift Keying (8-PSK) modulation; data rate of 59.2 kBit/s possible, maximum theoretical transfer rate 473 kBit/s, in practice maximum 220 kBit/s download and 110 kBit/s upload.
EIR	Equipment Identifier Register maintains a list of mobile phones that are identified by their International Mobile Equipment Identity (IMEI) which are to be banned from the network or monitored. It is often integrated in the Home Location Register (HLR).
EPC	Evolved Packet Core is the main component of the System Architecture Evolution (SAE). EPC serves as equivalent of GPRS networks via the Mobility Management Entity, Serving Gateway and PDN Gateway subcomponents.
E-UTRAN	Evolved UMTS Terrestrial Radio Access Network, a mobile radio standard, which was defined as UMTS's UTRAN successor, within the scope of 3GPP.
FDD	Frequency Division Duplexing means that the transmitter and receiver operate at different carrier frequencies. The station must be able to send and receive a transmission at the same time, and does so by slightly altering the frequency at which it sends and receives.
FDM	Frequency Division Multiplexing is a technique in which the total bandwidth available in a communication medium is divided into a series of non-overlapping frequency sub-bands, each of which is used to carry a separate signal.
GALILEO	European, open, global, and independent positioning system, which is intended to be compatible with other navigation systems such as GPS.
GERAN	GSM EDGE Radio Access Network, Radio Access Network for GSM/EDGE Standard.

GGSN	Gateway GPRS Support Node, Crossing of the GPRS net in a public Data Network (PDN) or Packing Data Network.
GMSC	Gateway Mobile Switching Centre, Interfaces with other telephone networks.
GPS	Global Positioning System (NAVSTAR GPS); is a space-based worldwide navigation satellite system, which provides reliable location and time information, regardless of weather conditions, at all times and anywhere on or near the earth; developed in the 1980s; initially launched by the United States Department of Defense. It orbits the Earth and makes it possible to pinpoint geographic location - location accuracy ranges from 10m to 100m - nowadays it is both a military and commercial programme.
GPRS	General Packet Radio Service is a packet-oriented mobile data service, developed around higher data rates. It is packet-oriented and uses the same channels as GSM, with theoretical data rate of maximum 171.2 kBit/s - all 8 channels are bundled up. Maximum practical speed 115 kBit/s; available to users of 2G cellular communication systems, GSM as well as 3G systems; a 2.5G mobile standard, typically adopted by GSM operators as a migration step towards 3G.
GSM	Global System for Mobile Communications is, a European-developed digital mobile cellular standard which allows for international roaming arrangements between mobile operators, whilst providing subscribers with the possibility of using their phones in many parts of the world. It is used primarily for telephony, for management-provided and package-provided data transfer, as well as short communication, and was developed at the beginning of the 1980s. It is used in more than 200 countries and has approximately 3.4 billion users. It is compatible with ISDN or other analogue telephone networks and uses frequency carriers of 900 MHz to 1800 MHz; low speed rate of 9.6 kBit/s to 14.4 kBit/s.
GTM	Grounded Theory Methodology: research methodology focusing on an inductive research approach.

HANDOVER	The process of transferring an ongoing call or data session from one channel, connected to the core network, to another channel. It is a process with which the Mobile Switching Centre (MSC) passes a mobile phone conversation from a radio frequency in one cell to another radio frequency in another, as a subscriber crosses the boundary of a cell. For example - the mobile station changes its radio cell from GSM to UMTS base stations during a conversation, or a data connection, without interruption to the connection.
HCI	Human Computer Interaction involves the study, planning, and design of the interaction between people and computers.
HDTV	High-definition Television provides a resolution that is substantially higher than that of standard-definition television.
HFC	Hybrid Fibre Coax is a telecommunication industry term, for a broadband network, that combines optical fibre and coaxial cable.
HLR	Home Location Register is a central database that contains details of each mobile phone subscriber that is authorised to use the GSM core network.
HSCSD	High-Speed Circuit Switched Data is an enlargement of the GSM standard, used to speed up data transfer by the grouping together of several data channels. Besides this, data transfer rates, up to about 115.2 kbit/s (8×14.4 kbit/s), can be theoretically reached; through changes in the existing GSM infrastructure it is possible for the data rate to be increased by transference.
HSPA	High-Speed Packet Access, further development of (3.5G) UMTS, which is separated in HSDPA (High-Speed Downlink Packet Access) and HSUPA (High-Speed Upload Packet Access). Purpose: higher download speeds (2 MBit/s).
HSDPA	High-Speed Downlink Packing Access, data transfer procedures of the mobile radio standard UMTS, protocol allows for the increase of the data rates in a UMTS network.
HSUPA	High Speed Uplink Packing Access, data transfer procedures of the mobile radio standard UMTS. Protocol allows for an increase of the data rates in a UMTS network.
HTTP	Hypertext Transfer Protocol: a standard transport protocol for transferring 'web pages' from one machine to another.

ICT	Information and Communications Technology: ICT consists of IT, as well as telecommunication, broadcast media (all types of audio and video processing and transmission) and network based control and monitoring functions; often used as extended synonym for IT, but also to stress the role of unified communications and the integration of telecommunications (telephone lines and wireless signals), computers, middleware and software, storage, and audio-visual systems, which enables users to create, access, store, transmit, and manipulate information.
IP	Internet Protocol Address. A numeric value that serves to identify an interface that is connected to the Internet, in a unique way.
IMEI	International Mobile Equipment Identity. Unique serial number used for mobile phones, typically those connected to the GSM network.
IMS	IP (Internet Protocol) Multimedia Subsystem, collection of specifications of 3rd generation Partnership Project (3GPP), the aim of IMS is to enable access to the services of different networks.
IMSI	International Mobile Subscriber Identity, a unique number that is associated with all GSM and Universal Mobile Telecommunications System network mobile phone users. The number is stored in the Subscriber Identity Module (SIM).
ISC	International Switching Centre is a 3G core network element such as a Mobile Switching Centre (MSC) that controls the network switching subsystem elements on an international level.
ISDN	Integrated Services Digital Network. A digital switched network, which supports the transmission of voice, data and images, over conventional telephone lines.
IST FP6	Information Society Technologies aims to increase innovation and competitiveness in European businesses and industry; Framework Programme six.
ITU	International Telecommunication Union; the United Nations specialised agency for telecommunications. http://www.itu.int/
LBS	Location-based Services are mobile services that can provide information to the end user, by aid of data, dependent on position (e.g., data from the GPS-position regulation), and produce services of other kinds, for example, advertising services.

LDAP	Lightweight Directory Access Protocol is an application protocol for the access and the maintenance of distributed directory information services over an IP network.
LTE	Long Term Evolution, is a standard for wireless communication of high-speed data for mobile phones and end devices developed by 3GPP; based on GSM/EDGE and UMTS/HSPA network technologies with increased capacity and speed, using new modulation techniques.
M-COMMERCE	Mobile Commerce is similar to e-commerce, however the term is usually applied to the emerging transaction activity in mobile networks.
MGW	Media Gateway, Benefit data-transferring Authority on a UMTS network.
MMS	Multimedia Messaging Service provides more sophisticated mobile messaging than SMS. A global standard for messaging, MMS enables users to send and receive messages with formatted text, graphics, audio and video clips. Unlike SMS, it is not limited to 160 characters per message.
MOBILE IP	A network protocol standard that allows the change of a computer network to another network, whereby users of mobile terminals keep a firm IP address alongside, at the same time.
MS	Mobile Station or mobile telephone.
MSC	Mobile Switching Centre, mobile full-digital agency on the mobile radio network, component of GSM, UMTS or Long-Term Evolution (LTE) of mobile radio networks.
NFC	Near Field Communication: a set of standards for Smartphones and end devices for establishing radio communication with each other by linking them together, usually no more than a few centimetres; present and anticipated applications include contactless transactions, data exchange, and simplified setup of more complex communications such as Wi-Fi.
NGN	Next Generation Networks: one telecommunication network that transports all information and services (voice, data, media and video) by encapsulating these into IP packets.
NUDIST	Non Numerical Unstructured Data Indexing Searching and Theorizing: software product from QSR international which helps with the undertaking of qualitative research and is especially useful when a researcher is working with large amounts of data. It helps to structure the researchers' data in order to interpret it.

NVIVO	Is a data analysis software product from QSR international, designed for qualitative research by working on very rich text-based and/or multimedia information where deep levels of analysis of small, or large, volumes of data is required.
OMC	Operation and Maintenance Centre; company and servicing headquarters for telecommunication networks.
OMSS	Operation and Maintenance Sub-System, part of the Mobile Switching Centre.
OSI	Open Systems Interconnection, is an effort to standardize networking; started in 1977.
OSS	Operations Support System, Company Support System, Network Management System that supports automated service processes.
PAM	Pluggable Authentication of Module, is a mechanism for integrating multiple low-level authentication schemes into a high-level application-programming interface (API). It allows programs that rely on authentication to be written independently of the underlying authentication scheme.
PAN	Personal Area Network is a computer network implemented for the communication among computers and mobile end devices.
PDA	Personal Digital Assistant is a generic term for handheld devices that combine computing and communication functions.
PSTN	Public Switched Telephone Network, totality of all public management-engaged telephone networks.
QoS	Quality of Services refers to network traffic resource reservations and control mechanisms in computer environments.
RFID	Radio-frequency Identification is used for wireless non-contact systems, that use electromagnetic fields to transfer data from a tag, attached to an object, for the purpose of automatic identification and tracking.
RTP	Real-Time Transport Protocol, a protocol for the continuous transference of audio-visual data streams in IP based networks.
SAE	System Architecture Evolution is the core network architecture of 3GGG's Long Term Evolution (LTE) wireless communication standard.
SCE	Service Creation Environment in SPICE - Service Creation Environment on a Service-Delivery-Platform (SPICE).

SCTP	Stream Control Transmission Protocol, Session Initial Protocol (SIP) Transport Protocol is a reliable, connection-oriented transport protocol, which touches on a potentially unreliable package service without connection.
SDM	Space Division Multiplex, Space multiplex procedures, transference canals are bundled up in order to enable parallel, but exclusive use, by several transmitters and receivers.
SDL	Service Description Language: is a platform, programme and protocol independent description language for network services, for the exchange of messages, on the basis of XML.
SDP	Service-Delivery-Platform, Official development and execution platform, makes available services as a uniform program interface and shows a sub range of NGNs.
SGSN	Serving GPRS Support Node, SGSN has a similar function to a Mobile Switching Centre (MSC) for linguistic communication for GPRS data communication.
SIM	Subscriber Identity Module is a small printed circuit board that is inserted into a GSM-based mobile phone. It includes subscriber details, security information and memory for the personal directory of numbers. This information can be maintained by subscribers when changing handsets.
SIP	Session Initial Protocol, special net protocol from the Internet-protocol family for the construction, control, and dismantling of a communication meeting between two or more participants.
SLA	Service Level Agreement, agreement about the quality and price of a service contract.
SMS	Short Message Service; is a service available on digital networks, typically enabling messages with up to 160 characters, to be sent from, or received on, a subscriber's mobile phone via the message centre of a network operator.
SMSS	Switching and Management Sub-System: Mediation subsystem in a telecommunication system.
SOA	Service Oriented Architecture, architecture oriented structuring of services of IT systems; is a set of principles for designing and developing software in terms of interoperable services.
SON	Self-Organising Networks, self-curative/-optimising networks.

SPATEL	SPICE advanced service description language for telecommunication services, Enlarged, official description language for telecommunication services, a platform which simply allows the definitions of official parameters according to a standardised action.
SPICE	Service Platform for an Innovative Communication Environment, Collection of specifications with particular adjustment for user-centred, IP based services.
SSL	Secure Sockets Layer, is a cryptographic protocol that provides communication security over the internet and that encrypts the segments of network connections at the applications layer.
TCP	Transmission Control Protocol, Protocol for arranging which way data should be exchanged between computers, a reliable, connection-oriented, package-intermediatory transport protocol in computer networks.
TDD	Time Division Duplexing is the application of Time Division Multiplexing (TDM) to separate outward and return signals.
TDM	Time Division Multiplexing is a type of multiplexing in which two or more bit streams or signals are transferred apparently simultaneously as sub-channels in one communication channel, but are physically taking turns on the channel.
UBIQUI-TOUS COM-PUTING	The English term "Ubiquitous" means "everywhere". It refers to the development that computers are to be seen everywhere in our lives (from the modern pocket calculator to the Smartphone). Computers have played a role of increasing responsibility since the 1990s, with a trend towards Ubiquitous Computing. This means "completely piercingly"; it is difficult to separate either concept from another, therefore, they are summarised under "Ubiquitous Computing".
UBS	Ubiquitous Services are services that support human computer interaction in which information processing has been thoroughly integrated into everyday objects and activities.
UDP	User Datagram Protocol is a network protocol without connection.
UMTS	Universal Mobile Telecommunication System is the European term for third generation mobile cellular systems or IMT-2000 based on the W-CDMA standard. It is a third generation mobile radio standard; with clearly higher data transfer rates (up to 7.2 MBit/s with HSDPA; without maximum 384 kbit/s).

URL	Unique/Uniform Resource Locator. A naming system for web resources.
USIM	Universal Subscriber Identity Module (card). A printed circuit board (similar to a SIM) that is inserted into a mobile phone. Adopted by W-CDMA operators for 3G mobile. Capable of storing information, with sophisticated security functions, in comparison to SIMs. Also referred to as User Identity Module, or USIM.
UTRAN	UMTS Terrestrial Radio Access Network is a hierarchically built up radio access network in a mobile radio network according to the UMTS standard.
VLAN	Virtual Local Area Network is the concept of partitioning a physical network, so that distinct broadcast domains (is a logical division of a computer network, in which all nodes can reach each other by broadcast at the data link layer) are created.
VLR	Visited Location Register is a database of the subscribers who have roamed into the jurisdiction of the MSC (Mobile Switching Centre) that it serves.
VoIP	Voice over IP: phoning in computer networks that are built up according to internet standards.
VHE	Virtual Home Environments is a system to support GSM roaming.
WAP	Wireless Application Protocol - A licence-free protocol for wireless communication, which enables the creation of mobile telephone services, and the representation of internet pages on a mobile phone, and is therefore the mobile equivalent of HTTP (Hypertext Transfer Protocol).
WEARABLE COMPUTING	Computer or electronic components one carries directly on the body.
WIDGET	Component of a graphic window system: Widgets are always integrated into a certain window system and use this for interaction with the user, or other windows system Widgets.
WLAN	Wireless Local Area Network: local radio network according to the standard of the IEEE-802.11 family.

Wi-Fi	Wireless Fidelity: wireless systems that provide internet connectivity, this refers to Wireless Fidelity, the 802.11b specification for Wireless LANs, laid out by the Institute of Electrical and Electronics Engineers (IEEE). It is part of a series of wireless specifications that also includes 802.11a, and 802.11g. Sources: International Telecommunication Union (2003) and Home Office (2003b).
WPAN	Wireless Personal Area Network is a personal area network for interconnecting devices centred around an individual person's workspace, in which the connections are wireless.
XML	Extensible Mark-up Language of structured records, in the form of text data.

1 Introduction

This Chapter seeks to illustrate the background and scope of the research. It identifies the problem statement, and sets out the underlying motivation for engaging in research on this topic. Furthermore, it clarifies the specific aim and the objectives of the study, as well as the main contributions of this study and the methodological project procedures applied. Moreover, it provides a short list of the author's publications during research and a comprehensive outline of the structure of the thesis.

1.1 Background and Scope of this Research

The future of Information and Communication Technology (ICT) infrastructure will increasingly focus on international, national, regional, and local needs, for both the social and economic development of society, whilst pursuing technical innovation and development in the IT sector. The term ICT defines collaborative information processing and communication. In general, the rapid development of information systems floods the market with legions of new ICT systems, applications and services and necessitates a manageable handling of the increasing complexity and diversity, in terms of those, new as well as, existing systems, applications and services.

Pavlovski and Plant (2007), defined Service Delivery Platforms (SDPs) as operator solutions that provide a unified middle ground for the optimised exchange of services between users, operators, service and content providers. A Service Delivery Platform is an intelligent web-based platform that supports ubiquitous communication between mobile users, by using Information and Communication Technologies. Furthermore, SDPs support service development and the execution of a variety of applications and services in a simple way (Ahson and Ilyas, 2011).

Johnston *et al.* (2007), outlined that SDPs are coming into their own, as key instruments for enabling and streamlining the operator service offerings, focussing on management and sales. Market forces and technological developments are respectively driving and enabling modern SDP initiatives, to deliver improvements to operators, users and content and service providers, across various devices and networks. The SDP technology is described in Section 2.3 in detail.

Trick (2002), argued that the general requirements of the communication between different society groups, should be supported by technical infrastructure to meet the goals of a qualitative and quantitative improvement of the quality of life. Trick and Weber's (2009) model identifies requirements of the economy, work, education, environment, technology and everyday life as important criteria in the planning and creation of future communication platforms from a general perspective. These essential requirements consolidate all challenges for the development of an ICT infrastructure.

According to Trick and Weber (2009: pp. 8-13), general requirements define that support communication between different social groups - men, women, children, young and old, national citizens, foreign nationals, the wealthy, the poor, and so forth, are done in the best possible way, by providing a relevant information and communication environment. These requirements are listed as follows (Trick and Weber, 2009; Johnston *et al.*, 2007; Pavlovski, 2007):

- Universal access to public infrastructure,

- Well-manageable risks,

- Infrastructure for future-oriented services,

- Integration of all social groups,

- Service variety,

- Private sub networks,

- High network reliability and availability,

- Safety, protection and privacy,

- High mobility,

- Promotion of productivity and automation,

- Usability,

- Protection against violence, racism and pornography,

- Access to public networks, for example in schools and libraries,

- Access to work from home and also mobile everywhere,

- Low-cost access to knowledge and information,

- Low-cost network access and end devices,

- Equal access to networks in urban and rural environments,

- Multimedia applications,

- Multi-lingual functionality,

- Observation of regulatory requirements,

▨   Integration of existing infrastructure,

▨   Low resource of energy consumption during production,

▨   Low energy consumption during operation,

▨   Low ecological damage during production, operations and disposal of waste,

▨   Low operational costs,

▨   Low system costs in new sub network installations,

▨   Low initial operational costs in new sub network installations.

Usability, operability, context-awareness, mobility, and availability are drivers for the deployment and development of SDPs in the area of cloud-based or ubiquitous services (Cordier, 2006b).

A cloud-based service is an IT service, offering the user functionalities based on a Service Level Agreement (SLA), using an SDP, thus eliminating the need for users to have their own infrastructure to communicate on a variety of ICT systems, applications and services. With the integration of SDPs within communication systems in general, basic drivers can be improved due to the power of new innovative technologies, such as IP Multimedia Subsystem, Session Initial Protocol, Universal Mobile Telephone System or Long Term Evolution within these systems, central internet platforms or portals (Ahson and Ilyas, 2011).

The usability of cloud-based ICT systems has been enhanced through improved accessibility, increased and better functionalities, quick preparation of specific services for different user-groups, higher availability through new ICT technologies, easy adaptability, etc. (Talukder *et al.*, 2005; Ahson and Ilyas, 2011).

Johnston *et al.* (2007), demonstrated two of the principal functions that SDP's play as being, to manage and sell services, and to track service usage. From an operator vantage point, SDPs embody an organised technical and business strategy for offering, managing, controlling, and optimisation of the services offered to customers. Operator SDP methods usually span multiple elements of their systems and business process environments. Therefore, by operating with broad SDP methods and implementations, operators gain efficiencies in managing and selling what they have currently got, and improve on innovations and diversify their products.

According to McLean, *et al.* (1993), end-user computing dominates the organisational use of information technology worldwide. Its growth has been driven by the availability of inexpensive hardware and IT systems, increasingly powerful and easy to use software, and user demand for control of information resources.

Users however, notice the advantages of in depth SDP implementations, as they are able to effortlessly identify and differentiate available services, subscribe to and purchase them more efficiently, irrespective of networks and devices, and can also better understand promotions and invoices. SDP's facilitate in flattening the hierarchical hurdles that exist between users and services, from an administrative and technical perspective. This then adds to, the improvement and expediency of services, usage, customer satisfaction and repeat business (Johnston *et al.*, 2007; Tarkoma *et al.*, 2007a).

The fact that user needs are important for today's design and development processes, Magedanz and Sher (2006), argued that the need for a common, multi media SDP is driven by new technical standards for open service platforms. In an SDP White Paper (2006), SDP enablers, mentioned above, facilitate the operator in embracing unlimited amounts of services and automatically matching them to user needs. Usability and convenience adapts the navigation structure of mobile portals for individual users, based on the accumulated user profile and intelligent processing of navigation and usage data.

Osorio Luis *et al.* (2011), argued that the growing complexity of information and control systems has created new challenges for the manufacturing sector, and even bigger challenges for collaborative manufacturing. This growth in complexity of the ICT when coping with innovative business services, and is based on collaborative contributions from multiple stakeholders. This requires novel and multidisciplinary approaches. Service orientation is one of the strategic approaches used to deal with such complexity from a technical perspective.

While Roy and Langford (2008), argued that the integration impetus was assisted by rapid development of electronic technologies designed to provide tools to track and analyse user needs and integrate this information with service provision processes for example, Bertin and Crespi (2009) made it clear in their work, that users' needs are the driver of the next generation of telecom services, and therefore the involvement of user's in the development process is an important approach.

This research analysis incorporates user experience, to design ICT infrastructures, raised by web-based SDP technologies. The author has investigated individuals' perspectives of user needs by adding to and/or contradicting, current research, on technologically-driven studies, in terms of SDP topics. A qualitative study was employed to explain, and investigate, the challenges that are met in a user-driven study. The following Section outlines the problems that the researcher focused on, and the motivation of what to investigate in this research.

1.2 Problem Statement and Motivation for this Study

Interoperable ubiquity between different types of user devices and core systems enables the operation and the development of mobile services anytime and anywhere. Mobile and wired/wireless applications and services have become commonplace, but the challenge lies in helping users make their everyday lives easier (Klemettinen, 2004). ICT applications in our everyday lives generate very high demands on hardware and software architectures in core back-end systems, due to the need for round-the-clock accessibility of mobile services and applications. Trick and Weber (2009), and Jonston *et al.* (2007), both mentioned challenges, in Section 1.1, focussed on within this study, particularly from the user's perspective.

On a technological level, network users are routed to different core networks. On a client level, interoperable mobile services distribute applications to different client types. One problem that arises is that the development and operation of such services depends on the types of application fields and often addresses specialised groups of users. Converging platforms and infrastructures, such as the web, Smartphones, laptops and other end devices, increase the sensitivity of the data generated. A service architecture model supporting the concurrent development and operation of different technologies and platforms is extremely challenging, however it is a necessary precondition for dealing with mobile application scenarios in our day-to-day lives, and is presented in Section 2.3, in detail.

At present, various architecture models such as Java, .NET, Service Oriented Architectures (SOA), Web Services, Galileo (European Satellite Navigation System), Global Positioning System (GPS, U.S. Satellite Navigation System), Universal Telecommunication System (UMTS), High Speed Packet Access (HSPA), IP Multimedia Subsystem (IMS), Long Term Evolution (LTE) and so fourth exist for the purpose of dealing with ICT and mobile communication issues based on a common platform technology and SDP approach (Umar, 2004). These architecture technologies do not, as yet, suffice to support the interoperability of applications and services on different requirement levels.

The next generation of applications and services will have to be extremely user friendly, due to the fact that ICT systems and related services cannot be observed independently, from those who use them. For this reason the identification of challenges and aspects, with particular consideration of user needs for ICT environments are the focus in this study.

1.2.1 Problem Statement for this Investigation

Multimedia services evolution for mobile and wired ICT operators, is driven by user and enterprise needs. Users expect to be able to do increasingly more with communication services and are attracted by services that offer them access to a wide range of communication information and entertainment services, in a user-friendly, cost-effective way. Users also want to enjoy constant connectivity in the best possible way. They demand access to services wherever, whenever, and however they wish (Talukder *et al.*, 2005).

Technologies, such as broadband access, Voice over IP (VoIP) and wireless LAN (WLAN or WiFi) are reducing the entry barrier to new service providers in both the wired and mobile communication industries. As such, today's operators need to find ways of making their services more appealing to users, whilst maintaining customer relationships and profits. They need to optimise their current technology investments, whilst embracing new opportunities, in order to create service packages that are both easy to use and attractive for subscribers (Umar, 2004).

According to Norros and Savioja (2004), there is a need for deepening the relationship between usage and design. Usage is also the driver in design process technology, plant's safety, instrumentation and control, and the design of man-machine interface. This collaborative activity is called activity-oriented design. To enable activity-oriented design, the creation of design methods are needed, in terms of driving the design activity. The criteria for evaluating what is good design, is not currently available in present standards. Norros and Savioja (2004), argued that criteria for good tools and practices must consider human in a favourable role in the various tasks of operating an industrial plant as opposed to the view of humans being a source of error. This is the way to create an optimal system, which takes advantage of the unique capabilities of both the human operators and the automation systems.

Taking usability into account, SDPs then have to be designed to be more end-user friendly both from a deployment and operational perspective. This is because such environments tend to address technically orientated people. SDPs, such as SPICE (Service Platform for Innovative Coomunication Environments), lack that user perspective, where the aim of this research is to identify the challenges supporting SDPs (services and interfaces) from different technological platforms, with particular consideration of both the development and the operation of those services from a user's point of view. A number of challenges defined in Section 1.1 have to be met, so that SDPs become a truly user-focused technology.

These challenges, with a particular emphasis on user-needs, enterprises, operators and regulators alike, are to be addressed in the following four Paragraphs:

▦ User needs

    a) Today's ICT users are increasingly demanding. They are more individualistic, independent, well informed and involved, than ever before. They welcome services that appeal to their emotional, as well as, to their practical needs (Nielsen, 2004). Users enjoy the advantages of thoroughly thought out SDP implementations, as they can identify and understand service offerings better. Likewise, services are then available across different networks and devices (Johnston *et al.*, 2007).

    b) New, exciting services and enhancements to existing services play a key role in breaking down the experiential differences between digital communication and face-to-face interaction. New, advanced terminals and communication mechanisms adapted for user needs enable this without over-burdening the user with technical complexity behind them (Cordier *et al.*, 2005).

    c) Users are under the impression that SDPs can streamline the administrative and technical obstacles that exist between them and services. This, in turn, contributes to increased service uptake, usage, customer satisfaction and retention (Johnston *et al.*, 2007). People and individuals, working in enterprises, wish to have control, and demand flexibility as being able to move, add, and change user information. In this case, enterprise's needs are as relevant as users (Dix *et al.*, 2004).

▦ Enterprise needs

    a) Enterprises always have to take costs into consideration and seek new ways of enhancing operational efficiency. There are some requirements that are specific to, or more apparent in, the enterprise world. These needs are tailored to the work group or work environment (Shneiderman and Plaisant, 2009). New technologies enable different, more flexible ways of working, such as, promoting the remote worker, who - although a relatively new phenomenon - is becoming increasingly commonplace. Working from home, at airports or on the road, is very convenient when one has access to the same services as in the office, such as buddy lists, presence of and stored information (Umar, 2004).

b) It has to be possible to reach remote workers using a single name or number, regardless of location or access device, and with the advent of long-distance working and international business relationships, enterprise users need intelligent ways of bridging the distance with smart tools, such as collaborative working and file sharing (Cordier *et al.*, 2005).

c) Employees need to have secure access to functionality from their mobile devices in the IT environment, and as such the provision and management of applications must be carried out in a secure and efficient manner. Communication between enterprises and their customers is critical, particularly for call centres offering help and support services becoming increasingly significant (Rolan and Hu, 2008).

d) In this case, capabilities such as video communication will help drive forward personal services, and assist in problem solving. Multi-national companies - large enterprises in particular - need to ensure interoperability within legacy systems, such as in their telecommunication system and IT environment. They wish to migrate from their existing systems to new IP- and SIP-based functionality, comprising of telephony, messaging, presence, conferencing and collaboration, etc. (Cordier *et al.*, 2005).

■ Operator-, Service- and Content Provider needs

a) Operators see SDPs as embodying an organised technical and business strategy by offering, managing, controlling, and optimising services to customers. They are able to flexibly integrate existing operator systems and resources into a compounded whole and therefore act as an enabler in opening network functions and self-service features, both to developers and partners. Operator SDP strategies usually span across multiple parts of their systems and business process environments. Operators can become more efficient by managing and selling what they have, and gain innovative strides introducing new offerings onto the market by working with broad SDP strategies and implementations (Johnston *et al.*, 2007).

b) A successful SDP implementation facilitates service and content providers to participate in the service-exchange ecosystem, and promotes, sells, monitors and securely receives payment through operator networks. Service and content providers are thus enabled to sign up as operator partners and discover network and service capabilities exploiting the SDP supply-chain-management features (Johnston *et al.*, 2007).

c) In general, operator, service and content providers, look for efficient and adaptable paths to respond to new business opportunities. Operators need to be able to deliver a seamless and consistent user experience, wherever and however the services are accessed (Cordier *et al.*, 2005), as users are now expanding their voice telephony behaviour to multimedia services. Moving to a paradigm to regulate ICT infrastructure and the rights to operate, regulators are being installed to regulate and standardise the preliminary development and implementations of these environments in different markets (Rolan and Hu, 2008).

■ Regulator needs

a) Beyond users' and operators' own individual needs there is a wider community of interest that must be served by any public communications system – for example, in areas such as consumer protection, service quality, safety and security (Dix *et al.*, 2004). Regulatory and standardisation bodies are working to ensure that IP-based communications serve the different – sometimes opposing – needs of various members of the global community. Specific issues that are, or will need to be, addressed include universal service obligation, number planning, number portability, reliability, voice quality, emergency services, inter-carrier compensation, data protection and lawful interception (Shneiderman and Plaisant, 2009).

The question now arises as to what extent an SDP (see Section 2.3), such as the Service Platform for Innovative Communication Environments - SPICE (see Section 2.3.4), can be integrated into the sphere of existing systems, in order to achieve maximum usability for the single user within the ICT system. As a starting point, the requirements of any future telecommunication infrastructure have been set forth in Section 1.1 (Trick and Weber, 2009: p. 8).

SPICE addressed unsolved problems in terms of designing, developing and putting into operation, efficient and innovative mobile service creation and execution platforms, for networks beyond 3G. Therefore, SPICE principally addresses the technical challenges in design of SDPs. It is an SDP architecture, already specified, that solves the problem of simultaneous operation and deployment of services, from a technical perspective. SPICE uses Internet Protocol Multimedia Subsystem (IMS) as reference-architecture, which works as a link between IT and mobile communication networks (Cordier, 2005). This is illustrated in Sections 2.3.4 and 8.3.2 to 8.3.6, in detail.

The SPICE project (http://www.ist-spice.org/), was carried out by the European Union to fund research in the field of ICT. European research projects were structured around consecutive programmes – the Framework Programmes. The Sixth Framework Programme (FP6) investigated the EU's research on technological development and demonstration activities for the period 2002-2008, and thus a set of common criteria reflecting the major concerns of increasing industrial competitiveness was identified, as was the quality of life for European citizens in a global information society.

This PhD focussed on a subset of the FP6 study and investigates qualitatively, by interviewing the SPICE experts (three groups of SPICE end-users, developers and architecture experts, defined and described in Section 2.3.4.3).

The project researched, prototyped and evaluated extended overylay architecture and framework to support, simple and efficient service creation, test and deployment of intelligent mobile communication and information services. The SPICE platform supported multiple heterogeneous execution platforms, which allowed new and innovative services to spread across different operator domains, across different countries, realising a variety of business models. For users, operators and service providers, the SPICE project contributed to turn today's confusing heterogeneity into an easily manageable and rich service environment, by exploiting the diversity of device capabilities and fostering service adoption (http://www.ist-spice.org/).

Today's end-users want to control their various IT problems in a fast and uncomplicated way, with a single administration console, for instance. Therefore, it is beneficial to incorporate user experience in SDP, alongside technical innovations. This research extends the SPICE project, investigating the creation, provision, deployment and delivery of services from a technical viewpoint, with the user's perspective of SDP technology, supporting everyday tasks and complementing the technical approach that SPICE recommended.

1.2.2 Problem Findings and Challenges of SDPs

The problem findings and challenges of SDPs, particularly SPICE (described in Chapter 2) can be summarised as follows (Bergaus, 2005; Bergaus, 2006; Bergaus, 2010b; Cordier, 2005; Cordier et al., 2006b; The SPICE Project: http://www.ist-spice.org/):

- ■ ICT systems support, to a higher degree, proprietary systems and interfaces than standardised applications, services and networks out of necessity because there is a broad range of environments in the field, but too few standard technologies and interfaces. The use of Internet standard technologies to control and operate these ICT environments can help to change that.

- ■ End-users do not have the possibility of using IT services and mobile communication services from the same end devices, on demand, however and whenever they want.

▨ The explosion of mobile services and the mobile Internet has increased, and will continue to increase, the development and implementation of new proprietary solutions.

▨ The Internet is currently the most important platform for user application and services and it is continuing to grow in importance. Issues of Internet mobility and end device independence are becoming increasingly relevant.

▨ The growing hype surrounding Internet and ICT technologies, allows the technical initiatives to grow, but with little focus on the needs of users and their perspectives.

▨ Current research projects on SDPs, mainly focus on the technical perspective that focuses on what is possible to implement, technical features or a concept of a technical design. There is currently little research available that focuses on the user's perspective, identifying and discussing the challenges and aspects from their point of view, in terms of SDP development.

ICT, and the technology hype behind it, support complex business scenarios, but there are not enough activities, to then perceive ICT and Internet technologies from the user's perspective, for support and control of applications, services, and business scenarios by using different types of end devices and networks by one single instance to drive the making of the daily lives of users easier.

According to Pastuszka *et al.* (2008), to succeed in this new environment, service providers must focus on knowing their end users better, than ever before. They also need to embed flexibility into their service delivery capabilities to exploit user needs, new trends and developments. Bertin and Crespi (2009), argued that there is widespread agreement that convergence in the telecommunications world is becoming increasingly more of a reality. This convergence occurs simultaneously on service, terminal and network levels, and is mainly driven by current technological and market trends and anticipated user needs.

Pastuszka *et al.* (2008), argued that misunderstanding end-user needs and their evolution could intimate knowledge of the subscriber base is critical to providing the proper service mix and experience, and therefore avoiding user dissatisfaction. However, by employing the right techniques and tools to identify and follow end-user preferences and changing behaviours, service providers can develop compelling offers and generate additional revenue. Based on the argument of Pastuszka *et al.* (2008), user needs are important success factors to design and develop information systems. Unfortunately, system design for user needs is driven by techniques that focus on technically driven development of information systems.

Based on the arguments of the related literature referenced, and the problem findings and challenges of SPICE described above, the problem is that the concentration of the perspective of users when designing and developing web-based platforms (SDPs) is lacking in current studies. Users need to be more involved, especially when designing and developing information systems to support the end-users everyday tasks. Current research studies are primarily focusing on technical feasibility, quantitative studies and user need analysis, in terms of existing technical concepts and systems. The combination of technological aspects on one hand, and concentrating on user needs from their perspective on the other, opens up a necessary field of research, touched upon in this thesis. This inspired the author to undertake qualitative research on design aspects for SDPs, investigating a system for user needs from the their perspective.

1.2.3 Motivation for this Research

This research investigates in a strong involvement of users in technically driven development processes and the perspective of users in terms of SDP-based ICT development of future cloud and web-based SDP technologies. The underlying motivation behind this research is to investigate the development of services on SDPs and the development of SDPs themselves from a user perspective. The SPICE platform, in particular, is the SDP that has been researched, from an end-user, developer and architecture expert perspective. Within the context of this qualitative research study these were the three representatives of the SPICE experts group that participated. Based on the information garnered from interviews with these different groups, a substantive GT and a GT category-based model was developed, describing the challenges and design issues faced in developing SDPs according to the perspective of usability. Usability is described as the learnability of a man-made object (Nielsen, 2004).

This object of use can, for instance, be a software application, website, book, process, or anything with which a human being can interact. It is widely used in communication and knowledge-transfer objects (see Section 2.4). The model that focuses on the issues faced in developing SDPs from a user's perspective was compared with a second model, based on structured and grouped literature data that was developed from the results of the literature-based study. The results of this study provide guidance on how to develop services and applications on SDPs, in order to better meet user needs and expectations, whilst fully considering the basic requirements of the communication infrastructure (see bullet points in Section 1.1).

This study focuses on problem findings, and can result from general SDP discussions particularly in terms of the outcome of the FP6 SPICE project. Furthermore, it outlines the research, starting with the problem statement and the description of building a conceptual framework, to the point of a proposed solution and an architecture prototype definition, based on a functional architecture.

The selected research methods are based on applied-science, using a positivist research paradigm (see Section 3.2) to develop a theory, and modelling for justification of the theory. In this dissertation the design aspects of a web-based platform (such as an SDP) for the future, as seen by SPICE experts (developers, users and architecture experts), will be analysed and discussed, based on an empirical, and supported by a qualitative, study.

Bergaus and Stottok (2010), investigated Human Interaction in Railway Telematics and SDPs, researching the possibilities of increasing security and availability of railway telematic systems through the implementation of innovative technologies such as SDPs. That study differs from the PhD thesis, as it is a separate qualitative study where train drivers and SDP experts were interviewed to investigate specific scenarios in implementation of innovative technologies, to increase security and availability of railway telematic services, from the train driver perspective. This PhD thesis investigated general research of challenges and design issues of SDP-based ICT development, from the perspective of SPICE experts.

The study focuses on the development of a model, which is based on Grounded Theory categories, and reflects the viewpoint of SPICE experts. Based on this model, a framework of functional requirements of the said respondents was then defined, depicting design guidelines from a users' point of view.

1.3 Aim and Objectives

The research subject of this study is based on the subject areas of ubiquitous and cloud computing. The term Ubiquitous computing identifies the ubiquity of computer-based information processing. Cloud computing designates an abstract, highly scalable and administered ICT infrastructure platform, and runs customer applications with a correlative billing model (Mell and Grance, 2001). Both subject areas are important in terms of supporting end-users with interoperability of ICT and mobile communication technologies, as well as the Internet, in order to operate and deploy applications and services using SDPs in any network on any device. The following diagram illustrates the aim of this investigation:

Figure 1: Aim of this study

The aim outlined in the illustration above is presented as follows.

1.3.1   Aim: Identify challenges and design issues and develop a model / framework from the perspective of users to make everyday tasks easier

Challenges from the perspective of the potential user of web-based platforms had to be identified within this study, to deliver services and applications in general, independently of the technology used, as these challenges are not fully represented within the available literature. Research is primarily undertaken from a technological point of view. In this case, the technical aspects of the user study was an alternative approach, and supports a user-specific view.

These challenges are essential for identifying the requirements and the meta-model for web-based platform design issues from a user's perspective, to simplify everyday tasks. The final categories and functional design aspects obtained from the interview data are related to aspects from literature. Furthermore, the aim of this research is to develop a model, related to Trick and Weber's (2009), requirements of the communication infrastructure shown in Section 1.1 and the problem findings described in Section 1.2.

The focus of this study is user needs, challenges and design aspects, which together form the basis for defining and developing a web-based platform, in order to deliver services and applications in general (for example an SDP), independent of the technology used, and allows for applications supporting the users' daily life operating on different networks and end devices, ubiquitously. The following illustration, Figure 2, outlines an example with regards to the relation of empirical aspects to such as from the literature.

Figure 2 also depicts the representation of empirical data in form of codes developed during this study and data generated by doing a literature review and structure and group data (literature-based study and the Mapping Process), a relation can be shown between the data. This is explained in detail in Chapters 3, 4, and 5.

A substantive Grounded Theory (GT, see Section 3.4) was developed to identify guidelines for the development of ICT systems with a relation to web-based platforms, based on the challenges identified in the study. GT is a research methodology for generating a theory from data. The final categories created by a Grounded Theory Methodology (GTM) approach helped to map and identify a generic framework in the form of a functional model. This model specifies the challenges and requirements for designing web-based platforms in general, with regard to the use of this technology in ICT environments, as indicated from users' perspectives.

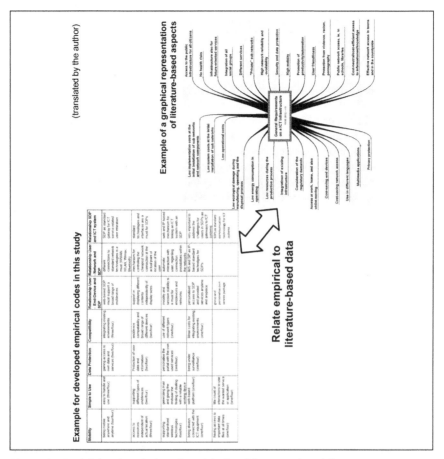

Figure 2: Explaining the relation of empirical and literature-based data

The defined aim (Identify challenges and design issues and develop a model / framework from the perspective of users to make everyday tasks easier, see Section 1.3.1) relates to the four objectives of this investigation (presented in Figure 3 below) in that the identification of challenges and design issues of SDP-based ICT systems can be undertaken, by investigating the relationship of different groups of users and SDP-based ICT systems, and also identifying the current technological situation in terms of SPICE, supporting user tasks (relating to Objectives 1 and 2).

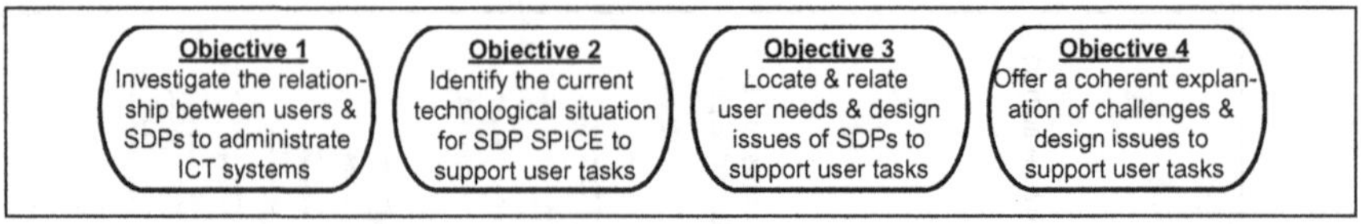

Objective 1	Objective 2	Objective 3	Objective 4
Investigate the relation- ship between users & SDPs to administrate ICT systems	Identify the current technological situation for SDP SPICE to support user tasks	Locate & relate user needs & design issues of SDPs to support user tasks	Offer a coherent explan- ation of challenges & design issues to support user tasks

Figure 3: The four objectives of this investigation

The four objectives outlined in the illustration above are presented as follows. The aim of the study corresponds to the stated objectives and investigates the relationship between user and SDPs. Objectives 2 and 3 state, the current technical situation in terms of supporting user activities (Objective 2), and the proposed user needs (Objective 3). Objective 4 investigates and explains the support of everyday activities when using SDPs.

Moreover, the development of a model / framework from a user's perspective relates to Objectives 3 and 4 in terms of locating and relating user needs and design issues, when designing SDPs and offers a coherent explanation of identified design issues. Detailing and specifying the aim represented above, the four objectives for advancing the research purpose are presented in the following Paragraph.

1.3.2 Objective 1: Investigate the relationship between users and SDPs to control and operate ICT environments from an individual's perspective.

Objective 1 investigates the relationship between users and SDPs on how to administrate (control and operate) Information and Communication Technology (ICT) environments, from an individuals' perspective. It is necessary to identify and illustrate the needs of different groups of individuals, in terms of technological influences on a web-based platform, such as an SDP, independently from the technology, since the viewpoints of different groups of individuals (end-users, developers, and architecture experts) will surely have an effect on the challenges, design issues, and policies regulating a future-based ICT infrastructure. In order to learn about individuals' awareness of challenges and design issues, data and the impact on people's everyday lives in terms of new ICT technologies, empirical data will be collected using a qualitative research approach. The study will focus solely on a users' perspective. The methodology guiding the collection of data is discussed in Chapter 3, and the findings from the data collection are presented in Chapter 4.

1.3.3 Objective 2: Identify the current technological situation regarding user needs and design issues of SDP SPICE in terms of supporting user's everyday tasks.

Objective 2 identifies the current technological situation regarding user needs and design issues for SDPs (SPICE) in terms of supporting user's everyday tasks and activities. In order to fulfil the second objective, it is necessary to identify and discuss the current technological background regarding the Service Delivery Platform SPICE, observed from the perspective of various groups of individuals - so-called SPICE experts. This group of participants includes end-users, developers, and architecture experts, who have a connection to the development of the SPICE SDP (Bergaus, 2006). This will be supplemented with a review of relevant developments in the SDP environment, as well as the representation of general requirements in the literature. The objective will be met by conducting an extensive review of the relevant literature (SDPs, especially SPICE). The ICT infrastructure definitions, which are commonly used in and taken from the literature, will be critically evaluated in the light of the analysis of empirical data, to be provided in Chapters 4 and 5. The objective is to paint a picture of the dynamics involved in developing a general framework for ICT infrastructure, whilst considering the viewpoints of the various people involved.

1.3.4 Objective 3: Locate and relate user needs and design issues of web-based platforms to support daily user activities.

Objective 3 locates and relates user needs and design issues in terms of web-based platforms towards ICT infrastructure requirements from the individual's perspective to support daily user activities. To locate and relate challenges and design issues it is necessary to relate the developed results of this study with those from academic literature. In this case it is necessary to implement a procedure that allows a comparison between empirical and literature-based data in a simple way. Literature-based data researched by the author in the literature review were structured to a comparable representation to relate both types of data. This objective is primarily addressed in Chapters 4 and 5. In Chapter 4, empirical findings are related to the relevant literature. A limited number of interviews with SPICE experts in this area serve to supplement the review of the literature, and accordingly the findings and results of this help to illustrate a theoretical model based on the categories discovered. This is then addressed in Chapter 5.

1.3.5 Objective 4: Offer a coherent explanation of challenges and design issues of web-based platforms and ICT systems to support individual's everyday activities from an individual's perspective.

Objective 4 offers a coherent explanation of the individuals' views of challenges and design issues in relation to web-based platforms and ICT technologies to support users' everyday lives. The final objective addresses the challenges and design issues from the users' perspective, the SPICE participants of this study. The respondents' views were summarised as a guideline, to address design guidelines, from a user viewpoint to develop web-based platform controlled ICT systems of the future. This will be achieved through the development of a theoretical model, using the Grounded Theory, that maps out the relationship between web-based platform parameters of information, and communication infrastructure design aspects. The theory is based on Grounded Theory categories and concepts, and their respective relationships. This objective is addressed in Chapter 5.

The identified and specified objectives investigate the research purpose to meet the goal of this study, to develop a conceptual model for analysing the design aspects of an SDP as a single instance to control and operate ICT systems of the future, described in Section 1.3.1. Thereby, empirical data, and developed categories, based on the findings of the individual's perceptions of using SDP-based ICT infrastructure, were established. Instead of focusing on a technical study by using simulation and software modelling tools, the author focused on the perspective of a special group of individuals from the Sixth Framework Programme (FP6) Information Society Technology (IST) SPICE project (see Section 2.3.4), a European research programme for specifying and standardising SDP architecture from a technical point of view.

The study seeks to develop a theory of how future-oriented technology can be used to support peoples' everyday activities, by using innovative ICT technologies, and how those systems can positively influence individuals' confidence. To this end, interviews were conducted with end-users, developers and architecture experts from the SPICE project. These interviews express their views pertaining to SDP-related challenges and design aspects. Grounded Theory Methodology (GTM) has been used to illustrate patterns and topics that are useful in understanding broader discourses concerning SPICE data, in terms of the challenges, design aspects, technology and policy settings. To achieve the goal of this investigation the next Section 1.4 outlines the research methodology and procedure followed, and illustrates the phases of the research procedure.

1.4 Project Overview

The project research methodology undertaken for the purpose of this dissertation contains various aspects based on a qualitative research paradigm. A Qualitative study, is a process of inquiry, whereby the goal is to understand a social or human problem from multiple perspectives, conducted in a natural setting, with the aim of building a complex and holistic picture of the phenomenon of interest (Blaxter *et al.*, 2001). For the current study, data has been taken from the semi-structured interviews of three groups of participants (end-users, developers and architecture experts). Grounded Theory Methodology (GTM) is appropriated for the data analysis.

Based on the qualitative research approach, a pilot interview phase and two semi-structured in-depth single interview phases were used for the purpose of collecting data in three stages. This was done to overlap data collection and analysis in three phases to facilitate access to, and time taken with, the international interviewees who participated in this study. This was addressed in Sections 3.9.5 and 3.9.6.

To make the results viable and comparable, a common interview guide (Patton, 1987), was applied to ensure a transparent and high-quality research process. The coding comprised of open, selective and theoretical coding for analytical purposes, and memo writing required the researcher's own interpretation of the data, written in his own words. Theoretical sampling was employed which allows the future replication of the research and data collection for further analysis, which is necessary in the process of developing a theory (Semiawan, 2006). All the components of the methodology are discussed in relation to GTM. How these were applied in producing the findings of the research will be discussed and made clear in the Chapters 4 and 5.

Firstly, the author began this study by inductive research during the pilot interviews. Then the researcher adopted an abductive research approach for phases 2 and 3 for variety, with tasks in the research procedure, and to further validate a developed substantive GT (Strauss and Corbin, 1990; Strübing 2005). The author formulated four questions based on research challenges apparent to user needs of SDP-based ICT systems. These questions were developed after looking deeper into the literature (interview phase 2 and 3). This is described in detail in Section 3.9.4.

The research procedure follows various stages: a. Literature Review, b. Data Collection, c. Data Analysis, d. Development of Model and e. Results/Conclusion, described in the following Paragraph and depicted in Figure 4:

Figure 4: Phases of the research procedure applied

a. Literature Review: The selection of literature available on the topic of SDPs was reviewed, in order to identify relevant information, to explore existing knowledge, and to form a sound foundation for the qualitative study. An overview of the significant background and literature on the research areas of SDPs, NGNs and UBSs as well as usability, requirement engineering and design for testability proved to be very useful both in theoretical and practical terms. Once a research perspective has been clarified on the basis of existing literature, the challenges for SDPs from a user perspective could be identified.

The literature review started after the pilot interviews and took place in research interview phases 2 and 3. This was the idea for introducing the literature-based study to better understand research topics and build up the literature-based criteria catalogue.

b. Data Collection: Semi-structured pilot interviews were carried out which served to illuminate the status quo of SDP use within ICT systems. Interviews were conducted with participants working in these specific areas, and who were therefore more engaged within this area. The participants were part of the technical project at SPICE. Five interviews were carried out and transcribed at this stage. Semi-structured interviews were conducted in a way that allowed focused communication regarding the status quo of SDPs within a specific target group of SPICE experts (end-users, developers, architecture experts - described in Sections 2.3.4.3, 3.9.6 and 3.10).

The results of the pilot interviews were considered. All of the fifteen interviewees were people responsible for the use or development of SPICE, or were experts in architecture models, in this field. The main focus of the semi-structured interviews was the practical approach to the subject of the development of SDPs, particularly SPICE. The fifteen interviews were firstly recorded and then later transcribed.

GTM was central to the current study, as it is a methodological tool that offers a framework for qualitative analysis and can thus be used to develop new theories, based on the data collected. For this dissertation, initial data was gathered in the pilot interviews, which involved identifying the challenges and requirements of SDPs, in four semi-structured interviews. Fifteen in-depth interviews were conducted, to examine individuals' perceptions to the SDP SPICE.

All interviews were coded and analysed using Grounded Theory Methodology. The lack of existing theory regarding SPICE, in the context of usability aspects, justified the use of GTM as a suitable research methodology. The gathered empirical data was also analysed by using GTM.

c. Data Analysis: The data obtained was coded and interpreted, and formed the basis for the development of a model with the three different target groups (end-users, developers of SPICE services, and architecture experts). The data analysis was undertaken using a new coding technique, referred to in this dissertation as colour coding, developed by Stottok (2010a). The mapping process, used for validation of the collected data, is also a new technique, developed by the author to validate GT-based findings from data analysis, using a mapping procedure, so as to structure and group literature-based data.

d. Developing a Model: The development of the model was based on empirical data, gathered from the interviews with the SPICE experts. The data was validated and compared to the literature-based data, which was collected and developed. A criteria catalogue, resulting from the categories generated from the literature, together with the categories from the empirical data study, were compared and validated.

The developed categories, which arose from the GTM approach in this study, are highly relevant to the development of the interview-based and the literature-based model as well as the generic framework of an SDP-based ICT system (presented in Chapter 5) within this investigation.

e. Results/Conclusion: The results, consisting of the findings from the semi-structured interviews and the mapping process, in conjunction with the research objectives, are based on an empirical approach. In conclusion, it should be noted that the motivation behind this investigation, namely the value generated through SDP technologies in new and modern ICT systems, is the focus of this dissertation, and thus the value generation relates to the aim of this investigation.

During the course of this study, the researcher developed a unique mapping process and a colour coding system. Both methods helped collect data in an easier and more efficient way. Using Grounded Theory-based research, the study indicates the way in which usability factors should be incorporated into any future SDP. GT was chosen to generate a theory from the empirical data collected. Therefore, this study is of interest to the usability, and those interested in the practical application of Grounded Theory.

1.5 Main Contribution to this Research Study

The main contribution is illustrated in the six developed Grounded Theory categories and their relations (exploratory framework), which present the views of
the interview participants in design issues of SDPs. A relation of a specific category to other categories is subsequently illustrated in the same colour. These
categories were developed by collecting and analysing, empirical data from fifteen interviews then justified in seven different justification stages (described in
Section 3.12). A detailed description is given in Sections 3.3, 4.5 and 5.3.

The EMPLIT methodology used within this study consists of an empirical
part, using an adapted form of GTM with a Colour Coding approach for the
analysis and coding of interview data. This data is depicted in a mind map and a
model visualisation was developed. The literature-based study uses the mind
mapping technique to group and structure the literature-based data. The mapping
process aided in justifying the qualitative data of the study. The application of
the EMPLIT methodology aided the researcher in developing and justifying the
substantive contribution within his research.

EMPLIT is an unexpected finding of this investigation and a prototype of an
alternative methodology, researching user needs of technical systems, should this
system or concept of this system not exist, when starting the research. This is
described in Sections 0 and 0.

This study presents an alternative to investigate user needs with a user-
based study. SDP development can be improved when starting SDP-based ICT
development, through the application of individuals' view of SDP before investigating technical feasibility.

1.6 List of Publications

This Section gives an overview of the most relevant papers and publications
printed during the entire research study. The following list illustrates the pertinent publications and papers of the author relevant to this research investigation
and sets them in context of the current dissertation:

■ Paper 'Architecture Model for a Service Delivery Platform supporting mobile distributed services in interoperability networks shown by the example
  of mixed reality applications', published in research in progress papers
  2006, Leeds Metropolitan University
  [Internet] http://www.leedsmet.ac.uk/inn/bergaus.pdf

▨ Paper 'Information Roaming in Interoperable Networks', published in Research in progress papers 2007, Leeds Metropolitan University
[Internet] http://www.leedsmet.ac.uk/inn/M_Bergaus.pdf

▨ Master Thesis 'Verbesserter Nutzen von Telematiksystemen im Schienenverkehr durch Bereitstellung innovativer Service-Delivery-Plattformen' published together with Mr. Bernd O. Stottok to obtain Master of Science in Applied Science and Research 2010, Department of Interactive Media and Education Technologies, Danube University Krems
[Internet] http://stottok.rollsport-nuernberg.de/

▨ Paper 'Colour Coding: an Alternative to Analyse Empirical Data via Grounded Theory' published together with Mr. Bernd O. Stottok and Mrs. Andrea Gorra at the 10th European Conference on Research Methodology for Business and Management Studies 2011, 20-21 June, Normandy Business School Caen, France
[Internet] http://www.academic-conferences.org/ecrm/ecrm2011/ecrm11-home.htm

▨ Paper 'Validation of Grounded Theory Based Data by Means of Analytical Mapping Techniques', published together with Mr. Bernd O. Stottok and Mrs. Andrea Gorra at the 11th European Conference on research Methodology for Business and Management Studies 2012, 28-29 June, University of Bolton, UK
[Internet] http://www.academic-conferences.org/ecrm/ecrm2012/ecrm12-home.htm

1.7 Outline of Chapters

This guide to the following Chapters provides an outline of the thesis structure, which consists of six main Chapters, logically structured, with the purpose of supporting the reader in understanding the structure of the dissertation, illustrated in Figure 5 below. This thesis consists of six parts corresponding to the respective Chapters: 1. Introduction, 2. Literature review, 3. Research procedure, 4. Analysis and findings, 5. Results and discussion, and 6. Conclusion:

Figure 5: Phases of subsequent chapters

The purpose of Chapter 1, is to describe the overall context and rationale of the thesis, including background and scope of this research, the problem statement, and motivation of the study, the aim and the objectives, the main contributions to this research, as well as an overview of this research project.

Chapter 2 outlines the background of the topics discussed, and presents an in-depth literature review, grouped into three significant areas. Firstly, the connection of ICT and SDPs is described. Secondly, definitions of SDP technologies and an overview of SPICE are given. Following this, definitions on usability, user-centred design, requirement engineering, design for testability, and human-computing interaction are given, in terms of system design for user needs. The fourth area presents a review of related research of technical and user-oriented studies, including a small bibliography of related papers published, by the author, within the context of the research. Finally, based on the literature review, the research gap was identified and research questions defined and formulated.

Background and essential information regarding information and communication technologies is presented, with a focus on mobile communications technologies. Secondly, definitions of the most important technologies are described.

The methodological paradigm for this study is described in detail in Chapter 3, along with the rationale for this methodological choice. An adapted version of GTM forms the basis for the methods used for data collection and analysis. It is pivotal to the way in which this thesis examines empirical evidence. In addition, mind and concept mapping techniques are presented, and two new research approaches - the colour coding system for the analysis of the data in terms of GTM and literature-based study with a mapping process for the justification of the empirical data with the help of a literature-based data are presented. Finally, the research methodology, and its application, is presented, including a dual-layered justification process (a process to structure and support the justification of the research problem of this investigation by validating research results and the research process itself) validating both the intermediate and final results of this study.

Chapter 4 is split into three parts and focuses on the analysis and presentation of findings. Part 1 illustrates how the procedures of colour coding, the creation of literature-based criteria catalogue, and justification of intermediate and final results, was done, with examples. A detailed example of the overall coding procedure is also shown. Part 2 draws and triangulates the results from the literature-based criteria catalogue together with those from the three phases of the empirical study. Empirical findings are compared to the literature, and synthesised, so as to provide a holistic interpretation of the research objectives. Part 3, then presents the development of the GT categories, and illustrates the relationships between them.

Chapter 5 reports on the outcomes and findings of the empirical data collection. The findings are presented with reference to the different stages of data collection: pilot- and in-depth interviews. Visual displays of ideas provide an insight into how each of the six final categories was developed. The views of respondents are discussed as well. The last part of Chapter 5 explains the divergence between an individual's view of the research topics and those predominantly discussed in the literature.

The final Chapter, Chapter 6, summarises these results and findings and sets about the conclusions drawn from the study, in relation to the aim and the objectives identified above. It draws on all data and interpretations, discusses the results and includes suggestions for further research.

The following, Chapter 2, presents background information on SDPs and the SPICE project, as well as design systems for user needs, which was vital for this research investigation. Additionally, related literature and research questions are set out.

2 Literature Review: ICT, SDPs and System Design for User Needs

Chapter 2 provides a literature review, together with theoretical topics pertaining to Information System Theory, Information and Communication Technologies (ICT), Service Delivery Platforms and System Design for User needs, and relates current literature to all of the these topics within this investigation.

Section 2.1 introduces the study and its context. Related research to Information and Communication Technologies and the Information Systems Theory is introduced in the second part of this Section. Service Delivery Platforms (SDPs), as one possible application of general web-based platforms are introduced, and their possible fields of applications are presented using the example of SPICE - Service Platform for Innovative Communication Environments, within the third Section (2.3) of this thesis. Different approaches in terms of user needs, for designing a system, together with system design aspects when designing ICT systems, is introduced in Section 2.4 of this Chapter. This Chapter then puts this PhD thesis into context with other research studies, and lists publications done by the author.

Finally, Section 2.5 summarises a conceptual framework for developing web-based platforms, with the example of an SDP in terms of ICT environments for the future, being introduced. The concepts of human-computing interaction and the conceptual framework from Trick and Weber (2009) were briefly introduced. The research gap is presented and a handful of research questions are presented and formulated to illuminate the research problem outline in Chapter 1. All literature research is distributed within Chapter 2 systematically. All relevant background information to the essential related technology and the complexity of these are presented in Appendix A - Sections 8.1 to 8.3.

2.1 Introduction

This Section provides a literature review of the relevant topic areas, providing explanations about the related research, and further defining and introducing important terms and definitions.

Ubiquitous Computing, also described as ubiquity of computers, was initially formulated in the article "The Computer for the 21st Century" by Marc Weiser (1991), who, at the time, was head of the Computer Science Laboratory at Xerox PARC. Computers should unobtrusively support a person in their daily tasks, whereby they should remain seemingly invisible, in the background, yet should be available, always and everywhere. This idea has fundamentally revolutionalised the way we think about, and work with, computers. The computer disappears as the focus, and in its place steps the human being surrounded by computers, which have to support him on a daily basis, and take over many of his day-to-day tasks (Wohltorf, 2004: p. 91).

To be able to achieve this target, downscaling quantity of machines and more efficient use of energy, or the development of new sources of energy, is necessary. Above all however, the computer should actively sense its environment, and should be able to adjust to any situation that arises. This requires the vast use of sensors that can deliver the necessary information over the available environment, and therefore instruct the computer, by using these indicators, which actions it must take. The term Sentient Computing was created for this special form of ubiquitous computing (Wohltorf, 2004: p. 91).

Pervasive Computing (lat. pervadere = interfuse) can be understood as a synonym of Ubiquitous Computing. It describes the fusion of everyday life with connected, intelligent objects, able to communicate with one another. Pervasive Computing, is therefore, frequently regarded as a form of the industry-named variation of Ubiquitous Computing. This technology supports people with personalised services and is universally accessible and obtrusive (Burkhardt *et al*, 2001: p. 24-25).

Wearable computers are miniature electronic devices that are either worn under, with or on top of, clothing of the bearer. This class of wearable technology has been developed for general, or special, purpose information technologies and media development. These types of computers are particularly useful for applications that require more complex computational support, than just hardware coded logics. One of their main features is that one does not need to turn it on or off, as it is always active.

Another feature is its ability to multi-task. There is no need to stop what you are doing in order to use the device. These devices can be incorporated by the user to act like a prosthetic. It could be an extension of the user's mind and/or body (Starner *et al.*, 1995).

Cloud computing has been defined as being the practice of using a network of remote servers hosted on the Internet and stores. It manages and processes data as opposed to a local server. It relies on sharing of resources to achieve coherence and economies of scale, similar to a utility, over a network. Three types of cloud computing can be defined (Armbrust *et al.*, 2010; Voorsluys *et al.*, 2011):

■   *Infrastructure as a Service (IaaS):* This is a cloud service model whereby cloud providers offer computers as physical or virtual machines. A hypervisor runs these virtual machines as guests. The management, of pools of hypervisors by the cloud operational support system, precipitates the ability to scale a large number of virtual machines. Other resources in IaaS clouds include images in a virtual machine image library, raw (block) and file-based storage, firewalls, load balancers, IP addresses, Virtual Local Area Networks (VLANs), and software bundles. These resources are maintained in large pools found in data centres, and can be supplied on demand by IaaS cloud providers (Voorsluys *et al.*, 2011). To deploy their applications, cloud users then install operating system images on the machines along with their application software. According to this model, it is the cloud user who is responsible for patching and maintaining the operating systems and application software. IaaS does not refer to a machine that does all the work, but rather to a facility provided to businesses, which offers users the advantage of extra storage space in servers and data centres (Voorsluys *et al.*, 2011).

▪ *Platform as a Service (PaaS):* The PaaS model allows cloud providers to deliver a computing platform that typically includes an operating system, programming language execution environment, database, and web server. Application developers are able to develop and run their software solutions on a cloud platform without bearing the costs and complexity of buying and managing the underlying hardware and software layers. Some PaaS offer functions in such a way, that the cloud user does not have to allocate resources manually, by scaling the underlying computer and storage resources automatically in order to match application demand (Voorsluys *et al.*, 2011).

▪ *Software as a Service (SaaS):* According to this model, cloud providers install and operate applications in the cloud, and cloud users access the software from cloud clients. It is not the task of cloud users to manage the platform and infrastructure on which the application is running. Due to this there is no need to install and run the application on the cloud user's personal computers. This saves maintenance and support time. A cloud application is elastic, and this renders it different from other applications. This elasticity is brought about by cloning tasks onto multiple virtual machines at run-time, in order to keep up with changing work demands. Load balancers distribute the work over the set of virtual machines. This process is inconspicuous to the cloud user, who only sees a single access point. To accommodate a large number of cloud users, cloud applications can be multitenant, which means that any machine is able to serve more than one cloud user organisation. Specific types of cloud-based applications are often referred to, as software with a similar naming convention: desktop as a service, business process as a service, test environment as a service, communication as a service (Voorsluys *et al.*, 2011).

Being able to develop and implement applications and services in the current century, extremely flexible architecture is needed, in order to support the concepts of ubiquitous computing and others described above. One possibility is to use a Service Oriented Architecture (SOA).

Service Oriented Architecture is an architectural paradigm that can be used to build and facilitate infrastructures, in line with consumer's needs, and with provider's capabilities to interact via services, across different domains of technology. Services act as main facilitators of data interchange, but in order to function, additional mechanisms are required. Several new trends within the computer industry rely on SOA as an enabling foundation. The automation of Business Process Management is included together with composite applications (applications that aggregate multiple services to function), various new architecture and design patterns generally referred to as Web 2.0 (Valipour *et al.*, 2009; Voorsluys *et al.*, 2011).

Service orientation demands, services with operating systems, to be loosely coupled with other technologies that support applications. SOA defines functions as distinct units, referred to as services which developers make accessible over a network. This is done to allow users to combine services and then reuse them in the production of applications. In fact, SDPs are based on Service Oriented Architecture concepts. SOA is a set of principles and methodologies for the design and development of software services. These services are defined business functionalities that are constructed as pieces of software codes or data structures that can be used for different purposes. The design principles of SOA are used in developing and integrating systems (Bieberstein *et al.*, 2005).

SOA increases awareness of the available SOA-based services, defines various ways of integrating contrasting applications for Web-based environments, and uses multiple implementation platforms. SOA defines the interface in terms of protocols and functionality. These services, and their respective consumers, communicate with one another by passing data in a well-defined, shared format, or by coordinating an activity between two or more services (Valipour *et al.*, 2009). Service Delivery Platforms (see Section 2.3) are designed and implemented on the concepts of SOA. The next Section introduces the reviewed literature regarding Information Communication Technology (ICT) it describes important terms and discusses what other researchers did, in this field of study.

2.2 The Connection of Information and Communication Technology (ICT) to SDPs

The following Sections describe the different technological areas, Information Systems Theory and Information Communication Technology, with appropriate definitions, and present an analysis of the up-to-date academic literature based on the current state of the art. This related topic focused on technical research, with an emphasis on the technical perspective. Related research from the user's point of view does not exist, except with another application on work of the author himself, focusing on Service Delivery Platforms to improve Railway Telematics Systems. This study was also done from the perspective of the user and investigated the use of Railway Telematics. Details of this related research application and the context for this PhD study, will be explained in Section 2.4.5.3 – Thesis in Context.

2.2.1 Basic concepts

Information Technology (IT) is a branch of engineering that deals with the use of computers to store, retrieve, and transmit information. The acquiring, processing, storing and dissemination of vocal, pictorial, textual and numerical information by a microelectronics-based combination of computing and telecommunications are its main fields. Modern and new fields of IT include next generation web technologies, bioinformatics, cloud computing, global information systems, large scale knowledge bases, to name a few. Progress is mainly driven in the field of computer science, built on an evolving electronics' infrastructure, promulgated by Engineering, Physics/Mathematics, Defense (military) expenditures, public/private R&D, and the consumer product marketplace (Melody *et al.*, 1991).

System Theory (ST) is the foundation of a generic understanding of the world. The concept 'system' is a universal analogy used for anything, regardless of its particular properties, origin or substance. It therefore provides a synergistic force to counter the fragmentation, or analytical aspects, of science and empirical knowledge. It can also be used to translate and unify ideas throughout fragmented, and somewhat estranged, fields of knowledge (Bailey, 1994).

System theory postulates that everything is a system, signifying that the concept system is applicable to everything in a meaningful and practical sense. Everything is a system that is composed of sub systems, which interact to create that system. Thus, ultimately, there is only a field of primitive systems, and the information that mediates their interactions. Through their permutations and combinations, they build up the successive levels of systems. Every system is a sub-system within larger systems, and interacts with other systems passing information, coordinating, organising, cooperating, competing, etc., thus forming a higher-level super-system, and so on, up to the universe as a whole, which is a single, unified, and coherent system (Weinberg, 1975).

Information Systems (IS), is the study of the complementary networks of hardware and software that people and organisations use to collect, filter, operate, create, and distribute data (Lee, 1991). The study links business and computer science, using a theoretical basis of information and computation so as to study various business models and related algorithmic processes within a computer science discipline. Computer Information System(s) (CIS), is the field of study of computers and algorithmic processes, including their principles, software and hardware designs, applications, and their impact on society (Benbasat and Zmud, 2003).

The history of information systems coincides with the history of computer science that began long before the modern discipline of computer science emerged in the twentieth century. With respect to circulation of information and ideas, numerous legacy information systems remain today and are continuously updated so as to advocate ethnographic approaches, ensure data integrity, and improve the social effectiveness and efficiency of the whole process. Generally, information systems focus on processing information within organisations, particularly within business organisations, and the benefits are shared with modern day society (Agarwal, 2005).

Silver *et al.* (1995) provided two perspectives on Information Systems (IS). The IS-centred viewpoint includes software, hardware, data, people, and procedures. Another managerial outlook includes people, business processes and Information Systems. There are different types of IS, for example: transaction-processing systems, office systems, decision-support systems, knowledge-management systems, database-management systems and office-information systems. Users criticise many information systems that are typically designed to allow humans to perform tasks for which the human brain is not well suited to. These tasks cover areas like dealing with large amounts of information, performing complex calculations and controlling many simultaneous processes.

Silver *et al.* (1995) defined Information Systems as systems, implemented within an organisation for the purpose of improving the effectiveness and efficiency of that organisation. The capabilities of the IS and the characteristics of the organisation, its work flow, human resources, and its development and implementation methodologies together define the extent to which that goal is achieved (Benbasat and Zmud, 2003). Several IS scholars have debated the nature and basis of Information Systems, which have their roots in other reference disciplines such as Computer Science, Engineering, Mathematics, Management Science, Cybernetics, and so forth.

Information systems research is primarily interdisciplinary, focused on studying the effects of information systems on the behaviour of individuals, groups and organisations. Hevner *et al.* (2004), categorised research in IS into two scientific paradigms comprising of behavioural science and design science. The purpose of the former is to develop and verify theories that explain or predict human or organisational behaviour. The latter stretches the boundaries both of human and organisational abilities by creating new and innovative history.

The term Information System Theory (IST) was used to describe theoretical computer science, where a computer was a system that processed information. Here, information is far more general than simply the contents of computer files or data structures. Each system comprises of information and additionally processes information, regardless of the form, that information takes, regardless if its medium is a computer file, light rays, particles of matter, etc. (Lee, 1991).

The term Information and Communication Technology (ICT) refers to the convergence of audio-visual and telephone networks, with computer networks through a single cabling or link system. Significant economic incentives are in place, based on minimising costs by eliminating telephone networks and merging of audio-visual, building management and telephone networks with computer network systems, by using a single unified system of cabling, signal distribution and management. This has initiated the increase of organisations using the term ICT in their company names, to draw attention to their specialisation in the process of merging the different network systems (Melody *et al.*, 1991).

The Internet is a global system of interconnected computer networks that use the standard Internet protocol to serve billions of users worldwide. It is a network of networks, consisting of millions of private, public, academic, business, and government networks, on a local and global scope, that are linked by a broad array of electronic, wireless and optical networking technologies. It consists of an extensive range of information resources and services, such as the WWW's interlinked hypertext documents, and an infrastructure that supports different services i.e. email, chat, and TV. ICT standards are very important to enable technological systems to interoperate with each other. This is especially relevant as the main idea behind ICT, is that information storage devices can communicate with communication networks and computing systems in a media-frictionless manner (Melody *et al.*, 1991).

ICT systems and environments are an extension of Information Technology (IT), and they have broadened the term IT via the integration of telecommunications and focussing strongly on unified communications. Telecommunications focus on telephone technology and systems operating, both with wired and wireless signals. The scope of IT is wide, beginning with the integration of computers and crucial organisational software, middleware, storage systems and including audio-visual systems. This allows users to create access, store, transmit, and manipulate information and data. Basically, ICT consists of IT in addition to telecommunications, broadcast media, all types of audio and video processing and transmission, as well as network-based control and monitoring functions (Melody *et al.*, 1991).

March and Smith (1995) suggested a guideline for the research of different aspects of Information Technology, including output of the research (research output) and activities to carry out the research (research activities). They identified research output as follows:

■   Constructs as concepts forming the vocabulary of a domain and that include a conceptualisation utilised in describing problems within the domain and specifying their respective solutions.

■   A model consisting of proposals or statements expressing relationships between constructs.

■   A sequential method made up of a set of steps (an algorithm or guideline) utilised in performing a task. Methods are based on a set of underlying constructs and a model of the solution space.

■   An instantiation is the realisation of an artefact in its environment.

Other research activities include:

■   Constructing an artefact to perform a specific task.

■   Assessing the artefact to determine if any progress was made.

■   In terms of an assessed artefact importance on determining reasons the artefact worked, or conversely did not, within its environment allows for theorising and justifying theories about IT artefacts.

Although Information Systems, as a discipline, have evolved over the past 30 years, the focus of IS research continues to be subjected amongst scholars. Two main viewpoints surrounding this debate are: a narrow perspective that focuses on the IT artefact as the central subject matter of IS research and a broad perspective focusing on the interplay between the social and technical aspects of IT that are embedded into a dynamic evolving context (Agarwal, 2005). Given that information systems fall under the auspices of an applied field, they are expected, by industry practitioners, to generate findings that are immediately applicable in practice. However, this is not always possible, as information systems researchers frequently explore behavioural issues in more depth than practitioners would expect them to. This may render information systems research results difficult to understand, and in turn face criticism (Ron, 2002).

2.2.2 Convergence and ICT4D

Telecommunications convergence, network convergence, or simply convergence are terms, generally used to describe newly formed telecommunications technologies and network architectures used to move many communications services into one network. This particularly entails converging previously distinct media, such as telephony and data communications, into common interfaces on single devices. Rajendra and Siddhartha (2010), define convergence, in their Policy Initiative Dilemmas on Media Convergence: A Cross National Perspective, as integration and digitalisation.

Integration, in this case, is defined as "a process of transformation measure by the degree to which diverse media such as phone, data broadcast and information technology infrastructures are combined into a single seamless all-purpose network architecture platform". Digitalisation is not solely determined by its physical infrastructure, but by the content or the medium.

Convergence is defined by Blackman (1998), as a trend that exists in the evolution of technology services and industry structures, and then later further defined as the merging together of telecommunications, computing and broadcasting into, a single digital bit-stream. Mueller (1999) disagreed with the statement, that convergence is really a takeover of digital computers of all forms of media. There are different types and classes of computers, which are constantly developed providing the easiest and fastest way to handle different forms of media information. Convergence services including VoIP, IP-TV, Mobile TV, and so forth, will eventually replace old technologies and are posing a threat to current service providers. IP-based convergence is inevitable and will cause new services and demands on the market. Once old technology converges into common public, IP-based services become independent of access or less dependent on access. The old service is access-dependent (Bores *et al.*, 2001).

Information and Communication Technologies for Development (ICT4D) is a general term that refers to the application of Information and Communication Technologies (ICTs) within the fields of socioeconomic development, international development and human rights. The basic hypothesis behind this approach is that increasingly, more and enhanced information and communication, development of a society (either through improving income, education, health, security or other aspects of human development). Presently, the most tangible and effective ways to improve information and communication flows in a society is to adopt ICT, therefore ICT4D (Sutinen and Tedre, 2010).

The aim stated that ICT-for-development is to make use of this ongoing transformation by actively using the enabling technology to improve the living conditions of societies and segments of society. Historically, social transformations of this kind, such as the industrial revolution, the resulting dynamic are interplays between an enabling technology, normative guiding policies and strategies, and the resulting social transformation. With ICT4D, this three-dimensional interplay is shown as a cube. Following the Schumpeterian School of thought (Michaelides and Milios, 2008), the first enabling factor for the associated socio-economic transformations is the present technological infrastructure: hardware infrastructure and generic software services. In addition the human requirements for making use of these technologies include capacity and knowledge of these foundations (horizontal green dimension in Figure 6). They are the basis for the digitalisation of information flows and communication mechanisms in different segments of society.

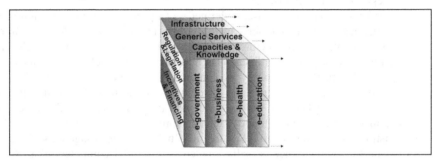

Figure 6: ICT4D cube: interplay between technology, society, and policy (Hilbert, 2011; source: http://www.martinhilbert.net/HilbertCube.pdf)

When part of the information flows, and communication processes in these sectors are carried out in electronic networks, the prefix "e-" is often added to the sector's name, resulting in e-government, e-business and e-commerce, e-health, and e-learning, etc. (vertical blue dimension in Figure 6). This process of transformation represents the basic requirements and building blocks; however, they are not enough for development. The mere existence of technology is not sufficient to achieve positive outcomes because there is no technological determinism. ICT for Development policies and projects is geared at promoting normatively desired results of this transformation, minimising negative effects, and removing probable bottlenecks.

There are basically two types of interventions: positive feedback (incentives, projects, financing, subsidies and so forth that accentuate existing opportunities) and negative feedback (regulation and legislation, etc.) that limits and tames negative development (diagonal yellow-red dimension in Figure 6) (Hilbert, 2011; Naismith et al., 2004). Although ICT4D is primarily dependent on technology, one should heed that the concepts and applications of ICT4D also require a clear understanding of issues of community development, poverty, agriculture, healthcare, and basic education. The acronym ICT4D contains a divisive disciplinary discussion by Richard Heeks (2009). As atomised by

Heeks, the "I", is related to "library and information sciences", the "C" is associated with "communication studies", the "T" is linked with "information systems", and the "D" stands for "development studies".

The dominant term used in this field is "ICT4D" or "ICT4Dev" (ICT for development). Alternatives include ICTD (ICT and development, which is used in a broader sense) and development informatics (Sutinen and Tedre, 2010). The concept of ICT4D can be interpreted as dealing with disadvantaged populations anywhere in the world, although it is more typically associated with applications in developing countries as it is concerned with directly applying IT approaches to poverty reduction. ICT can be applied either in a direct sense, whereby their use directly benefits the disadvantaged population, or in an indirect way, whereby they assist aid organisations, non-governmental organisations, governments or businesses, in order to improve general socio-economic conditions (Unwin, 2009).

The field is gaining recognition as an interdisciplinary research area, made obvious by the growing number of conferences, workshops and publications. This type of research has been spurred, in part, by the need for scientifically validated benchmarks and results, which can be used to measure the efficiency of current projects. There is also a – somewhat loose – community of both technical and social science researchers that has grown up around the annual ICT4D conferences (MCNamara, 2003).

Driving this incessant force of creative destruction is technological change. While the key carrier technology of the first industrial revolution (1770–1850) was based on water-powered mechanisation, the second (1850–1900) was enabled by steam-powered technology, the third (1900–1940) was characterised by the electrification of social and productive organisation, the fourth by motorisation and the automated mobilisation of society (1940–1970), and the most recent by the digitalisation of social systems.

Each of these "long waves" has been characterised by a sustained period of social modernisation, most notably by sustained periods of increasing economic productivity. According to Carlota Perez (2005): "this quantum jump in productivity can be seen as a technological revolution, which is made possible by the appearance of the general cost structure of a particular input that we can call the 'key factor', and which fulfils the following conditions:

- clearly perceived low and decreasing relative cost

- unlimited supply for all practical purposes

- potential all-pervasiveness

- a capacity to reduce the costs of capital, labour and products, as well as to change them qualitatively".

Digital Information and Communication Technologies fulfil those requirements and therefore represent a general-purpose technology that can transform an entire economy, leading to a modern, and more developed, form of socio-economic and political organisation. This is often referred to as the post-industrial society, information society, digital age, and network society, among others.

The world's effective capacity to exchange information through two-way telecommunication networks grew from 281 petabytes of (optimally compressed) information in 1986, to 471 petabytes in 1993, to 2.2 (optimally compressed) exabytes in 2000, and to 65 (optimally compressed) exabytes in 2007. This is the informational equivalent of 2 newspaper pages per person per day in 1986, and 6 entire newspapers per person per day, by 2007. Given this growth, telecommunications play an increasingly important role in the world economy and the worldwide telecommunication industry's revenue was estimated to be $3.85 trillion in 2008. The service revenue of the global telecommunications industry was estimated to be $1.7 trillion in 2008, and is expected to touch $2.7 trillion by 2013 (Suinen and Tedre, 2010).

2.2.3 Ubiquitous Technologies

Recently, developments in mobile computing and communication have led to the proliferation of mobile phones, tablet computers, Smartphones, and netbooks. Some of these consumer electronic products, such as netbooks and entry-level tablet computers, are often priced lower than laptops and desktop computers, since the target market of these products reside in emerging markets.

This has made Internet and computing more accessible to people in these markets, and developing countries, where most of the world's poor reside (Sutinen and Tedre, 2010). Furthermore, these consumer electronic products are often equipped with basic mobile communication hardware, such as WiFi and 2.5G/3G Internet USB sticks. These have allowed users to connect to the Internet via mobile and wireless networks without owning a landline or an expensive broadband connection via DSL, cable Internet or fibre optics (Unwin, 2009).

According to the International Telecommunication Union, mobile communications and technology have emerged as the primary technologies that will link the least developed countries. This trend is further highlighted by the positive sales reports of technology companies that sell these electronic devices in emerging markets, and include some of the least developed countries. In fact, some multinational computer manufacturers, like Acer and Lenovo, are focusing on bringing cheaper netbooks to emerging markets like China, Indonesia and India (Perez, 2005).

The Section showed a few technical and organisational challenges that could be faced in the 21st century in designing, developing and implementing ICT systems of the future. The author concludes with a citation by Roy Amara

(Pescovitz, 2008): "We tend to overestimate the effect of a technology in the short run and underestimate the effect in the long run". Technology is, and will be, important for solving challenges and problems of our daily tasks, but it is not only technology that we should focus on. A very important point is reliability.

Software errors of complex systems can endanger human life, e.g. a software failure of a hydrofoil vessel in Vienna, August 2012, resulted in eight people being injured, because the machines were switched off by the system and for an estimated fifteen seconds the hydrofoil was uncontrollable. The analysis resolved previously unexplainable software failures. Such incidents are not unique.

Another example of a software error was the Boeing crash of the Austrian airline, Lauda-Air, in 1991. The aircraft disintegrated at 2,000 metres, because system failure caused in-flight deployment of the thrust reversal, and it consequently crashed into the jungle and exploded. All passengers and crew were lost (Cockpit Voice Recorder Database, 1991). The author defines, exactly, the focus of his research on the user perspective of developing guidelines to complement technical system development with aspects arising from users.

The next Section describes Service Delivery Platform technology. Related technological challenges and technologies, that are pivotal and closely related both to Information and Communication Technology systems and Service Delivery Platforms, is presented in Sections 8.1 and 8.2 of the Appendix.

2.3 Service-Delivery-Platforms

In the future, network operators and service providers will face the enormous task of offering new services (value-added services), quickly, simply, and cost efficiently. New communication demands are being created by customers, due to future, principally unlimited, technical possibilities. Therefore, for network operators and service providers, it is essential to produce capable service platforms, or Service Delivery Platforms (SDPs), with which, in the shortest time and with as little effort as possible, new applications can be developed and introduced onto the market (Trick and Weber, 2009: p. 474).

A Service Delivery Platform can be specified as a concept of an IT-based platform, used by telecommunication providers, to provide services to a variety of customers. These services include, traditional telecommunication services, such as telefony for example, and advanced data services, such as location-based services for instance. According to Ahson and Ilyas (2011) a minimal set of SDP requirements are expanding this definition:

■   SDPs are service-oriented as they manage service creation, provisioning, execution and billing.

■   Support delivery of services in a network in a device independent manner, by abstracting the underlying network infrastructure.

■   Provide a single standardised point for devices to find and use diverse service enablers and content.

■   Provide external developers and IT using enterprises with open and secure access to telecommunication capabilities (Ahson and Ilyas, 2011; The Morina Group, 2004).

A detailed overview of technical definitions, technological background information and the capabilities of SDPs are given in Appendix A - Sections 8.1 to 8.3.

2.3.1 Mobile Software Applications

Today's evolution with respect to software applications, and the hype regarding mobile applications, is changing the paradigm (anytime and anywhere to any network on any device), as the intelligence of application software becomes ever more important in its shift from server-related intelligence to client-related intelligence, because the users are getting more capable. Application software (short apps) is computer software designed to help users perform specific features and tasks. A mobile application, or short mobile app, is a software application designed to run on Smartphones, tablet computers and other mobile end devices. It is available through application distribution platforms, which is typically operated by operation and service providers such as Apple Store, Google Play, Windows Phone Marketplace and Blackberry App World. This development was pushed during the last three to five years on the market, making the end devices more capable and powerful (Pagani, 2005).

Earlier, end devices did not have enough computing power to run complex applications with good performance or availability. These applications and their development were initially different from today's developments. Besides the applications for powerful computers, a second application for the identical business process was usually developed for the execution on mobile environments, as these did not have the capability, power, storage space and speed needed. This promulgated powerful applications and services, to be more server-oriented in the past than they are today. However, as this study focused on the viewpoint of Service Delivery Platforms and user-oriented ICT system design, the specific implementation is transparent to the user. Additionally, ubiquitous applications are expected to be more stable and reliable than the specific technical implementation, from the users perspective.

2.3.2 SDPs in Terms of Core Technologies

According to Grech *et al.* (2002), the 3GPP UMTS networks promise to deliver an abundance of advanced, innovative, and feature-rich applications to end-users in a 3G wireless environment. A core network IP multimedia subsystem was introduced, as part of the 3G wireless environment. Grech *et al.* (2002) argued that it aims to enable the convergence of, and access to, voice, video, messaging, data and Web-based technologies for the wireless user. The goal was to combine the growth of the Internet with the growth in mobile communications. The service control architecture for the IMS was summarised as consisting of an application server, providing the execution environment for the applications, and communicating with the call state control function that handles the session control and mobility management functionality. They introduced three general sets of standardised platforms for service control in the UMTS IMS, each one addressing particular needs, from legacy service support to light weight, SIP based support.

Frattasi *et al.* (2005) argued that, even though the successor of the previous cellular generations, the fourth generation of wireless mobile communication systems (4G), is predominantly presented as a convergence platform that provides clear advantages in terms of coverage, bandwidth, energy consumption and a variety of heterogeneous services, ranging from pop-up advertisements to location-based and interactive or IP data casting to network architectures in the past. Based on this vision of 4G, they proposed innovative services and architectures that may achieve enhanced security, energy efficiency, and just-for-you and just-in-time content delivery. Furthermore, since the state-of-the-art technologies do not appropriately cover the needs required for 4G, a context sensitive service discovery that both operates in a wireless and wired network environment, ranging from local to global distances, is described and applied to the case of the proposed services.

Schaefer *et al.* (2006) argued that, telcos today experience a tremendous hazard to their business models. Legacy switched voice and carrier-related data-services threatened by new applications and service providers, carrying on their business "over the top" of the ubiquitous open packet switched IP-transport platform, the Internet. Until recently, carriers used to be the only ones able to offer telecommunication services like voice, because all services were tightly fixed to network structures; additionally, transport and service were an integral whole and minute-based revenues used to be a stable cornerstone of their business.

With the availability of the "Esperanto" Internet as an open accessible transport platform and with the introduction of various services on top of that platform, including voice carriers, like Skype, carriers are therefore forced to confront the challenge of either rescueing part of their minimum or of finding new sources of revenue or both. The first alternative then is a direct strategy against over-the-top VoIP-providers ("pure play"). With an IMS service platform based on an NGN-network, a premium voice product, called VoNGN, can be offered, which can only salvage a part of the voice business. What is even more critical for a future strategy is enlarging the product concept for all-embracing communication, presence, and multimedia services.

According to Baldoni et al. (2009), embedded systems are specialised computers used in larger systems or machines to control equipments such as automobiles, home appliances, communication, control and office machines. Pervasivity is particularly evident in immersive realities, i.e., scenarios in which invisible embedded systems need to continuously interact with human users, in order to provide continuous sensed information and to react to service requests, from the users themselves. The SM4All project investigates an innovative middleware platform, for inter-working of smart embedded services in immersive and person-centric environments, through the use of composability and semantic techniques for dynamic service reconfiguration. This is applied to the challenging scenario of private homes and home-care assistance in the presence of users with different abilities and needs (e.g., young, able-bodied, aged and disabled).

Jin et al. (2010) argued that vvirtual worlds have been linked with e-learning applications to create virtual learning environments. While they can support many educational activities that extend both traditional on-campus teaching and distance learning, they were used primarily for learning content, generated and managed by instructors. With the evolution of Internet technology, social virtual worlds were able to facilitate more social interaction, efficient visual communication, integration of rich media and sharing of student-generated content. They offered the prospect of lively interactive virtual communities in which users interact through their emotional avatars, in a 3D virtual world. Social virtual worlds were increasingly embedded into e-commerce and e-learning, and challenge our ideas about the next generation of virtual learning environments.

Jin et al. (2010) outlined the impact of emerging social networking technologies on the Internet, revealing the convergence between social networking and virtual worlds for technology-enhanced and examined the way in which social virtual worlds were transforming the nature of learning as a social practice. They introduced a design and the implementation of an innovative social interactive learning platform that augments social virtual worlds and other social networking services, with conventional learning management and student support systems.

Niculescu and Pana (2010) argued that the scientific development of different disciplines at the beginning of the 21st Century could only be conceived, in an interdisciplinary context. This fact implies both in-depth documentation and cooperation among the scientists in the diverse knowledge spheres. Knowledge workers are not linked to a unique organisation, but instead they are in touch with people belonging to other organisations. In this complex relationship system, the employers are involved concurrently in similar working situations, and are also constantly learning. They argued that this is why Internet technologies have improved to sustain this net society, whilst being adapted, simultaneously, to individual needs and profiles. The creation of conditions for organisational culture of academic communities' development, presupposes a suitable sociotechnological framework as a communicational and social framework, in addition to an ethical and axiological one.

This multi-framework set, allows for the knowledge worker's creativity, besides improvement of the value system and managerial ethics based on transparency, to foster communication and understanding. Such efforts include the exchange of information and experience, the building of consensus, the creation of new knowledge through collaboration and rapid decision-making. Niculescu and Pana's multiframework set, gives possibilities for new knowledge creation: innovative solutions in unpredictable situations, provided by human and social factors. Their research proposes a modular architecture of this multi-framework set, namely a knowledge management experimental system for scientific communities. Knowledge work necessitates continuous learning together with constant teaching and knowledge sharing.

Arnaud *et al.* (2011) argued that heterogeneous communication devices were emerging, and changing the way of communication. Innovative multimedia applications are now accessible through these embedded systems. The 3GPP IP Multimedia Subsystem provides a basic architecture framework for the NGNs supporting the convergence platform for service provisioning in heterogeneous networks. ETSI TISPAN standardisation effort, focuses on delivering IPTV services on such a platform.

However, IPTV on IMS standardisation suffers from a lack of efficient user-centric network management mechanisms, as the end-user could consume IPTV services from different access networks, on different mobile devices, at anytime. User's Perceived Quality of Service (PQoS) or Quality of Experience (QoE) of IPTV service may also suffer from wireless access network impairments. The research from Arnaud *et al.* (2011) paper, introduced new functionalities in IPTV over IMS architecture, which optimise satisfaction of the end-user and resource utilisation of the operator's networks. A context-sensitive user profile model was used to deliver IPTV streams, adapted to the user's environment. Additionally, they introduced a multimedia content management system that was proposed, to perform dynamic cross-layer adaptation of the IPTV stream based on PQoS measurements on the end-user side.

Verdot *et al.* (2011) argued that, improvements in network, software, and hardware capabilities have leveraged the development of rich Internet applications, which offer new and better user experiences. This new deal in the landscape of Internet technologies led them to reconsider the integration of telecommunication on the web. Instead of creating yet another artificial bridge between Internet and various telecommunication architectures, they tried to design an innovative communication model adapted to the intrinsic properties of the web. Verdot et al. (2012) implemented a prototype built on an innovative container-based mechanism, providing this new web-telco infrastructure with a high degree of flexibility and complete adaptability to its environment. They defined open interfaces to guarantee fine-grained control and personalisation of the communication sessions and finally, they tested this new approach through a live experimental platform in order to measure the impact of their model in real conditions.

According to Wang et al. (2012), various network virtualisation techniques have been proposed for flexibly supporting heterogeneous services, over virtual network platforms. In their research they argued that systematic views on how virtual network resources could be practically managed in open environments was missing. To fill the gap, they presented a two-dimensional architecture, for end-to-end virtual network resources management, from distinct viewpoints of service providers and network providers. In terms of the horizontal dimension of virtual network resource management, service providers are allowed to bind virtual network resources rented from heterogeneous network providers to form unified end-to-end service delivery platforms.

The vertical dimension of virtual network resource management enables network providers on the other side to perform cost-efficient allocation of virtual network resources to requesting service providers, but without necessarily forcing themselves to collaborate with each other. This provided virtual network resource management architecture, complementing existing network virtualisation platforms, and accelerating the realisation of virtual resource sharing in future Internet business marketplaces.

Villegas et al. (2012) presented a layered Cloud service model of software (SaaS), platform (PaaS), and infrastructure (IaaS) that leverages multiple independent clouds by creating a federation among the providers. The layered architecture leads naturally to a design in which inter-cloud federation takes place at each service layer, mediated by a broker, specific to the concerns of the parties, at that layer. Federation increases consumer value and facilitates providing IT services, as a commodity. They argued that this business model for the Cloud, is consistent with broker mediated supply and service delivery chains in other commodity sectors, such as finance and manufacturing. Concreteness is added to the federated Cloud model, by considering how it works in delivering Weather Research and Forecasting service as SaaS, using PaaS and IaaS support. Weather Research and Forecasting is used to illustrate the concepts of delegation and federation, the translation of service requirements between service layers, and inter-Cloud broker functions, needed to achieve federation.

2.3.3 SDPs to Drive the Alignment of Web-Platforms and Applications

Pavlovski (2007), outlines a wide set of capabilities that accommodate both IMS and current IT based aspects of SDP deployments. Together the results provide some insight showing how IMS based SDP solutions could be designed to accommodate several parameters, including multimedia services that are highly sought after, the scalability and integration requirements, trends for transaction growth, and the integration of IT capability.

Zhdanova *et al.* (2007) argued, that current mobile service platforms and systems are rather limited in their capabilities and as a result, mobile devices are not used optimally, although enablers and systems, when combined, can achieve innovative, value-added services. They explored ways to improve and enhance a user's experience with mobile systems, experimenting with an ontology-enabled combination of several enabling components. They illustrated the motivation and outcome using a specific scenario, on learning and adapting modality output, according to the user's habits and needs. The main contribution of their work was that functional components adapted to mobile communications settings, showing an ontology-enabled approach to integration of components.

According to Quiao *et al.* (2008), network heterogeneity and service convergence are the main characteristics of future network. Providing self-adaptive, intelligent, integrated services has become the pursuant goal of network carriers and value-added service providers. Dynamic discovery and composition of services are the critical enabling technologies for self-adaptive integrated services. In the service discovery and composition process, semantic interoperability is a key issue. Ontology, as a semantic interoperability and knowledge sharing foundation, has in fact received increasingly more attention. The telecommunication service field, however, consists of a large number of concepts, terminologies and relations. The challenge then, lies in how to abstract sharing domain concepts and reasonably organise them.

Quiao *et al.* (2008), presented a practical domain ontology modelling approach for telecommunications service field. Based on this approach, they constructed an open telecommunication service domain ontology repository to support the knowledge sharing and reuse. They partly facilitated the semantic interoperability of the telecommunications networks and the Internet in the service layer.

Villalong *et al.* (2007), introduced a standardised mobile ontology for mobile service delivery, in NGNs. The main goal of this ontology, was to provide enough flexibility and extensibility while trying to converge to a standardised semantic model, for use in SDPs at the same time.

Begic *et al.* (2009) presented that open, decentralised networks, such as the Internet, are increasingly heterogeneous and dynamic. Applications running over such networks must be able to cope with resource restrictions and operate under the most diverse conditions. Providing multiple services over the same network, has an enormous effect on scalability, performances and cost of this network. Selecting a proper concept of network for mass market has a capital importance for telecom operators. This is even more important for group communication applications, since the differences among group participants must also be taken into consideration. The research from Begic *et al.* (2009), analysed the support mechanisms for group communication applications, which adapt to available network resources.

Models used in this paper are simplifications of real discreet stochastic systems, which represent one of the most popular research areas. Subscriber's behaviour, and dynamic network evolution, are taken into account as key variables before implementing new ideas and innovations. Innovative elements refer to an active node involvement, in forming distributional platform based on IP (Internet Protocol) with elements of multiple services offerings in new generation networks.

In his research, Christian (2011) presented the implementation of a framework, using standard-based service enablers and interfaces, supporting an IPTV application that illustrates the adaptability of the framework so as to generate SDP architectures. Its implementation further facilitated, in evaluating standard-based service enablers and APIs applicable to the SDP framework.

The TeleManagement Formum SDP reference architecture, according to Schülke and Misu (2011), is a generic architecture that integrates SDP technology experiences from various industry groups then represents an applicable service delivery model for both traditional and cloud-based service delivery. Differentiators for SaaS aggregation platforms are shown through the multi-tenancy support in cost reduction, ensuring customer separation, openness for different reselling models, trustworthy operating processes, and open APIs, various business model support and a degree of flexibility allow personalisation of user segments for a customer.

Today, these new, evolving, cloud types and models are in the forefront and investigated by the industry. Success within the market however, has yet to be realised. For this to be achieved, architecture and infrastructure that allows applications to run on more than one device across devices and domains, is both defined and provided. This is also applicable to device features. New APIs are also provided to allow access to local and remote device and network resources in the Cloud.

The next Section introduces, as an example for a Service Delivery Platform, the Service Platform for an Innovative Communication Environment (SPICE).

2.3.4 A Service Platform for an Innovative Communication Environment (SPICE)

The Service Platform for Innovative Communication Environments, or SPICE, is an architectural model that illustrates the problem of the operation and deployment of services together, on one common platform. SPICE makes use of the services of IMS as reference architecture, and is also an IMS-based architecture, that supports convergence features. These two architectures have the potential for dealing with interoperability, as well as operation and deployment aspects, which can be viewed as the initial research areas in this study (Cordier *et al.*, 2005; Bergaus and Stottok, 2010).

2.3.4.1 A Technical Overview of SPICE

The SPICE platform is basically a Service Delivery Platform, based on a service architecture, which provides services supporting convergence, and the adoption and creation of existing and new services, in a simplified way. The SPICE platform is, from a technical perspective, a framework with the following base functions (Cordier *et al.* 2006b: pp. 2-3, Bergaus 2007: pp. 1-2):

▪ Facilitating of the use of mobility at any time, on every network, and at every location, by using telematic services on an SDP, SPICE integrates the connection between the IT and telecommunication world with the IP multimedia subsystem (IMS).

▪ Middleware software, for the support and stabilising of distributed services, in particular the facial point of mobility and interoperability, in order to enable the use of different networks and end devices.

▪ The simple and quick creation of intelligent mobile services, and the supply of official composition tools, such as service description language, service creation environment and service runtime engines, for varying execution platforms.

▪ An integrated content management and content delivery framework that is part of the SDP environment.

▪ Access control framework for the support of convergent authentication mechanisms and the integration of High-Level-Service-Level-Agreements (SLAs).

▪ Development of a set of intelligent service enablers, for the support of services with content awareness functionality, in order to be able to provide specific content on different final device formats.

■   Service roaming functionality that is necessary for the improvement of the stability of services. It also speeds up the availability of services. Furthermore, the use of IMS-based broadband technology is supported.

One of the most important features an interoperable network can offer is support of mobility that includes the capacity for roaming and handover (see Paragraph 8.1.1.2). The term handover refers to the capacity to continue an ongoing session, even in the case of changing point of access of the telecommunication network. By using a roaming service, the mobile subscriber is able to gain access to a telecommunication network, in the visited networks, outside of his Home Service Provider's domain (see Sections 8.3.4 to 8.3.6).

In order to provide the subscriber with access to, and support of, the subscribed services in the home network (service provider domain), different concepts and approaches were proposed, and eventually standardised for further developments (see Sections 8.3.4 to 8.3.6). The following types of mobility can be distinguished (ITU Draft Q.1706, WWRF Vision of System Concepts of Wireless World): Terminal mobility, network mobility, personal mobility, service mobility, profile mobility and session mobility (see Paragraph 8.1.1.5).

SPICE addresses the problem of designing, developing and putting into operation, efficient and innovative mobile Service creation/execution Platforms, for networks beyond 3G. SPICE investigates novel platform features, such as distributed communication sphere management, intelligent service enablers, service roaming, adaptive content delivery and multi-domain access control.

Research undertaken on technical feasibility in the SPICE EU project, shows SPICE technology as a technical-driven SDP platform. The following section summarises project background information describing the author's motivation to investigate user perspective.

2.3.4.2   The IST SPICE FP6 Project

The Information Society Technologies (IST) work programme was a part of the FP6 and set out in detail, the objectives, scientific and technological priorities of the IST priority thematic area, of the FP6 Specific Programme for "Integrating and Strengthening the European Research Area". It defined the objectives and technical content of calls for proposals, the implementation plan and the criteria that was used for evaluating proposals responding to these calls (Information Society Technologies Research – IST in FP6, http://cordis.europa.eu/ist/).

The SPICE project was coordinated by France Telecom and other large European companies. It was also part of the Wireless World Initiative (WWI). The focus of this project was the design and prototype implementation of a development and execution platform for mobile 3G (3rd generation) services. Within the project, an overlay architecture and framework, for the easy and quick development/creation of services, was developed and evaluated. Furthermore, testing and installation of intelligent mobile communication and information services was supported by the SPICE platform.

In terms of the improvement of Information Technology, the SPICE platform supported various heterogeneous execution platforms. In the future it will be possible to enable new and innovative services across borders, within the networks of different telecommunication operators. Frontiers will disappear, diffused, and through this, it will be possible to create a multiplicity of new business models (Cordier, 2005; Cordier et al., 2006b; Zhdanova et al., 2006). SPICE focused on technical feasibility of developing an interoperable, web-based platform, that supports use and handling, of a variety of mobile services and applications.

The SPICE project addressed the unsolved problem of designing, developing and putting into operation, efficient and innovative mobile Service creation/execution Platforms, for networks beyond 3G (3rd generation). SPICE researched, prototyped and evaluated an extendable overlay architecture and framework for the rapid creation and deployment of intelligent and personalised Mobile Communication, Content and Information Services (Cordier, 2005). SPICE also faced key challenges in seeking to overcome major hurdles faced when creating and delivering mobile services. Examples of such hurdles are (Cordier, 2005; Cordier et al., 2006b):

- Time to market for new services developments is too long,

- Users own many different communication devices and are surrounded by many access technologies, but they usually cannot deal with the complexity of accessing their services via several of these devices,

- Service provisioning increasingly involves more parties – telecommunication content/service providers, third party networks, service providers, and even end-users – increasing the complexity of the environment for service operation.

The expected impact for end-users, operators, and service providers, is that the SPICE project will turn today's confusing heterogenity, into an easily manageable and rich service environment, by exploiting the diversity of device capabilities and fostering service adoption. The SPICE approach will broaden business opportunities in the communications and associated business sectors. The SPICE solution will benefit the service developer community, by offering them opportunities for multiple sales, or the acquisition of service components; it will benefit network and service operators, in that the cost of generating, deploying, and operating new services will be reduced; and it will benefit society and the user community in that socially beneficial and enjoyable services will be widely available at affordable cost levels.

The SPICE Service Delivery Platform with open service architecture and innovative enablers will facilitate the creation and deployment of mobile services easily and rapidly, also by non-professional users and commercial service and application providers (Cordier *et al.*, 2006b; Zhdanova *et al.*, 2006).

SPICE addresses challenges, with regard to the design and development issues of service creation and execution, for networks beyond 3G (3rd generation), and puts these into operation in an efficient way. This project researched prototypes, and evaluated an extendable overlay architecture and framework for supporting easy and fast service creation, test and deployment of intelligent mobile communication and information services. Building on significant advances in IT technologies, the SPICE platform will support multiple heterogeneous execution platforms, allowing for new, innovative services, to be spread across different operator domains and over different countries, whilst accommodating a variety of business models (Cordier, 2005).

Some of these mobility types are already fully available within today's interoperable networks, while others are standardised, but only partly included, or entirely left out of, commercially available networks. The support of all these types of mobility, as well as a select combination of them, will be required, in order to provide an information platform able to offer services within next generation networks. In addition to the different types of mobility, an improvement of service provision, service delivery, and of the dynamic service composition within one domain (e.g. home domain), in visited domains or even across domains, will also be a requirement.

The SPICE project discusses preliminary information, roaming definitions, assesses objectives and problem findings, and outlines the research emanating from the outset. It makes use of case definitions, and undertakes a requirement definition process, that clarifies the fundamentals of the service mobility architecture model from a technical point of view. The following Sections discuss possible applications of SDPs especially from the SDP SPICE viewpoint.

2.3.4.3   Definition of the Interview Participant Group of SPICE Experts

According to Van Bossuyt *et al.* (2008), the main value of next-generation, mobile service platforms for users, has been identified, by taking into account lessons drawn from cases mentioned in the previous paragraph. Users can be split into service developers (both professional and non-professional), who create new services using service enablers and modules, found on the platform, and end-users, who then consume those services.

In this study there were three groups of interviewees selected. This group of experts comprised of SPICE architecture experts, developers and end-users. The motivation to interview three groups of people, so closely knit to SDP SPICE, was promulgated by the classical, "Plan-Build-Run" approach. According to

Zarnekow and Brenner (2002), in the broad system of IT management, three stages are basically described: 1. Plan, 2. Build, 3. Run, abbreviated to PBR. If new IT systems are planned, they must be planned and constructed before they can run. IT organizations are structured, and communicate largely, along these lines.

The author believes, that as a basic structure for understanding IT management, "Plan-Build-Run" addresses three necessary stages to develop ICT systems. PBR encourages waterfall thinking, the idea that a complex system just needs to be designed, constructed, and operated. Agile trends turn this from a one-off effort into an ongoing cycle, and this cycle is accelerating, challenging traditional IT organisations and methods. In the following Paragraphs a definition of the three groups is given:

- SPICE architecture experts

- SPICE developers

- SPICE users

SPICE Architecture Experts

SPICE architecture experts, are individuals that work in the SPICE IST 6th framework programme. They have extensive experience of ICT systems and are viewed as architects of ICT with a strong interdisciplinary skills-set. They were assigned to the SPICE project to help identify challenges on an architectural and blueprint level, and as experts in designing conceptual ICT architectures. These experts were interviewed with the premise of identifying any inter-related technology aspects, pertaining to the relationship of SDPs and ICT systems, from a common perspective. They were chosen based on their expected contributions to conceptual technical design. This group may be viewed as conceptual designers and planners of an SDP-based ICT system, drawing on PBR, described in 2.3.4.3.

SPICE Developers

The chosen SPICE developers that participated were familiar with development and implementation of ICT systems. Numerous experts contributed to the development and implementation of SPICE architecture. One could refer to them as the "Build" and "Run" parts of the PBR scenario, described in 2.3.4.3. SPICE developers implementing SDPs could also act as users, as an SDP can operate and provide new services simultaneously without any downtime.

SPICE Users

SPICE users are referred to as the classical users, and the "Run" part of the PBR scenario, described in 2.3.4.3.

2.3.4.4   Related Research Projects to SPICE

The European IST-FP6 project SPICE addressed the issue of designing, developing and putting into practice efficient and innovative mobile service platforms for the rapid creation and deployment of intelligent and personalised mobile communications and information services, according to Ballon *et al.* (2008). A major challenge faced, is the design and validation of lucrative business models for next-generation mobile service platforms. Within the realms of this paper, a business model is defined, as the architecture of a business, detailing how a company sets about exploiting a product or service, for financial gain or profit.

Strohbach *et al.* (2006) reviewed and explained, in their concept, that services can be developed in a cost-effective way with fast time to market. Where IMS (presented in Section 8.1.4) worked, based on heterogeneous network technologies and supported roaming, but didn't address the challenges of rapid development of mobile services. This was addressed using the new architecture of SPICE, integrating IMS to a service oriented architecture that addresses the needs of tomorrow's service platforms.

Tarkoma *et al.* (2007a) argued, that SPICE architecture depicts how existing IMS systems can be extended, to support knowledge-based distributed service provision. An example of service usage, based on a scenario with a video on-demand service, was used to illustrate component interactions. The knowledge layer of the SPICE architecture was discussed in more detail.

This layer, reduces the fragmentation of information and supports knowledge sharing. Additionally the proposed Mobile ontology supports this, by unifying several existing information models. Tarkoma *et al.* (2007b) concluded, that the SPICE project, designed and developed an innovative mobile service creation and execution environment, for networks beyond 3G. The emphasis was to support multiple execution platforms that enable new, innovative services. SPICE architecture consists of four well-defined layers, and is based on components that are discovered, federated, combined and executed, in a distributed environment, presented in Figure 69.

The Middleware Platform for Developing and Deploying Advanced Mobile Services project, or MIDAS, specifies middleware components and a service architecture, that makes it feasible to develop, and rapidly deploy services, on heterogeneous network infrastructures, which involve a large number of users. MIDAS aims to produce overall architecture and middleware building blocks, providing solutions to technical issues that must be addressed, in developing mobile services. It specifically addresses mobile service provision in situations where the network may need to be set up at short notice, or for limited duration, and where communications infrastructure may be unavailable for some users, necessitating the need for use of ad-hoc communications (Plagemann *et al.*, 2007). The middleware includes modules for establishing connectivity using heterogeneous networks, distributed data sharing in unreliable networks, generating synthesised context data, and context based routing of messages (The MIDAS Project).

The project, Mobile Terminal Information Value Added Functionality, or MOTIVE, proposes a monitoring architecture, containing data capturing devices and servers. Based on this monitoring layer, a service layer can then be developed, for example: end-to-end user experience, ubiquitous terminal assisted positioning, and anonymous mobile community services. The key objective of the MOTIVE project is to develop and demonstrate a multi-layered open system architecture and functionality addressing issues such as terminal local processing, user control (when and how information is revealed), data transfer load, network side processing/storage and real time versus off-line information collection modes. MOTIVE system will exploit the information collected at the mobile terminals in order to provide enhanced services and applications in the B3G networks (IST-MOTIVE Deliverable D2.2 - MOTIVE system architecture).

According to Botha et al. (2010), Open Platform for User-centric service Creation and Execution (OPUCE) was an Integrated Project that started in September 2006, funded by the European Union's FP6, and ended in February 2009. The purpose of the project was to produce an open service infrastructure that could enable users to easily create and deploy services in heterogeneous environments. The OPUCE open platform allows traditional information services to merge with communication capabilities, through a user-centric platform, which is supported by Web 2.0 technologies, and a user generated Service paradigm. This allows non-technically skilled end-users to create and share their own Internet/Telco service Mashups.

Mobicents was started as an open source VoIP middleware platform then evolved, to become the first, and only, open source platform to be certified for JSLEE 1.0 compliance. It is a communication platform that has architecture for creating, deploying and managing services and applications, by integrating voice, video and data, across a range of IP and telecom communication networks. In 2007, Red Hat made a firm commitment to enter the emerging Telco middleware market, by doubling investment in the JBoss middleware offering, and officially backing the Mobicents project. They now offer a carrier-grade middleware platform, based on the Mobicents project, that falls under the JBoss Communications platform brand (Botha et al., 2010).

In their article, Magedanz and Sher (2007) gave a summary of the how SDPs have evolved in the last decades. It should have been evident that in face of converging networks and emerging interconnected multi-domain IP networks, the provision of an SDP is a daunting task, with integration work a prerequisite. They outlined that IMS is currently considered the ultimate SDP approach, exploiting the inherent use of IP-centric protocols. The deployment of IMS is driven by the need to interwork with access networks as well as SDPs, such as for example IN/CAMEL (Intelligent Network/ Customized Logic for Mobile Enhanced Logic) and OSA/Parlay (Open Service Access/Parly) API allow, if desired by the business model, third party application providers to make use of the network.

Magedanz and Sher (2007), indicated adopting OSA/Parlay as a unifying service framework instead of CAMEL, and/or IMS could merge the service being provided throughout differing and converging networks. According to Domingue *et al.* (2010) SOA4All (a collaborative European research and development project, is pioneering advanced web technology that will allow billions of parties to expose and consume IT services online) could facilitate the realisation of the world wherein a multitude of parties expose and consume services through advanced web technology.

The result of the project will reflect a comprehensive framework and software infrastructure, which will integrate complementary advances into a coherent and domain-independent worldwide service delivery platform. To achieve such a scalable and widely adopted infrastructure and framework, SOA4All is based on four core principles namely: SOA, semantics, the web and Web 2.0. Present technologies are going to be validated in various real-world applications, including the telco scenario referred to above.

Almeida *et al.* (2008), investigated an approach to the SPICE project in relation to Service Creation. This consisted of a language that leveraged reuse through platform-independent service composition; tools that support the definition of services and their deployment to a target Service Execution Environment and a Service Execution Environment that effectively allows, combining different technologies described in the next Section.

The INDENICA task aspires to provide infrastructure constituents and tools to assist in efficiency and effective creation of domain-specific Virtual Service Platforms (VSP). The Service Platform Infrastructure Repository represents a core aspect needed to achieve these goals at design, deployment and run times. With design time, the repository acts as an infrastructure component library fostering reuse, decreasing development and integration times respectfully, and shielding investments in the INDENICA platform. The repository then maintains deployment descriptors and environment configuration information, enabling easy (re-) deployment of VSPs and their components, at deployment time. The repository also affords the movement of pertinent design and deployment time information to the runtime environment. This then allows runtime components, for example monitoring and adaptation facilities, to take additional information about the deployed VSPs and their infrastructure into account, facilitating greater control over the runtime characteristics of VSPs and their environment (INDENICA Research Project, 2010).

Webinos Project Deliverables (2012), defines the deliverables of the European research project. Users who own devices that, are more connected, expect applications to store preferences and status information, which is synchronised across devices in different domains, has increased. The webinos project was motivated by the need to define and deliver an open source platform, that would facilitate web applications and services to be used and shared stability and over a wide spectrum of connected devices.

According to Almeida *et al.* (2008), Service Creation Environment (SCE) architecture supports different pluggable transformers, to automate the translation of the SPATEL specification into platform-specific code, for different target execution platforms. Examples are JSLEE, J2EE, .NET, as well as BPEL scripts, for orchestrating service compositions in the Service Execution Environment (SEE).

The SCE facilitates efficient service creation both of basic and complex service compositions; selection of reusable services can be based on actual QoS, cost and other non-functional properties, which have now been made accessible because of SPICE SCE, both to end-users and to a broad spectrum of application developers. The SPICE SCE, together with the SPATEL language and the SPICE SEE, add value to the community of developers, in utilising this new method of reusing components, they are then provided with advanced telecommunication services. This will ease the service creation process, diminishing time-to-market, for the new services.

According to Demeter (2008), SPICE proposed enablers and middleware solutions for enriching the SOA landscape for telecommunication services. It developed a semantic discovery and publication middleware, coupled with a service brokering architecture, in order to provide automatic service composition. The Service Roaming Manager concept extended the operation of service composition, over the operator's boundaries. This is described in the next Section.

The purpose of a part of this dissertation is to analyse the SPICE platform (a special SDP supporting the operation and development of ubiquitous services for convergent environments) and to find a model that solves all research issues, from a usability point of view. This research work is constructed on SDPs and more specifically based on SPICE. The participants interviewed in the study are SPICE experts who have worked on European Union funded SPICE research project. SPICE covers only the technological view and potential of a Service Delivery Platform. This investigation focused on the user-centred perspective.

From the researcher's perspective information in what SPICE can offer is lacking, and which user target group it is geared at when they are using SPDs in general. The author is of the opinion that technological features are too complicated for normal end-users as the requirement definition process is also too technically-driven. The author attempted using an alternative means of this requirement definition, by focusing on a user-driven study to further analyse and then define user needs, before investigating the technical feasibility of such systems. For this to be realised, three different groups of SPICE users, defined as SPICE experts (described in the next Section), participated in a qualitative study.

2.3.5   Contribution of SPICE and Critical Treatment of SDPs

The attributes of SPICE architecture and key achievements of the SPICE project are summarised and shortly discussed in the following Section. According to the SPICE project (http://www.ist-spice.org/), these attributes and key achievements are presented in Table 1, following, and cross-referenced with the current SDP literature. Table 1 also shows the relationship to the problem findings, outlined in Chapter 1. Additionally, a short critical review and discussion of the SPICE contributions is presented.

Table 1 presents the SPICE contributions by listing the attributes and key achievements of the SPICE project, in the left column, and cross-referencing them to the current SPICE and SDP literature, shown in the middle column. The challenges are then related to the attributes and problem findings outlined in Chapter 1.

The listed references of current literature focus on technical feasibility studies, using quantitative research methodologies, employing techniques that focus research only on the technical objectives of theses studies. From a critical literature review however, the author is of the opinion that a more user-focused view, employing innovative, technical procedures, could benefit and sustain the implementation of such environments.

As is outlined in Section 1.2.1, for example, Johnston *et al.* (2007), argued that users enjoy the advantages of thoroughly thought out SDP implementations, in that they are able to identify and understand service offerings better. Users are under the impression that SDPs can streamline the administrative and technical obstacles that appear between them and services. This, in turn, contributes to increased service uptake, usage, customer satisfaction and retention (Johnston *et al.*, 2007).

Table 1: SPICE attributes cross-referenced to current SDP literature

SPICE Attributes and key achievements	Cross-Reference to Current Literature on SDPs (examples)	Relating to Problem Findings and Challenges of SDPs (outlined within Chapter 1)
• Service Delivery Platform Architecture linking to IP Multimedia Subsystem (IMS) and embedding a knowledge layer • The SPICE Project: http://www.ist-spice.org/)	• Evolution of service delivery platforms (Johnston et al. 2007) SPICE – Evolving IMS to Next Generation Service Platforms (Tarkoma et al., 2007a) • SPICE: A Service Platform for Future Mobile IMS Services (Tarkoma et al., 2007b) • Service Delivery Platforms in Mobile Convergence (Pavlovski and Plant, 2007) • Service Platform perspective: Overview of the Service Platform for Innovative Communication Environment proposal (Cordier, 2005)	• The hype around the Internet and ICT technologies initiate more and more technical-focused projects with little focus on user needs. • ICT systems support more to a higher degree of proprietary systems because there is a broad range of environments in the field

• Component-based middleware layer ensuring the inter-working of distributed service components:
  o Full components life-cycle management guidelines
  o Semantic publication and discovery infrastructure for components; Service brokering function (to dispatch incoming service requests)
  o Service Roaming Manager functionality
• (The SPICE Project: http://www.ist-spice.org/)
	• Advanced Beyond 3G service delivery environment the SPICE service platform design principles (Cordier et al. 2006a)
	• Mobile Service Platforms Cluster White Paper Mobile Service Platforms – Architecture Whitepaper (Demeter, 2008)
	• Service and information roaming – architecture and design aspects (Zoric et al. 2006)
	• Service business processes for the next generation of services: a required step to achieve service convergence (Bertin et al. 2009)
		• Current SDP research mainly focused on technical features or technical design.

• Advanced semantically-enhanced service creation and composition tools:
  o Service description language (SPATEL) and its graphical notation
  o Service creation environment comprising a Developer Studio, and
  o End-user Studio, an automatic Service Composition Engine and a deployment tool
• (The SPICE Project: http://www.ist-spice.org/)
	• Addressing the challenges of Beyond 3G service delivery the SPICE service platform (Cordier et al. 2006b)
	• Advanced Language for Value added services composition and creation (Belaunde et al. 2006)
	• Service Delivery Platform: Critical Enabler to Service Providers' New Revenue Streams (Schulke et al. 2006)
	• Service Creation in the SPICE Service Platform (Almeida et al. 2008)
	• An Algorithm for Automatic Service Composition (Goncalves da Silva et al. 2007)
		• Explosion of mobile services and applications with the help of the mobile Internet
		• End-users do not have the possibility of using different applications and services from the same end devices on demand

• Definition and Setup of a distributed Service Execution Environment with different execution engines • (The SPICE Project: http://www.ist-spice.org/)	• Scenarios for the representative next generation communication and information services (SPICE deliverable 1.2, 2006) • Convergence – An outlook on device, service, network and technology trends (3G Americas, 2005) • Adaptive IPTV services based on a novel IP Multimedia Subsystem (Arnaud et al. 2011) • Defining a Service Delivery Platform Architecture by Reusing Intelligent Network Concepts (Rolan and Hu, 2008) • Enabling Service Delivery in Next-Generation Networks towards Service Clouds (Schulke et al. 2011)	• Current SDP research mainly focused on technical features or technical design.

SPICE Attributes and key achievements	Cross-Reference to Current Literature on SDPs (examples)	Relating to Problem Findings and Challenges of SDPs (outlined within Chapter 1)
• Content management and delivery framework integrated in the SDP. Definition of a multi-faceted mobile service ontology, used throughout the project. • (The SPICE Project: http://www.ist-spice.org/)	• Mobile Ontology: Towards a Standardized Semantic Model for the Mobile Domain (Villalonga et al., 2007) • Service Program Mobility Architecture (Lundqvist et al., 2006) • Mobile Service Platforms Cluster White Paper: Mobile Service Platforms – Architecture Whitepaper (Demeter) • The Service Web: a Web of Billions of Services (Domingue et al., 2010) • Cross-Case Analysis of the User Value Proposition for Next-Generation Mobile Service Platforms (Van Bossuyt et al., 2008)	• Internet is today the most important platform for user application and services

• Distributed Communication Sphere Management System, comprising:
  o A widget-based interface on the mobile to search and access services (Dynamic Desktop)
  o A terminal manager and a resource discovery system
  o A group management system and a terminal user rules engine
  o A multimodal delivery and control system
• (The SPICE Project: http://www.ist-spice.org/)
	• A Service Integration Platform for Collaborative Networks (Osona et al., 2010)
	• SPICE: A Service Platform for Future Mobile IMS Services (Tarkoma et al., 2007b)
	• Development and Publication of Generic Middleware Components for the Next Generation Mobile Service Platform (Bhushan et al., 2007)
	• Service Delivery Platforms – Developing and Deploying Converged Multimedia Services (Ahson and Ilyas, 2011)
	• Service Delivery Platform: Critical Enabler to Service Providers' New Revenue Streams (Schulke et al., 2006)
		• Current SDP research mainly focused on technical features or technical design.

• Access control framework
  o Supporting convergent authentication mechanisms
  o Integrating high-level service SLAs and privacy - Supporting charging of composite services
• (The SPICE Project: http://www.ist-spice.org/)
	• A Comparative Study: Service-Based Application Development by Ordinary End Users and IT Professionals (Namoun et al., 2010)
	• Service Delivery Platforms in Practice (Pavlovski, 2007)
	• Service Platform for Innovative Communication Environment – Functional Architecture (SPICE Project Deliverables 1.3, 2006)
	• A Brief Survey of Software Architecture Concepts and Service Oriented Architecture (Valipour et al., 2009)
	• Cloud Federation in a Layered Service Model (Villegas et al., 2012)
		• End-users do not have the possibility of using different applications and services from the same end devices on demand.

• Development of a set of Intelligent service enablers
  o Knowledge discovery, exchange and interpretation enablers
  o Personal information and attentive services enablers
• (The SPICE Project: http://www.ist-spice.org/)
	• Mobile Ontology: Towards a Standardized Semantic Model for the Mobile Domain (Villalonga et al., 2007)
	• A Service Integration Platform for Collaborative Networks (Osorio Luis et al., 2010)
	• A Service Delivery Platform for End-to-End Value Web Enablement (An SDP Alliance White Paper, 2006)
	• Towards the automation of the service composition process: case study and prototype implementations (Shiaa et al., 2008)
	• Service Delivery Platform - A Directory Service Evolution (iwwiteware™, 2010)
		• Current SDP research mainly focused on technical features or technical design.
		• End-users do not have the possibility of using different applications and services from the same end devices on demand.

2.3.6 Summary

This Section described the Service Delivery Platform technology concentrating on the SPICE architecture, emphasising their potential, for use in different environments. Based on Service Oriented Architecture and cloud computing concepts the architecture of an SDP, and the architecture of SPICE were described and presented. SPICE can be seen as a special SDP with a convergent approach (connection of IT and mobile environments).

A literature review of current SDP and SPICE literature was presented. The author presented additional literature of SPICE relationships, related SPICE attributes and key achievements to current literature, as well as to challenges and problem findings, which were outlined in Chapter 1. Furthermore it was stated that much research is undertaken from a technical perspective but little from that of users. The group of SPICE experts (users, developers and architecture experts) was also defined.

At this point, all relevant aspects have been defined and illustrated. The following Section describes the related research to this PhD thesis in context. This entails that state-of-the art literature research is presented, both from a technical and a user point of view, and relate to the work of this thesis.

The listed references of current literature focus on technical feasibility studies, using quantitative research methodologies, employing techniques that focus research only on the technical objectives of theses studies. From a critical literature review however, the author is of the opinion that a more user-focused view, employing innovative, technical procedures, could benefit and sustain the implementation of such environments.

The next Section discusses and presents a system design with a strong involvement of users perspective.

2.4 System Design for User Needs

Evaluating user perspective, in terms of ICT systems is important. Traditional methods of user testing are expensive and tedious to operate cross culturally, over various numerous geographical locations. The challenge that exists is engaging users successfully within different implementation and testing methodologies (Greenbaum and Kyng, 1991). The entire concept of User Centred Design (UCD), and the participation in different testing methodologies, challenges international software development teams, however, input from user perspectives creates the opportunity for development guidelines to be established for individual cultures and frameworks (Nielsen, 2004).

2.4.1   The Importance of Usability is Increasing

'User friendly' is often the term used as a synonym for usable, and could additionally refer to accessibility. Usability describes the quality of user experience across websites, software, products, and environments, and no agreement exists with the relation between human factors and usability terms. Karwowski *et al.* (2011), brought to light the consideration of usability as the software specialisation of the larger topic of ergonomics. Some see these subjects as tangible, with ergonomics emphasising physiological matters e.g., turning a door handle, and in recognising that a door can be opened by turning the handle would then focus on the psychological.

Usability is also vital in website development (web usability). According to Jakob Nielsen, "Studies of user behaviour on the Web find a low tolerance for difficult designs or slow sites. People don't want to wait. And they don't want to learn how to use a home page. There's no such thing as a training class or a manual for a Web site. People have to be able to grasp the functioning of the site immediately after scanning the home page - for a few seconds at most." Alternatively, passers-by just leave the site and browse, or shop, elsewhere (Shneiderman and Plaisant, 2009).

Karwowski *et al.* (2011), stated that usability is the ease of use and the learnability of a man-made object. This focus could be a software application, website, book, tool, machine, process or anything a human interacts with. A means of measuring, such as needs analysis, and the study of the principles behind an object's perceived efficiency or elegance, is encompassed by 'usability'.

Usability studies are undertaken with elegance and clarity in HCI and computer science, with respect to interaction with a computer programme or when a web site is designed. Usability differs from both user satisfaction and experience because usability additionally takes into consideration usefulness (Nielsen, 2004).

ISO defines usability as "The extent to which a product can be used by specified users to achieve specified goals with effectiveness, efficiency, and satisfaction in a specified context of use." In this case then 'usability' refers to ways of streamlining ease-of-use during the design process. Jakob Nielsen and Ben Shneiderman have both written about a framework of system acceptability, where usability is a part of usefulness, and is composed of (Nielsen, 1993):

■ *Learnability:* Centres on the question of how simple it is for users to accomplish basic tasks the first time they encounter the design?

■ *Efficiency:* How quickly users can perform tasks once they have learned the design?

- *Memorability:* After not using the design for given time, how quickly can they re-establish proficiency, when they return to it?

- *Errors:* What is the number of errors, how serious are they and how easily can they recover from the errors?

- *Satisfaction:* Is it easy and simple to use the design?

In evaluating user interfaces for usability, the definition is as simple as how a target user perceives its effectiveness and efficiency. Every part can be measured subjectively with criteria, e.g., principles of user interface design, to provide a metric, often expressed as a percentage. Distinguishing between usability testing, and usability engineering, is essential. Ease of use of a product or piece of software, is determined by usability testing, contrasting with usability engineering (UE) which is the research and design process which ensures a product with good usability (Gloud and Lewis, 1985). Usability is a non-functional requirement, and in so saying with other non-functional requirements, usability cannot be directly measured but should instead be quantified by means of indirect measurements, or attributes such as, the number of reported problems with ease-of-use of a system, as an example (Gloud and Lewis, 1985).

2.4.2 User Centred Design

Complex computer and information systems enter our everyday life, where simultaneously, markets are saturated with competing brands. As companies realise the benefits of researching and developing their products with user-oriented methods instead of technology-oriented methods, usability has increased in popularity in recent years. In understanding and researching interaction between the product and user, usability experts are able to provide an insight unattainable by traditional, company-oriented market research. The usability expert may identify needed functionality or design flaws that were not anticipated, after observing and interviewing users, as an example. A method called contextual inquiry does this in a natural context, within users environment also known as User Centred Design, abbreviated to UCD (Holm, 2006).

UCD has been constantly discussed in terms of providing the user with easier access and application of the information. In the current type of UCD, computers actively provide information, which users passively receive. It should be recognised what the importance is of getting the user involved by applying interactive technology (Greenbaum and Kyng, 1991). A prerequisite to interface development and testing is defining user culture, including their characteristics, types, levels of expertise, and user task descriptions. As new media allows us to interact at a higher, than simply the information-processing levels, attention to individual differences will increase in importance and detail. An example, as the

Web interface incorporates video technologies, we must pay attention to individual and cultural differences in facial expressions, gestures, and demeanour (Nielsen, 2004).

Human Computing Interaction (HCI) specialists have, for a long time now, stressed the importance of User Centered Design (UCD), and it has recently become a focal point in terms of mainstream software development methods, such as extreme programming and DSDM (Beck, 2000; Stapleton, 2003). In the UCD paradigm, its intended users are constantly considered during design, whereas with user-driven or participatory design, some of its users may become part of the design team or participatory (Dix et al., 2004).

User Centred Design (UCD) recommends that, design should begin on an abstraction level that facilitates designers, to make the essential connection between the user's goals and the specific ways of meeting those goals. This could involve discovering the optimal device or program to assist users in achieving their objectives (Hackos and Redish, 1998). What is paramount and beneficial in eliciting experience requirements, particularly if the same service is provided through different interface technologies, is that Technological independence and a focus on user roles and expectations prior to any choice of a specific interaction platform is made, (Patrício et al., 2003).

The participation of users during a design and implementation project is vital to the successful development of computerised ICT systems. System analysts are also essential in developing useful information systems. As software development teams become more international in their composition, so then are users becoming more important. This entails that there is a greater focus on working with users of software when analysing business performance, problems and objectives, and on distributing this communication of the planned system to all stakeholders. This is a component of a method called Requirement Engineering presented in the following Section.

2.4.3 Requirement Engineering

It seems as though software development has become a business requirement for a number of reasons, which include cost, availability of resources, the need to position developments nearer to customers, time-to-market acceleration, improving additional knowledge, and improving operational efficiency. The increase of software development globally, has created software engineering challenges due to time zones, diversity of culture, communication or distance. Some of these challenges were identified and published in a framework by Ramachandran and De Carvallo (2010), mentioning the following attributes:

■ Cultural diversity and cost management, time-to-market, and complexity,

■ Communication project management and customer-driven quality,

■ Software development, tools, techniques, platforms and time zones.

Requirements Engineering (RE), is a systems and software engineering process that enfolds activities involved in discovering, recording and maintaining a set of requirements, for a computer-based system. In the traditional waterfall model of the systems or software engineering process, RE is presented as the first stage of the development process, with the result being a requirements document.

RE can, therefore, be considered a continual process during the lifetime of a system where requirements are tentative and new requirements have to be drawn, then recorded, and actual requirements maintained, during the lifespan of the system (Kotonya and Somerville, 1998). RE processes, facilitate a requirement to be defined as a condition or capability, that must be fulfilled by a system, to satisfy a contract, standard, specification, or other critical documents. A system should be correct, consistent, verifiable and traceable, for the requirements to be defined.

RE is the process of eliciting, understanding, specifying and validating both customer and user requirements. It further identifies under which technological restrictions the application should be constructed and run. It is an iterative process with the objective to analyse the problem, to document the results in a variety of formats and evaluate the precision of the results produced (Shams-Ul-Arfif, Khan *et al.*, 2010).

When a software application is built, the development team has to be informed about the application's requirements and the problem domain. It is a complex process acquiring the elicitation and specification of these requirements, as it is necessary to identify the functionality that the system has to fulfil in order to satisfy the user's and customer's needs (Chakraborty *et al.*, 2012). According to Hull *et al.* (2005) two classes of requirements were described:

■ *Functional requirements:* The functional requirements determine what a software program does. These are made up of statements of services the system should provide, how it should react to particular input, and how the system should react in particular situations.

■ *Non-functional requirements:* Non-functional requirements describe the attributes of a software program. This entails constraints on services or functions offered by the system, such as timing constraints, constraints on the development process, standards, security requirements, and performance.

Leffingwell and Widrig (2003), argued two types of requirements when designing a software application:

■ *User requirements:* These are statements in natural language, including diagrams of the services the system provides and its operational constraints written for customers, from their perspective.

■ *System requirements:* These are structured documents, with detailed descriptions of the system's functions, services and operational constraints.They what should be implemented, and may form part of a contract between client and contractor. This could be seen as the technical system's-related perspective.

2.4.3.1   Different Views between Users and Developers

According to Saiedian and Dale (1999) and McAllister (2006), some major problems occurred when separating views of different groups of users, such as developers and end-users with the requirement process, as each had their own conflicting perspective. A few examples are, that developers often see users being unable to articulate what they want, or that users have too many needs that are politically motivated, and want everything immediately; that users can't prioritise needs, or refuse to take responsibility for the system. In some cases they are unable to provide a usable statement of needs, and in others they are not committed to system development projects; are unwilling to compromise and cannot remain on schedule. On the other hand, users see developers that don't understand operational needs; that place too much emphasis on technicalities, and try to tell users how to do their jobs; that cannot translate clearly-stated needs into a successful system; that constantly reply negatively or exceed the budget and do not deliver on time.

They ask users for time and effort, even to the detriment of the user's important primary duties; set unrealistic standards for requirement definitions; are unable to respond quickly to legitimate changing needs. DeBellis and Haapala (1995) offered four reasons, why users and developers misunderstand requirements:

■ Paper-based documents are typically used to capture and convey requirements, which are prone to ambiguity, omissions, and misinterpretations.

■ Users and developers have a conflicting frame of reference and do not invest time, building a common language for dialogue.

■ Users may not understand the real requirements, themselves, until they have interacted with early versions of the information system.

◼   Even if requirements are understood, the time between requirements deter-
     mination and deployment of the information system, allows for require-
     ments to change.

Combining both user and developer views, is intended to deepen the understanding of requirements. There are discrepancies of viewpoints between the two
different groups involved in RE and the software life-cycle process (illustrated in
the last Section 2.4.3): Functional user requirements are high-level statements of
what the system should do. Functional system requirements describe the system
services in detail (Pandey *et al.*, 2010).

The author is of the opinion that, by specifying a high level functional user
requirement, of what an ICT system should deliver, is of significant importance
for the whole system design, before describing the system services in detail
(functional system requirements).

2.4.3.2   Requirement Engineering Process

Chakraporty *et al.* (2012) described a framework for requirement engineering
process as follows:

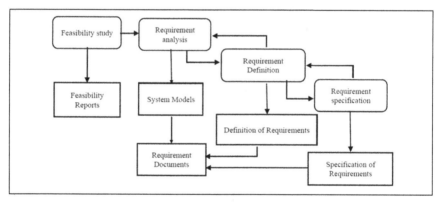

Figure 7: A framework for requirement engineering process (Chakraporty *et al.*, 2012)

A framework for the RE process is presented above in Figure 7. A feasibility report is produced and proceeds to the output as defined and specified by the
prerequisites of Requirement Analysis, Requirement Definition and Requirement
Specification. The feasibility study process results in a feasibility study report.
After getting requirement acquisition, which is the input of the statement of requirements, requirement modelling is performed and then proceed to the requirement model process; finally the requirement is validated (Chakraporty *et
al.*, 2012).

Requirement elicitation is an iterative process, involving domain understanding, requirement collection, classification, structuring, prioritisation and validation, according to Alexander and Stevens (2002). Information systems have many stakeholders with different requirements, therefore, social and organisation factors influence the system requirements. Requirements validation is concerned with checks for validity, consistency, completeness, realism and verifiability. Business changes adapt to changing requirements, where the management thereof includes planning and change management.

2.4.3.3   Feasibility Studies

Feasibility studies determine whether a proposal for a system is viable. If the system contributes to organisational objectives, or if it is possible to engineer it using current technology, and if that system can be integrated with other systems that are in use, then a feasibility study checks this. The implementation of the study is based on information assessment and the impact of the system on all stakeholders, e.g., users, developers, management, contracting organisation, funding sources (Alexander and Stevens, 2002).

2.4.3.4   Requirements Elicitation and Analysis

Requirement elicitation and analysis, facilitates technical evaluation and analysis of the requirements. According to the interview participants, the analysis is seen as an interactive process in which participants with market competence, and those with technical understanding, negotiate requirements. There are different methods of undertaking requirement elication, and the most relevant to this study will be described in the following Paragraphs (Pandey *et al.*, 2010).

Interviews

Formal or informal procedures are undertaken in an interview, by the requirement engineering team. They pose questions to stakeholders about their existing ones, which need to be developed. Scenarios are taken from real-life examples of how a system can be used, and include: A description of the initial situation, as well as, a description of the normal flow of events. Furthermore, a description of foreseeable challenges is presented, including information about concurrent activities, and a description of the final stage.

Use-cases are an example for the application of a scenario-based technique. Often, UML is used to identify the actors in a role-play, then afterwards the interaction is described. A set of use-cases should describe all possible interactions with the system. Sequence diagrams may be used to add detail to use-cases by showing the sequence of event processing in the system (Alexander and Stevens, 2002).

Questionnaire

This is an effective tool requiring minimum effort, and produces a written document reflecting the key evaluation questions. It examines a large number of respondents simultaneously and gets customised answers. Furthermore, it allows one sufficient time to answer, give applicable answers, and is a simple tool consisting of open and/or closed questions. In order to get the right results and responses, the questionnaires must be clear, defined and concise, with respect to the domain of the system to be developed. Questions should focus on the problem, and redundancy in questions must be avoided (Shams-Ul-Arif *et al.*, 2010).

Observation (Ethnography)

Social scientists invest a considerable amount of time observing and analysing how people actually work. People do not have to explain or articulate their work. Indeed, important social and organisational factors are observed. Ethnographic studies have shown that work is usually richer and more complex than suggested by simple system models. Prototype development, results in unanswered questions which, focus on the ethnographic analysis. The problem with ethnography is that it studies existing practices with some historical basis, which may now be irrelevant.

Requirements derived from the way that people actually work, rather than the way in which the process defines it, suggest that they ought to work with cooperation and awareness of other people's activities. Software systems are used in a social and organisational context, which can influence or even dominate the system requirements. Social and organisational factors are not a single viewpoint, but are influences on all viewpoints. Good analysts need to be sensitive to these factors, but at present no systematic way to tackle their analysis exists (McAllister, 2006).

Interviews, as well as Ethnography in qualitative scenarios, can also be done with focus groups, for example, users or customers as part of a development team. There are some problems with Requirements Elicitation: the parameters of the system are ill-defined, irrelevant design information may be given, stakeholders do not have a full understanding of their requirements, or have a poor understanding of computer capabilities and limitations. Software engineers could have poor knowledge of the problem domain and stakeholders and/or software engineers may not speak the same languages.

"Obvious" information is omitted. Different stakeholders have conflicting views. Requirements are vague and not testable, such as "user friendly" and "robust". Requirements are volatile and change over time (Chakraborty, *et al.*, 2010).

2.4.3.5   Requirements Specification

Requirements state what a system should do, and design describes how it does this, in practice, requirements and design are inseparable. System-architecture is designed to structure requirements, and inter-operates with other systems that then generate design requirements, where the use of a specific design may be a domain requirement. Most systems need to inter-operate and the operating interfaces must be specified as part of the requirements of an interface specification. Three types of interfaces need to be defined: Procedural interfaces; data structures that are exchanged; data representations (Nguyen and Swatman, 2000).

Requirements specification document

A requirements specification document is produced after successfully identifying the requirements. The document describes the final product rather than the process of its development. It is a formal statement defining what is expected from system developers. It contains a complete description of the external behavior of a software system. This document includes both, a definition of user requirements and a specification of the system requirements, but it is not a design document. Ideally it should set out what the system should do, rather than how it should do it (Pandey *et al.*, 2010).

2.4.3.6   Requirements Validation

A validation of requirements is done in order to reflect concern that requirements define a system that customers really want. Requirements error is expensive, so validation is critical in as far as addressing requirement errors post delivery, and cost more than fixing an implementation error. For this reason, requirements are validated. The system provides functions that best support the customer's needs, in terms of consistency and traceability. To ensure and check completeness, customer requirements must be included, then checked if they can be implemented, within the allocated and pre-specified budget and technology.

Another important check-point is adaptability: can a requirement be changed without a significant impact on other requirements. As with the techniques used for requirement validation, requirement reviews by means of systematic manual analysis of requirements, is used as well as prototyping. In this case, an executable model of the system (test case generation) is used to check requirements. Test development for requirements is done, to check the testability. Requirements must be understandable, non-prescriptive, correct, complete, concise, formulated in consistent language, unambiguous and testable, traceable, feasible, and ranked in order of importance and stability (Gilb, 2003).

From the author's perspective, the requirements document focuses intensively on those that are technically oriented. Yeh and Tsai (2001) studied the conflicts between users and developers, citing previously researched reasons for these conflicts. These included: intergroup hostility, poor communications, negative perceptions of the other group, and frequency of interpersonal interaction.

They examined conflicts that were substantive in nature (related to practices, policies, procedures, roles, and responsibilities) with those that were emotional in nature (related to personal perceptions and feelings). Due to those differences noted between users and developers, conflicts are expected to be common during the development of an information system.

2.4.4   Design for Testability of Software Architectures

Design for Testability (DFT) is a definition for design techniques that add certain testability features to a hardware product design. The premise of the added features is that they make it easier to develop and apply manufacturing tests for the designed hardware. The motivation for producing tests is to ascertain if the product hardware contains no defects, which could adversely affect the product's optimal function (Scheffer et al., 2006; IEEE Std 1149.1 (JTAG) Testability Primer, 1997).

Tests are applied at several steps in the hardware manufacturing flow and, for certain products, may also be used for hardware maintenance, in the customer's environment. Generally, tests are driven by test programs that are executed in automatic test equipment or, in the case of system maintenance, inside the assembled system itself. In addition to finding and indicating the presence of defects (i.e., the test fails), test log diagnostic information, about the nature of the failures found that the diagnostic information is used to locate the source of the failure. The response of patterns from a good circuit is, therefore, compared with the response of patterns from a device under test. If the response is the same as, or matches, the circuit it is good, otherwise the circuit is faulty (Scheffer et al., 2006).

DFT plays a significant role in the development of test programs and as an interface for test application and diagnostics. Automatic test pattern generation is much easier if appropriate DFT rules and suggestions are implemented. DFT affects, and depends on, the methods used for test development, test application and diagnostics. One key objective of DFT methodologies is to allow designers to compromise between the amount, and type, of DFT, and the cost/benefit (time, effort, quality) of the test generation task. Another benefit is diagnosing a circuit in case any future problems emerge. This is similar to adding some features, or provisions in the design, so that device can be tested in case of any fault during its use (IEEE Std 1149.1 (JTAG) Testability Primer, 1997).

Building reliable software is an important issue, seeing that computer applications are now used in various environments, including those where human life depends on the computer's correct functioning. Software is considered reliable if it has a low probability of failure, when it is used (Hamlet, 1994).

When faulty code in the software is executed then failures occur. Identifying these faults in the software is done through formal proofs or through selective or exhaustive testing (Ramamoorthy and Ho, 1975). Formal proofs are rather complicated to perform and exhaustive testing is not feasible because of the large number of execution paths that exist, even if the software comprises of relatively few lines of code. Selective testing, dynamic testing, or simply software testing, is the most common method used to improve confidence in the reliability of software.

Software testing involves executing software and observing how it reacts. If the softwareconforms in behaviour, confidence in its reliability is increased, and software testing progresses from being a post-development activity, to an activity that is integrated throughout the development phases. In the traditional waterfall software development life cycle, software testing was done after a software system had already been built. More recently defined, software development methodologies and processes recommend that testing be done at various stages throughout the development cycle. The V-model, for example, recommends that testing should be done at unit, integration and system levels (Black, 2007). At each testing level of the V-model, a different level of granularity of software component is subjected to testing activities.

Test-driven development is another, recently defined, software development methodology, used for the development of unit tests, even before the functional code is written. After creating unit tests, the developer writes the functional code necessary, to ensure that all the previously created unit tests pass. Once the unit tests have all passed, and developers cannot think of any more to create, the development work is considered complete. Test-driven development improves the quality of software, by forcing developers to take certain design decisions based on the testing needs. Also, written tests provide a form of documentation for the software (Beck and Andres, 2004).

Regardless of how testing is integrated into a software development cycle, there are a number of difficulties incurred when testing software. Software testing is based on assumed inputs, that may give false test results if the assumptions are wrong (Voas, 1992). Testing may reveal errors, but not necessarily help with, pointing out where the faults in the software are located. Moreover, testing requires that there is an oracle present to specify what the expected results, from the test, are. In worse case scenarios, testing may not even reveal failures because the faults either do not get executed, or get executed but deceptively, give correct results for the inputs that were chosen (Binder, 1999).

Size of software systems also affects testing. As size of systems increases, so does the cost of testing. Estimate cost of software testing, ranges from 40% up to 80%, of the entire development cost (Zaidman et al., 2007). Unit testing, for example, is very expensive in terms of effort, to maintain the test code. Besides test code maintenance, relatively large parts of the entire system have to be tested, even for small additions to the overall source code base. Finally, the additional software units may seem correctly implemented, only to discover functions after they have been composed together and tested at sub-system level. Software testing can, therefore, be viewed as an economic problem that is driven by either a predefined reliability target, or by resource constraints (Binder, 1994). In the former, resources are devoted to the testing until the reliability target is achieved, whereas in the latter instance, testing is performed until the resources dedicated to testing, are depleted.

Voas and Miller (1995) introduced software testability, as the third piece of the reliability puzzle, alongside the previously mentioned formal verification and software testing. They defined testability as: the probability that the software shall fail on its next execution. Testability is defined in the IEEE glossary of software engineering as (IEEE, 1990):

■ The degree to which a system or component facilitates the establishment of test criteria, and the performance of tests to determine whether those criteria have been met.

■ The degree to which a requirement is stated in terms that, permit establishment of test criteria, and the performance of tests, to determine whether those criteria have been met.

Testability can also be thought of as a characteristic, or property, of a piece of software that makes it easier to test. Binder (1994) and Freedman (1991), adapt the notions of controllability and observability from hardware testing into the software context. Controllability is the ability to manipulate the software's input as well as to place this software into a particular state, while observability deals with the possibility to observe the outputs and state changes that occur in the software. Based on their definition, a piece of software is said to be testable if it has these two properties. Other work adds extra characteristics like understandability, traceability and test-support capability to the testability notion (Gao and Shih, 2005).

Besides being a characteristic of software, testability can be defined in terms of the software development process that is relative to the testing phase, for example, integration test, relative to an activity of the test phase, for example, test case creation, and as a characteristic of the architecture, design, and implementation of a piece of software (Kolb and Muthig, 2006). Binder (1994), talks of six major factors that result in testability during the development process. The factors are: characteristics of the design documentation, characteristics of the implementation, built-in test capabilities, presence of a test suite, presence of test tools and the software development process capability/maturity. Some of the characteristics of the documentation that can enhance testability include: unambiguity in requirements, thoroughness of detailed design, traceability of the requirements to the implementation and, separation of concerns. These characteristics are not only related to testability and also refer to fundamentals of design practice (Binder, 1994).

Testability complements software testing, as it eases fault finding in software, by helping to focus the testing efforts on areas that are most likely to yield these faults (Voas and Miller, 1995). However, resources for developing software are typically limited. Testability enables achievement of greater reliability in such a resource-constrained development environment. In a reliability-driven development environment, testability also reduces the overall costs needed to attain a predefined target. Testability, therefore, facilitates making testing more effective and efficient.

The testability characteristic of software, leads to the idea of design for testability. Binder (1994), defines design for testability as "a strategy to align the development process so that testing is maximally effective". As an example, this strategy involves incorporating certain features, in software implementations and/or software designs, that should improve on the testability of software.

2.4.5 Related Research in Terms of System Design for User Needs

This Section relates the research of this thesis and presents that there is an abundance of technical research work on systems and technical possibilities, but only several directly related research papers along the lines of this thesis, with the focus on the user perspective in developing web-based platforms, such as SDPs to administrate future-based ICT systems.

There is much work in terms of SDPs, on technical topics, regarding standardisation and reference frameworks. There appears though to be little work on SDPs and their deployment characteristics, with respect to services and service growth, seen from the perspective of users. A detailed analysis of the mobile Internet content provider model, was studied, with a focus on the Japanese market experience (Devine, 2001). The findings highlight the importance of operator and external content service provider relationships, in terms of content provisioning and effective revenue sharing, models. The view of the end-users was an integral point to focus on, within this research.

Building test capabilities into software implies, that certain features that are not necessarily in the functional specifications of software, are added to the software to ease testing. For example, having extra set/reset methods that allow classes in object oriented software to be placed in a desired state. Besides having extra methods, built-in test capabilities could also incorporate hard coding test cases, into the software. Testing tools that automatically execute test scripts, record execution traces, log state and performance information and, report test results, makes it easier to handle testing.

Being committed to software testing within an organization that produces software, reflected in the resources dedicated to testing, like capable staff, presence of a systematic testing strategy and integration of testing, throughout the entire development process (Jeon *et al.*, 2002). Implementing high quality software testing increases cost. Leffingwell and Widrig (2000) cite two reasons for this increasing cost:

▪ time invested in all other activities (e.g., design, coding) is wasted if requirements are incorrect, and these activities have to be redone,

▪ and the natural assumption that errors discovered during testing or inspection are related to design, which wastes valuable time until it is realised that they are from errors in requirements.

The cost of requirement errors is not limited to the price of creating the system. If the requirements are wrong or incomplete, the system is redundant, or lowers productivity.

2.4.5.1   Related Research - Technical-Oriented Studies

Funk (2000) points out that partnerships built on standards are a key success factor, with particular support for IT systems such as billing and presenting content via external service providers. Pavlovski (2002), presents a platform outlining service delivery environments to deliver multimedia content and services to mobile devices for alternative networks such as GSM. Pavlovski and Staes-Polet (2005), also address capabilities to support both wired and mobile networks, peer-to-peer services, and other enhanced multimedia services. Related work on delivery of services to the home using a delivery platform to enable third party services is also proposed in Lee *et al.* (2006).

The importance of IT system components including Customer Relationship Management, content management, billing for content partners, service and user growth was researched by MacDonald (2003). IMS as a basis for service delivery platform has been suggested by Bushnesll (2004) and in Magedanz *et al.* (2005) a service delivery platform that extends IP multimedia systems was developed. The authors outline a test bed architecture that integrates SIP and Parlay (another network connecting protocol – it enables software developers to use the capabilities of an underlying network) with the telecommunications network to deliver multimedia services.

Patel and Ramachandran (2010), claimed software development, which addresses customers needs and expectations, is the ultimate goal of the software development methodology. In order to meet these demands, one has to perform requirement engineering so as to identify and structure the requirements, using historical user data and story cards aided by agile requirements engineering. It is uncommon for customers to have a general mental overview of requirements or systems, which raises problems related to requirements. These are requirement conflicts, missing requirements, ambiguous requirements, and do not address non-functional requirements from the exploration phase.

With such emphasis put on understanding requirements, it is unsurprising then, that numerous approaches have been introduced to improve requirement identification, and consequently understanding the requirements of users and developers. A number are more user-oriented techniques, such as a natural language approach (Lu et al., 1995), while others are more developer-oriented techniques, such as employing intelligent computer aided design (Williamson and Healy, 2000).

'Voice of Customer' is the intended technique to help developers understand the needs of users and used in customer-focused methodologies (Griffin and Hauser, 1993). As such, it is a philosophy of development rather than a specific technique. Simply, it captures the needs of users in their own words, and prioritizes the importance of each. It is evident in quality management strategies, such as Total Quality Management, as it is often equated to user satisfaction.

Preece et al. (2002), identifies usability and user experience goals respectively, for interaction design which allows the trend towards a more goal-oriented analysis of user needs. Usability goals are concerned with the optimal interaction between users and systems, addressing specific usability criteria, such as effectiveness, efficiency, safety, utility, learnability, and memorability. User experience goals are concerned with how users experience an interactive system from their perspective, which differ from usability goals. Interactive systems that offer an optimal user experiences are satisfying, enjoyable, fun, entertaining, helpful, motivating, aesthetically pleasing, supportive of creativity, rewarding and emotionally fulfilling.

According to Klockner et al. (1999), one of the more serious communication problems, is caused by developers: "Designers (developers) had a tendency to defend the features they designed, which could be a hindrance to understanding the user perspectives to this feature, as opposed to pure user advocates, who could concentrate on the users' perspectives". Klockner et al. (1999) proposed employing a user advocate to improve understanding of requirements, and to bridge the gap between users and developers. A user advocate concept, understands that users are not system designers and developers are not users (Nielsen, 1993), and provides an interface, or bridge, between the two different perspectives of these groups. The user's advocate acts as a translator instead of asking users and developers to learn a new language, which may be required in modeling, interviewing, or workshop approaches.

During requirements, elicitation, including a user advocate has many advantages. Developers believe they help communicate a sense of ownership and pride in the software. Although these are positive qualities, unabated, the developers' sense of ownership and pride could hinder the development of quality software. Requirements and design work may need to be radically altered or completely abandoned in favor of a new direction, and users may be intimidated by the developers' enthusiasm. User advocates can encourage the tendency of users to view ideas in a "yes, but" manner, which can draw out true requirements (Leffingwell and Widrig, 2000).

User advocates can act as a moderating influence and stop developers from rushing into a development, before the software requirements have been fully analysed. This can help cut down on costly errors that may not show up until later in the development process. Users may not appreciate how difficult it is to create a software system and expectations may be unrealistic, in terms of ease, in making changes. They view their involvement in requirements elicitation as something that can happen later, after they see the developed system. User advocates can help users understand that even though the system is developed with software it is not simple, timely, or cheap to make changes to the system (Leffingwell and Widrig, 2000).

Liberal *et al.* (2009) pointed out that future Internet will have to cope with undetermined terminals and services (even users), in a number and heterogeneity never seen before. So, flexibility or adaptability will be considered as one of the most important design principles. This flexibility will demand different kinds of awareness, both in the ends and in every node in the service supply chain, while targeting users' satisfaction as the final goal of any management process.

According to Blum (2010) the philosophies of Web 2.0 and SOA serve different user needs and thus expose differences with respect to the design and used technologies of real world applications. Tools for analysing user needs and mechanisms to define and manage access to personal information, as published location information or accessibility, based on context information.

The key motivation at this point of the research work was to focus on the user view and steer away from the technically driven aspects of SDP related research projects, as the technology is both complex and complicated. This technology has to be transferred in a user-friendly manner for potential end-users. New requirements and new technologies are getting more common with the rapid development of NGNs and Web 2.0 technologies. There were user-focused methods also, with a strong tendency toward technology environments, in form of processes and software programs to analyse user needs. There is a set of new challenges the multimedia marketplace could face and need to address from the user's perspective (Zheng et al., 2011).

Related research in terms of user-focused studies is illustrated in the following Section.

2.4.5.2   Related Research - User-Focused Studies

This Section describes the related research of users and how they perceive the use of SDPs and SPICE, and the perspective of users in designing a system for user needs. Current research and existing studies are essentially driven by technological feasibility, and numerous quantitative studies exist on the research topic of SDPs, focusing on the technology level.

Magedanz and Sher (2006) argued that the need for a common multimedia SDP for converging networks and the proven commercial usability of distributed object oriented platforms, is driven by new technical standards for open service platforms. One of the main reasons is the option to map the API to different network types and thus to run the services seamlessly across different networks. The value for the end-user is access to a wealth of services and content, which can be offered by an SDP. In an SDP White Paper (2006), SDP enablers mentioned above, facilitate the operator in embracing unlimited amounts of services and automatically matching them to user needs. Usability and convenience adapts the navigation structure of mobile portals for individual users, based on the accumulated user profile and intelligent processing of navigation and usage data.

They argued that this reduces click-distance (the number of scrolls and clicks to reach desired content and services), reduces navigation effort and significantly improves portal/service access and usability. These enablers monitor user activity, construct detailed user profiles, and actively personalise the access portals for each individual user, while dynamically adapting individual menus in response to the needs and preferences of each unique visitor. This is achieved by lending 'intelligence' to different aspects of access portal interaction. The user experience is thus significantly enhanced and is ultimately more productive, both for the end user in terms of reaching their service consumption objectives, and the operator in terms of driving service usage and revenues.

According to wwiteware™ (2010), addressing customer-centricity, the best practice is to start the system design with the managed services, as required and seen by the customer: to design the deliverables up front. The significant advantage of this approach means that design is focussed on core business, operational and usability of the system in its inception stage. With respect to information engineering and service platforms, two dimensions should be considered: SDP functionality within a system's architecture and SDP functionality and its underlying managed infrastructures. All IT systems need to be managed, and with customer-centric systems, it is even more important that management functions are designed up front, where system deployability and usability are implicated (similar to the process of designing a business).

According to 3G Americas (2005), convergence is a complex and multifaceted topic. It is a technology and industry trend, impacting on almost all communications and information industries. It promises great changes to the way we, as customers, consume communication services – anytime, anywhere, any device. It comprises of four key components – service, terminal, network, and industry convergence – all of which are interrelated and critical to the success of the others. In the end though, if convergence does not deliver on the basic end-user needs, its success will likely continue to be elusive. Convergence will need to simplify the customer's interaction with their information and communications data, provide multiple compelling devices and the ability to seamlessly move between devices while keeping consistent data and look and feel, plus simplify and optimise the network all at once.

Chappell and Graham (2009), argued that predicting the future of consumer services in the information, communications and entertainment (ICE) sector, is fraught with difficulty. Many recent Web and Internet service successes, including people to people (P2P) file downloading, YouTube and Facebook, were not predicted by anyone, and seemed to emerge from nowhere, creating whole new service categories from scratch. A major reason for this inherent unpredictability is the Web itself: a hugely creative service development environment, spawning new ideas daily, some of which succeed massively, some of which flare brightly and then die, and many of which make no progress at all. Only the fittest survive, as in the wild, so it is on the Web, predicting which features and qualities confer survival benefits, is a risky exercise. But if we cannot safely predict which new services will have caught the public imagination in 3-7 years' time, they argued the prediction of what kinds of attributes they are likely to have. Among these, they believe that more services developed by end-users, as well as widespread adaptation of existing services to suit end-user needs, will be probable developments.

While Roy and Langford (2008), argued that the integration impetus was assisted by rapid development of electronic technologies designed to provide tools to track and analyse user needs and integrate this information with service provision processes for example, Bertin and Crespi (2009), made clear in their work that user's needs are the driver of the next generation of telecom services. Founding the services on users' needs requires that various services cooperate together to meet specific needs. As a consequence, services should no more be developed as "silo" but with combinable service enablers. This enabler paradigm raises the issues of the identification of the enablers and of the consistency of a service composed from various enablers. These aspects must be addressed by considering the service from the user point of view: what is the added value for the user and through which perceived steps is this added value provided? Such service business processes are then a key tool, to identify enablers and to ensure the coherence of composed service.

Bertin and Crespi (2009), argued that from their perspective a service business process must be specified in a comprehensive way by considering the service from the user point of view to identify enablers and to ensure coherence of a composed service. This task is not endless because the key services offered by a telecom service provider are limited when considered from a user point of view (the added value for the user) and not from a commercial point of view (the product catalogue).

The fundamental problem in designing information systems, is to focus on real user-related needs of a system that is defined by users of a target solution, in terms of cost and complexity. There are different possibilities (e.g. RE) supporting user-oriented design and development of information systems. The author is of the opinion that, these can be strongly supported by a target-oriented qualitative user study to focus on the real need what users expect when information systems are designed and developed.

The next Section presents related research don by the author and peers in terms of technical-driven and user-focused studies.

2.4.5.3   Related Research done by the Author

The author's key motivation to investigate these challenges and design issues for developing SDPs as a single instance to control and administrate ICT systems of the future, was focused on the perspective of users when designing such systems and environments. Therefore, the author identified the research questions (derived from the literature review in Section 2.5.3.1 and in Section 3.9.4) within the literature that require attention in emerging user-focused SDP development.

There was another empirical study done by the author, with a strong focus on user-centred SDP development. According to Bergaus and Stottok (2010), a group of train drivers, based on a user study, was interviewed to investigate the discussion of increasing security by providing SDP related technology in combination with railway telematic systems, from the train driver's perspective.

(Bergaus 2006), investigated the technical architecture of an SDP, such as SPICE, and researched enlargements to the field of complex distributed applications, such as mixed reality applications. This is a technical study with a focus on the application of establishing a technical architectural model and thus not related to this PhD study, which is a qualitative, user-centric study.

(Bergaus 2007), researched service roaming techniques, and the possible applications of SPICE with roaming information, in convergent networks. This study was written from a purely technical viewpoint, and contrary to this PhD study, did not account for qualitative user needs.

(Stottok et al. 2011), investigated the methodological approach for coding by using colours within GTM. GTM with a Colour Coding approach, was also taken into account for the analysis of the data within this study. However, there have been expansions to Colour Coding in this PhD study.

(Bergaus *et al.* 2012), investigated a methodological approach for empirical data validation by using a unique Mapping Process, developed by the author himself. Literature data is structured, grouped and transferred to a visual Mind Map representation to compare and validate empirical data at different data collection and analysis stages. This PhD study uses a similar methodology.

(Bergaus *et al.* 2012b), investigated, in depth, a methodological approach for empirical data validation, by using his own unique Mapping Process developed and discussed some possible applications and limitations. This German paper is currently under review. This PhD study uses a similar methodology.

A master thesis (Bergaus and Stottok, 2010) was written together with the author's colleague Bernd O. Stottok who conducts research in Human Interaction within the railway telematics field of research. The idea was to conduct qualitative research in the area of Railway Telematics and SDPs, by researching the possibilities of increasing security and availability of railway telematic system, through the implementation of innovative technologies, such as service delivery platforms and communication technologies. This study differs from the PhD thesis, in that it is a separate qualitative study where train drivers and SDP experts were interviewed. The methodology used in the master thesis was also GTM. Colour Coding was developed with strong connection to this master thesis. It could be seen as an introduction of colour coding, and the Mapping Process to a specified application such as the railway telematics, in order to implement innovative technologies and increase security and availability of railway telematic services from the train driver perspective.

The empirical study also evaluated the use of SDPs in the area of the empowerment of Railway Telematics systems, conducted by Bergaus and Stottok (2010). This study researched telematic systems in railway applications to transport goods more efficiently, faster, more cost-effectively and safer. To increase the adoption of railway telematics systems, a combination and enlargement with innovative technologies like NGSs and SDPs was done, in this study. To reach this goal it was necessary to show how users and operators could create benefits for themselves.

Usability, handling, mobility and availability, are drivers for the use of such technologies in railway telematics. With the replacement of the Global System for Mobile Communications – Rail by Ubiquitous Computing technologies, such as SDPs, further beneficial enhancements of telematics systems were gained through improved access and functionalities, for example faster allocation of services for specific user groups. This research study focused on the aspects and challenges of a railway telematics system of the future as seen by train drivers; and SDP expert's perspectives were analysed and discussed with an empirical study. The study pointed the way that usability factors should be incorporated into any future telematics system using Grounded Theory based research.

Nowadays, technical development brings higher demands for hardware, software, service architecture, electronics, and security and environment protection. Computer and Software technologies are responsible for innovative telematics systems of the communication and navigation, as well as, for multimedia services.

They offer extensive multimedia uses and the query, processing, ready position and representation of data, of the most different data origins. An increasing need for data transfers particularly online, but also offline, is sensible. Hence, telecommunication enterprises and technologies such as UMTS and IMS play an essential role in the telematics sphere today. This is connected with risks, primarily with data transfer delays, for example. A new infrastructure is necessary for the construction of a Pan-European UMTS network. The concurrent adjustment on telematics uses, causes high capital costs. They are not yet prepared, nor willing to pay, in high measure of telematics service (Bergaus and Stottok, 2010).

Modern communication technologies can serve to make the daily work of train drivers easier. With the help of onboard terminals, also mobile phones, status announcements and communications can be transmitted to headquarters. Communications can be sent directly near a data terminal or navigation system, and status announcements, delivery data and arrival times can be administered. Free services on the Internet and the "opening" of the Internet and the IP based data processing by inclusion of SDPs in a railway transport telematic systems, let's assume potentially boundless possibilities, which should be controlled.

Nevertheless, fulfilling the security level and avoiding an explosive increase of possible services, the performance, availability and actual winding up of the commercial processes, should remain with the railway driver of a vehicle where possible (Bergaus and Stottok, 2010).

The research from Bergaus and Stottok (2010), analysed a specific group of railway people, specifically train drivers, to investigate the need for new technologies such as SDPs within the environment of railway telematics systems, as the existing environments, are proprietary and technologically outdated. The goal was to investigate the research on the possibility of supporting train drivers through new technologies. This could be seen as an added value, as drivers could determine the degree of supporting themselves, bearing in mind that a number of functions have already been automated.

The role of a driver evolves, from that of an operator, to that of a manager. One of the difficulties for designers is to derive a means of holding the driver's attention during a journey, through integration and careful delivery, regardless if a higher degree of automation is necessitated.

This PhD study differs from the Master study, in terms of the research content. The topic of this investigation is complete as the PhD thesis investigates the challenges and design issues of web-based systems (SDPs) for the administration of ICT systems from a users' perspective. Additionally, the PhD thesis is more comprehensive in comparison to the master thesis. The PhD thesis investigated the challenges and design issues of SDPs in terms of ICT systems whereas the master thesis investigated one specific case, and SDPs were discussed, to integrate this technology in Railway Telematic systems.

2.4.6 Summary

This Section described System Design for User Needs and presented the methodologies, requirement engineering and design for testability of software architectures. Based on user-centred design, the author related this research to other studies by illustrating the connection of technical and user-oriented studies. At the end of this Section the related work, done by the author, was overviewed.

At this point, all relevant aspects are defined and illustrated. The following Section describes a framework to develop SDP-based ICT systems from the perspective of users. This illustrates some initial concepts and ideas to justify the research problem. The research gap was identified and research questions conducting the qualitative research study were formulated, based on the aim and objectives of this investigation.

2.5 A Conceptual Framework to Develop SDP-based ICT Systems from a User's Perspective

This Section provides an insight into the framework, relevant for the development of web-based platforms (SDPs), to administrate future oriented ICT systems. The subsequent Paragraphs review the needs of users for the development of SDP-based ICT environments in general, based on the literature researched. Main characteristics for human-computing interaction are presented, as well as, a cooperative partnership between human and computer. A related research Section is illustrated, to summarise related work in terms of technical-oriented and user-focused studies, related to the research topic. The research gap is identified and four research questions were formulated during this study, in interview phases 2 and 3 following the research approach of this study and are closely linked to the aim and the objectives of this study.

2.5.1 Human-Computing Interaction

Human-Computing Interaction (HCI) describes the interaction between people and computers. According to Harper *et al.* (2008), a characteristic and successful methodology for predicting and analysing user behaviour – the idea that a user needs to fit the computer – is through the application of Fitt's Law (1954). This is a model of human movement, which is used by researchers to predict, for example, the time required for a user to click on a given size target, using a mouse. It has been used widely as a method for evaluating systems where the time to physically locate an object is critical to the task in hand, or where there is limited space on the device for the placement of digital objects in an interface.

As HCI has developed, so has the emphasis on aspects of the mind and less on the behaviour of the body; less on pointing and clicking with fingers, and more with how people understand and come to recognise objects and processes. At the start of the 21st century, HCI was an interdisciplinary field, which underwent enormous change. In terms of a science, or a discipline, these changes have occurred over a very short time. HCI now encompasses many philosophies, perspectives and types of expertise. There are multiple and overlapping groups of researchers, some emphasising design, others evaluation, and others user modelling (Harper *et al.*, 2008).

A further distinction in HCI is made between adaptable and adaptive systems: in adaptable systems the user chooses between different behaviours, while adaptive systems provide automatic modification of the behaviour according to the user needs (Fink *et al.*, 1998). According to Zhang *et al.* (2004), HCI development in this phase includes: prototyping, that is also part of system analysis and design, summative evaluation, before system release and use evaluation, after the system is installed and being used by targeted users for a period of time. Summative evaluation, takes place after the system is developed to confirm whether the evaluation metrics or other industry standards are met. User evaluation collects feedback in understanding the actual behaviour toward system use. This understanding helps in developing new versions or other similar systems.

Harper *et al.*, (2008), pointed out that HCI needs to move forward, from concerns about the production and processing of information, toward the design and evaluation of systems that enable human values to be achieved. Doing so requires HCI to shift its epistemological constraints, away from their psychological roots towards other approaches, such as the philosophical, where conceptual sensitivity to meaning, purpose and desire is possible. This suggests adding a fifth stage to HCI's conventional design/research model: a stage of conceptual analysis where we consider the human values we are trying to support or research. This affects the whole cycle of research and design, including how we understand the user, how we conduct studies in the field and the laboratory, how we reflect on the values sought in design, how we build prototypes and how we evaluate our designs. Finally, HCI researchers need a larger assembly of skills and know-how if they are to succeed, which has implications for the concepts, frameworks and theories of HCI.

The HCI concepts presented in terms of system design for user needs leads to the models of Christoffersen and Woods (2002), and Klein *et al.* (2004), which supported HCI related concepts in other studies, and which are the starting point and basis for the models the author will present, in the Section 5.4.

2.5.1.1   Main Characteristics for Human to Computer Interaction

With consideration to the answers of the questions to the development from automated systems, and people who use those systems to real team players (referring to a team consisting of human and ICT system), Christoffersen and Woods (2002: pp. 1-2) ascertained, that through progress in technology positive effects in terms of economic efficiency and security were realised. Unfortunately, however with the increase in automation, new problems have arisen.

More than 30 years of research on the factors of human influence on human computer interaction, has led to the development of two basic requirements. The advocates of one school of thought argue that human ability is fundamentally limited, whilst opponents of this view argue that the real problem lies in a reduction of automation. The truth probably lies somewhere in the middle. Human beings must operate in coordination with automated design, as a combined system (Hutchins, 1995: pp. 117-118).

The quintessence of the research is that for the successful application of every non-trivial degree of automation, it is important to guarantee a harmonious and coordinated interaction between the human end-user and the automated system. Automated systems and end-users have to work together as team players. For example, SDPs and ICT systems must be designed in a friendly, easy to handle way that those systems and their end-users can operate together with ease. Christoffersen and Woods (2002: pp. 2-4), described two main characteristic features illustrating how this aim can be achieved.

Both concepts were seen as the main characteristics of the inner circles of the model in this investigation (shown in Figure 48 and Figure 49), as every effort to fulfil the requirements, should allow for measurement of both of these characteristics. According to Stottok (2010b: p. 6), the terms observability and directability can be understood in the following ways:

- ▓ *Observability:* Increases in the complexity and independence of the computer agent requires a corresponding increase in the feedback mechanisms, for their human partners, regarding their activities. Statements that serve to support this process must offer a comprehensive, dynamic picture of the instantaneous situation and the agent's activities, and indicate how these will develop in the future.

■ *Directability:* The human actor must be able to direct the computer partner, easily and efficiently. The human actor must be able to exercise discretion and strategic control, and this control must remain protected so as to manage the automated activities in such a way that they support the overall effectiveness of the human-computer collaboration

2.5.1.2 Cooperative Partnership between Human and Computer Agents

This Paragraph describes the cooperative partnership model between humans and computers forming the base concept of the model development in Chapter 5. Computer agents have become team players. Both basic abilities (Observability and Directability described in Paragraph 2.5.1.1) must be guaranteed, as they are key to a cooperative partnership between the human being and the computer agent, in a common system (Christoffersen and Woods, 2002: p. 1-2).

Klein *et al.* (2004: p. 91), define a common activity as that consisting of coordinated actions, understood by a group of people who interoperate with each other. They also state that a common activity contains at least four basic requirements that must be fulfilled. These four basic standards, shown in the middle "white" ring of the following model, can be described as follows (Stottok, 2010b: pp. 7-8):

■ *A Basic Agreement:* The participants must come to a basic agreement, in which they work out and establish how they wish to work together. This is often an implicit, unspoken agreement, which supports the process of working together with a common perspective, and has the aim of avoiding breakdowns in team coordination.

■ *Mutual Predictability:* During the course of the common activity, coordination can take place. The team members rely on the fact that mutual predictability exists to a reasonable degree. With strong dependencies upon one another's activities, it is only possible to plan one's own actions, including coordination activities, if one can predict precisely what others are thinking or doing.

■ *Directability (Allocatability):* Team members need to be subject to mutual control mechanisms. This refers to the conscious ability to value the actions of other parties in a common activity, and to make modifications, as soon as conditions and priorities change. Unfortunately, the concept of directability is used in the literature once again, in a different meaning (see Paragraph 2.5.1.1). This is the reason why "Directability" is also referred to as "Allocatability" to differentiate it from the second use of the acronym.

■ *A State of Common Characteristics:* This common ground covers the pertinent knowledge, views and acceptances, which are shared by the participants involved. Common ground enables every party to understand the messages and signals which help to co-ordinate common actions, and to continue coordinating them. Klein *et al.* (2004: p. 94), reflect on the way in which challenges, that they have laid out in their work, can be looked at, from different points of view:

a) They show a blueprint for the design and evaluation of intelligent systems. The fulfillment of the requirement helps with successful coping of problems so as to avoid disturbances or breakdowns in coordination.

b) They can be seen as warnings, for how used technologies coordinate duties and can interrupt them instead of supporting them.

c) They can be extracted from as a challenge or a requirement for realisable human computer systems. They help to develop systems in such a way that they become real assistants for the people in the common team.

These challenges have been discussed in terms of air-traffic and railway-traffic-system discourse, and will be replaced by the categories developed in this study, to reflect the challenges pertaining to SDP and ICT systems (Christoffersen and Woods, 2002: p. 1-2; Stottok, 2010b).

Based on Chistoffernsen and Woods' work in combination with Klein *et al.*'s criteria, the author shows a model related to these criteria in combination with the extended developed GT criteria (empirical model) and literature-based categories (literature-based model) in Chapter 5.

The final part of this Section, introduced the related research of developing SDPs, in terms of ICT systems of the future, as relevant to having a single instance tool for the administration of different ICT environments.

2.5.2 A brief introduction to Trick and Weber's Conceptual Framework

Trick and Weber's (2009) model outlined in Section 1.1, defined general requirements that support the communication between different social groups by providing a relevant information and communication environment. The general demand of their research was to define a technical infrastructure model (representing the network view) that supports the communication between social groups of our society in the best possible way. To define a model that present the requirements of a communication infrastructure from a technical point of view Trick and Weber (2009) answered, in their research, the question "What are the identified social groups and society areas need to have an optimal communication for their further development." Thereby, the goal was to improve the qualitative and quantitative life quality including all people in the society communication process model, presented (Trick, 2002).

In the development process of their model they mapped the general requirements to concrete technical aspects from a network perspective. Some of their researched aspects, were that future oriented networks represented with

NGNs (see Paragraph 8.1.2.3) must support multimedia communication with high broadband and a network must be independent from, services and applications employed by their end users. An additional, significant, point was the connection and interconnection of the network. Each social group should have the possibility to use private networks within the Internet, for instance. Unfortunately, the basis for cost-efficient access must be an optimal utilisation and arrangement of the access technology (Trick and Weber, 2009).

This led the author to question, applications and services when constructing a model in terms of the ICT infrastructure of the future, and how it is possible to communicate and administer these applications and services for the end-user.

2.5.3 Research Framework

According to Hilbert's cube (see Section 2.2.2), an interplay between an enabling technology, such as SDP and ICT systems, normative guiding policies and strategies, and the resulting social transformation, are depicted in a three-dimensional interplay is shown, and described. Based on the ideas described above, the following Paragraph discusses the use of SDPs as single instance tool for the administration of ICT environments.

Various groups involved in discussions regarding public or private cloud models, PaaS, internet portals and other useful tools, for controlling and administrating ICT environments, have acknowledged, that a single instance is helpful to operate different types of ICT systems, using the Internet, to operate services and applications (see Sections 2.2 and 2.3) against the use of SDPs in terms of ICT systems of the future.

2.5.3.1   Research Questions

Research Question 1: Can SDPs be used to support people's everyday activities when using innovative technologies?

Research Question 1 highlights the question of using SDPs to support daily activities of its potential users, in term of ICT technologies. This question is noteworthy to better understand if present day, technology-driven aspects, meet the goals of future-oriented ICT environments? This question addresses the ability for designing and developing ICT systems to meet the goal of SDP-based ICT environments.

According to the CTIT Progress Report (2011) the telecommunications and Internet industry has highlighted the high costs of diverse IT and communication environments, over the last two decades. Today, there is no need for pure technology-based developments that are very cost-intensive and not within reach of common end-users. The Internet Service Providers Association expects costs of more than 60 billion U.S. dollars a year for the setting up sufficient infrastructures with regard to ICT environments, such as free hotspots; to support everyone's needs in public (CTIT Progress Report, 2011).

It is important to discover ways to develop end-user focused solutions, with specific goals that meet the needs of a broader range of potential users. The Internet, for example, is ubiquitously present in our lives; the underlying infrastructure is largely accessible at all times, yet there is a large number of non-homogeneous systems for supporting different types of users. The goal should be to support everyones needs and goals with a common, easy to use, easy to understand, and universally affordable ICT infrastructure (CTIT Progress Report, 2011).

The fact that more and more technology-driven applications are appearing on the market for shorter periods, is a reflection of markets becoming quickly saturated and users being rapidly forced to adapt their needs, to technology-driven procedures, specifically in terms of mobile and Internet applications and services. In the article Smart Cities (2010) the authors argue that, by putting a stop to technology-driven high-tech developments, developers can begin to focus much more on the users' perspectives.

According to Project Fireball (2012) the European Union Research project "Fireball" from the 7th framework programme (FP7-ICT-2009-5) published in 2012 the article "D2.1 - Landscape and Roadmap of the Future Internet and Smart Cities (M24)", which describes a more user-focused development of IT and communication systems.

The article outlines that the user needs more attention than what technology is trying to deliver. This leads to the viewpoint of human-computing interaction (usability-driven) development, and how the perspectives of potential users of a system are becoming increasingly important necessitating a focus on them. The authors of "Fireball" argue that information and communication technologies serve as everyday means of communication, in private and business lives in Europe, and the rest of the world. They are essential elements of modern life, and it is argued that individuals can be discouraged from taking part in essential interactions with friends, family, businesses and employers when trying to avoid the use of modern means of communication (Project Fireball, 2012).

The requirement of application and communication service providers to build-up this type of infrastructure, in up to three to five years, and the costs associated with it, could also affect global competitiveness of the European, and worldwide, industry. User-centred and user-focused design and development have an effect on consumer confidence, as people might avoid using ICT, in order to avoid having their everyday lives affected by ICT technologies (Project Fireball, 2012).

The author is of the opinion that this research question is important, as it sets the scene for user-centred development of ICT systems by using SDP technology and could therefore become one of the motivation aspects for other researchers to further investigate qualitative studies and research, on SDP and ICT technologies, from a user's perspective. The following research questions are reviewed and addressed again in Section 5.8.1, in terms of this research.

Research Question 2: Where are the difficulties of engaging an optimal interaction between technical environments and end-users?

Research Question 2 points out, that the fast growth of ICT makes it necessary, but very difficult, to provide services and applications that engage an optimal interaction between technical environments and end-users. Where are the difficulties, and what can we do to proceed?

Nowadays, an explosion of applications and services on ubiquitous technologies can be observed, which thus increases the challenges on IT design and communication systems in order to meet the goal of future-oriented environments. The exponential growth of Internet applications and controlling and operating different kinds of ICT systems by one single platform is very difficult to handle (Selwyn, 2011).

Human Computing Interaction (described in Section 2.5.1) is a discipline that addresses the interaction of technical environments, with an emphasis between computers and humans. It entails the study, planning and design of interaction between people (users) and computers; it is often regarded as the intersection of behavioural sciences and design of study. A computer has an abundance of qualities and uses, and this takes place in an open-ended dialogue between user and computer. This interaction occurs on the interface and includes software and hardware. The input received from users via peripherals and other user interactions with large-scale computerised systems is processed by a computer system. HCI could be seen as a discipline concerned with the design, evaluation and implementation of interactive computing systems for human use and with the study of major phenomena surrounding them (Sears and Jacko, 2007; Stuart *et al.*, 1983).

Today's services and applications are more user-oriented as a broad range of users is addressed in this respect, through commercial aspects within a hard competitive market. According to Dubey and Rana's (2010) definitions of usability, the ongoing study of the optimalisation of technical environments in terms of the perspective of the user, is increasingly important, in order to meet the needs of the end-users (ICTs for e-Environment - Final Report, 2008).

Research Question 3: Why are the purposes of Internet platforms changing if users want more support in their daily lives?

Research question 3 highlights that the purposes of Internet platforms are changing due to the individuals increased dependence on other technologies, in their daily lives. Internet application development has increased in importance in today's software development, due to the web's rapid growth.

According to Haythornthwaite and Wellman (2002), information sharing and methodologies are constantly changing and evolving. Previously, human networking was limited to face-to-face contact, now media breakthroughs continue to extend the reach of our communications. From printing press to television, each development improves and enhances our ability to communicate. Previously separate and distinct communication forms have now converged into a common, homogeneous platform. This platform provides access to a wide range of alternative and new communication methods that enable people to interact directly with each other almost instantaneously.

Internet technology is perhaps the most significant change agent in the world of today, and it dissipates national borders, geographic distances, and physical limitations. The creation of online communities for the exchange of ideas and information has the potential to increase productivity opportunities globally (Ahson and Ilyas, 2011). The web connects people and promotes untainted communication. It facilitates running businesses, dealing with emergencies, informing individuals, supporting education, science, and many more topics, in our daily activities. It is astounding just how rapidly the Internet became an integral part of our daily lives. The complex interconnection of electronic devices and media that comprise the network is transparent to the millions of users who make it a valued and personal part of their lives (Selwyn, 2011).

Research Question 4: What is the impact of rebuilding today's ICT infrastructure in terms of using new ubiquitous services? What extent of SDPs (from the example of SPICE) can be integrated into the sphere of existing ICT systems, to achieve maximum usability for the single user of ICT systems?

This research question highlights the impact of rebuilding ICT infrastructures, to use new ubiquitous services. This question answers, what the important increases are in existing SDPs and ICT systems, preparing for new ubiquitous services from the users perspective, to achieve maximum usability.

There is no definite link between SDPs and ICT environments to address a broad range of potential end-users in our society. The telecommunications and Internet industries, and also Long Term Evolution (LTE) technology, have emphasised the high costs for technical infrastructures to rebuild infrastructure environments.

Technologically speaking, the Internet Service Providers Association expects annual high costs to set up sufficient replacement measures for application and service providers, rebuilding or enlarging their infrastructure environments, to remain state-of-the-art. The reason for this is, ICT and the topic of convergence and compatibility, become very high requirements on new and existing infrastructures (CTIT Progress Report, 2011).

The requirement of communications service providers, to build new infrastructure and fulfil customer needs and the costs associated with it, could also affect global competitiveness of European and international industries. "The only constant is change, continuing change, inevitable change that is the dominant factor in society today.

No sensible decision can be made any longer, without taking into account not only the world as it is, but the world as it will be" (citation by Isaac Asimov, 1990). The information and data generated by provided services and applications are used and stored by different users on an SDP. Although communication information and data can serve as evidence for planned crimes, with help of communications technologies, undoubtedly a link between the device that was used for communication and an individual cannot be established with any certainty and further investigations, (Walker and Akdeniz, 2003).

Data from the ITU's measuring the Information Society, 2011 report, shows that mobile phones and other mobile devices are replacing computers and laptops, for accessing the Internet. African countries have also recorded growth in using mobile phones to access the Internet. In Nigeria, for example, 77% of individuals aged 16 and above use their mobile phones to access the Internet compared to a mere 13% who use computers to go online. These developments and growth in mobile communication, and its penetration in developing countries, are expected to bridge the digital divide between the least-developed countries and developed countries. However, there are still challenges evident in making these services affordable (Sutinen and Tedre, 2010).

SDPs and ICT environments cannot be linked without any certainty to a personal identity, as the control and operation of ICT systems should be done by services and applications that control ICT systems. This is dependent on what the end-user wants to do and also which type of end device they want to use (CTIT Progress Report, 2011).

Based on these research questions, it is necessary to consider the viewpoints of SDP end-users and developers, as well as designers of these systems and their environments, for example architectural experts, as these groups can offer information about the daily requirements of mobile environment users. That was at the centre of debates around the challenges and design issues of Service Delivery Platforms to administrate future-oriented ICT environments. According to the CTIT Progress Report (2011), the multi-disciplinary nature of the subject area of SDPs and ICT technologies, and the aspects and challenges of developing a framework for web-based platforms as an administration tool for ICT environments in general, has been addressed.

This Section has outlined four research questions relevant to the design and development of user-centred administration systems, focusing on Internet based ICT systems. These research questions were relevant and necessary for the research, and were the author's motivation for doing this empirical study. These research questions are revisited in Section 5.8.1, to relate the aim and the objectives, to outcomes and findings, of this investigation. The research questions are addressed in Section 3.9.4 in detail. The reason why the research questions were developed after the pilot interviews, was due to research design (pilot interviews – inductive; interview cycle 2 and 3 abductive), and is described in detail in Chapter 3.

The next Section describes the research problem outlined in Section 1.1 using data derived from the literature researched.

2.5.3.2   Research Gap

According to Johnston *et al.* (2007), outlined in Section 1.1, users reap the benefits of well thoughtout SDP implementations because they can more easily find, and make sense of, service offerings, subscribe to and consume services across different networks and devices, and understand promotions, discounts and bills. SDPs help flatten the administrative and technical hurdles that stand between users and services. This, in turn, contributes to increased service uptake, usage, customer satisfaction and retention.

With available technical concepts or systems in terms of SDP-based ICT systems it is possible to select a quantitative or qualitative research study, as technical studies also work with methodologies to analyse user needs (i.e. Requirement Engineering or Design for Testability for software architectures presented in Section 2.4). The emphasis here is that technical parameters must be available in the form of a concept or a technical pilot environment. The researcher can also select a qualitative study to design a system for user needs and start to develop the interview guideline with the existing technical parameters. But what happens when a technical concept or system does not exist? This is what is lacking in existing research studies, which are strongly technology driven.

According to the Report from the Information Society Technologies Advisory Group (ISTAG) (2006), the constitutive character of ICT requires a new research offering, one that combines perspectives from technology, business models and user needs without sacrificing the deep knowledge within each area. This applies, as much to specifying which societal challenges should be solved, as to developing the solutions. The next generation of ICT will enable the creation of systems that are more intelligent and personalised, and therefore more centred on the user. The future is knowledge-based and ICT's should be allowed to shape it. To do this, users need to be able to "think ICT from the outset" and to better accommodate the user perspective in future developments of the technology.

Based on the arguments and research questions, given within this Chapter, it is fact that current research studies are primarily focusing on technical feasibility, quantitative studies and user need analysis, in terms of existing technical concepts and systems. The combination of technological aspects on one hand, and the concentration on user needs from a user's perspective on the other, opens up a necessary field of research, touched upon in this thesis.

Based on the fact, that many researchers investigated technical-driven projects, as well as the fact that of the importance of user needs increasing when developing complex information systems, the author was therefore inspired to undertake qualitative researching on design issues for SDPs, investigating a system for user needs from the user's perspective. Hence, the problem findings and challenges from the SPICE project outlined in Section 1.1, the problem statement (see Section 1.2), and, the aim and objectives, and the research questions, were formulated at the start of the initial research setup, for this study.

In summary, and to the best of the researcher's knowledge, to date, no specific framework or model of SDP-based ICT development from the perspective of users exists. As discussed within Chapter 2, many technical studies related to SDP development were shown and presented. User-focused studies in technical environments were primarily shown employing technical-oriented methodologies such as requirement engineering or system design for testability of software architectures and studies employing user-centred design were not found in the environment of SDPs and SDP-based ICT development. However, the summarised results of the literature review showed, that it was not exactly the case that a research investigated in user perspective of SDP-based ICT development.

SDP-based ICT development, from the perspective of user's, makes it an interesting case to investigate as to how the users view of design issues for SDPs can influence the common development process. Hence, the author explored this research study further and presents the research methodology, analysis, and their results. The research methodology described in Chapter 3, is based on a qualitative research study, developing a set of design issues within an exploratory framework for SDP-based ICT systems, from the perspective of individuals.

2.5.4 Summary

The last Section illustrated a framework to develop SDP-based ICT systems from a user perspective. Therefore, human-computing interaction was introduced and the main characteristics were presented, based on a model from Christoffersen and Woods (2002). Furthermore, a cooperative partnership model between human and computer agents was illustrated, using the model from Klein *et al.* (2004). The author also addressed Trick and Weber's research (2009), to explain their technical communication infrastructure model (outlined in Section 1.1) to support communication within different social groups.

Based on these concepts and related research (Sections 2.2 to 2.4), the author discussed SDPs, in terms of a single instance control tool to administrate ICT systems. A research framework was then introduced that defined specific questions, which underpin the research of the user's perspective, and the research gap was identified.

2.6 Chapter Summary and Conclusion

Chapter 2 introduced the terms and definitions used in this study, the related research to ICT, Service Delivery Platforms and System design for user-needs topics. SDPs in general, and the SPICE platform as an application example of an SDP, were introduced by a literature review. System design for user needs and related research in context of this PhD thesis, was discussed. A conceptual framework was introduced to develop SDP-based ICT systems form the user perspective was introduced.

Similar definitions of the technologies related to the academic literature, were given in this Chapter, and the needs of users for the development of ICT environments were set-up and discussed. Essential information to the technology is described in Appendix A (Sections 8.1 to 8.3). Several predominant concepts and technologies regarding the design and development of SDPs in terms of ICT environments, were discussed, and presented. Additionally, different methodologies analysing user needs were illustrated using technical and user-related concepts introduced. These are technically driven and aimed at designing a technical system. Both, the SDP and user literature, identify with the related research Sections 2.3 and 2.4 that those design and development aspects, are strongly technically driven and lacking design aspects of SPDs, in terms what users really need. Technical studies researched SDPs by following the aim of designing and developing a technical system or a concept of an information system. The focus was clearly the development of technical features and the discussion of user needs had little priority, shown within the SPICE project.

In Chapter 2 the author describes the related research (Sections 2.3 to 2.5) in context to this PhD thesis. However, much research and many papers exist with technical backgrounds on the topic of SDPs, but little research focuses on a user-needs background, for SDPs. This Section focused on recent technological developments and background information regarding the technologies, followed by a discussion of web-based platforms, such as SDPs, especially SPICE, in the literature. Using the presented information, the research problem was identified and research questions formulated, based on what was currently lacking in SDPs, in terms of the user perspective. SDPs are an inherent part of mobile communication technologies and advances in ubiquitous computing technologies have facilitated the convergence of IT and communication technologies. The following, Chapter 3, presents in detail, the methodology used in this research investigation.

3 Research Methodology

Chapter 3 describes the research methodology used in this study. Firstly, fundamental background information of the research paradigm and strategy (Section 3.2) and a general overview of the research methodology (EMPLIT framework, Section 3.3) and the research project (Section 3.3.5), is given. Moreover, information and guidelines on the different approaches to Grounded Theory Methodology (GTM, Section 3.4), and mapping techniques (Section 3.6), are provided. The Colour Coding approach within GTM is discussed in terms of classical coding methods and stages are addressed in Section 3.5. The feedback procedure presenting the results to the participants of the empirical study is described in Section 3.7. The concept of a Literature-based study is used to analyse the related data from the literature review, together with the data from the empirical study, illustrated in Section 3.8. Consolidating all described concepts, EMPLIT methodology used in this study, is presented in Section 3.3 from a general point of view. Sections 3.9 and 3.10, presented the setup for this study and illustrated the application of EMPLIT methodology within the study. Section 3.11 shows some examples from the analysis process in terms of the application of EMPLIT by providing data extracts from coding and the literature-based study. The last Section (3.12) describes the justification of empirical data during the research process, and the final results of this investigation.

3.1 Introduction

According to Carter and Little (2011), method, methodology, and epistemology are intimately and intricately connected, supporting one another in research planning and implementation. Constructing a qualitative research study, the epistemology position has to be chosen. Secondly, variants of a methodology, or elements of existing combined methodologies, has to be employed. Thirdly, methods within the chosen epistemology and methodology, that should produce the best data to answer the research questions, have to be selected, where quality debate is the most important application of this approach.

Based on the research problem outlined in Chapter 1, further elaborated on in the paragraphs illustrated in Chapter 2, the research methodology developed and used in this study is described both from a general, and an application of EMPLIT, perspective. Additionally, the justification process of this qualitative study is described deploying different activities, split into two stages, to reflect the evidence of this investigation.

The following Section describes the epistemology and underlying philosophy within this research investigation.

3.2   Underlying Philosophy of the Research Paradigm

According to Bassey (1990), research can be seen as a network of coherent ideas about the nature of the world, where different functions executed by a group of researchers, conditions and thinking, underpins their research actions. Within this context, a research paradigm is seen as a broad framework of perception, understanding and belief, within which theories and practices, operate. A research design is a plan for assembling, organising, and integrating information (data) and its results in the findings, derived from the research. This will be discussed in next section.

Qualitative methods can be seen as positivist, interpretivist or critical (see Section 8.5), depending on the underlying epistemology (Klein and Myers, 1999), whereas GTM can be influenced by different underlying epistemologies (theories of knowledge; it questions how knowledge is acquired). GTM is independent not only of the type of data used, but can also be appropriated by researchers with different assumptions. This property of the method allows researchers with conflicting epistemological stances, to succeed in using it (Urquhart and Fernandez, 2013).

Positivists generally assume that reality is objectively given, and can be observed and described from an objective viewpoint (Levin, 1988), by measurable properties, which are independent of the researcher and his instruments. They believe that phenomena should be isolated and that observations should be repeatable. This often involves manipulation of reality variations, only in a single independent variable, to identify regularities in relationships between some of the constituent elements of the social world. Positivist research studies generally try to test theories in an attempt to increase the predictive understanding of phenomena.

Orlikowski and Baroudi (1991), classify Information Systems research as positivist, if there is evidence of formal propositions, quantifiable measures of variables, hypothesis testing, and drawing on inferences of a phenomenon, from the sample, to a stated population (Avison and Pries-Heje, 2005).

In contrast to psychoanalysis, a scientific theory is one that can be empirically falsified, known as the falsification principle, and is the core of positivism. Hence, positivism differentiates between falsification as a principle, where a negating observation is all that is needed to cast a theory out, and its application in the real world, through methodologies recognising that observations may themselves be erroneous. It is therefore, widely accepted in practice, that more than one observation is needed, to falsify a theory (Avison and Pries-Heje, 2005).

According to Urquhart (2012) an objective social world originates, existing independently when issues of validity related to coding arises if Grounded Theory Methodology (GTM) is used, within a positivist paradigm. From a research design perspective, the interpretations of the results conducted with a positivist paradigm should not be subjective and the view of only one respondent considered, but of several. Orlikowski and Baroudi (1995), argued that positivist information system researchers, assume an objective physical and social world, that exists independently of humans, and whose nature can be relatively unproblematic ally apprehended, characterised, and measured. The role of the researcher is to "discover" the objective physical and social reality, by crafting precise measures that will detect and gauge those dimensions of reality that interest the researcher.

This then motivated the author to use interviews within a positivist paradigm, where fifteen different participants, in three coding stages, using an additional third party, to code the data collected. At the end of each coding stage, the same interview transcripts coded by the researcher, were then coded by the third party, cross-checking and archiving inter-coder reliability.

The next Section describes the research framework developed and used within this research study. This includes a qualitative study, in the form of semi-structured, in-depth interviews (empirical study), and a literature-based study. Based on all these single methods and techniques, the EMPLIT (empirical and literature-based) framework and its application, together with the specific study setup for this investigation, are presented.

3.3   EMPLIT Research Framework

The author developed, and utilised, a new methodology in this study; EMPirical and LITerature-based study (EMPLIT), by merging different, existing, and newly developed methodologies and techniques. This methodology is generally applicable for the justification of qualitative, empirical data in a multilayered validation procedure illustrated in Figure 8, below.

The EMPLIT framework consists of different methodologies and techniques in order to collect, analyse, and validate empirical data by more than one justification stage. The justification was done taking results from the literature-based study and by validating the research questions.

The last justification phase, based on the results of the empirical study, was delivered in a presentation and feedback session with the interview participants, at the end stage of the research project.

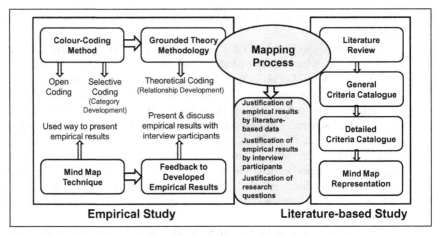

Figure 8: EMPLIT research framework of this research study

The EMPLIT framework has given the author justification to directly address the complex field of SDPs, by applying GTM as research methodology, collecting and analysing empirical data inductively, by using Colour Coding. It was used for generating open and selective codes, followed by categories, to investigate user needs from the perspective of SPICE experts to deal with the research problem. The EMPLIT framework, used within this study, is a framework for abduction research.

After the development of the final GT categories and their sub-categories, Theoretical Coding helped establish relations between the six major categories. Categories and their relations represent the views of SPICE experts in this study and are an alternative to investigate user needs of SDP-based ICT systems traditionally (presented in Section 2.4).

The results were presented to the interviewees, and a final discussion about their views of the results was established, validating the research results. The Mind Mapping technique was used to summarise results from the three interview phases and to have a benchmark in terms of comparing and validating empirical data in literature-based aspects. A literature-based study was therefore established to handle the complexity and data volume of SDPs and systems design, for user needs. Moreover, documented references of different detailed aspects of the literature review in a summarised form facilitated a third-party coder to step-in to the coding work, immediately. The mapping process was used to justify and validate the data to establish whether some existed in the literature, or not, and how it confirmed, extended or contradicted existing literature aspects. Moreover, the results from the feedback session with the respondents and validation of the research questions, was also established to validate the empirical results.

3.3.1 Empirical Study

The empirical study of the EMPLIT framework is based on GTM with a Colour Coding approach. The whole coding follows open, focused (selective) and theoretical coding stages to generate codes. Selective coding is done to develop Grounded Theory categories. Following Charmaz's way of conducting GTM, the literature review was done parallel to the data collection, and analysis, started in interview phase 2.

This was done to make a comparison of codes and categories from the empirical data and aspects from the literature collected. The aspects, from the Mind Maps, validate the empirical codes and categories and the researcher is therefore able to visualise and justify collected and analysed data at each phase in the empirical study (see Figure 8).

3.3.2 Literature-based Study

The literature-based study of the EMPLIT framework is based on the aspects gathered from the literature review. The general and detailed criteria catalogue grouped and structured literature-based data from SDP-related fields. Ready structured and grouped criteria catalogues, were transferred to mind map representations, described in detail, in Sections 3.8 and 3.11.3.

3.3.3 Theoretical Sampling to Intermediate the Integration between Empirical and Literature-based Study

Theoretical Sampling, described in Section 3.4.2, was employed in this study to ensure that integration of the empirical study and the literature-based study intermediated. Theoretical Sampling influences the next data collection phase of each phase, dictating which sample to take from next, based on the outcome of the analysis after each phase. This also influenced the focus set for the next interview phase, in terms of topic areas, who and how many interview participants were selected, from the three different groups of the SPICE experts.

Additionally, the results of the non-commital literature review, which began in the second interview phase and done over phase two and three, was also based on Theoretical Sampling. The reason for sampling the literature was to ensure using EMPLIT, that the outcome of the literature-based study and the literature-based criteria catalogue made sense, to focus on theoretical areas, in terms of the wide field of complex literature initiating the mapping process. Unfortunately, this has to be done with the respect the GTM requires so that the researcher does not impose theoretical concepts on the coding process. With respect to the information the author decided that the most effective way forward, was to do a non-comittal literature review, recommended by Urquhart and Fernandez (2006), ensuring that the theory that emerged was relevant to the literature reviewed.

Theoretical Sampling with regard to the literature was also based on the outcomes of each analysis stage in interview phases two and three.

In this investigation, the process of Theoretical Sampling leads to where to sample from next, as well as which literature topic has to be reviewed in interview phases two and three. Then, to intermediate integration in both the empirical and literature-based study, the following had to be done: deciding which part of the literature topic to focus on, which literature research and which SPICE expert group (users, developers or architecture experts) to sample in the next inteview stage. The developed interview guideline, was adopted for the next phase, transforming empirical and literature-based results to a mind map representation, as the mapping process helped compare and justify these two types of data.

3.3.4 Mapping Process

The Mapping process, developed by the author, defined the procedure to establish different stages of justification and validation, justifying collected and analysed empirical data. An important point pursued by the mapping process, was comparing the empirical data using codes and categories, from the literature-based results gathered from the literature-based study. The results from the literature were then structured into general and detailed requirements for SDP based ICT systems, because this study focussed on general aspects of SDP and ICT related topics.

The mapping process allowed for development of a criteria catalogue for the requirements and design aspects of general ICT systems of the future, which use an SDP. Furthermore, the justification of the results from the empirical study, according to how a model based on the criteria catalogue and empirical data can be developed, was important.

This justification stage highlights, how the researcher followed the step-by-step analysis of the collected data. The starting point was the development of a general and detailed criteria catalogue, described in Section 3.8.

Collection of the data and the GT-based analysis, using Colour Coding, was conducted according to the following procedure, throughout the three data collection and analysis stages, as described in Figure 9 below.

The mapping process began in Interview Phase 2 to be data sensitive and to avoid being too influenced by the literature-based data, at the start of the empirical data. In terms of Theoretical Sensitivity (described in Section 3.4.6) the author was able to maintain the integrity of the data analysis and development of focused codes, having the raw data double-checked by a third-party researcher, who then coded empirical data again objectively and without prejudice.

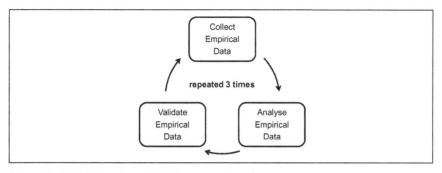

Figure 9: Validation of empirical data throughout 3 stages

The first stage started with collecting data from the in-depth interviews (from phase 2 and 3), followed by a GT-based analysis using Colour Coding. The collected and analysed codes were justified from the literature-based criteria catalogue. The second phase (seven interviews) was justified employing the same procedure as the one in the pilot interviews: collecting and analysing data and validating empirical data by using the literature-based criteria catalogue. The same was done in the third interview phase with another four interview participants. This procedure of validation is also part of the mapping process, and justifies empirical data by means of relevant literature.

The justification of the empirical results, by presenting them to the interview participants, discussing their view of the results and getting their feedback, described in Section 3.7 was one justification step. Another was the validation and discussion of research questions (presented in Section 3.9.4) addressed in Chapter 5. (Bergaus *et al.*, 2012) describing an earlier version of the detailed procedure of the literature-based Mapping Process.

The following Sections, describe the data collection and analysis phases of this study, from a methodology point of view.

3.3.5 Overview about the Research Project Process

This process started with an inductive approach by collecting data in pilot interviews. At this stage the author sharpened the research investigation, by focusing on user aspects of SDP based ICT systems, formulating four literature based research questions. From this point on, the researcher followed an abductive approach in interview phases 2 and 3, adopting Charmaz with respect to GTM.

Data collection was carried out in three interview stages: pilot interview phase (1), second interview phase (2) and third interview phase (3). Initially, the collected data from the interviews was analysed by using GTM with Colour Coding, and then categories were developed after each collection phase, within the framework of the literature-based criteria catalogue. Thereby, empirical data was validated on the basis of literature-grounded data taken from the literature-based data, conforming to the literature-based criteria catalogue:

- *Collect Data Interview Phase 1:* Data from the pilot interviews was gathered and transcribed.

- *Analysis Data Interview Phase 1:* Pilot interview data was analysed. In the interview phase 1 (pilot interviews) there was no literature-based study and Mapping process because of the inductive approach.

- *Collect Data Interview Phase 2:* Data from the second interview phase was collected and transcribed. The author conducted the literature-based study and Mapping Process, in interview phases 2 and 3, adopting an abductive approach.

- *Analysis Data and Mapping Process Interview Phase 2:* Interview data was analysed. Additionally, the gathered literature-based data from the literature research was structured, grouped and mapped as described in Section 3.8.

- *Collect Data Interview Phase 3:* Data from the third interview phase was collected and transcribed.

- *Analysis Data and Mapping Process Interview Phase 3:* Interview data was analysed. Additionally, the literature-based data gathered from the ongoing literature research were structured, grouped and mapped as described in Section 3.8. and empirical data was validated.

Semi-structured, in-depth, interviews together with a literature-based study, were employed for collecting and analysing empirical data. Data was collected and analysed in multiple sequences to develop a substantive Grounded Theory. To confirm and check the reliability of the intermediate data, the researcher established a dual-layered justification process described in the Section 3.12.

The consolidated results were presented to the interview participants for feedback. This was an important and beneficial element of the GTM. The data collection and analysis phases, as well as, the justification steps are presented in the following Table 2.

From the onset, four pilot interviews were analysed using GTM (see Section 3.4) and Colour Coding (see Section 3.5). The results of these first pilot interviews are presented in Section 4.2. A large number of initial codes were assigned to every interview. Additionally, two further sets of in-depth interviews were conducted and assigned with focused codes, presented in the interview phases two and three. Theoretical memos were written during the entire process of collecting and analysing data, as this facilitated reflection on the collected data.

Table 2: Data collection and analysis phases

Phase	Data Collection & Analysis	Codes & Categories / Method	Interpretation	Timeline
1 (Pilot)	Empirical study – pilot interviews: Conducting and transcribing 4 pilot interviews (2 users; 2 developers)	Initial Codes: Analysing empirical data by using colour coding	Memo writing; third-party coding	Jun09 – Aug09
		Developing Initial Categories		Nov09 – Jan10
2	Empirical study – in-depth interviews: Conducting and transcribing 7 interviews; (3 users; 3 developers; 1 architecture expert)	Focused Codes: Analysing empirical data by using colour coding; development of categories	Memo writing; third-party coding	Apr10 – Sep10
		Developing Further Categories		Oct10 – Nov10
2	Literature-based study & Mapping Process: Literature review regarding NGNs and SDPs; structuring and mapping literature-based data	Literature Research: Structure and group relevant literature; generate structures mind maps; mapping codes and categories	Compare empirical codes by the use of literature-based data	Dec10 – Mar11
		Theoretical Samling to Intermed Integration between Empirical and Literature-based Study		Apr11 – May11
3	Empirical study – in depth interviews: Conducting and transcribing 4 interviews(1 user; 1 developer; 2 architecture experts)	Focused Codes: Analysing data by using Colour Coding; Development of Categories; mapping codes and categories	Memo writing; third-party coding	Jul11 – Sep11
		Developing Further Categories		Oct11 – Nov11
3	Literature-based study & Mapping Process: Ongoing literature review regarding NGNs and SDPs – structuring and mapping literature-based data	Literature Research: Structure and group relevant literature; generate structures mind maps	Compare empirical codes by the use of literature-based data	Dec11 – Feb12
		Developing Final Categories		Mar12 – May12
		Theoretical Samling to Intermed Integration between Empirical and Literature-based Study		May12 – Jun12
4	Presenting the consolidated study results to the interview participants: Justify the final results	Presentation of Results: Present categories developed and models to the interview participants to get their feedback	Justification of the final results	May12 – Jun12

A number of memos are shown throughout Chapter 4, in order to demonstrate their importance in the development of the final GT categories, and description with the models, illustrated in the Sections 4.5 and 5.9. The literature-based study and the mapping process phases between the interview phases two and three, were used to justify the analysed codes and check their reliability within each phase as outlined in Table 2. No changes were necessary after the feedback was received.

The empirical study was done in 3 phases, where fifteen interviews were conducted. Codes and categories were developed based on the data analysed. In addition data was justified based on the literature, to confirm codes and interpret data, by writing theoretical memos, in phases two and three. At the end of the empirical study a workshop with all interviewees was held to present the results of the study, and to discuss feedback. These different phases were done between June 2009 and June 2012 (see Table 2).

Theoretical Sampling was employed to analytically decide from whom to sample from next, in interview phases 2 and 3. That meant, which interview participants (out of the three presented groups, see Paragraph 2.3.4.3) were selected for interviews in the next stage and which field or topic was going to be reviewed within the literature based study.

The next Sections, 3.4 to 3.8, describe all the methodologies, methods and techniques used in the EMPLIT framework, which were presented in Section 3.3. The following Section also gives an overview of Grounded Theory Methodology, describing the fundamental base of the specified methodology used within this research project.

3.4 Grounded Theory Methodology (GTM)

Grounded Theory (GT) is a flexible, qualitative, research design, processing a systematic research procedure that works to develop a process, an action or an interaction of a substantive topic, primarily used in qualitative research. Grounded Theory Methodology (GTM) is a systematic methodology in social science, involving the discovery of a theory, through the analysis of empirical data (Cresswell, 2012).

Glaser and Strauss (1967: p. 9-13), wanted to show verifiable qualitative research results using their research method. Over the last 40 years, since the "discovery" of GT, there have naturally been improvements and simplifications in the theory, and variations in the procedure, depending on the research purpose (Goulding, 2002: p. 170). Today, GT is one of the most common approaches to qualitative research, and is used in addition to sociological research, in other disciplines, such as psychology, education and information systems research.

GTM has undergone transitions since it was presented, by Glaser and Strauss (1967). One of the first signs of a deviation in interpretation was in the work of Strauss and Corbin (1990). In practical terms, Glaser emphasized the emergence of concepts, while Strauss and Corbin (1990), more systematically, provided the researcher with several analytical tools to choose from, to "create" and "construct" a theory, from the stories told by the participants. This difference, was later discussed by Glaser (1992), as the polarities of emergence versus forcing (Glaser, 1992).

Interestingly, while Strauss and Corbin's (1990) version of GTM has been seen as systematic tools that have procedural affinity to positivism (Locke, 2001), others find characteristics of post-positivism, in Strauss and Corbin's emphasis on context and complexity. Inspired by this emphasis, Clarke (2005) argued, that she moved the grounded theory around postmodern turns by developing a situational analysis, focusing on discourses, narratives, and historical analyses. Charmaz (2006), stressed that the connection to the researcher should be visible as the theory is a construction, and results from the interplay between the researcher and the respondents.

Where Glaser (2002), insisted that codes and categories emerge directly from data, Strauss and Corbin (1990), argued that theoretical pre-knowledge flows into data. Initially the author followed Glaser's inductive approach during the pilot interviews, but in phases 2 and 3, adopted the Charmaz approach to GTM. The author therefore formulated research questions (presented in Section 3.9.4) based on literature (literature-based criteria catalogue and the literature-based study) and further included abductive approach within the second and third interview and analysis phases.

Both Strauss and Corbin (1990) and Strauss (1991), take into account that observation and development of theory, are necessarily theory guided. Moreover, scientists should be in a position to modify or reject during, and due to, observation. This facilitates researcher to systematically control or validate their qualitative research results when using GTM (Reichertz, 2010). According to Glaser, GTM accentuates induction or emergence, and the individual's creativity is seen in clear stages, whereas Strauss focuses more on validation criteria and a systematic approach.

The author followed Peirce's approach to abduction research and formulated research questions (in the interview cycles 2 and 3) based on a non-commital literature review in phase two, of the qualitative study. A non-commital literature review emerges on the upcoming theory the relevance of the literature being researched (Urquhart and Fernandez, 2006). These questions are answered and discussed in the Chapter 5. The motivation for continuous justification of developed research questions during data collection, analysis and restarted data collection, theoretical sampling and writing theoretical memos was to assure the level of quality (Strübing, 2004).

Though GTM is used to generate theories and for collecting and analysing data using its procedures, this investigation used GTM primarily as a coding process rather than as a theory creation tool, by leveraging GTM techniques. The motivation for this investigation arises from a combination of the academic and practical experiences of the author in the subject matter. As a PhD candidate, the author's interest was drawn to GTM while shifting from technical oriented SDP-related research, to a more user-focused research. Given his experience within the study project topics, it seemed appropriate to conduct a GT study within the field of information systems. The result was to study SDP-based ICT-systems from a user's point of view.

3.4.1 Introduction to Grounded Theory

It is believed that GT theories emerge slowly from data, in a process of gradual abstraction. One of the most famous quotations from "The Discovery of Grounded Theory" is: "Clearly, a Grounded Theory Methodology that is faithful to the everyday realities of the substantive area is one that has been carefully induced from the data" (Glaser and Strauss, 1967). Popper (1959), already proved the inaccuracies of inductive procedures, in general, and with respect to GT, by Kelle (1994, 2005), and Strübing (2004) in particular.

Grounded Theory (GT), refers to a specific scientific research style, in which social reality is explored, using scientific theory. GT offers researchers the possibility to systematically combine various methods and techniques with which to deal with empirical data, starting from the processing of the analysis, through to the compilation of data, and its eventual conceptualisation. The available methods and techniques have no rigid instructions, but are practical research "recipes" (Strauss and Corbin, 1996: Preface).

The systematic approach of GT is based on an iterative process of research, where the phases of data collection and analysis are considered as involving mutual co-operation (Fendt and Sachs, 2008: p. 431). The aim is to discover a previously designated set of methods and techniques, by systematically applying a theory that finds justification in empirical data (Fendt and Sachs, 2008: p. 431). The development of the theory is thus based on real experiences, which lead to insights, which in turn provide the source of the theory (Semiawan, 2006: p. 2).

The data set, created throughout the research process, is constantly expanding, and is the most important component of the overall research process, in terms of general categories and relationships. Subsequently, attempts to develop statements about the relationships of concepts are made. These are called categories, and are to be understood as a form of classification of concepts, whereby theses, drawn by the comparison of concepts are combined within a single category. The concepts and categories developed are only considered meaningful if their connection is clear, i.e. if they are closely linked (Strauss and Corbin, 1996: p. 219).

Turner (1983: p. 347) proposes two criteria, so as to benchmark the quality of the theoretical outcomes: firstly, if the theoretical account fit closely and apply to the social environment it is concerned with, and secondly, if it is true, legible and enlightening to individuals who are familiar with the social phenomenon being researched.

One of the most important benefits of the GT Methodology is the ability to derive theory from the context of collected data. However, this can be painstaking for the researcher due to their lack of knowledge in interpreting data, and the knowledge to recognise when saturation has been achieved (Esteves et al., 2002). According to Urquhart (2007: pp. 339-360) the potential of GTM as a tool for Information System research, documented useful adaptations of GTM regarding the interaction of individuals and the technology. The recommended adaptations are (Urquart, 2007):

- Initial literature review to familiarise oneself and not for defining a framework

▨   Coding for theory generation as opposed to superficial coding

▨   Memos used for aiding the theory building process

▨   Building emerging theory and engaging with other theories

▨   Clarity of procedures and chain of evidence

Weber (2003) pointed out, that the interaction of individuals and technology, and the potential of GTM for theory building, is untapped in the field of information systems. GTM requires researchers to develop a newly generated theory, with other theories and allows great discussions after the theory generation about building formal from substantive theories. Urquhart *et al.* (2009), recommended GTM, applied as a tool for qualitative research, within the Information Systems scope instead of a theory-building tool. In their paper, Shannak and Aldhmour (2009), present a theory about ICT developed GT.

In the author's opinion, GT provides the optimal method to be used in this study. The author sought to embrace and promote openness to pragmatic approaches, in this study. All empirical research is "grounded" in data.

3.4.2   Characteristics of GTM

GTM is often seen as a theory building process, where researchers often leverage GTM for coding procedures. This is why Glaser and Strauss (1967), distinguish between substantive and formal theories. A substantive GT pertains to the phenomena being studied and makes no general claims beyond that particular phenomena. A formal theory focuses on a high level description of conceptual entities. Glaser and Strauss (1967), argued that it should be possible to build a formal theory from a substantive, by using theoretical sampling, to widen the scope of the theory.

Theoretical Sampling is a very powerful idea of GTM, in deciding analytically where to sample from next, thus showing that the theory can quickly adapt, based on emerging concepts. Urquhart (2012), argued that one common way to increase the scope of the theory is to sample unlike groups, while increasing the explanatory powers of the theory, researchers sample diverse and less saturated concepts. Theoretical Sensitivity is based on being steeped in the field of research and associated ideas, so researchers understand the context in which a theory is developed, (Glaser, 1978). It is also very important for the selection of data. Glaser and Strauss (1967), reflected the fact, that different kinds of data, gives researchers different views to understand a category or develop its properties. This entails that researchers should constantly sample data from the phenomena, in order to build the theory out and upwards.

Theoretical sampling enables one to focus on a developing theory, ensuring that the theory is truly grounded in the data. It is a key tool of GTM, and can be used to extend the scope to generalise the GT, where emerging concepts from the analysis enable sampling other datasets, to help extend and build the theory. By conscious selection of sample groups that are either similar to, or very different from, the original group, and looking at either diverse or similar concepts in the data, expand and densify the theory (Glaser and Strauss, 1967).

Information technology stresses the importance of deciding analytically, where to sample from next in the study. It helps to ensure the comprehensive nature of the theory and that the development is truly grounded within the data (Urquhart, 2012). Theoretical sampling is used in an iterative conceptualisation to relate categories to each other through an iterative process, the theoretical coding, described in 3.4.4.3. Reliability checks, only when the theoretical saturation (results are in a stable mode, without changing or bringing new results) is reached.

The procedure distinguishes itself, above all, by its openness and flexibility at the beginning, and is to be regarded at as important, because this serves the generation of categories (Charmaz, 2006: p. 186, 240). Demolition occurs as soon as a saturation of the categories becomes evident. Theoretical sampling works with theoretical coding and the generation of theoretical memos. Theoretical sorting, as well as theoretical writing, follows the development of base drafts (Charmaz, 2006: p. 186, 240).

Researchers should not look at the existing literature when starting their empirical study. According to Glaser (1992), the dictum in GT is, that there is no need for reviewing the literature in the substantive area under study. According to Charmarz (2007), it is helpful to look into the literature, consider construction of meaning regarding the data, but following ways to compare the data with due consideration, before imposing other theories on it.

Constant comparison, introduced by Glaser and Strauss, facilitates ongoing analysis. What is important, is that the imagery of research being grounded in the data was unfortunately bound to elevate data to prime position, precisely at a time when the term data, itself, was increasingly problematic (Charmaz, 2007). According to Urquhart (2012) comparitative analysis is the process of the constant comparison of instances of data, labelled in one category, with other instances of data being labelled for that category.

The initial stage of coding in GTM is more detailed based, thus scaling down the level of the theory. Researchers in turn run the risk of being embroiled in the detail due to the bottom-up nature of coding, within GTM. Overcoming and surpassing this challenge, and to move forward from this point is to group categories into successively larger themes so that the emergent theory is at a sufficient level of detail. Both, Glaser and Strauss (Glaser 1978; Strauss, 1987), suggested having one or two core categories for the substantive GT in order to get the theory to a reasonable level of abstraction. This is a process of scaling up the emergent theory to a sufficient level of abstraction engaging it with other theories in the field (Urquhart, 2012).

3.4.3 Criteria for GT Studies

Charmaz (2006), outlines the following criteria that GT studies should attempt to fulfil, emphasising that a combination of credibility and originality enhance both the resonance and usefulness of the research:

Credibility

■ Strength of correlation between the data gathered and the argument?

■ Enough data to validate claims?

■ Sufficient range, within categories, of empirical observations?

■ Has the research provided enough evidence for the researcher's claims to allow the reader to form an independent assessment?

Originality

■ Do the categories offer new insights?

■ What is the social and theoretical impact of this research?

■ How does grounded theory challenge, extend, and refine current ideas, concepts and practices?

Resonance

■ Do categories portray the entirety of the studied experience?

■ Does GT make sense to the participants?

■ Does analysis offer them deeper insights into their lives and worlds?

Usefulness

■ Is there ground and motivation for further research within significant areas?

■ How does the research investigation contribute to knowledge?

■ Does the analysis offer interpretations for lay people to use in their daily lives? (Charmaz, 2006, p. 182)

The criteria for GT studies are revisited in Chapter 6.

3.4.4   Coding and Analysing Content with GT

In fact, although GT is often referred to as a qualitative method, this is incorrect as it is a general method. It is the systematic generation of theory from systematic research. It is a set of rigorous research procedures, which lead to the emergence of conceptual categories. These categories are related to each other, as a theoretical explanation of the actions that continually resolve the main concern of the participants, in a substantive area. GT can be used with either qualitative or quantitative data.

According to Charmaz (2006), the use of GTM in information systems research, is to clearly identify what it is used for: 1. a coding method or 2. a method for theory generation. There is ample evidence in information systems literature for the first use, but less for the second. One useful benefit of using GTM in information systems research, could be a much more detailed consideration of the role of theory and generation, of our own theories specific to information systems (Charmaz, 2006).

GTM uses bottom-up coding, where codes are suggested by the data, not by the literature. The importance of an open mind cannot be over-emphasised. GTM requires researchers to consciously put their knowledge of literature aside, so that pre-conceptualisations are not imposed on the data (Dey, 1993).

When using GTM, data collection and analysis follow a cyclical process using early data analysis to shape on-going data collections (shown in Figure 10 below). By reading through the transcribed interviews, the author identifies concepts and relations between different elements in the text. In GT these are typically known as categories, whereas codes refer to keywords or short sentences that are assigned to elements of the text.

By coding the interview text, the researcher identifies phenomena and links, and can group different codes into larger, more meaningful categories (Charmaz, 2006; Blaxter *et al.*, 2001).

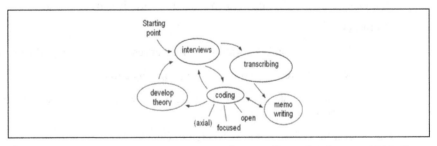

Figure 10:   Steps in developing a GT (According to Miles and Huberman, 1994; Gorra, 2007, 2008)

Typically, the following methods are used for the coding of data: open coding, focused coding, and optional axial coding. The process assigns codes to participants' words and statements, in order to develop concepts at the onset of the analytic process. This initial coding phase allows the researcher to compare events or situations with others, and develop more abstract concepts based on these events (Charmaz 2006: pp. 80-81). The second, commonly employed stage, involves assigning focused codes. These are not assigned to every single line of interview transcript, but can make use of some of the initial concepts that focus on specific issues identified in the previous coding stage. Focused coding is a non-linear process and may require the researcher to review previously coded statements and other events several times to confirm previous assumptions (Charmaz, 2006: pp. 245-269).

An optional coding stage is axial coding. It identifies key categories and their relationships to others, as well as "the act of relating categories to subcategories, along the lines of their properties and dimensions" (Strauss and Corbin, 1996: p. 123). The initial results of this coding stage can be used to influence the selection of further respondents, by a process known as theoretical sampling, and to locate further evidence for the central category and the developing theory. The process of coding and developing categories is supported by memos, which are constantly maintained and updated throughout the interview process in order to provide a record of thoughts and ideas for the researcher.

Coding can also be described as a process of describing and summarising the detailed materials using more and more abstract and general terms. This process is important, as it allows the researcher to extract the underlaying concepts that will help to build the theory. The coding process is done in three interrelated steps adopting Charmaz's coding methods: open, selective (focus), and theoretical coding (Müller and Olbrich, 2012).

3.4.4.1 Open Coding

Open coding is concerned with the principal identification of codes from the text describing the observation in the field. It includes element and concept indicators, which direct the coding process and allow for anything and everything to be coded (Müller and Olbrich, 2006). The researcher asks three general questions about the data:

- "What is this data a study of?" This leads to discovery of the "core variable." The core variable becomes the focus of the research and theory. The core variable is the variable that accounts for the most variation.

- "What category does this incident indicate?"

- "What is actually happening in the data?"

The process of open coding, or line-by-line coding, assigns codes to participants' words and statements in order to develop concepts, constituting the start of the analytic process. This initial coding phase allows the researcher to compare events or situations to others, and to develop more abstract concepts, based on these events (Charmaz, 2006: pp 80-81).

3.4.4.2   Selective Coding

Once categories and their properties have been established, Selective Coding will identify categories that are somewhat central to the understanding of the observed phenomenon (Müller and Olbrich, 2006). It covers core categorisation and integration of the theory or elements of the theory. This usually occurs when core variable and major dimensions and properties have been discovered. Closed coding involves limiting the coding to those things related to the core variable.

The second commonly used coding stage, involves assigning focused codes. These are not meticulously assigned to every single line of interview transcript, but can make use of some of the initial concepts that focus on specific issues identified in the previous coding phase. Focused coding, is not a linear process, and may require the researcher to repeatedly go through previously coded statements or events, to confirm assumptions that have previously been made (Charmaz 2006: pp. 245-269).

This process results in an "abstract representation of an event, object, or action/interaction, that a researcher identifies as being significant in the data" (Strauss and Corbin 1996: p. 103), its outcome should be the development of more abstract categories. In classical GTM, focused coding is denoted as selective coding. The stage identified or developed in the categories that are central in the understanding of the observed phenomenon, such 'core categories' can help to connect and explain the varous categories, their properties and their relations better (Müller and Olbrich, 2012).

To this end, a series of successive levels of coding steps was applied (Flick, 1996: p. 197). Through the initial "open coding", data was abstracted from the concrete context. Open coding involves breaking down a text into individual, meaning-based elements. This is also named "line-by-line analysis" (Semiawan, 2006: p. 8). The next step, involved "selective coding", or "focused coding", analysing possible key categories, specifically in terms of their relationship to other categories and sub-categories.

3.4.4.3   Theoretical Coding

Theoretical coding is the final stage of coding in Glaser's version of coding and establishes relationships between categories and-/or theoretical codes. These codes conceptualise how the substantive codes relate to one another, establishing new connections and making ideas relevant. At this stage codes were related to each other fulfilling the theory given that any theory consists of categories. The theoretical code has to fit with the emerging theory (Glaser, 1978). According to Urquhart (2012), a theoretical code is one that defines the relationship between two substantive codes. These codes are presented as focused codes, within this study shown in Chapter 4.

The Theoretical Coding stage identified key categories, and their relationships to others, as well as "the act of relating categories to subcategories along the lines of their properties and dimensions" (Strauss and Corbin 1996: p. 123). The initial results of these coding phases can be used to guide the selection of further respondents, known as theoretical sampling, and to find further evidence for the central category and the developing theory.

Lehmann (2012), recommended in relation to different GTM coding levels of abstraction in generic coding levels of qualitative data analysis after Miles and Huberman (1994), that coding happens in three levels in GTM, as well as in other social research:

▪ Initially, communalities in the data are captured in descriptive codes to clearly capture the essential attributes of the phenomenon.

▪ Secondly, as more data and codes are available, interpretive codes are abstracted from the idiographic confines of the concrete incidents, to help understand what is going on behind the data.

▪ Lastly, inferential pattern codes, now abstract of space and time and etic, to the substantive range of the research, are conceptualised. They are explanatory and often predictive (Lehmann, 2012).

In comparison to the different GTM schools these three levels of coding are different (Lehmann, 2012):

▪ Glaser and Strauss (1967), described the first discriptive step as 'Open Coding'. The second interpretive step was named 'Selective Coding' and the last pattern level, described as 'Theoretical Coding'. This is to reduce the number of concepts that make up the final theory.

▪ Strauss and Corbin (1990), restrict relations between categories, because it forces concepts rather than letting them emerge. They named the three levels: 1. Open Coding, 2. Axial Coding and 3. Selective Coding.

▪ Charmaz (2006), designated three levels of descriptive coding: a. Open Coding, b. Focused Coding, and c. Axial Coding, and as level of interpretive coding: 'Theoretical Coding'.

Further developments of Strauss and Corbin (1990), and Charmaz (2006), defined their own labels, including interim steps, where they differ obliquely from the three universal coding levels described before. Focused Coding focuses either on a subject or an object group. Axial Coding looks for a relationship between data, and this can be seen as more a function of Theoretical Sampling than of coding (Lehmann, 2012). This study focused on Charmaz's focus of coding using four coding stages Open, Focused, Axial and Selective Coding. In Section 3.4.4, the Colour Coding System used in this research study, was shown. According to Morse and Richards (2002), Theoretical Saturation is the phase when analysed qualitative data which researchers have continued sampling and analysing to the point where no new data appears, and all links between concepts have been verified from the theory, and no additional data is needed.

3.4.5 Theoretical Integration

Theoretical integration is the process of relating the emergent theory to other theories, in the same or similar field of research. Supporting this integration, theoretical memos are used for the theorising and present theoretical write-ups of ideas about codes and their relationships during coding. Researchers focus on their own way, of interpreting data by using their own words. Data collection, analysis and memo writing are ongoing and overlap. Memo writing should take precedence because it is the actual write-up of what emerges from the data and analysis. Data is always available and can be analysed at any time. Ideas are fragile, and they should be written down at the earliest possible opportunity to ensure reliable recollection (Charmaz, 2007).

Whilst writing memos, one should think and write theoretically, in a "stream of consciousness" fashion, with no concern about grammar, spelling, etc., thus minimising 'writer's block'. Theoretical Memos are always modifiable as the researcher discovers more about the topic and begins to integrate the literature. Once confident with the theory, one can begin to analyse and integrate this into relevant existing literature. Theoretical material from the literature must earn its place in the theory, the same way as any other theoretical construct (Paris and Hürzeler, 2008).

Sorting and theoretical outlining refers to the conceptual sorting of memos into an outline of the emergent theory, showing the relationships between concepts and relationships. This process often stimulates memos, and sometimes further data collection. The completed process constitutes a first draft write-up. From this point on it is merely a matter of refining and polishing the product into a final draft (Paris and Hürzeler, 2008).

Integrative diagrams show the integration of the developed GT categories in relation to each other. Without focusing on the relationships between the categories, the researcher cannot claim to be building a theory. Integrative diagrams are used in the final stage of Theoretical coding by developing the final categories and the theory. It is more about the relationship between the categories than the categories themselves, it is when researchers theorise about the data (Urquhart, 2001; Urquhart, 2012).

3.4.6 The Role of the Researcher

Some authors have classified GTM as a positivist methodology (Charmaz, 2006), whereas others have considered it to be an interpretive methodology (Brown, 1995; Goulding, 1998). When conducting research, an important aspect to bear in mind is the issue of reflexivity, which could be understood, as the process of critical self-reflections on the biases of the researcher, theoretical predispositions, as well as the entire research process. In positivist research this is particularly important in establishing validity of accounts gathered from participants and possible bias on the part of the researcher (Urquhart, 2012).

The approach researchers take in obtaining aspects is of great importance within GT. An approximation, without preconceived opinions or personal feelings, should be sought. Therefore, a detailed study of relevant existing theories is planned before the start of the study. Recommended in certain literature, such as Glaser (1987: pp. 12-13), this explicitly requires one to refrain from the influence of another's opinion by looking at the literature before collecting and analysing the data.

In contrast, Charmaz (2006: p. 178) recommended the interference of doing literature research parallel to the empirical data study. Written memos by the researcher should contain analytical ideas, which are for documenting the cognitive progress that takes place during the research process. As memos, they are understood as being crucial aids to the analysis and distinguish, in detail, between coding memos and methodological memos. Coding memos include the category name, a text code (extract), and references.

The objective attitude of the researcher should be characterised by a marked sensitivity to the data found in the correlations, known as "Theoretical Sensitivity". The designated property of the researcher allows him to establish categories of phenomena, and thus ultimately arriving at the discovery of a theory (Paris and Hürzeler, 2008: pp. 3-4; Glaser, 1978; Smith and Bryant, 2000). It is assigned to sensitise researchers on what is happening with the phenomenon that they are studying.

Theoretical Sensitivity relates to the personal quality of the researcher and indicates an acute awareness of the subtleties, of the meaning, of data. One arrives at a research situation with varying degrees of sensitivity, depending on previous reading and experience with, or relevant to, a given area.

It can be further developed during the research process. Theoretical Sensitivity refers to the attribute of having insight, and the ability to give meaning to data, the capacity to understand and to separate, what is from what is not pertinent, conceptually rather than on concrete terms. It is theoretical sensitivity that allows one to develop a theory that is grounded, conceptually dense, and well integrated – and to do this more quickly than if this sensitivity were lacking (Strauss and Corbin, 1990).

The researcher's assumptions about the phenomenon being explored are therefore, critical to the research and should be clearly stated in the research report. In GT, researchers have to demonstrate "Theoretical Sensitivity" to the nuances of data, by being engrossed in professional literature together with professional and personal experiences (Glaser, 1978). Theoretical sensitivity is enhanced via four techniques, outlined in Strauss and Corbin, (1990):

■ Basic questioning of the data (i.e., who, when, why, where, what, how, how much, frequency, duration, rate, and timing).

■ Evaluation and assessment of meanings and assumptions of a single word, phrase, or sentence.

■ Create new means of comparisons promoting non-standard aspects of looking at the data and making provisions a denser theoretical conceptualisation.

■ Probing absolute terms such as never and always (Brown *et al.*, 2002).

In qualitative research, a conscious effort to maintain a balance between the participant and observer role is made, by the researcher, who then carefully examines their own, subjective thoughts, feelings and experiences. The level of inter-subjectivity, or interactions between the researcher and participants and its impact on the findings of a study, needs to be monitored during the study so as to maintain neutrality and unbiased points of view (Glesne, 1999).

Additionally, researchers need to manage the multiple roles they, and the respective roles of the participants, play during the research process (Glesne, 1999). The researcher may additionally function as a supportive listener, a volunteer worker across different contexts, and needs to be cognisant of their roles and try to be in tune with the participant. Outlining exact role management enhances the rigor of a study and precisely portrays the perspectives and experiences of the participant (Glesne, 1999; Rossman and Rallis, 2003).

The author combined both his academic and practical experience in this subject matter, and as a PhD candidate became intrigued with the nature of GTM, enthusiastically pursuing subsequent postgraduate studies researching technical aspects of SDPs.

Given the practical experience gained as a practitioner in teaching mobile and ubiquitous technologies, management consulting and the development, pre-sale and sales from state-of-the-art technologies in different fields of business, it seemed appropriate to combine theoretical and practical areas of his expertise and interests, by conducting a GT study within the field of SDPs, from a user's point of view to investigate in this PhD study

While conducting GT research, the author developed an interest in philosophical underpinnings of this methodology. Intrigued by these conflicting opinions and curious to gain more knowledge about the philosophical antecedents of this particular methodology, the author began studying the philosophy of science in general terms, intending to obtain a broader philosophical understanding of the Glaserian nature of GTM. The perspective was to follow GTM in a positivist approach, starting with research on information systems to emphasise a general, universal substantive GT.

3.4.7 Limitations of the GTM

Researchers point out that GTM, as with other methodologies has its limitations. It is extremely time-consuming and complex, due to coding and memo writing procedures (Bartlett and Payne in McKenzie et al., 1997). The investigation at hand has followed the methodological guidance of Charmaz (2006), and Strauss and Corbin (1998), in terms of gathering and analysing the collected interview data. The use of GTM in explaining a phenomenon, or building a theory, is a highly subjective procedure. It relies on a researcher's abilities to build, develop and describe a phenomenon. Findings from the mapping process (criteria catalogue) are used to strengthen those findings based on interview data, with the aim of fulfilling the criteria for GTM as discussed in Section 3.4.3. Certain studies make use of the term GT inappropriately, and Bryant (2002) points out that the flexibility of the method can be used to provide a proof of studies lacking in methodological strength (Smith and Bryant, 2000).

3.4.8 Statement of Reasons for Choosing GTM in this Study

GTM is a method that can be used to generate theories, and to collect and analyse qualitative data, using codes attached to data by focusing on a bottom-up approach to define a new theory with the help of building relationships between concepts informed by the codes. The motivation for choosing to employ GTM in this research was that GTM is used as a coding and analysis process due to the structured procedure in analysing data rather than a theory, generating tool.

This investigation focuses on the user perspective, and for this reason the named group of SPICE-experts was interviewed. This was a group of three subgroups of potential users of SDPs. Driving and supporting the development of SDPs and ICT systems in general from an end-users perspective is an important issue, because these technical environments are becoming influential in our daily lives, and therefore a broad range of our population gets the possibility to use and to benefit from these systems for the fact that ICT becomes stronger in our everyday's life (Cordier et al., 2006b).

The researcher chose GTM for this study as this methodology supports an inductive procedure to conduct research on influence factors of the users' perspective to position an SDP, as a common control and communication instance for any ICT systems. GTM guided data collection and the different analysis phases. This work does not focus on GTM research per se. The GT methodology was only chosen as a guide, and to support the research methodology in three steps.

3.4.9 Alternative Methodology

Another qualitative research method is the Actor Network Theory (ANT). In the following Section, a short overview about ANT is given. ANT is a theory of social science, focused on the meaning of interdependencies and the consequences of science and technology for human society. The most well known representatives of ANT are French social scientists, Michael Callon and Bruno Latour, and the British scientist John Law. ANT owes its originality to the fact that technology and reality, are not socially built. Society, nature and technology, are no longer perceived as separate units, rather people, natural and artificial, perceived as a part of the social world. According to this perspective, the social does not present itself as purely social rather than the term "the social" describes a connection type (Latour, 2006: p. 17).

This combination type is a fundamental indicator for the process of connection, translation and association of human and non-human beings, namely from heterogeneous units which are not themselves, social, technical and natural objects taken into the ANT to observe their influence on society. Scientific and technological developments are not caused by natural, technical or social factors (Latour, 2006).

Initially, when developing this research methodology, the author researched GTM and ANT and found that in ANT there are two main ideas, according to Tatnall and Gilding (1999): "Many methodological approaches we think are binaries which often leads us to designate an entity as either technological or social, and then we attribute specific properties to that entity, in order to explain its behaviour, thereby adopting an essential position. Research studies that follow GT often adopt this approach, but ANT does not distinguish between the social and technological, and sees properties as network effects rather than innate characteristics of an entity" (Tatnall and Gilding, 1999).

ANT was not applied in this study due to negative criticism it had received. According to Tatnall and Gilding (1999), some critics argue that research, based on ANT perspectives, remains entirely descriptive and fails to provide explanations for social procedures, which this study strongly investigates.

The next Section describes the Coding System used in this study.

3.5   Colour Coding System

The process of coding and developing categories, is supported by written memos, which are a set of notes kept on the person constantly, providing the researcher with a record, of thoughts and ideas. While the process of Colour Coding, introduced in this Section, has the iterative data collection and analysis of the "traditional" Grounded Theory coding process is common, the approach described differs significantly, in the way the interview data was coded.

For the purpose of this investigation, a coding system described as Colour Coding, developed within the context of other studies, was employed. It follows the tradition of various coding methods found in GT and described in the previous Section. It is of particular relevance for people who possess distinctive visual orientation (Stottok, 2010a: p.7-10). The idea of Colour Coding was developed by Stottok, Bergaus and Gorra (Stottok *et al.*, 2011), and subsequently refined, as it offered a way of moving quickly from open coding to the next step of focused coding of data from transcribed interviews and is a concept of supporting open, selective and theoretical coding within GTM research. A log of all codes, concepts and categories identified in the interview data was kept in the "Fact Finding Tool" (see Section 3.5.2), which is a Microsoft Excel file consolidates all data analysis related codes and texts (Bergaus and Stottok, 2010; Stottok, 2010a). To demonstrate the difference between traditional GTM numerical coding and Colour Coding, Table 3 provides an overview of both methods.

Table 3: Example of a comparison between numerical and colour coding

Coding Methods	Examples
Numerical Coding (based on assigned bracketed numbers)	"Freedom to do what you want (legally)" [33]. "It doesn't exist – big brother is always watching!" [127]. "Respecting my family life as opposed to my work life" [15].
Colour Coding (based on the colours pink, sea green and blue)	"Freedom to do what you want (legally)". "It doesn't exist – big brother is always watching!". "Respecting my family life as opposed to my work life" .

According to Gorra (2007: pp. 172-173), three examples were displayed in the upper line with numerical coding, including their numerical codes, whereas in the lower line, the same text passages were presented by means of colour coding. The sentence in pink represents the code belonging to the numerical code "Freedom to do what I want (legally)" ([33], pink).

Respectively, the sea green sentence belongs to the numerical code "It doesn't exist - big brother is always watching!" ([127], sea green), and the blue sentence is assigned to the numerical code "Respecting my family life as opposed to my work life" ([15], blue).

The reason the author chose to apply Colour Coding within this study reflects the thoughts of Strauss (Strauss and Corbin, 1996), which states that every researcher must find their own way to analyse data, based on their creativity and the availability of data. Colour Coding is a pragmatic approach that supports effective data analysis and processing, and the author found it easy to use. The method was considered to be very suitable since it was possible to efficiently develop categories and sub-categories, and to switch from open, to focused, coding, at an early stage (Stottok *et al.*, 2011).

Colour Coding follows the tradition of the different coding methods used in GT and it supports the use of induction as well as abduction, a way of forming and confirming a hypothesis. This is because the method of Colour Coding helps to move quickly from the phase of open coding to focused coding. A log of all codes, concepts and categories identified in the interviews is kept in an Microsoft Excel file, which will be defined as the "Fact Finding Tool" (described in Section 3.5.2). This tool consolidates all data-analysis-related codes and texts. The following Section shows with help of specific examples, how this visual method of text coding is used in this research study (Bergaus and Stottok, 2010).

3.5.1 Initial Coding by Using Qualitative Analysis Software

To analyse the initial interview data by using GTM, one pilot interview was coded using NVivo and another, using NUD*IST, to identify the differences and to ascertain the advantages and disadvantages, of those specific qualitative analysis software coding tools.

NVivo

NVivo is a qualitative data analysis software tool developed by Tom Richards in 1999. It contains tools for fine, detailed analysis, and qualitative modelling, and was designed for qualitative research facilitating researchers working with large text based, multimedia information, where deep levels on small or large volumes of data are required. NVivo helps users organise and analyse unstructured data, allowing users to classify, sort and arrange information.

The software supports the coding process of empirical data. The researcher can test theories, identify trends and cross-check information, in various ways, using search engines and query functions. NVivo accommodates a wide range of research methodologies including GTM (QSR International, 2012; Gibbs, 2002).

NUD*IST

NUD*IST – Non Numerical Unstructured Data Indexing Searching and Theorising, is a software tool that supports qualitative research, especially GTM. It is based on the concept of building a logical hierarchical system of nodes, where each node is logically related to other nodes. This is done by flagging a text search, to construct a possibly large and highly structured hierarchical database, indexing into the documents, which have to be analysed. Node search uses seventeen operators, including Boolean, proximity and other operators, generating new nodes to build hierarchical indexing categories encouraging the generation of new ideas. NUD*IST indexes and annotates both online and offline documents, and helps to evolve, and confirm, theories based on widely varied and unstructured sources (Fielding, 1998; Lamont-Mills, 2004).

Summary

The first phase of coding proved to be unsuccessful. More than two hundred codes were assigned during a 30 to 40 minute interview, with some codes only being used once or twice. In addition, some codes resembled topics from the literature but were not explicitly mentioned by the interviewees. Also, the author found both NVivo and NUD*IST very complicated in that these tools included many detailed functions, which proved time-consuming to work with. As a result of these problems, the researcher decided to take an alternative manual approach to coding the interviews, by using a colour-coded schema, used in previous studies (Bergaus and Stottok, 2010).

The author adopted the colour coding approach to save time in learning the text analysis software described above, focussing on the relevant research topic and step-in coding, instead of spending time mastering new software tools and manually setting parameters with these tools, to find relations between these hundreds of codes. Based on this decision, the initial two interviews were repeated, only this time using the more time-efficient colour coding approach. Colour coding follows the typical steps of Charmaz (2006), described in Section 3.4.4.

The researcher used Colour Coding and not text analysis tools such as NVivo and NUD*IST, to expedite time taken in the preparation stage of coding as the complexity of these software products was high, and learning software tools too time intensive. These products are also inefficient and time consuming, operationally and administratively. Furthermore, many technical terms that were used in the interviews, needed to be interpreted because of the special expressions (Slang) used by some of the participants.

3.5.2   Fact Finding Tool

For analysis, along with the original transcribed interviews, a special analytical tool, the "Fact Finding Tool" (FFT) introduced by Stottok (2010a: pp. 7-10), was used. A file was created in Microsoft Excel Format, in which the GTM-based categories identified during the course of the interviews (sorted according to colour coding), were inserted so that each found category could then be analysed. The Fact Finding Tool is used for the analysis process of the transcribed interviews, in addition to the file containing the transcribed interviews.

This tool showed which codes and sub-categories belonged to the respective category, and also to which category the respective codes and memos had been allocated, efficiently and effectively. Furthermore, text passages could be taken from the tool and put into the results Section of a publication, either as summaries or citations.

A consistent width for all the columns, to keep the subsequent analysis simple was predefined. The number of cells in each column was equal in each interview the researcher undertook. Due to the cell space limitation, the maximum length of content that could be inserted into that cell was defined. Therefore, the researcher split the text passage into as many cells as were needed to reproduce and insert the complete passage (Bergaus and Stottok 2010: pp. 7-10; 128). This tool and other colour coding systems, are particularly appropriate for the visually orientated researcher. This tool shows which codes and sub-categories belong to which category, and which code memos could be arranged. In the FFT summary, texts and verbatim quotes could be extracted, for result presentation.

In the FFT, a tab page for each category identified in the interview transcripts was created, then after the first tab within this file was opened, and the name of the category was added in the first line. Below that, the name of the first detected sub-category, together with additional, explanatory information was added. Additional sub-categories, that were identified during the continuing analysis process, were also added in the lines below the first sub-category, in the relevant category tab. In the first line underneath these explanatory lines the information, from which interview the text passages in this column was taken, was inserted (Stottok *et al.*, 2001). An example of this process is shown in Section 3.11.1.

When another text passage in the first transcribed interview was identified, the researcher found it suitable to be subordinated to the already existing first category. This procedure equates to focused-coding as per GTM, and again this text was copied in the interview.

Furthermore the re-colouring for the first category with the defined colour, was done and the text was pasted into the next free cells in the first column, for the first interview in the first category tab of the FFT.

The researcher repeated the steps for all parts of texts during the coding process from the first subordinated data to that category. The author concluded after completely going through the first interview searching for codes that could be identified and sub-categories that could be created from these codes, as long as they were found to be suitable; belonging to the first defined category (Bergaus and Stottok 2010: p 128). Creating the Fact Finding Tool in Microsoft Excel had similar advantages for the researcher. Memos could be added to the cells containing relevant text passages and the same colour range was used, as in Microsoft Word, for colouring. For this reason the author was able to use the identical colours in the explanatory lines, in the tabs of the FFT that were originally used for coding text passages in the interview file. These lines carry the name of the category, and its subordinated sub-categories, including the name of the text that the passages were taken from. In Section 3.11.1 and the two figures (Figure 15, Figure 16) show this procedure. In the first image (Figure 15) an excerpt from a Fact Finding Tool tab where the colour "red" displayed, was used for the explanatory lines.

The next Section gives an overview of Mind and Concept Mapping techniques, in order to describe the visual presentations of empirical and literature-based data.

3.6   Mind- and Concept Mapping Techniques

Mind and Concept Mapping can be carried out to graphically illustrate representations and various other summaries. Different visualisation techniques make it easier to learn about and comprehend specific topic areas existing. Mapping techniques are especially useful when they offer advantages over other forms of visualisation, particularly when they are not specific to a certain area, and can therefore be applied in various different fields (Buzan, 2003; Novak and Gowin, 1984).

3.6.1 Mapping Techniques

Mapping techniques, for example a *Mind Map*[1] can be seen as a form of thoughts. A *Concept Map*[2] can be seen as a conceptually and hierarchically structured cognitive plan. Mapping techniques serve to make visual, abstract, and complex connections. These techniques, lead to a new form of thought model, and encourage creativity, because our brain responds to them in its entirety, with both parts of the brain being challenged. The main difference between Mind Maps and Concept Maps is observed in their exterior forms. Concept Maps are ordered forms that are hierarchically constructed, and within which the connection lines between the various concepts, are explicitly shown.

The main concept is not often found in the middle of the Maps, as is usual in Mind Mapping but at the top of the map, in order to represent its hierarchical importance and position. The primary difference, between *Mind Maps* and *Concept Maps,* is the different theoretical view of the representation of knowledge in the brain. Tony Buzan, the developer of *Mind Maps,* focused, above all, on the associative structure of memories, and thereby attempted to support the process of association. In contrast to this theory, Novak and Gowin, the developers of Concept Maps, assumed that knowledge in the brain is hierarchically ordered and founded on concepts, and thereby attempted to support the process of hierarchical structuring (Brühlmann, 2007: pp. 3-7).

3.6.2 Advantages of the Mapping Techniques and their Functions

Mind and Concept Mapping are techniques for external visualisation. With every 'map', an attempt is made to offer a visual presentation of an idea, in order to make it accessible to the viewer. In linear reading of a text only one half of the brain is involved, whereas through visualisation, both hemispheres of the brain are activated.

Interaction between the left and right hemisphere of the brain, when learning with and drawing up of 'maps', is definitely one of the important advantages for quickly considering new, complex topics, and then structuring them. With the drawing up of every 'map' a profound assimilation of the subject content is achieved, and therefore a connection between previous knowledge and new information brought about, because the information structure has to be reduced to reflect the most important points. Therefore, connections hierarchies and causal connections within the subject under inspection, are worked out. Furthermore working and learning with 'maps' is a meta-cognitive function.

---

[1] All trademarks and trade names are the properties of their respective owners.
[2] All trademarks and trade names are the properties of their respective owners.

With the drawing of a 'map', the learner becomes aware of what they already know, about the given material, and whether they have actually understood it, since the learner has to turn every concept into an understandable connection for himself. A third characteristic of external visualisation, is the promotion of multiple representation functions. When the content of a text is made visual within a 'map', then this representation, in form of an image, must be reconsidered. Thereby, a form of translation of one representation code into another takes place. Within a 'map' the key information within the learning content, and the connections between pieces of information, is immediately obvious. The learner, therefore, does not have to filter this out of the text (Brühlmann, 2007: p. 8-13; Renkl and Nückles, 2006 p. 139-142).

An additional advantage of the Mapping Technique is its attractiveness. Mapping Techniques are as attractive for those who produce them as they are for those who are presented with them. During the creation of a map there is no limit on the imagination. As a result of this 'maps' are increasingly being used in presentations. Colours and images motivate the audience to listen more intently. The information is more easily and quickly readable, and therefore easier to pass on. The time needed to register the learning material is reduced, because only the relevant terms and not entire sentences are noted, read and repeated (Buzan and North, 1999: pp. 32-39).

The time saved in comparison to linear notes, is stated as being 95%, in terms of reading 90%, and in terms of repetition also 90%. Therefore, learning with 'maps', effectively saves time. An additional advantage of Mapping Techniques is that they match the brain's natural tendency to create countless associations. This advantage is particularly relevant for Mind Mapping. Through its appearance, a *Mind Map* creates the feeling that countless further branches could be added. Yet it can also be seen in its entirety, Buzan speaks about "radiant thinking", which can be explained as circular, radiating thought (Brühlmann, 2007: pp. 12-13).

The mapping process in this study and the resulting 'maps' offer the advantage of researchers being able to quickly grasp complicated subject areas and at the same time being able to structure them, whilst being able to assimilate links, hierarchies and causal connections.

3.6.3 Use of Mind Maps in this Study

Mind Maps are used in this study for two different representations. Firstly, Mind Maps were generated within the literature-based study, where aspects were mapped to a Mind Map representation after structuring and grouping, and generating the general and detailed criteria catalogues. It represents literature-based aspects or criteria for the justification with the empirical codes and categories. This is shown in Section 3.8.4

A second representation of Mind Maps is shown in Chapter 5, for the generic framework of SDP-based ICT systems of the future. The functional requirements developed from the validated empirical categories in combination with the literature based data created also two Mind Map representations. These results were created in terms of subjective and intuitive open/focused/axial and selective coding, described in Sections 4.5 and 5.5.

The following Section illustrates the presentation and feedback session done with the interview participants to present and discuss the final results of the study.

3.7   Feedback to Developed Empirical Results

The phase presenting the results to the interview participants was undertaken to confirm if the respondents' views were valid in terms of the empirical results of the research. To justify the final results of the study, the author initiated an additional phase with all the interview participants, to further justify the empirical results, from their viewpoints. The aim was to clarify whether the results of the study and the opinions of the empirical data were going to be confirmed or not. This was done in a workshop and group discussions with all participants giving them the chance to be informed about the results and in return for them to comment on the results.

The justification of research results was done in different ways: Presentation and discussion of the results, group interview and a feedback session regarding their thoughts, checking the reliability of the empirical results was essential to reflect these results in final categories and their relations (shown in Section 4.5) and present the models and ultimate findings (presented in Section 5.4) to the respondents. The reflection of the respondents' view was shown and discussed in Section 5.7.6. The following, Figure 11, shows how the workshop procedure was planned and delivered with the interview participants:

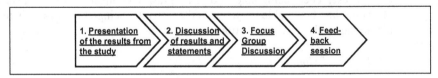

Figure 11: Steps of the result presentation workshop with respondents

The workshop started with a presentation of the study research objectives, described the procedure and presented the methodology, which was done before the researcher presented the final results in form of the GT categories to the interview participants. Here it was important to give the respondents the possibility to comment on the results of the study. For this reason a discussion in the plenum as well as with each of the interview groups (users, developers, architecture experts) was done. In the last step, a feedback session regarding the results and the whole workshop day, was done.

The next Section is an overview of the literature-based study undertaken in this research project.

3.8   Literature-based Study

The Literature-based study describes a technique developed by the author, to quickly learn about complex and extensive topics, while documenting researched literature, transparently. This study provides a procedure that starts at the beginning of the research investigation and ends with the justification of the empirical data, by using the literature-based data.

3.8.1   Literature Review Phase

The literature review phase starts with the collection of literature-based data to develop an initial criteria catalogue, and continues throughout the second and third phase of the research process to develop and improve the literature-based criteria catalogue. Additionally, this helped to formulate the research questions. All literature-based data must also have respective data to be afforded the possibility to then compare this data with that taken from the empirical study, and for validation.

3.8.2   Literature-based Criteria Catalogue

Reviewing and analysing the literature by searching for existing information, regarding challenges and design issues of SDP-based ICT systems, various groups and loosely-structured bullet point lists, with reference to original literature from academic papers, dissertations, articles and books, were generated. The author named this list, literature-based criteria catalogue, and it represented a list of general and detailed criteria in terms of the research topics around SDPs. It was developed in two steps, together with details of sources, containing the link to each literature reference.

3.8.3   Phases from the Literature-based Study

The literature-based study was carried out in the following, basic, four sequential expiry phases:

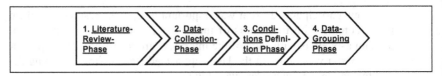

Figure 12: Phases from the literature-based study

1. Literature Review Phase

Books, dissertations, theses, and professional articles on the subject areas of NGNs and SDPs were investigated and read then, suitable data sources were extracted and recorded. Based on reviewing literature the author collected and documented relevant literature for this study from the very beginning until the end of this investigation. Importantly, it should be mentioned that the researcher followed the outline of Charmaz (in 2006: p. 178) – "... looking in the literature before data analysis ends ...", and along with the empirical analysis of data also consciously considered the literature. This began in the second phase of conducting empirical data and also in the last interview stage.

2. Data Collection Phase

Once clear subject areas were identified (SDPs, SPICE, NGSs, user-centred design, etc.), based on the technical main topics of this study, outlined in Sections 8.1 and 8.2, data was collected through a preliminary structured process.

3. Conditions Definition Phase

Conditions, concerning the subject fields and single areas of SDPs and ICT systems were defined, and the demands concerning design issues were elaborated upon (e.g. demands specific to the target group, from the point of view of operators, customers, manufacturers, and end users).

4. Data Grouping Phase

The data-grouping phase, assigned specific requirement groups and requirement aspects to each situation, within the scope of the condition definition phase, to ensure clear and well-structured Mind Maps.

3.8.4   Visualisation of Literature-based Data via Mind Map Representation

The analysis of literature by searching existing information regarding challenges and design issues, group and structured mind-maps, was generated to visualise the literature-based data. Traditionally, the technique of Tony Buzan's Mind Mapping (Buzan, 2003) was provided to visualise the literature-based criteria catalogue. From the list of criteria, visual transformation took place in form of maps. The aspects of a generated map are summarised as a broader category and serve as a basis for the validation of empirical data.

The preparation of literature-based data collected during the literature review was sorted, grouped and structured by using two tools described before, the literature-based criteria catalogue and Mind Map representations. The literature-based criteria catalogue is a word collecting and structuring tool, which was used to structure research related topics in bullet point, form including a reference to the original literature. This criteria catalogue is split into two parts, to allow the researcher to work with large volumes and complex unstructured literature review data, as follows:

▪ *General criteria catalogue:* Group and structure relevant aspects from the literature of the research topics roughly. The goal of this catalogue was to simplify the topic in form of creating significant groups, and reducing the complexity of the topic through a structuring procedure.

▪ *Detailed criteria catalogue:* Detailing aspects from the general part in the form of a detailed grouping and structuring procedure. For visual oriented researchers, mind maps help to offer them literature-based data compactly and simply. The general and detailed criteria catalogue was transferred to a Mind Map, and the main and detailed objects were subdivided.

This was necessary, having more than two hierarchical levels, as it became impossible to read the illustration in A4 format. Transfer criteria catalogues to a mind map representation is additional and not a prerequisite. After conducting and analysing empirical data, the literature-based criteria catalogue facilitated a comparison between data sets to validate the interview-based data by the literature-based data. It is possible to do more than one phase, where empirical data is conducted and analysed.

This procedure helped the researcher to structure and group voluminous and complex literature-based data with the existing relation to original data sources (papers, dissertations, books, articles, etc.) and is used as a literature research and validation tool, in several stages in this study. Also, if more researchers work on the same research project this is an effective communication tool for the researchers concerned, especially if some researchers lack expertise on certain topics related to the research project as a whole, or if a code verification needs to be undertaken by a third party researcher. Mind Maps help them to better and faster grasp the themes, and a transparent communication line between researchers is then possible.

The advantage of this method is that the researcher was able to systematically extract general aspects, balance voluminous literature by taking the Criteria Catalogue (general and detailed) and Mind Maps with their generated aspects. Combinations, hierarchies, and causal relations within a topic, are graphically set out, and intricately complex themes can be understood quickly and be simultaneously structured, and used to validate empirically gathered data. One limitation of this method though is that extensive literature cannot be displayed in one map alone. Experts, therefore, on the respective subjects compile maps from their own fields of research independently, and make them available to others (Bergaus et al., 2012).

The literature-based study helped justify the results from the empirical study (interviews) with data derived from the literature. The mapping process was investigated in the validation of empirical data by literature-based data after the second interview phase and after the final 3rd interview phase, as well. The critical criteria catalogue was collected, then split into general and detailed requirements, then clearly grouped and structured, on a mind map basis (Bergaus et al., 2012: pp 4-8).

The next Section describes the research study setup, used within this investigation, outlining the actual setup undertaken for this research project.

3.9   Research Study Setup

This Section describes the specific setup of the research study, starting with the selection of the interview participants for the target groups. The development and preparation of the interview guideline, the research project background information sheet and statement of confidentiality is presented and illustrated. Background information of the participants is also presented, together with the recording and transcription procedure, used in the interviews. The aim of this investigation was to gain an insight into the underpinning development of SDPs, with improved use, for prospective ICT systems.

3.9.1 Pledge of Confidentiality

The author explained that all those interviewed would be informed about the study, and further explained the way their data would be processed and used. The statement of confidentiality for all interview groups is set out in Section 9.2. All interviewees agreed to the use of their data, extensively, and for all purposes.

3.9.2 Sample and Ethical Consideration

The participants (SPICE experts) were selected based on the researcher's judgement. Six users, six developers and three architecture experts were chosen to participate in the study, ensuring that all participants represented the SPICE project. Due to the small sample size of the participants (15 in three stages), the study cannot be seen as a representative of the whole population.

This study was guided by the ethical principles on research with human participants set out by Leeds Metropolitan University (Research Ethics Policy, 2012). Aim and objectives of the pilot project, together with details of the data collection process were explained to the participants. The participants were informed that they could withdraw from the study at any time without being questions. All data collected was anonymous, by replacing their names with ascending code numbers (e.g. p11_u and p12_d) in the order of the initial interviews. Appendix B (Section Cover Letter/Email to Participants of the Interviews) shows the email that was sent out to participants, before receiving their agreement, to take part in the pilot interviews.

For the second and third interview phase, the participants were contacted informally, then by email explaining the study's aim and the interview procedure that would follow suit. The email assured participants about anonymity and confidentiality of data collected, and informed them that the interview was recorded for transcription purposes (see Appendix B, Section 9.1 - Email sent out prior to interviews). The interviews were recorded using a digital voice recorder and the files were transferred to a PC for transcription. When transcribing the interviews, participants' names were replaced with code numbers. Participants of the pilot study were assigned the codes p11_u, p12_d, p13_u and p14_d. "u" indicated users and "d" stands for developer. This is described in the Section 3.9.6.

The codes for respondents of the second and third interview phase followed the same system, starting with number p21_u, p22_u, p23_d, p24_u, p25_d, p26_d, p27_ae, p31_u, p32_ae, p33_ae, p34_d where "ae" indicates architecture experts. In addition to the four pilot study interviews, eleven more in-depth interviews were conducted within the interview phases 2 and 3. An interview lasted around 30 to 40 minutes. Respondents were selected based on initial findings. The pilot study ha,d for example, highlighted strong end device but also network related topics. A list of respondents, including some characteristics can be found in Table 4 and Table 5 within the Section 3.9.6.

3.9.3 Background Introduction Information about the Research Project

With today's innovative technology such as SDPs, it is possible to positively influence the further development of ICT systems, e.g. for improved usability. The target of this analysis was to extract answers from the interview data secured from the group SPICE experts. For the research purpose, a background information sheet was created, and given to the interview partners (see Section 9.3).

3.9.4 Research Questions for Developing Web-Based Platforms (SDPs) in Terms of ICT Systems of the Future

This Section provides an insight into the framework, relevant for the development of web-based platforms (SDPs), to administrate future oriented ICT systems. The subsequent Paragraphs review the needs of users, for the development of ICT environments in general, based on the literature researched. Four research questions were formulated during this study in interview phases 2 and 3 following the research approach of this study and are closely linked to the aim and the objectives of this study.

The research questions in the discussion about the design and development of ICT environments are presented. Based on the literature review and the concepts presented in Chapter 2 (specifically Paragraph 2.5.3.1), the following questions in terms of researching the user perspective when investigating SDP-based ICT systems materialised:

- Can SDPs be used to support people's everyday activities when using innovative technologies?

- Where are the difficulties of engaging an optimal interaction between technical environments and end-users?

- Why is the purpose of Internet platforms changing when users want more support in their daily lives?

- What is the impact of rebuilding today's ICT infrastructure in terms of using new ubiquitous services? What extent of SDPs (on the example of SPICE) can be integrated into the sphere of existing ICT systems, in order to achieve maximum usability for the single user of ICT systems?

The research questions formulated were helpful for justification of the research problem outlined in Chapter 1. The reason the author defined these research questions at this stage of the methodology, was that their development had not been undertaken from the onset, as the researcher began looking at the literature from interview phase 2 onwards, when the inductive approach changed to an abductive research paradigm. This is why the research questions were presented in Paragraph 2.5.3.1 based on the literature review and revisited in Chapter 3, and incorporated in the research methodology. The author has described the detailed content in Chapter 2 and the process-related parts in Chapter 3.

3.9.5 Theoretical Sampling and 3-Stage Research Design within this Study

Theoretical Sampling (see Section 3.4.2) is a concept to make analytically based decisions of where to sample from next. The researcher has overlapped data collection and analysis, using three sequential interview phases, due to time constraints. Access to the interview participants and the organisation of the interviews had to be conducted over 4 days in Austria, Germany and Switzerland. Additionally, the pilot interviews were collected and then preliminary analysed for any emerging topics. This provided the researcher, the opportunity to generate ideas for new or adapted interview questions, and which aspects to follow, in the next interviews.

Theoretical Sampling was also used to ensure the integration between the empirical and the literature-based study. This was discussed and shown in Section 3.3.3, and Section 3.3.5 in Table 2. Based on the analysis of the pilot interviews, which involved 2 SPICE users and 2 SPICE developers, Theoretical Sampling contributed to the decision of the interview participants i.e: 3 SPICE users and 3 SPICE developers, including an architecture expert. From the pilot interviews through to interview phase 2 and 3, the ground for including architecture experts as a third part of the participant group, was due to their ablility to provide data, in terms of showing the overall picture, building a bridge between user-related and development-related, data.

Another argument was having a decision possibility to interview additional participants, suggested by the interviewees of the previous phase. However, the author decided to work with a three stage interview design, to ensure the concept emerging from the first phase, influenced sampling in the second and what emerged in the second phase, influenced sampling in the third stage.

3.9.6   Interview Participants of this Study

The interviews were conducted in German, as the fifteen respondents were German native speakers and were located either in Austria, Germany or Switzerland. Due to this criteria, background information and guidelines were prepared in German. Responses included specific informal German-language expressions and it was therefore important that all interviews were conducted and transcribed in German.

Based on that, the analysis of the data was also conducted in German, as was the transfer of all analysed texts into the Fact Finding tool. For the current purpose of presenting this thesis, all information regarding findings, analysis and data collection shown in it was subsequently translated into English at the end of the research process.

3.9.6.1   General Information about the Interview Participants

At this point it is important to highlight that respondents came from multinational companies, operating in these three countries. As a result, the findings discussed here, with regards to the Information Society Technologies (IST) SPICE project of the sixth framework programme (FP6) represents a universal principle, and not any country-centric or Central European-centric, bias. The IST thematic priority aims to increase innovation and competitiveness in European businesses and industry and to assist all European citizens so that they can fully benefit from the development of the knowledge-based society (The SPICE Project: http://www.ist-spice.org/). An overview of the SPICE project and the technical aspects is given in Sections 2.3 and 8.3.2 to 8.3.6.

In three interview phases participants from the SPICE community were interviewed. The participants' names were substituted with code numbers to ensure anonymity. For example participants in the pilot interviews were assigned the numbers p11_u, p12_d, p13_u and p14_d, where "p" indicates participants, "u" stands for user and "d" indicates developers. The codes for the respondents of the second and third interview phases followed the same coding systems, starting with number p21_u and p22_ae, where "ae" indicate architectural experts. The next Paragraph will give some background information about the fifteen interview participants.

3.9.6.2   Demographics and Background Information of the Interview Participants

This Paragraph specifies demographics and background information of the fifteen interview participants participated at this investigation. The following, Table 4, shows an overview of all interview participants, their gender, age, and their role within the SPICE project. More information about their experience is presented in the three phases of as follows.

The rationale for interviewing each group of SPICE participants, was that these three groups of SPICE experts (end-users, developers and architecture experts) are experienced with SDP-based ICT systems, and can contribute important aspects, when designing those systems, in terms user needs.

Pilot Interviews

All four participants (2 users, 2 developers: p11_u, p12_d, p13_u and p14_d) had between 2 and 5 years experience within the specialised SDP topic area and had worked more than 2 years in the SPICE European research project. The users, p11_u and p13_u, had little experience in comparison to the two developers, p12_d and p14_d. Both of them had also worked more than 2 years in the SPICE research project and had approximately more than 10 years experience in designing and developing ICT hard and software systems.

Table 4: List of interview participants and some information

Interview-Cycle	Participant	Gender	Age	Participants' Role	Description of the Role
Pilot (First)	p11_u	Male	28	SPICE end-user	IST SPICE FP6 core-team member; user of mobile end-devices
	p12_d	Male	34	SPICE developer	IST SPICE FP6 core-team member; developer in portal solutions
	p13_u	Female	31	SPICE end-user	IST SPICE FP6 extended-team member; user of mobile communication applications & services
	p14_d	Male	43	SPICE developer	IST SPICE FP6 core-team member; developer of network solutions
Second	p21_u	Female	46	SPICE end-user	IST SPICE FP6 extended-team member; m-commerce and e-business applications
	p22_u	Male	25	SPICE end-user	IST SPICE FP6 core-team member; mobile and convergent technology systems
	p23_d	Male	52	SPICE developer	IST SPICE FP6 core-team member; developer of SPICE applications
	p24_u	Male	37	SPICE end-user	IST SPICE FP6 extended-team member; user of location-based service applications
	p25_d	Female	41	SPICE developer	IST SPICE FP6 core-team member; developer of SPICE and cloud services
	p26_d	Male	49	SPICE developer	IST SPICE FP6 extended-team member; developer of network systems
	p27_ae	Male	23	SPICE architecture expert	IST SPICE FP6 core-team member; expert in ICT solutions
Third	p31_u	Female	27	SPICE end-user	IST SPICE FP6 extended-team member; user of mobile Internet applications
	p32_ae	Male	54	SPICE architecture expert	IST SPICE FP6 core-team member; expert in IT architectures
	p33_ae	Male	47	SPICE architecture expert	IST SPICE FP6 extended-team member; expert in mobile and converging technologies
	p34_d	Male	32	SPICE developer	IST SPICE FP6 core-team member; developer of portal solutions

In-Depth Interviews 2nd Phase

All seven participants (3 users, 3 developers, and 1 architecture expert: p21_u, p22_u, p23_d, p24_u, p25_ d, p26_d and p27_ae) had between 2 and 5 years' experience within the specialised SDP topic, and had worked more than 2 years in the SPICE European research project. The users, p21_u and p22_u, had a lot of experience, along with the developers, p23_d and p25_d. The user, p24_u, had little experience in the SPICE project, but was well experienced in testing ICT systems. The developer, p26_d, and the architecture expert, p27_ae, were experienced on a senior level, and had worked for more than 12 years in the field of ICT hardware and software systems.

In-Depth Interviews 3rd Phase

All four participants (1 user, 1 developer, and 2 architecture experts: p31_u, p32_ae, p33_ae and p34_d) had between 2-5 years experience working on the specialised SDP topic, and had worked for more than 2 years in the SPICE European research project. The user p31_u and the developer p34_d had a great deal of experience, along with the architecture expert p32_ae and p33_ae. All of them were highly experienced in testing and developing ICT systems.

The timeline of the when the interviews took place is illustrated in Table 5. It relates the interviews and participants for this research investigation, in terms of their nationality and the timeline of the interviews.

Table 5: List of interview and timeline

Interview-Cycle	Interview Nr.	Participants	Nationality	Timeline
Pilot (First)	1	p11_u	Austrian	Jun 2009
	3	p12_d	Austrian	Jun 2009
	2	p13_u	German	Jun 2009
	4	p14_d	Swiss	Jun 2009
Second	5	p21_u	German	Apr 2010
	6	p22_u	Dutch	Apr 2010
	7	p23_d	Finnish	Apr 2010
	8	p24_u	German	Apr 2010
	9	p25_d	French	May 2010
	10	p26_d	Swedish	May 2010
	11	p27_ae	German	May 2010
Third	12	p31_u	French	Jul 2011
	14	p32_ae	Swiss	Jul 2011
	15	p33_ae	Austrian	Jul 2011
	13	p34_d	German	Jul 2011

Information of the selection process of interviewees is described in the following Paragraph.

3.9.6.3   Selection Process of the Interview Participants

Experts from the SPICE project were chosen as interviewees representing the target group for this study, because they were able to provide the necessary expert's assessment from a technological perspective, and were familiar with SDPs. End-users were also questioned, as were SPICE project developers. A total of fifteen participants from the Service Delivery Platform area (six SPICE users, six developers and three architecture experts – overall fifteen participants) were interviewed.

The potential participants for the SPICE expert's interviews were all SPICE users and developers who showed sufficient system experience in the areas of Network infrastructure, Service Delivery Platforms and mobile device computing. An address pool was first developed in order to identify suitable candidates for the interviews. In terms of SPICE experts, individuals from "ist-fp6 Integrated Project" – a European research project - were selected, between January 2006 and June 2008, as a part of the Wireless World Initiative (WWI).

After an address pool of all suitable interviewees had been developed, SPICE users and developers were contacted by phone as part of a random check method.

3.9.7   Interview Guideline

Basically, there were three types of guidelines: non-directive, semi-directive and directive guidelines (Donaghy, 1990: p.4). Semi-directive guidelines were used for the purpose of this investigation. They were constructed in such a way that those chosen, were interviewed according to the interview question group catalogue. In this way, only a few of the possible questions were asked within the question group, and depended on the situation. Within a given topic area single questions had to be logically ordered. General questions were asked first, in order to arrive at thematically restricted ones later. This was done as to be able to positively use the influence of earlier-posed questions on the answers to subsequent questions. Questions were constructed in an easy, clear and concise manner without being concrete or suggestive (Huber and Mandl, 1994: p.27).

The following Paragraphs describe the development of the interview guidelines and the connected preparations for the semi-structured interviews undertaken with the interview group of SPICE experts.

3.9.7.1   Development of the Interview Guidelines

An interview guide (see Section 9.4) was developed for the SPICE experts, and a distinction was made between SPICE end-users and developers. First, a short introduction was provided in the form of background and introduction information about the project, and information about the secrecy of the data. In addition, the interview partners were also given a written pledge of confidentiality (see Section 9.2), and a general background information sheet (see Section 9.3). The guide was tested for content completeness during the test interviews by two representatives from each of the interview groups, a SPICE end-user and a SPICE expert.

Approximately ten minutes were required for each thematic area, and an interview was not to include more than six thematic areas (see Section 9.4), due to limitations of human concentration (Donaghy, 1990: p.8). After the topics were established, their possible sequencing was discussed with two representatives from the SPICE experts' interview group, to ensure that all necessary content was covered, and that the interviews were adequately comprehensible.

Themes and sub-themes for the interview guidelines were worked through in written form, and were orientated towards the generated requirements taken from literature sources. At the end of the interview, the interviewees were presented with a short written questionnaire with personal questions relating to age, position in the company, educational qualifications, number of years in the company and so on (also presented in Section 9.4).

3.9.7.2   Critical Incident Technique (CIT)

Flanagan (1954: p. 327) developed Critical Incident Technique (CIT), named the technique of "Critical Incidents", an observation method used to identify critical incidents with regards to situative conditions (Farrero and Argüelles, 2005: p. 4). The main target of this technique is the discovery of actions, which enable declarations about a person's competence, as well as about future behaviour (Flanagan, 1954: p. 327). In the interview guidelines, a sequence was chosen, according to logical viewpoints and difficulties. At the beginning, rather more easy-going themes were addressed, i.e. the principles of SDP. Later on, themes based on those before, or more sensitive themes were dealt with, i.e. the question of access possibilities and business indicators for SDPs.

An interview guideline (see Section 9.4) was developed for SPICE experts, where differentiation was made between users and developers. Initially, a short introduction including background and introduction information took place and information was given about the statement of confidentiality. The purpose of the interview was explained and the interviewee informed, that it was possible to stop the interview at any time. Interview partners were given a written statement of confidentiality, to be co-signed (see Section 9.3), and an information sheet with general background information.

The guidelines were tested in the pilot interviews. CIT was used to structure the interview guidelines as well as the literature-based general and detailed criteria catalogues due to the complex aspects of SDPs, so that the language focused on as many incidents and occurrences as possible. In this way, the author lay down the basis, for a delayed analysis of the interviews, in order to maximise relevant content from the topics.

3.9.7.3   Structure of the Interview Guidelines for the SPICE Experts

The guidelines for the SPICE expert interviews were developed according to recommendations worked out for the SDP platform developers. These will, therefore, be described according to their content. As both users and developers were interviewed, it was necessary to include, in the intended guidelines, focus points for each of the groups.

These were based on the content-based materials from Chapter 2 - Literature Review. Both groups received the same information:

■   Introduction to the interview

■   Questions about the network infrastructure

■   Questions about service delivery and availability platforms

■   Questions about the applications of SDPs from a user perspective

■   General final questions (see Section 9.4)

The first group of questions for the SPICE experts, "Introduction to the Interview", concerned itself with the conception, the consideration of data ano-
nymisation, the representation of the initial situation, a short overview on background information, and the representation of the targets for the interview which
was to follow. The second group of questions, "Questions about the network
infrastructure and access possibilities", concerned itself with both named points
of focus, whereby the focus was on the aspects of access to the network infrastructure, for the integration of as many social groups as possible, and cost effective installation and operation of the network infrastructure.

The third group, "Questions about service delivery and availability platforms", focused its questions on the SDPs themselves, dealing with the issue of
access to SDPs through standardised interfaces to core networks, as well as making available standardised interfaces, in order to attain a high degree of coverage
in the area of end devices. The services developed and made available on SDPs,
should allow operation quickly, simply and cost effectively. Questions about
user-friendliness, user privacy, and cost considerations were also presented.

The fourth group of questions, "Questions about uses and services from a
user-centred perspective", was concerned with how end devices achieved access
on the SDP, and were able to exchange content-conscious data. The user-
friendliness of the end device is important in relation to the interaction with services made available on the platform. Aspects concerning costs were a central
focus. The final question group, "Questions about the conclusion" involved general questions relating to SDP and SPICE.

3.9.8 Recording and Transcription Procedure

All qualitative interviews were recorded in digital audio format with an electronic recording device. Audio records of the interviews enabled the researcher
to capture the sensivity of the conversations. Parallel to carrying out interviews,
a transcription was carried out, from the beginning, with an appropriate mechanism, the colour coding method, in order to facilitate quick coding. The transcription of a text involved making written records of the conversation with fixed
notation rules (Depperman, 2003: p.39).

The recorded conversations were anonymised during the transcription, in
line with data protection conditions, and the texts were stored using cryptic
names. Also, when necessary, in the transcription texts, location and names were
replaced. The interviews were transcribed word for word, without consideration
of gap filling sounds, such as "ah", "hm", "mm". Additionally, contrary to many
studies, long pauses, changes in tone or sentence melody were not characterised

in the transcription text, e.g. in order to save space, and because these pauses do not contribute anything to this study.

The interviews and all pertinent information were originally done in German, as all participants were German native speakers from Austria, Germany and Switzerland. The interviews were also done in German and the transcriptions are accordingly German transcripts. All examples used in this study were translated, from German into English, by the author.

3.10 Application of the EMPLIT Methodology within this Study

This Section describes the application of the EMPLIT methodology by presenting the GT based colour coding system within EMPLIT, and the application of the literature-based study. The four phases of EMPLIT and the detailed research procedure developed and used in this research study are presented.

3.10.1 Data Collection and Analysis

Qualitative data was collected through a combination of interviews of the participant group of SPICE experts. An analysis was conducted, to determine the direction of the research and to give an indication of what to look for next, in the data collection. Pilot and in-depth interviews were carried out in three stages, constantly collecting and analysing data. Theoretical Sampling underlines the potential for further analysis and data collection needed to complete the entire process of developing a theory.

3.10.2 EMPLIT in Four Phases

The research study focused on qualitative research approach, and used an adapted form of GTM in four sequential phases for collecting and analysing the data shown in Table 6 below.

The collection of data used semi-structured interviews in three interview phases, after that, one feedback phase follows: first, the pilot interviews for testing the research design, followed by a second and a third interview phase. The results generated from this study were presented to the participants at the end, and discussed with them. The experiences gained from each concluded phase provided valuable input for the next interview phase. Below, the general data collection phases shown, in Table 6, are briefly elaborated on, in terms of their relevance to the empirical part of this study:

Table 6: Overview of data collection and analysis phases

Research Study Phases	Data Analysis Techniques and Methodologies
Phase 1 Empirical Study: Conducting, transcribing and analysing 4 pilot interviews (2 users; 2 developers); Developing initial codes and categories	Adapted GTM with colour coding approach Mind map technique to visualise and present the data
Phase 2 Empirical Study: Conducting, transcribing and analysing 7 interviews (3 users; 3 developers; 1 architecture expert); Developing focused codes and further categories Literature-based Study: Generating literature–based criteria catalogue; map, group and structure literature-based criteria and transfer it to mind map representations	Adapted GTM with colour coding approach Mind map technique to visualise and present the data Mapping process to compare and justify empirical codes by the use of literature-based data; Application of EMPLIT to justify empirical data
Phase 3 Empirical Study: Conducting, transcribing and analysing 4 interviews (1 user; 1 developer; 2 architecture experts); Developing focused codes and final categories Literature-based Study: Further generating literature–based criteria catalogue; map, group and structure literature-based criteria and transfer it to mind map representations	Adapted GTM with colour coding approach Mind map technique to visualise and present the data Mapping process to compare and justify empirical codes by the use of literature-based data; Application of EMPLIT to justify empirical data
Phase 4 Presenting the consolidated study results (developed categories and models) in a workshop to the interview participants to validate the final results and get their feedback	Justification of final emprical results by the respondents

Phase 1: Pilot Interviews and Analysis

Four pilot interviews were carried out on the basis of semi-structured interviews. The interviews were conducted, transcribed, and analysed using an adaptive form of GTM in a qualitative evaluation. Initial categories based on the collected data were developed. The development of a model based on the data, gathered from questioning of different target groups (end-users, developers of SPICE and architecture experts).

For the purpose of this investigation the interview method was chosen in order to gain a very in-depth understanding of the interests of the interviewees. This decision was supported by the fact that qualitative research consists of open rather than closed questions. In contrast to using questionnaires, interviewees in qualitative research programmes are able to answer quickly and in detail, and it is possible for the interviewer to react flexibly to interviewee responses. In ex-plorative research, in particular, interviews can be used to gain a broad appreciation of a specific field of knowledge. In this work, the semi-structured interviews, based on the demands generated from the pilot study, that in itself was based on the literature review and processed using mind mapping, proved invaluable. The semi-structured interviews were target group-oriented, designed with SPICE experts, end-users, developers and architecture experts in mind.

The data collected in the pilot interview was based on a pre-developed interview guideline. Four participants were interviewed, two end-users and two

SDP developers. Based on a developed coding procedure and concepts, the collected data was prepared and consolidated with the use of the Fact Finding tool for data analysis. At this first stage, grouped codes and concepts were developed.

Phase 2: In-depth Interviews and Analysis

Seven semi-standardised interviews were conducted and recorded, and were transcribed as a starting point for the qualitative evaluation. The interview guidelines were adapted on the basis of the experiences gained in interview phase one, in order to optimise the procedure of collected data. In this interview phase seven participants were interviewed, three end-users, three developers and one SDP architecture expert. The transcribed data from interview phase 2 were analysed, and compared with the results from analysis step 1. The data was grouped into topics in the Fact Finding tool, and grouped codes and concepts were further developed (see Sections 3.11.1 and 10.2).

Phase 3: In-depth Interviews and Analysis

An additional three, semi-standardised interviews, were carried out. These were also resumed and transcribed in a qualitative evaluation. The improvement of the model based on additionally generated data, stemming from more questions of different target groups (end-users and developers of SPICE services, architecture experts), strengthening of the data gained during the analysis.

The interview guidelines were adapted again, also based on the outcomes of interview cycle two, in order to optimise the procedure of collected data. In this interview cycle, four participants were interviewed, one end-user, one developer and two SDP architecture experts.

The transcribed data from interview cycle 3 was analysed, and compared with results from analysis steps 1 and 2. Data was grouped in the FFT, by topics and grouped codes, and concepts were further developed.

Phase 4: Presentation of the Consolidated Results to the Interview Participants

Triangulation of the results of the pilot interviews and the in-depth interviews from the interview phases 2 and 3 took place, as well as comparison and validation with the literature based data. The empirical data was then coded. A comparison and consolidation of the empirical data collected was done using GTM coding with stages open, selective, and theoretical coding (described in Section 3.4.4) and the development of the final categories.

A validation of the results of this qualitative investigation was done in this phase 4, as a reflection of the results together with all participants helped to validate the results. In the last interview phase all fifteen participants were presented with the research results and consequently the outcomes of the study were discussed with them.

The information sent out before the interview included some background information to the planned study and research project. The aim was to inform the participants about the research project to familiarise themselves with the subject area. From the researchers point of view this seemed necessary, as early pilot interview findings showed that the majority of people had a strong technical focus within the SPICE research project and had the opportunity and sufficient time to think about various scenarios related more focused on the user perspective.

3.10.3 GTM Colour Coding Procedure within EMPLIT

The Colour Coding System described in Section 3.5 refers to a new approach conducting bottom-up coding within GTM, in terms of the EMPLIT methodology, used in this investigation. The application of the Colour Coding system and its function is explicitly described in Section 3.11.1 using solid examples undertaken in this study.

3.10.4 Application of the Literature-Based Study

The literature-based study described in Section 3.8, illustrated dealing with data collection during the literature review, in terms of complexity and material volume in SDPs. Applying the study, how the general and detailed literature-based criteria catalogue was created, including the group, structure and how the clustering procedure worked, is illustrated in a detailed example in Section 3.11.3.

In this study, mind maps that dealt with various aspects from the literature on NGNs and SDPs, from varying perspectives, were developed and transferred from the literature-based criteria catalogue to map a representation, based on mind and concept mapping technology (according to Tony Buzan), and were visually structured. Besides this, group-specific Mind Maps were developed within the scope of the learning and understanding of the subject areas (NGNs, SDPs, User-centred services, ICT systems etc., described in Chapter 2).

This produced a map of thought in which correlations were shown in groups and sub-groups (see mind and concept mapping techniques in Section 3.6). The resulting mind maps were put together during the analysis process and were used to compare empirical codes with literature-based aspects collected in this mind map representations.

Furthermore, the mind maps developed from the general and detailed literature-based criteria catalogue, generate ideas for the justification and validation of focused codes, created from empirical data. This afforded the author a comparison of intermediate data in the form of codes, drawing from the literature, to acertain if data created from the interviews fitted in with aspects from the literature, or not. It is another possibility to validate codes.

In addition, the structured aspects from the literature-based study already available, could be called upon as focus code indicators, and thus gives the researcher a feeling whether the outcome of the empirical study is comparable to the literature or not. Besides the advantage of having indicators already prepared for the intermediate data of the next text analysis, it was also possible to validate empirical data with literature-based data. This gave the added advantage of being able to validate, by open and focused coding, work on focused code indicators derived from the literature-based study.

3.10.5 Detailed Research Procedure of this Study

This Section describes the research methodology used within this study in detail and shows how the researcher followed the qualitative research procedure step-by-step based on the study setup described in Section 3.9. Qualitative analysis was employed in the collection and analysis of the data. The procedure includes the following detailed steps; activity steps, activity input and activity output, illustrated in Figure 13 and Figure 14.

1. Formulation of Research Aim and Objectives

In formulating the research aim and objectives, input included the research question and the problems identified in the research area of SDPs (including NGs and User-centred services). Important components are the research questions, which outlined and stated the problems in the research area named. The output of this first activity included three to six research aims and objectives and a detailed discussion of the problem statement.

2. Development of Literature-Based Criteria Catalogue

Following Charmaz's (2006) approach of doing GTM, the literature review started at the beginning of the study. Based on research literature, the initial development of general and detailed literature-based criteria catalogue began and included inputs such as SPICE and corresponding challenges. User-centred service challenges were also presented and discussed, along with NGN challenges. The output was catalogued using bullet points on the literature, and identified challenges and aspects within the topics.

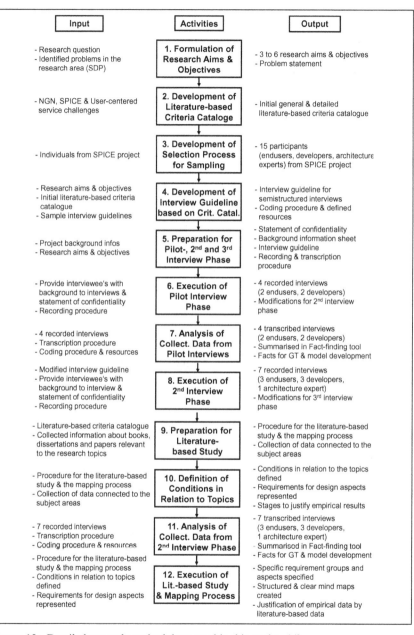

Figure 13: Detailed research methodology used in this study - 1/2

3. Development of Selection Process for Sampling

The input of the step "Development of Selection Process for Sampling" included contacts and individual respondents from the SPICE project for the qualitative study. The SPICE project and the author's motivation to research design issues for SDP-related ICT environments of the future, focused on the user's perspective of technical experts from the SPICE project, was to research user perspective on SDPs. These experts, represented by three different groups, are seen as experts in terms of SDP technologies. The output of this research step was the selection of fifteen participants (end-users, developers, architecture experts) from the SPICE project.

4. Development of Interview Guideline based on Criteria Catalogue

The input for this activity included the defined research aim and objectives, the initial literature-based criteria catalogue, based on the challenges described in the literature in terms of the topics, and sample interview guidelines. The output included an interview guideline for the semi-structured interviews, coding procedure as well as defined resources needed.

5. Preparation for Pilot and 2nd Interview Phase

The preparation for the pilot, second and third interview phases included input about the project background information. It also included the research aim and the objectives. The output covered the statement of confidentiality as well as a background information sheet. An interview guideline was presented along with the recording and transcription procedure.

6. Execution of Pilot Interview Phase

The input required for the execution of the pilot interview phase included an overview of the interviewee's background, the interview, and statement of confidentiality, as well as the recording procedure. The output consisted of four recorded interviews, involving two users and two developers, as well as modifications for the second interview phase.

7. Analysis of Collected Data from Pilot Interviews

The input covered four recorded interviews, transcription procedure, coding procedure and resources. The output covered the four transcribed interviews done with the two users and two developers, and a summary including Fact-finding tool and facts for GT and model development.

8. Execution of 2nd Interview Phase

The input for the execution of the second interview phase included a modified interview guideline, as the analysis of the first pilot interviews brought some consolidated first findings, that were relevant for the study and for the next interview phase, and was done because one of the seven participants in interview phase 2 was an architecture expert and there were also two senior developers interviewed. This made it necessary to reorganise the interview guidelines for the second round, only in exacting the SDP parts and relevant information on the interviewee's background. It also included a statement of confidentiality and recording procedure. Output included seven recorded interviews (3 end-users, 3 developers, 1 architecture expert) and modification for the third interview phase.

9. Preparation for Literature-Based Study (Mapping Process)

The input for this activity included the CIT-analysed literature-based criteria catalogue and all information on collected books, dissertations and papers, with regard to the research topic. The output outlined a procedure for the literature-based study and the mapping process as well as the collection of categorisation of data, into the subject areas defined through the initial structuring process (CIT-analysed criteria catalogue).

10. Definition of Conditions in Relation to Topics

With the help of the procedure for the literature-based study, the mapping process and the collection of data connected to the subject areas, conditions in relation to theme fields and single areas, were defined. Additionally, requirements for the design aspect were represented, (i.e. target group specific requirements from the perspective of operators, customers and manufacturers), and different stages to justify and validate the empirical data with the aid of the mind map representation of the literature based criteria catalogue.

11. Analysis of Collected Data from 2nd Interview Phase

The input included seven recorded interviews as well as the transcription procedure and coding procedure and resources. The output covered the seven transcribed interviews with three users, three developers and one architecture expert. The transcribed interview data were analysed and summarised within the Fact-finding tool and built the facts for the development of GT codes and categories as well as the models.

12. Execution of Mapping Process 2nd Interview Phase

The input for this stage was again the procedure for the literature-based study and the mapping process and the conditions in relation to topics defined as well as the requirements for design aspects and issues represented. This phase sorted the specific requirement groups and aspects, specified in the frame of the conditions definition phase, so that clear and structured mind maps could be created.

The justification of the intermediate data (empirical codes and initial developed categories) was done with the help of data from the literature-based study.

13. Execution of 3rd Interview Phase

The input in this stage included a modified interview guideline again, as the analysis of the interviews brought some consolidated findings that were relevant to the study and for the last interview phase, and was done with the help of one user and one developer, and two architecture experts.

This necessitated reorganising the interview guidelines for the second round only in exacting the SDP parts and relevant information with the interviewee's background information and statement of confidentiality, as well as the recording procedure. The output included four recorded interviews (an end-user, a developer and 2 architecture experts).

14. Analysis of Collected Data from 3rd Interview Phase

Input included four recorded interviews (an end-user, a developer and 2 architecture experts), and included the summarised Fact Finding questionnaires. Output included four coded interview transcripts, summarised in the Fact-finding tool, and structured facts for the GT and the model development.

15. Execution of Mapping Process 3rd Interview Phase

In this stage the procedure for the literature-based study and mapping process is chosen, as input, and the conditions in relation to topics defined, as well as, the requirements and design issues again. This involved ordering the specific requirement groups and aspects, specified in the frame of the conditions definition phase, so that clear and structured mind maps could be created. Moreover, the justification step with the final codes and categories, was done using mind map representation of the literature-based data.

16. Detailed Analysis of Interview-Based Collected Data

The input included facts for model development and 15 recorded interviews (6 end-users, 6 developers, 3 architecture experts), as well as summarised Fact-finding tool, coding procedure and resources. The output included the coded interview data and developed theoretical written memos, which interpreted the researcher's understanding of the respondent views, and structured facts for the GT and model development.

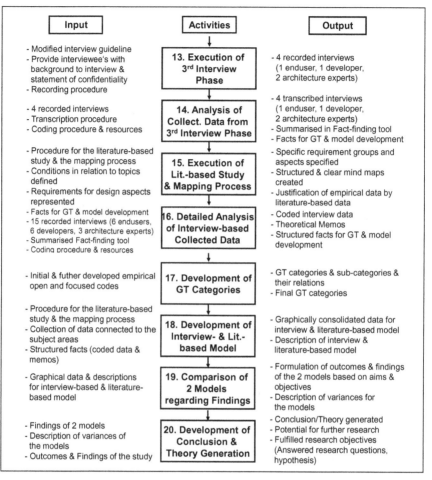

Figure 14: Detailed research methodology used in this study - 2/2

17. Development of GT Categories

Input included, initial and further developed empirical codes from the open and focused coding phase. Output included Grounded Theory categories and sub-categories including their relations. In this stage the final empirical GT categories were developed.

18. Development of the Interview-based and the Literature-Based Model

Input included the procedure for the literature-based study and mapping process, in particular the collection of data connected to the subject areas, structured facts in the form of coded data, and written theoretical memos. Output included graphically consolidated data for development of an interview and literature-based model, and description thereof. In this stage, two models were developed based on the GT categories, from the empirical study, and the literature-based aspects; collected, grouped and structured with the help of the literature-based study during the literature review.

19. Comparison of two Models In Terms of Findings

Input included graphical data and descriptions of the interview- and literature-based model, outlining the findings of the two models. Output included the formulation of the outcomes and the findings based on the aim and the objectives of this study. Both models were compared and discussed and for both a description of variances or consistencies was done.

20. Development of Conclusion and Theory Generation

Input included the findings of the two models and the description of variances or consistencies with the literature based model. The outcomes and findings of this study were summarised and thoroughly discussed. Output included the conclusion/theory, with the potential for further research, and the possibility to address any outstanding research questions.

Concluding the detailed research procedure, the EMPLIT methodology was applied by conducting and analysing data, in three interview phases with fifteen semi-structured interviews.

The previous Sections illustrated the application, and description, of EMPLIT, and all other relevant methodologies, and the techniques employed within this research. The setup for this study was also defined, where the conditions were described, including the parameters for the methodology used. The following Section will illustrate the relevant analysis stages through detailed examples, presenting excerpts from the coding, employing Colour-Coding method and an analysis of Literature-based data within this study.

3.11 Analysis of Data in EMPLIT

The following shows how the colour coding system is used with the EMPLIT methodology and describes the different coding stages using solid examples undertaken in this study. Moreover, the mapping process is shown in a concrete example, of developing the general and detailed criteria catalogue until these aspects are transferred to a mind map representation and mapped to the empirical codes and categories.

3.11.1 Analysis of Empirical Data Using Colour Coding System within EMPLIT

This coding method makes use of an effective way of coding and analysing interview-based empirical data. At the beginning, the entire interview transcription was written in black text on a white background. The text was then read from top to bottom, word-for-word, line-by-line, sentence-by-sentence, Chapter-by-Chapter. Once a word or paragraph, that appeared to be suitable for a code, became subjectively recognisable (Opening Coding according to GTM) it was marked in a different colour. After the marking of the text, the sub-categories were considered and were then sorted into next-level categories. Once, effectively identifying categories and sub-categories through Colour Coding of the text passage, in the interview text, that particular colour, came to represent a particular category, and sub-category, throughout the whole text.

This method was fixed for all further codes, allowing codes to be allocated inductively to the categories and sub-categories already established (Bergaus and Stottok, 2010; Stottok et al., 2011). As soon as the first category was identified and a colour code established, the analytical tool (Fact Finding Tool) was drawn up. The category was described in the very top line. The second line described the first sub-category that had been found. Underneath these explanatory lines, in the next line, it was noted from which base text the text passages originated. For example, in interview 01 (p11_u), the first code identified was copied from the interview text and inserted into the analytical tool (Bergaus and Stottok, 2010; Stottok, 2010a).

Category: Mobility
Sub-Category: Availability of networks and end-
devices
Sub-Category: Stability and session control
Sub-Category: Always on
Sub-Category: Any network on any device
Interview 01 (p11_u)
A: The advantage of an SDP, to offer and run services, is
from my point of view, that the user can gain access
independently from the location and the enddevice being
used. It is necessary that the user gains access with high
trustworthiness.
A: To offer services on an SDP allows the enduser to be on
any network, on any device, 24 hours a day.
A: A potential user must have the opportunity to gain access
by any network, independently from the location he or she is
at present and also independently from the used end-device.

Figure 15: Excerpt from the analysis tool (Fact Finding tool[3])

Red, in the Fact Finding Tool (see Figure 15) defines the category "Mobility", with their sub-categories (Stability and session control, Always on, any
network on any device). The following figure (Figure 16) shows an excerpt from
the coded interview text of "Interview 01 (p11_u)", where identification of the
first text passage from Figure 15 was possible as code and sub-category 'Any
network on any device':

Interview 01 (p11_u)

...

Q: What impact does mobility provide for SDP design aspects to support services?
A: Mobility is an important driver for today and I think it will take place more and more
in our lives. The advantage of an SDP, to offer and run services, is from my point of
view, that the user can gain access independently from the location and the
enddevice being used. It is necessary that the user gains access with high
trustworthiness. I think that ICT services can be offered about the internet by using
web-based and mobile security standards such as SSL and WPA2 for example to
meet the needs of a positive confidence of end-users.

...

Figure 16: Excerpt from a colour-coded interview after the 1st coding step

On completion of the first colour-coded interview, regarding the codes
identified, the same interview was analysed a second time from the top, based on
new codes discovered in following the interview coding procedures. In this second step a code was sought, that could be assigned to another category, as a new
sub-category, or to a different category with additional sub-categories, via interpretation or memo writing. Once a passage was identified that had already been
used for the first category, or an untouched part of the text, it was re-coloured.

---

[3] The process was applied, until all interviews had been analysed and color coded and all relevant
passages in the corresponding pages had been transferred to the Fact Finding tool.

If this new passage discovered and qualified for a new sub-category it was coded in the right colour and added in the Fact Finding Tool. If the newly qualified sub-category was not coded (coloured), a new colour was selected for this code. The re-colouring followed the same procedure as above (Bergaus and Stottok, 2010; *Stottok*, 2010a). The following, Figure 17, illustrates the Colour Coding procedure with two colours 'red' and 'blue'. The new blue colour indicated that the code 'Account and Data Protection' belongs to the category 'Security and Reliability'.

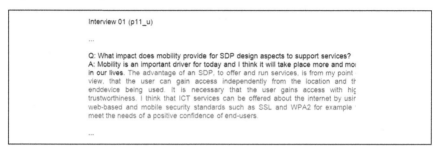

Interview 01 (p11_u)

...

Q: What impact does mobility provide for SDP design aspects to support services?
A: Mobility is an important driver for today and I think it will take place more and moi in our lives. The advantage of an SDP, to offer and run services, is from my point view, that the user can gain access independently from the location and tf enddevice being used. It is necessary that the user gains access with hig trustworthiness. I think that ICT services can be offered about the internet by usir web-based and mobile security standards such as SSL and WPA2 for example meet the needs of a positive confidence of end-users.

...

Figure 17: Excerpt from a colour-coded interview after 2 coding steps

If a text passage was already colour-coded, it could be possible that the re-colouring of such a passage resulted in the allocation of an additional code. In this case a mixed-colouring approach was employed in the form of an alternating colour mode, as illustrated in Figure 18.

The first word stays red for the code '*Any network on any device',* belonging the category *'Mobility'*. The second word was changed to green for the code '*Standard technologies'* belonging to the category *'Interoperability'*. The following word was then coloured alternatively with the appropriate colour (Bergaus and Stottok 2010, p.129; Stottok *et al.,* 2011).

The next step was to create another tab in the Fact Finding Tool for the second category and to add the explanatory lines for the newly detected category and sub-category, to create columns and to begin to fill the cells of the first column with passages from the first interview. The exact procedure as described above was adopted in order to check the complete transcription for the second category, and for any additional associated sub-categories.

After that, the analysis for the first interview thoroughly from top to bottom until no further codes, sub-categories and categories could be found. All information from the transcripts was transferred to the Fact Finding Tool after the colour coding process, after which the procedure was replicated for the second transcribed interview, and the content derived from the second interview data was integrated into the Fact Finding Tool (Bergaus and Stottok, 2010).

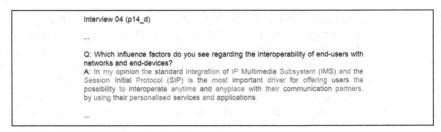

Interview 04 (p14_d)

...

Q: Which influence factors do you see regarding the interoperability of end-users with networks and end-devices?
A: In my opinion the standard integration of IP Multimedia Subsystem (IMS) and the Session Initial Protocol (SIP) is the most important driver for offering users the possibility to interoperate anytime and anyplace with their communication partners, by using their personalised services and applications.

...

Figure 18:   Excerpt from a colour-coded interview after 2 coding steps (including the alternation mode for 2 different codes)

Figure 19, below, shows an excerpt from the Fact Finding Tool tab for the category "Mobility", after the analysis and coding of three interview texts, of which the relevant text passages had been copied from the colour-coded interview transcripts and pasted into the tool:

Category: Mobility
Sub-Category: Availability of networks and end-devices
Sub-Category: Stability and session control
Sub-Category: Always on
Sub-Category: Any network on any device

Interview 01 (p11_u)	Interview 02 (p12_d)	Interview 03 (p13_u)
A: The advantage of an SDP, to offer and run services, is from my point of view, that the user can gain access independently from the location and the enddevice being used. It is necessary that the user gains access with high way.	A: The people who use an SDP can personalise their own services to use it at anytime and anyplace. It's important that this works in a stable and reliable way.	A: I think the mobility feature is one of the core topics that an SDP can be the communication control system for a broad range of ICT systems and components.
A: To offer services on an SDP allows the enduser to be any network, on any device, 24 hours a day.	A: I think it's necessary that a end-user must have control on over his or her application sessions all times. In this case the technology have to be support a stable and reliable	A: Nowaday's, mobile infrastructures must provide high availability by supporting scenarios, that users must be reachable all times.
A: A potential user must have the opportunity to gain access by any network, independently from the location he or she is at present and also independently from the used end-device	connection with a very good service quality A: Users must be available all times and the provided infrastructure must support this way by a good quality	A: This must support, that a networks must support stable connections for users.

Figure 19:   Excerpt from the Fact Finding tool with text passages from 3 interviews

The above mentioned procedure was followed repeatedly until all interviews were thoroughly analysed, colour coded, and relevant parts of text were transferred into the appropriate category tabs of the Fact Finding Tool and if there was more than one category or sub-category in one text passage, alternate colour coding was employed as described above (Bergaus and Stottok, 2010, p.130). Figure 20 shows an excerpt from a completely colour-coded interview. It shows four colours that indicate the four different categories to which the author allocated the text passages.

Figure 20 represents a colour coded interview with codes related to the category 'Mobility' in red, 'Security and Reliability' in blue, 'Interoperability' in green, and 'Applicability' in orange. The entire detailed procedure of Colour Coding is described in the attached paper 'Colour Coding: an Alternative to Analyse Empirical Data via Grounded Theory' (Stottok et al., 2011), published and presented by Stottok, Bergaus and Gorra at the European Conference of Research Methodologies (ECRM) in Caen, France, 2011.

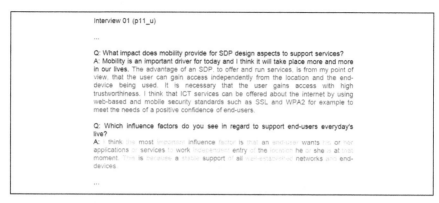

Figure 20: Excerpt from an entirely colour-coded interview

Colour coding has both advantages and disadvantages. One of the main advantages is that one file, a text file in which all interviews are transcribed and colour coded, helps the researcher gain a solid overview of categories and sub-categories, with regard to the entire analysis process. In the Fact Finding Tool, all aspects of importance to the GT were integrated and stored. These are representable, so that all information is given in a condensed form within the file. The interpretation of the discovered codes, developed categories and sub-categories, was supported with written memos. This makes analysis easier and also helps lay people understand all steps, that have been carried out.

This tool contains all sub-categories, coded text passages, and memos. It is necessary to observe that a new category, which, at a certain point in the study, has not yet been identified, or that has been overlooked in previous interviews, can be discovered at a later interview.

An analysis using this method can be time consuming, as text passages have to be repeatedly colour coded, once a new category or sub-category is found. There are limitations for people with colour blindness, daltonism or other related visual impairments such as achromatopsia; depending on the extent of the deficiency, the analyst affected can only use certain colours restrictedly, as these may only be observed as contrast (Bergaus and Stottok, 2010; Stottok *et al.*, 2011).

3.11.2 Overall Coding Process within EMPLIT

EMPLIT used GTM with a colour coding approach for the three general coding stages, described in Sections 3.4.4, 3.10.3, and 3.13. Inspired by Reid (2006), Figure 21 outlines an excerpt of the entire coding process within EMPLIT, using a coding diagram and outlines all coding stages, using the colour coded interview transcripts in depth.

Based on data slices from the colour coded interview transcript, open codes were generated in three phases to collect and analyse interview data. The selective coding procedure helped to develop focused codes, based on grouping and structuring of open codes, depicted in the second column. For grouping and structuring on a more general level, the major categories were developed.

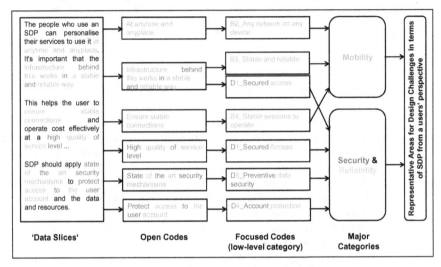

Figure 21: Excerpt of the overall coding process with each coding step

3.11.3 Analysis of Literature-based Data within EMPLIT

The literature-based study follows the procedure described in Section 3.8 and is a representation of mind and concept mapping. As with every map generated, the core information of a specific topic is visually presented to the viewer. In this way, the researcher is challenged to find an understandable connection for every term, and be able to create obvious key information for other researchers, in a quick and simple way. This method for the literature-based mapping process was developed by the author himself to support the analysis procedure by using GTM with a Colour Coding approach (Bergaus *et al.*, 2012). It therefore follows the outset of Charmaz (2006), and implies the procedure of phases 1-4: 1. literature research; 2. data collection; 3. definition of conditions, and; 4. grouping of data, as discussed in Section 3.10.4.

In this way, one or a number of structured maps are created for a given research topic, in which text passages with similar content are summarised in hierarchical graphs (Bergaus *et al.*, 2012), as is illustrated by Figure 22 below.

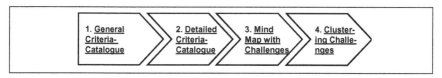

Figure 22: Phases for the literature-based study

1. General Criteria Catalogue

A general criteria catalogue was developed, by consolidating information and issues, in terms of challenges and possible design issues. These were noted in bullet-point form, specific to a topic area or sub-area. The referencing of original documents was essential at this stage.

2. Detailed Criteria Catalogue

A detailed criteria catalogue was generated by further detailed consolidating of information and issues, as above, in terms of challenges and possible design issues regarding a topic area or sub-area. Again, referencing was an important task at this stage.

3. Mind Map with Challenges

After consolidating information in terms of the general and detailed criteria catalogue, the literature-based data were transferred into grouped or structured mind maps, or into more hierarchical mind maps.

4. Clustering Challenges

Sub-issues were clustered into a group of issues in a hierarchical form, Figure 23, below, illustrates this procedure:

Step 1, presents an example of a general criteria catalogue for Service Delivery Platform Functions with aspects that are currently the most important SDP functions. The bullet points in "green" in Step 1 and Step 2 describe aspects regarding "Mobility". Step 2 presents an example of a detailed criteria catalogue with more detailed aspects of "Mobility", with regard to Beyond-3G systems.

Step 3 points out the result after the transfer from those aspects to a mind map and highlights the green aspects from the criteria catalogue after structuring and grouping. The last stage, Step 4 describes the clustering of highlighted aspects from differently created Mind Maps into the topic "Mobility". A more detailed description of the procedure and the analysed outcomes is presented in the next Paragraph 3.11.3.1.

The main reasons for the development and utilisation of the literature-based study were: firstly, that the complex and extensive topic investigated in the literature review was structured into clearly grouped, general and detailed aspects, and secondly, it afforded the possibility of justification of empirical data, with literature-based data (Bergaus, 2010a).

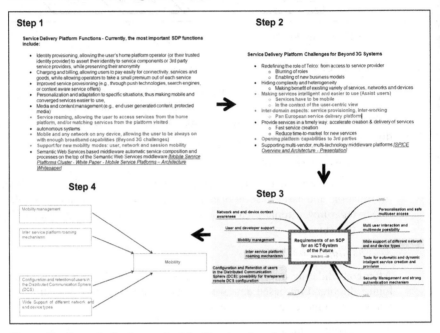

Figure 23: Example for the result of the literature-based study

The aims of this procedure were to develop a criteria catalogue for the requirements and design issues of SDPs for the support of future ICT systems; to structure and group the issues, to gain a fasterer understanding of the complex topics; to validate results from the empirical data study by means of the compiled criteria catalogue, to further develop a model based on the criteria. In this project, maps were provided within the scope of the Mapping Process, so as to look at different aspects of the literature regarding NGNs and SDPs, from varying perspectives. Furthermore, the various *Mind Maps* represent the results of the Mapping Process, in a specific situation (Bergaus *et al.*, 2012).

3.11.3.1 Development of the Literature-Based Criteria Catalogue

The mind maps created helped group and structure the collected literature, making it available for the validation of research aims, collected empirical data as well as focused coding over the whole investigation process. Different sources (publications, dissertations and Internet sites) discovered in researching the subject of SDPs were organised, grouped and structured. This allowed the researcher to efficiently track materials and process them, at a later stage. To summarise, collected materials from the literature review were checked, grouped and further summarised, as shown in Figure 24 (Bergaus *et. al.*, 2012):

Service Delivery Platform Functions - Currently, the most important SDP functions include:

- Identity provisioning, allowing the user's home platform operator (or their trusted identity provider) to assert their identity to service components or 3rd party service providers, while preserving their anonymity
- Charging and billing, allowing users to pay easily for connectivity, services and goods, while allowing operators to take a small premium out of each service
- Improved service provisioning (e.g., through push technologies, search engines, or context aware service offers)
- Personalisation and adaptation to specific situations, thus making mobile and converged services easier to use,
- Media and content management (e.g., end user generated content, protected media)
- Service roaming, allowing the user to access services from the home platform, and/or match services from the platform visited
- autonomous systems
- **Mobile and any network on any device - allowing users to be always on with enough broadband capabilities (Beyond 3G challenges)**
- Support for new mobility modes: user, network and session mobility
- Semantic Web Services based middleware automatic service composition and processes on the top of the Semantic Web Services middleware [*Mobile Service Platforms Cluster - White Paper - Mobile Service Platforms – Architecture Whitepaper*]

Figure 24: Excerpt from a general criteria catalogue with important aspects of an SDP (Bergaus, 2010b)

Figure 24 above, shows the initial step of the structuring of important functions for an SDP. In this first stage, a summary and grouping takes place. It is also important to retain the literature reference, from which the original document comes, in this case a *'Mobile Service Platforms Cluster - White Paper - Mobile Service Platforms - Architecture Whitepaper'* (see the underlined sentence in Figure 24). Requirements, such as SDP function, are represented in blue and are detailed and further developed in Figure 25 as below.

Based on the first step to create a general criteria catalogue, shown in Figure 24, a detailed criteria catalogue was created by focussing on the aspect highlighted in "blue" from Figure 24. A document reference was also incorporated in this kind of representation (Bergaus *et al.*, 2012). Figure 25 shows a deeper representation of the aspect "SDP challenges for B3G systems".

```
┌─────────────────────────────────────────────────────────────────────────┐
│           Service Delivery Platform Challenges for Beyond 3G Systems       │
│                                                                           │
│     •  Redefining the role of Telco: from access to service provider      │
│          ○  Blurring of roles                                             │
│          ○  Enabling of new business models                              │
│     •  Hiding complexity and heterogeneity                               │
│          ○  Benefiting from existing variety of services, networks and devices │
│     •  Making services intelligent and easier to use (Assist users)       │
│          ○  Services have to be mobile                                    │
│          ○  In the context of the user-centric view                      │
│     •  Inter-domain aspects: service provisioning, inter-working          │
│          ○  Pan European service delivery platform                       │
│     •  Provide services in a timely way: accelerate creation & delivery of services │
│          ○  Fast service creation                                        │
│          ○  Reduce time-to-market for new services                       │
│     •  Opening platform capabilities to 3rd parties                       │
│     •  Supporting multi-vendor, multi-technology middleware platforms [SPICE │
│        Overview and Architecture - Presentation]                          │
└─────────────────────────────────────────────────────────────────────────┘
```

Figure 25: Excerpt from a detailed criteria catalogue with representations of the aspects of Beyond 3rd Generation (B3G) system, with regard to an SDP (Bergaus, 2010b)

3.11.3.2 Development of Literature-Based Aspects (Categories)

The detailed criteria catalogue was transferred to a Mind Map, and the main and detailed objects were subdivided. This was necessary, as having more than two hierarchy levels, becomes impossible to then read the illustration in A4 format. In order to represent the general and detailed aspects of the requirement of the communication infrastructure, for the use of innovative, ubiquitous technologies for ICT systems, the results of literature research were included in the literature-based study. This was done to structure and group NGNs and SDPs. To give an example of this, both issues represented in purple in Figure 25[4] are further elaborated in the following Figure 26 (Bergaus *et al.*, 2012).

---

[4] ("Making services intelligent and easier to use Assist users: 1. Services have to be mobile; 2. The context of the user-centric view" and "Provide services in a timely way: accelerate creation & delivery of services: 1. Fast service creation 2. Reduce time-to-market for new services")

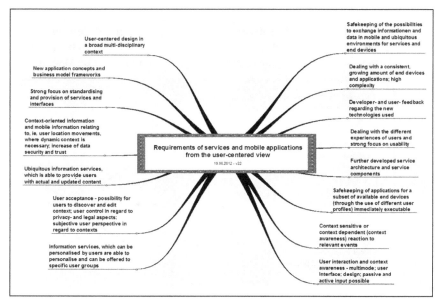

Figure 26: Requirements on the services and mobile applications from a user-centred perspective (Bergaus, 2010b)

3.11.3.3   Clustering Literature-Based Aspects

The developed categories from the empirical data were compared to the issues identified in the detailed criteria catalogue. The justification and validation was carried out using Mind Maps, created during the literature-based study, and from which single aspects could be clustered, into literature-based categories and sub-categories.

For example the aspects *'Interoperability should be possible on a network and device leve''*, *'Specific services for particular user groups or single users'*, *'User-centred design in a wide multi-disciplinary context'* and *'User acceptance for the possibility to recognise context to understand and process'* are derived from the Mind Map in Figure 26, and are combined with aspects from other mind maps to form the category *"Usability"*, as illustrated below in Figure 27 (Bergaus *et al.*, 2012).

This method was chosen and developed to establish the criteria catalogue based on Mind Maps, using the procedure highlighted in the Section 3.10.4. The literature was mapped over the general and detailed criteria in relation to the topics NGNs and SDPs, to a Mind Mapping view, and the "criteria/aspects" of these Mind Maps were then subsequently compared to the data (codes and categories) from the empirical study, thus enabling the validation of empirical data

by literature-based data throughout the three research phases; under consideration of Theoretical Sensitivity for GT-based research, as described by Charmaz
(2006). At this point, it was important that empirical research and analysis were
carried out in phases 1 and 2 prior to any literature review or Mapping Process.

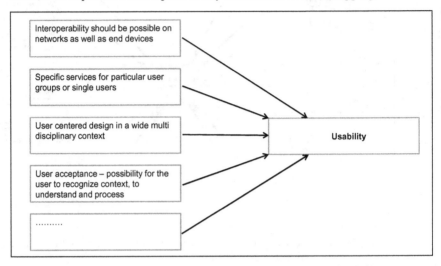

Figure 27: Clustering of aspects into a higher category (Bergaus *et al.*, 2012)

3.11.4 Third-Party Coding

A third-party coder, again, coded all fifteen interviews using the colour coding
system. This was also done in the three phases of interviews. In each phase the
recorded and transcribed interviews were coded, to confirm codes and check
reliability of the colour coding system. A separate third-party coded Fact Finding
tool, consolidated the results and the researcher then took these coding results to
compare with the subjective results of coding. The results of this comparison
were that most of developed codes were similar to each other in the interview
phases 2 and 3.

3.11.5 Memo Writing

A theoretical memo is used to theorise, allowing researchers the freedom to think
differently and creatively about what is transpiring in the collected and analysed
empirical data. From the researcher's point of view this procedure of theorising
is invaluable in the creation of ideas of research findings and relationships between categories and had to be written down in terms of the analysis process.
These memos are grounded with examples from the empirical data. This flexible

tool was used to support the theorising process in multiple ways. In this context, the researcher's own experiences were a combination of theoretical and integrative diagrams, which proved a powerful instrument to build a theorising process. A couple of theoretical memos with integrative diagrams are shown in Section 4.5, in terms of the development of categories.

3.11.6 Confirmation of Data within EMPLIT

To confirm and justify the empirical data within EMPLIT a comparison and confirmation was done based on different procedures, described in the following Section 3.12.

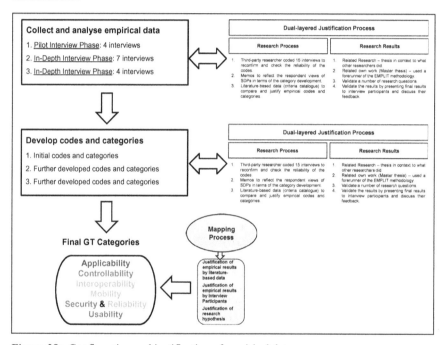

Figure 28: Confirmation and justification of empirical data

Figure 28 shows the entire procedure of confirming and justifying empirical codes and categories during the research study. Within EMPLIT the dual-layered justification procedure helped to confirm intermediate and final results based on codes and categories. This was described in Sections 3.3, 3.10, and 3.12 in depth.

The next Section concludes with justified results in a multi-layered procedure.

3.12 Dual-layered Justification Process

The analysis of the collected data and the development of the GT categories, with the justification of the preliminary and final results was done in different steps and phases. To ensure the integrity of the results of this qualitative study, the researcher established a chain of justification activities in two stages: 1. Justification of empirical data (codes and categories) during the research process; 2. Justification of the final research-results. This dual-layered justification process focuses on the goal to support the evidence of validating the EMPLIT methodology.

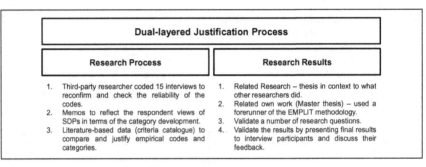

Figure 29:   The dual-layered justification process

3.12.1 Justification of Empirical Data During the Research Process

To justify the intermediate data of this study, different justification activities were done to ensure the integrity of the empirical data, within the study. A third party researcher coded all the interview scripts using the same coding procedure (colour coding) to reconfirm and check the reliability of the codes, developed from the empirical data, to add credibility and provide objectivity for the researcher. Memos were written by the researcher to reflect the respondents view on SDPs in terms of the category development. The literature-based data generated in structured mind maps within the literature-based study, were used to compare and justify the data (codes and categories), gathered from the interviews.

3.12.1.1   Third-party Coding

"Inter-Coder Reliability Test and Final Coding" Neuendorf (2002: p. 141) defines inter-coder reliability as "the amount of agreement or correspondence among two or more coders". She mentions two reasons why inter-coder reliability is important:

▓ to assure that, during the analysis process, the coding scheme is usable by more than one researcher, and

▓ to "calibrate" the coders against one another if a study comprises of multiple coders, which is not the case in this study.

Thus, another person, with similar results, following Neuendorf's argument, could apply the introduction of a second coder, aimed at re-assuring that coding scheme, as a measurement tool. The author involved a third-party researcher, who was already familiar with the Colour Coding system, to establish a procedure confirming developed codes and checking reliability of the colour coding system.

3.12.1.2 Memo Writing

The process of coding and developing categories was supported through a memo-writing process. Memos are sets of notes, which, kept continuously, support the researcher by providing a record of thoughts and ideas. Memos enable the researcher to reflect on the interviews and given codes, and to enter into a dialogue of the collected data. Initial thoughts are relevant, as they often spark the best ideas. Thus it is important to write memos immediately, whilst reading and coding the interview. At later stages in the research process, initial thoughts represented through memos can be revisited, reflected upon, and considered for the overall analysis. Memos can be used to ask questions, speculate on the potential meanings of interviewee's statements, and compare the concepts identified in interview transcripts against one another, and with the literature. Furthermore, this process helped the researcher confirm codes and categories and check the reliability of the empirical data as well.

3.12.1.3 Compare and Justify Empirical Codes and Categories

A comparison of the developed codes and categories was done using developed data, both collected, from the general and detailed literature-based criteria catalogue in terms of the literature review, during the entire study. Intermediate data (codes and categories) and final results, were compared after the second and the third interview phases, to justify these results. This was also done with the final results in the last interactive process stage.

3.12.2 Justification of the Final Research Results

For the justification of the final results of this study, a few different activities were adopted to ensure the integrity of the empirical results. Related research was undertaken to set the context of this thesis to that of other researchers. The master thesis "Verbesserter Nutzen von Telematiksystemen im Schienenverkehr durch Bereitstellung innovativer Service-Delivery-Plattformen" (Bergaus and

Stottok, 2010) used an older version of the EMPLIT methodology, in a special context of railway drivers and SDP technology to improve railway telematic systems and increase security and reliability of railway telematics. A final presentation and discussion with the research results was given to the interview participants during a one-day workshop, to show them the outcomes, support their satisfaction with the results of this study, and to get their feedback. Finally, a number of research questions outlined in Section 3.9.4 were validated and discussed.

3.12.2.1   Thesis in Context

This thesis and research investigation was discussed in the context of what other researchers have done regarding SDP-related ICT development. Sections 2.3 to 2.5 outlined a review in terms of the research topic.

3.12.2.2   Validate a Number of Research Questions

Section 3.9.4 addressed four research questions based on background information and related research in parts of Chapter 2. The validation of the research questions was done to support the evidence of the EMPLIT methodology and is stated and described in Section 5.8.1.

3.12.2.3   Validate the Results by Presenting Final Results to the Interview Participants

The justification, of the final results from the empirical study, was done by presenting those results to the interview participants and discussing the outcomes of the research study with them. Getting their feedback contributed significantly as it showed the evidence of EMPLIT and the developed GT categories. The procedure was described in Section 3.7 and how it worked will be shown in Section 5.7.6 supported by examples from the workshop.

3.12.3 Substantial and Methodological Results

Besides the expected substantial results of this investigation in the form of a 'substantiv' and Grounded Theory (presented in the Chapters 4 and 5), there are also expected methodological improvements. These improvements are the further development of the Colour Coding method for the GTM coding, as well as the Mapping Process. Colour Coding was developed for a more pragmatic way to start early with the analysis of the empirical data after gathering the pilot interview data. The Mapping Process structures, and groups, data gathered by reviewing the literature. The general and detailed criteria catalogue developed within the literature-based study structured data of the criteria catalogues were transferred to mind map representations. This procedure facilitated the researcher's understanding and grouping of the complex literature topic compare the collected coded and analysed empirical data in form of codes, and developed categories to the literature mapped data, consolidated in the Mind Maps. This procedure was done in the interview phases 2 and 3, to validate the actual empirical data. The methodological improvement developed in this research then verified codes and made literature research structured, transparent and comprehensible. The Mapping Process is a research and validation tool and, in terms of research groups, it can also be used as a communication tool between those researchers.

3.13 Development of the GT Categories

The following section describes the development of the six final categories and demonstrates the process of developing, justifying and validating categories. Three interconnected processes facilitated the development of the final categories in all three phases of empirical data collection and analysis, as is shown in the Table 7 below.

The development of the categories is based on open and selective Coding using the Colour Coding system. After the final evaluation of the pilot interviews, immediately following the first analysis phase, the first results were derived from the empirical data. These were developed in the analysis and reflected or interpreted using memos (Theoretical Coding) to establish relations between the categories. The categories and sub categories discovered were transferred into the analysis tool (Fact-Finding tool). Besides this, the discovered categories were defined as challenges that the participants identified in the interviews, used in SDPs in terms of ICT technology.

The pilot interviews generated initial codes, and these codes were justified prior to the category development. The first part involved the iterative process of coding, which used the Colour Coding approach, in order to help verify and reflect the codes. Memos facilitated establishing links between codes and tentative categories.

The mapping process phase was the last stage of each of the three phases, in which the developed categories were validated by the literature-based data, and summarised in categories by mind maps, as shown in Section 4.1 - Findings from Literature-Based Mapping Process.

Coding interviews constituted an important link between data collection and theory development. Grouping codes under different topics, and keeping written memos, helped to make sense of the respondents' statements. Particularly relevant codes have been further explored in-depth, by looking at their properties and dimensions. These could then be interlinked and related to other codes, in order to devise more abstract categories.

Table 7: The development process of the GT categories

Coding Phase	Task	Outcome	Reference
Iterative Coding Phase 1	**Colour coding**: 1. Open coding; 2. Focused coding; 3. Grouping and structuring codes; 4. Theoretical coding	Initial codes	Fact Finding Tool (FFT)
Code Reflection Phase 1	**Writing facilitated memos**: establish links between codes and tentative categories; **Justifying codes**: re-coding and intercoding by a 3rd-party researcher	Memos and links/relations between initial codes; justified initial codes; initial categories	FFT; Memo-File
Iterative Coding Phase 2	**Colour coding**: 1. Focused coding; 2. Re-coding pilot interviews; 3. Grouping and structuring codes again; 4. Theoretical coding	Focused codes	FFT
Code Reflection Phase 2	**Writing facilitated memos**: establish links between codes and tentative categories; **Justifying codes**: re-coding and intercoding of pilot interviews by a 3rd-party researcher	Memos and links/relations between focused codes; justified focused codes; further developed categories	FFT; Memo-File
Mapping Process Step 1	**Developing literature-based criteria catalogue**: general and detailed criteria; mind maps with grouped and structured categories; **Comparing codes/categories**: compare justified focused codes/ categories from the created mind maps	Literature-based mind maps; justified initial and further developed categories	FFT; Mind Maps
Iterative Coding Phase 3	**Colour Coding**: 1. Focused coding; 2. Re-coding pilot and in-depth interviews from phase 2; 3. Grouping and structuring codes again	Focused codes	FFT
Code Reflection Phase 3	**Writing facilitated memos**: establish links between codes and tentative categories; **Justifying codes**: re-coding and intercoding pilot and in-depth interviews from phase 2 by a 3rd-party researcher	Memos and links/relations between focused codes; justified focused codes; final categories	FFT; Memo-File
Mapping Process Step 2	**Further development of literature-based criteria catalogue**: general and detailed criteria; mind maps with categories; **Comparing codes/categories**: compare justified focused codes/ categories with data from the created mind maps	Further developed literature based mind maps; justified final categories	FFT; Mind Maps

Categories represent the basis for the developing GT, which aims to explain and sometimes predict phenomena based on empirical data (see Methodology Section 3.13). In order to offer an insight into this process, and to illustrate how the researcher arrived from the interview transcripts to the final categories, focused codes, memos and mind maps are presented, and explained in detail, in Chapter 4.

3.14 Chapter Summary and Conclusion

This Chapter introduced and justified the general research paradigm and strategy as well as the research project process of this investigation. The EMPLIT methodology used GTM and the Colour Coding System for theory generation and coding. GTM, together with mind maps, the feedback after presenting the developed empirical results to the interview participants, the literature-based study, the EMPLIT methodology, has been justified and presented as a suitable form of research methodology for this investigation. The specific study setup and the application of the EMPLIT methodology based in this research project, investigating web-based platforms and information systems illustrated topics on SDPs and ICT systems was presented, including the research justification process on multi-layers and the development process of the GT categories.

A research methodology was developed to provide an explanation of the phenomenon being studied: an alternative approach to investigate SDPs by analysing individual user needs when designing ICT systems. The methodology was specifically developed for this study and has been employed to offer an explanation of an individual's perspective of SDP-based ICT systems. Summarising the different methods of EMPLIT, the following research methods and techniques were provided: GTM; Colour Coding System; mapping techniques; the literature-based study and the mapping process.

The research questions presented were essential for validation in this qualitative research project. They related the aim and the objectives described in Chapter 1, to the outcomes and findings introduced in Chapter 5, with a focus on the user's perspective, and are particularly important for the empirical study. It is important to emphasise that, four research questions considered the viewpoints of SDPs from different perspectives, and fulfilled the user perspective criteria. A qualitative study was undertaken, by interviewing end-users and developers, and architecture experts, in a multiple-phases approach, as these groups offer information pertaining to daily requirements of mobile environment users, which is central to the debates on the challenges and design issues of SDPs, to administrate future-oriented ICT environments.

An empirical study collecting a series of interviews in three stages, a litera-ture-based study, a mapping process justifying and validating empirical data, and providing evidence of the developed EMPLIT methodology. The iterative phase of data collection and analysis is an essential element of the core research method GTM within this study and has helped shape on-going data collection.

Based generally on EMPLIT, the specific study setup, adhering to the re-search topics, was developed. The application procedure and a concrete research process for this application was described and discussed, and explored the analy-sis of data for the empirical and literature-based study. A solid example of cod-ing is given using the colour coding system within EMPLIT, showing how litera-ture-based data was generated, and how the mapping process works (Sections 3.11 and 3.11.6). The confirmation of data using EMPLIT was also illustrated.

The research methodology developed for this study was presented and de-scribed in detail, with all the necessary steps to reach the aim and fulfil the ob-jectives of this research, using EMPLIT methodology, described.

Chapter 4 presents and discusses the analysis and presentation of findings, within the empirical study, the GT theory and category development. The results for the literature-based study and the mapping process are presented, to justify and validate the empirical findings, in different stages.

4 Presentation of Findings

This Chapter presents detailed accounts of the findings from the three empirical data collection phases. Accordingly, this Chapter is structured in three parts. The first part focuses on the presentation of the findings from the literature-based and the empirical studies (Section 4.1). The second part then details the empirical findings and shows, for each of the three interview phases, the detailed results (Sections 4.2 to 4.4). The third part then discusses the development of the substantive GT by developing codes and categories (Section 4.5). GT codes (open and focused codes), theoretical memos and visual demonstrations of ideas (integrative diagrams) provide an insight into the development of the final GT categories. The methodology for this study, discussed and explained in Chapter 3, was used to guide the data collection phase, is illustrated in this Chapter.

4.1 Findings from the Literature-based Study

In the following, the results from the literature-based study are presented as Mind Maps. This visual representation of the literature-based data allows for the validation and verification of empirical data. The challenges and requirements are based on the theoretical background information, shown in Chapter 2, and the procedure described in Section 3.8 and following Sections.

4.1.1 Requirements for an SDP-based ICT infrastructure of the future

The following requirements have the theoretical basis as a starting point, and are to be seen in the context of the general requirements for an ICT infrastructure. The results of the literature research were integrated into a mind mapping process, in order to structure SDP and ICT system aspects. This was to show the general and detailed aspects of the requirements for the communication infrastructure for the application of innovative ubiquitous technologies, for ICT systems. Within the scope of the mapping process, these requirements form the essential criteria catalogue for design aspects for ICT systems of the future:

- *General Requirements for an ICT infrastructure:* General requirements, with regards to the ICT infrastructure, are presented.

- *Requirements for the ICT infrastructure of the future:* Requirements are shown in general, with regard to the ICT infrastructure, or with reinforced attention to the network infrastructure.

- *Requirements for the development, provision and execution of services:* These requirements consolidate the complete official development, as well as the provision of services, in the context of an SDP.

- *Requirements for the services and mobile applications focusing on the user-centred point of view:* These requirements arise from users' perspectives, as elaborated by the respondents.

All the Mind Maps created were the results of the Mapping Process described earlier in Section 3.8, in detail. All requirements in the maps are a part of the literature-based criteria catalogue and present the mapped representation of the general and detail criteria catalogue.

General and detailed requirements for an ICT infrastructure

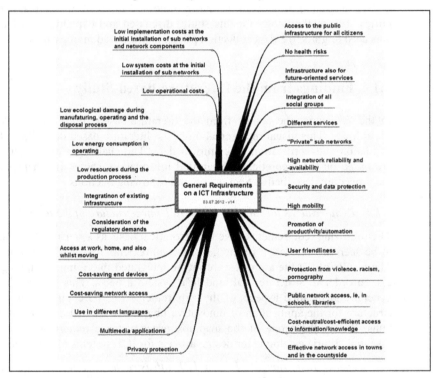

Figure 30: General requirements on an ICT infrastructure

Requirements for the ICT infrastructure of the future

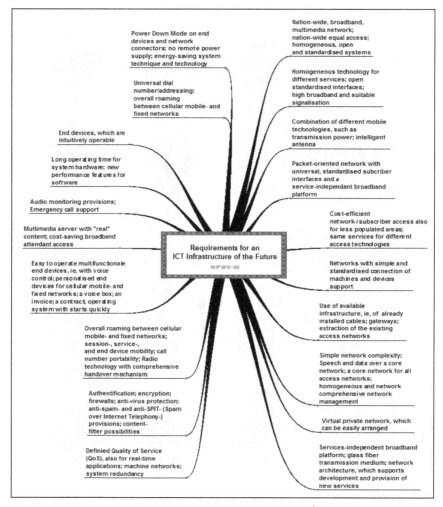

Figure 31: Requirements for an ICT infrastructure of the future[1]

---

[1] It is based on the literature researched and also the work of Trick and Weber (2009: p.14), explaining the requirements for an ICT infrastructure of the future.

Requirements for the creation, provision and execution of services

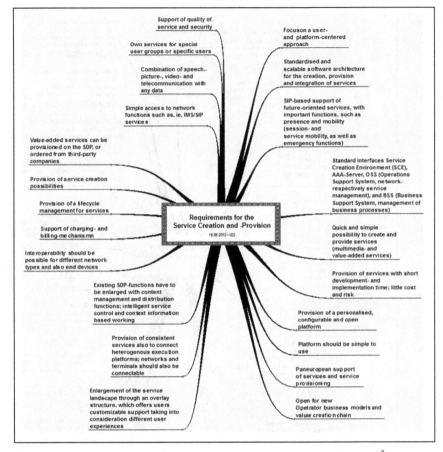

Figure 32: Requirements for the creation, provision and execution of services[2]

---

[2] The generic requirements for the official development and provision were set out.

Requirements for the services and mobile applications focusing on the user-centred perspective

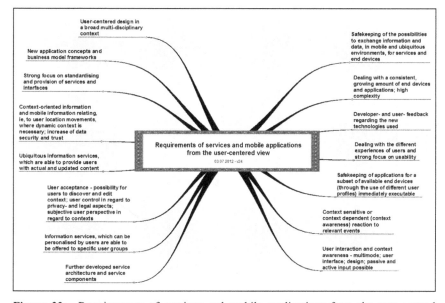

Figure 33:   Requirements of services and mobile applications from the user-centred perspective

4.1.2   Results of the Grouping and Structuring Procedure

All Mind Maps created were results of the Mapping Process described in Section 3.8. An additional step was structuring and grouping aspects of different Mind Maps to cluster the field of the research topic. This consolidated Mind Map represents aspects from the same type of themes in a 2-tier, or maximum a 3-tier, hierarchy. Limitations in presenting high multi-tier level on Mind Maps exist due to the constraints of an A4 page - the possibility to read these Mind Maps is therefore curbed, which is why the researcher used a maximum of a 2-tier level Mind Map in his representations.

Excerpt of the grouping and structuring procedure - requirements for the service creation and provisioning platform

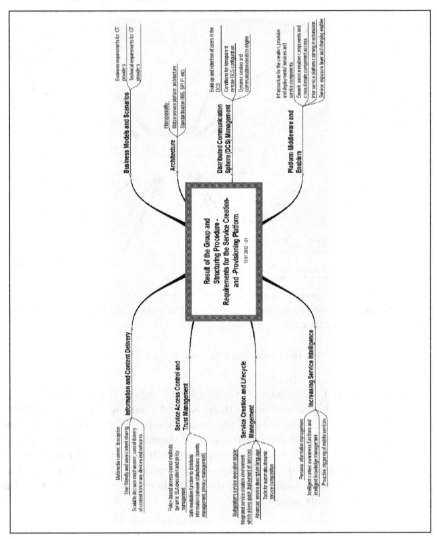

Figure 34: Excerpt of the grouping and structuring procedure[3]

---

[3] Requirements for the service creation and provisioning platform.

Further *Mind Maps* generated in the Grouping and Structuring phase of the Mapping Process are illustrated in Section 10.5. The following Sections 4.2, 4.3, and 4.4, outline the process of collecting, analysing and validating empirical data in three phases.

4.2 Findings from Phase 1: Pilot Interviews

Phase 1 - Pilot Interviews set out to achieve the following aim: To test the developed procedures and guidelines with the SPICE specialised groups of end-users and developers, and to find out about the participants impressions. Therefore, the pilot interviews involved a single data collection technique. Four participants were interviewed; two end-users and two SPICE project developers. A detailed analysis and the findings from the interviews are presented in the following Sections.

4.2.1 Aims of the Pilot Interviews

The target of the pilot interviews was aimed at learning about the participants' awareness of the challenges related to the design aspects of SDPs and ICT systems. It was conducted in one stage. The following interview aims were addressed:

▪ *Aim 1:* Awareness and attitudes towards the design aspects of SDPs and ICT systems of the future.

▪ *Aim 2:* Participants' definitions of design aspects regarding SDPs.

▪ *Aim 3:* Potential features to help end-users of ICT systems in making their lives easier.

The data from the interviews was arranged in content-analytic tabs in an excel file aptly named the Fact Finding Tool (described in Section 3.5). The complete Fact Finding Tool, showing all of the pilot interviews, is shown in Section 10.2 as well as on the DVD, see table of contents in Section 11.1 - Appendix D – DVD with Data Sources and Raw Data.

4.2.2 Summary of the Pilot Interviews

The four participants expressed similar thoughts during the interviews. Although the sample was limited to four participants, a range of SDP challenges and design-aspect-related opinions could be noted. Two participants, p12_d and p14_d, seemed to believe that mobility is an important aspect in the everyday life of an ICT system user: *"For me it is only of added value if I'm able to switch on my mobile phone or my laptop independently of the place where I am" (p12_d; translated by the author). "I think users must be able to have access to different services resources independently, using special end devices" (p14_d; translated by the author).* The two other participants, p11_u and p13_u, felt a bit uncomfortable with the use and look of dealing with different devices: *"When working with a laptop or PDA, and using services from an SDP, it is still necessary that the SDP platform remains easy to handle through the same procedure which is used in a wide range of end devices" (translated by the author).*

The following extract, taken from the empirical data from the pilot interviews shows, as an example, question Q23, with some of the answers the four participants gave on the topic of interoperability:

Table 8: Extract of the Fact Finding tool taken from empirical data of the pilot interviews (translated by the author)

Q23: Which influence factors do you see regarding the interoperability of end-users with networks and end-devices?			
p11_u	p12_d	p13_u	p14_d
I think the most important influence factor is that an enduser wants his or her applications or services to work independent entry of the location he or she is at that moment. This is because a stable support of all well-established networks and enddevices ...	The people who use an SDP can personalise their services to use it at anytime and anyplace. It's important that the infrastructure behind this works in a stable and reliable way. Standard networks such as WWAN and WLAN must be supported, and the automatic mechanism to connect has to be integrated by using standard technology IMS and SIP ... Developers have to make sure that ICT services meet the goal of a convergenced application by using push and pull mechanism to push for instance information to users in dependence of the actual location he or she is (location based sevice).	I think the mobility feature is one of the core topics that an SDP can be the communication control system for a broad range of ICT systems and components ...	In my opinion the standard integration of IMS/SIP is the most important driver for offering users the possibility to interoperate anytime and anyplace with their communication partners, by using their personalised services and applications ...

Regarding the influencing factors of interoperability, everyone agreed that mobility is a very important challenge to consider so as to be able, to work in a stable and reliable way with an SDP. In addition, the mechanism for ensuring that services work reliably anytime and anywhere was also seen as important. It is essential for the user to be able to integrate standard technologies, such as IMS and SIP. According to respondent p12_d, Location-Based Service mechanisms also need to be implemented, and p14_d expressed that the integration of IMS and SIP is a necessity, so that service and application operators are able to offer end-users a platform based on SDPs.

The application of SDPs is useful in making services more tangible for a broad range of users. However, all the participants stated that they see challenges in the areas of security and usability of such systems being implemented, at application or service provider level. The Fact Finding Tool proved to be useful in summarising the interview data and could also be used to support an in-depth analysis of further interviews and collected data. This supported the researcher's decision to use this approach, in order to guide further data analysis and collection, and to check analysed data again, should new codes or categories be found. For this reason, the pilot interviews were analysed again using GTM. The pilot interviews were coded and followed-up by further more in-depth interviews, based on the initial findings. A discussion of these early interviews, in relation to the relevant literature, will follow in Chapter 5 - Model Development and Discussion of Results.

4.2.3 Analysis of the Pilot Interview Data

The data analysis phase of the pilot interviews, by means of GT, involved the gradual implementation of the presented transcription and coding procedure, developed and presented in Chapter 3. During the pilot interview phase, four interviews were carried out and transcribed. On account of the mapping process a whole series of structured aspects and requirements had already been revealed. At this stage, open coding was executed immediately by using the Colour Coding scheme.

The next coding step was selective coding. This was conducted to find out about the relationships between created codes. Afterwards, the colour-coded data from the transcription texts, and the categories discovered were transferred into the Fact Finding Tool. Subsequently, categories were processed in the category sheets and partial memos were written to record the researcher's subjective thoughts on the aspects and issues identified.

The first interpretation of the results of this first analysis phase was conducted, and a summary of the results was compiled. This will be described in the next Section 4.2.4. With the help of this first interview-based data on the knowledge from the interviews with the SPICE experts, an initial model was developed following the analysis (the final model is presented in Chapter 5). The interview transcripts were coded with colour markers, on paper and thereafter transferred to the Fact Finding Tool, together with some comments. The codes were arranged in groups, which helped to identify patterns in the data (see Sections 3.5.2 and 10.6).

4.2.4 Summary of Initial Coding

The first coding of the pilot interviews provided some initial ideas (also called preliminary codes within the context of this study), which were used as guidance for the next stage of interviews. Most of the initial codes could be grouped into the four categories: *'Mobility'*, *'Simple to Use'*, *'Data Protection'*, and *'Compatibility'* (see Table 9). The numbers in brackets reflect how often the codes were used, for example "(two/four)" indicates that the code was used in two out of four interviews. At a later stage these preliminary codes and categories guided the development of the final categories (see 4.5). Moreover, the developed codes on the left side (column 'Mobility') have the most impact of the respondent views within the interview phase. The code on the right hand side (column 'Compatibility') had the minimal impact within the actual interview phase from the perspective of the respondents.

Table 9: List of initial (preliminary) codes for pilot interviews

Mobility	Simple to Use	Data Protection	Compatibility
• being mobile anywhere and anytime (four/four) • access to resources independent of actual location (three/four) • supporting standardised wireless technologies (two/four) • being always connected with the ICT equipment (two/four) • having access to important data files at all times (one/four)	• easy to handle and use (three/four) • supporting different types of end-devices (two/four) • creating confidence by the end-user and giving them the feeling of working with a reliable device • web-based platform (two/four) • litte count of interactions to use the wanted service or application (one/four)	• gaining access to own data and services (two/four) • protection of user data and information (two/four) • personalise the portal with the own used services (one/four) • being under surveilliance (one/four)	• integrating existing environments (two/four) • end-device compatability and broad range of different devices (one/four) • use of different network types (one/four) • minor costs for integrating existing environments (one/four)

The end-user's relationship to end devices was a phenomenon that was highlighted by the preliminary attributes. This relation varied from user to user, and seemed to be related to the ways in which the end device was utilised. The type of end device was particularly determined by the kind of service used. Some attributes in this area could be grouped together, as shown in Table 10 below.

Table 10 also shows some initial attributes as a result identified in the pilot interviews. These codes are related to the challenges and design issues of SDPs and ICT systems.

Table 10: Some initial attributes from the pilot interviews[4]

Relationship User - End-Device and SDP	Relationship User - Network and SDP	Relationship SDP and ICT system
• web-based SDP must support a broad range of enddevices (three/four) • support in displaying different contents independently of display sizes (two/four) • mobility and session stability is a must for enddevices and networks (two/four) • personalised access to SDP and provided services anytime and anyplace (one/four) • group and personalise own service package (one/four)	• different connections to standard network technologies is a must (WWAN, WLAN, Wimax, Bluetooth), (two/four) • mechanism for controlling the cheapest network connection at the actual point of location of the user (two/four) • automatic interaction with user, regarding connection possibilities within the networks (one/four) • IMS and SIP as IP-based standard technolgies for SDPs (one/four)	• SDP as standard gatway for ICT service-related user interation (two/four) • standard technologies and interfaces are a must for SDPs (one/four) • web and IP based mechanism for linking an ICT system with an SDP (one/four) • very important to address the challenges for users in SDPs as gateways to ICT systems (one/four) • SDPs as standard communication technology for ICT systems (one/four)

4.2.5 Justification of Initial Codes and Categories

It is important for the researcher alone to justify all codes and categories that are assigned to interview data, in order to ensure that they are applied consistently (Miles and Huberman, 1994). In order to justify the initial codes established through open and focused coding, by using the Colour Coding approach, a third-party researcher started afresh with coding the pilot interviews using the same method as before. The results from the third-party researcher were analysed and the relevant aspects and issues were compared with their own results. This meant that the categories and sub-categories, which had been previously developed, could now be compared and further elaborated on.

A comparison between newly and previously assigned codes, helped to clarify whether the codes were reliable and truly represented the empirical data. The comparison showed that past and present codes were similar to each other. However, initial codes were often either too narrow, too close to the interviewees' exact words, or seemed to mirror themes known from the literature. Hence the benefit of re-coding the interviews consisted of reconfirming and refining the codes. Memos were used to reflect changes in codes and the respondents' perspectives on the subject area. The next step was the collection and the analysis of seven interviews, with additional aims to those on hand, and this is described in the following Section.

---

[4] Relating to the challenges and design aspects of SDPs and ICT systems.

4.3   Findings from Phase 2: In-Depth Interviews

Phase 2 - In-Depth Interviews set out to achieve the aim of running the successfully tested interview procedure with the group of SPICE end-users, developers
and architecture experts, to gain a more in-depth impression of respondents'
perspectives and collect more data for the coding and analysis. The in-depth
interviews involved the same data collection method as used in phase 1. Seven
participants were interviewed; four end-users, four developers and an architecture expert from the SPICE project. The detailed analysis and findings from the
interviews are presented in the following Sections.

4.3.1   Aims of the In-Depth Interviews from Phase 2

Stage 2 interviews served to deepen the participants' awareness of challenges
related to design issues of SDPs and ICT systems. They were conducted in one
stage by considering the outcomes from the pilot interviews and focusing more
on the experiences of the SPICE experts to support the realistic design of SDP
for an ICT system of the future. The following interview aims were addressed:

- *Aim 1:* Awareness and attitudes towards design aspects of SDPs and ICT
  systems of the future

- *Aim 2:* Participants' definitions of design aspects concerning SDPs

- *Aim 3:* Potential features which could assist the end-users of SDP-based
  ICT systems in making their lives easier

- *Aim 4:* Identify challenges in relation to NGNs, SDPs and Ubiquitous Services.

- *Aim 5:* Participants' concerns regarding design issues for addressing challenges in the areas of SDPs.

The first three aims mirrored those in the pilot interviews, where the additional
two aims (aims 4 and 5) were defined to address challenges and design issues in
the context of SDP-related topics. The data from the interviews was also arranged in content-analytic tabs, in the Fact Finding Tool (described in Section
3.5.2). The complete Fact Finding Tool showing all interviews is shown on the
DVD, see table of contents in Section 11.1 - Appendix D – DVD with Data
Sources and Raw Data.

4.3.2 Summary of the In-Depth Interviews from Phase 2

All seven participants expressed similar thoughts during the interviews. A range of SDP challenges and design aspect-related opinions were noted. The participants p21_u, p23_d and p26_d echoed the opinions of the participants from the first phase, that both mobile and usability issues were very important for ICT system-users in everyday life. The participants p24_d and p27_ae came up with the topics of service landscape and the range of ICT services on SDP and also raised the issue of secure and reliable service-access for the user, independent from the network: *"An SDP could help to address a broad range of services and help to deliver those services to the end-users in an easy and effective way. Moreover, the access to a personalised user account has to be secure and reliable [...]"* *(translated by the author).*

The participants, p22_u and p25_d, raised new issues regarding the integration of existing infrastructures and infrastructure components, and cost awareness: *"It is necessary to use standard technologies and such environments which will be compatible with older existing equipment too. Only coming up with brand new technologies isn't realistic for implementing on a broad basis, in terms of the integration of existing environments – for example mobile basis stations or other end devices - in the field. Another important argument in this case is the cost issue"* *(translated by the author).*

The participants, p25_d and p27_ae, acknowledged another important aspect in terms of having the ability to use applications and services in a context-aware manner: *"In terms of many different end devices in the field, application and services have to be developed in a user-friendly way. This means, for instance that an application should have the ability to offer dynamic content for different end devices such as smart phones or laptops, as well as different types and sizes of displays"* *(translated by the author).*

Table 11 shows an extract of the empirical data from the in-depth interviews of the interview phase 2. It shows, as an example, question Q7 with some answers from the seven participants regarding the topic challenges of the network infrastructure.

Regarding the influencing factors of network-related issues, all those questioned agreed that stability and cost-efficiency were very important challenges, in terms of the network aspect of SDP. In addition, it has to be ensured that users have the possibility to actively decide to change network access points on the basis of performance or cost issues.

Table 11: Extract of empirical data from the in-depth interviews of phase 2 from the Fact Finding tool (translated by the author

Q7: Which challenges of a network infrastructure are essential for you as an user? Please state reasons.						
p21_u	p22_u	p23_d	p24_u	p25_d	p26_d	p27_ae
Essential for an enduser from a network perspective is: to have a stable connection and high performance access to a cloud-based web portal (SDP) with high availability of the services provided ...	I think for a user it is important that a broad range of network technologies, such as mobile phone network access as well as WLAN access, should be offered and easy to change for the user, in a cost efficient way. This means that if there is the possibility to use a free WLAN in a town, the user should be informed that switching to another network point saves costs or has the adavantage of higher performance, or the other way ...	Automatic gatway change mechanism and ambient services is a must in the development of an SDP and needs to be implemented by the operator. This helps the user to ensure stable connections effectively at a high quality of service level ...	From my point view as an user I need a stable connection from a fixed and a mobile perspective ...	I belive that the most important point here is that the user needs a connection at any network on any device. The user is not interested in configuring network connections by himself, he or she will only use differently available and broadband network types which work with his or her applications and services. In this case the developers have to make sure that such mechanisms are implemented in an automatic and cost-effective way for the users ...	Any network on any device has to be met and is the most important demand that an SDP will provide ...	I think that existing network architectures will solve many technical point of view, into focus, than we have to make sure, from a developers perspective, that users will operate their applications easily and cost efficiently. But there is a key point. If the automatism is to high graded, means too many decisions made by the system themselve, an SDP will get an acceptance problem because the user also wants to make decisions by him or herself, for instance all decisions in regard to cost topics and also performance

All seven participants perceived challenges in the fields of mobility, security and usability, as well as, in terms of the range of services to be implemented in such a system. The new aspects of infrastructure compatibility, and the issue of cost awareness, are also important issues when it comes to using an SDP as a basis system of ICT systems. The Fact Finding Tool again proved to be useful in summarising the interview data, and the data in this tool could also be used to support an in-depth analysis of further interviews and collected data for a last interview phase. This approach had to be taken again in order to guide further data analysis and collection. Analysed data had to be rechecked in case new codes or categories were discovered. In such a case, for example in phase 2, the aspect "Range of services", the pilot interviews as well as the interviews from the second phase were analysed again using the same approach. Both were coded and, based on the findings, followed-up by further more in-depth interviews.

4.3.3 Analysis of the Interview Data from Phase 2

The analysis of the interview data in Phase 2 was based on previous knowledge from the pilot interview cycle, again using the coding process (see Section 3.4.4) as discussed above. In this phase, a total of seven interviews were carried out, and transcribed in the same manner as the pilot interviews. The transcriptions were analysed in-depth and were once again open and axial coded, although only on a low extent, since the focused codes discovered in the pilot interviews provided the basis for a quick step-in to focused coding at this stage of analysis. After focused-coding the researcher turned back to open and then selective coding in order to discover further possible categories and sub-categories. The code verification was carried out in the same way as in the pilot interview cycle, by a third-party researcher who coded using the same procedure. Both coding results were compared. The result of the comparison was that both researchers identified the same type codes.

Afterwards, the colour-coded data from the transcription texts, and the categories or sub-categories discovered or justified from the pilot interviews, was transferred into the Fact Finding Tool again and processed to develop categories in the category sheets. Partial memos were written again to record the researcher's subjective thoughts on the aspects and issues identified. The interpretation of the results, of this second analysis phase, was conducted and a summary of the respective results compiled. This is described in the next Section 4.3.4.

4.3.4 Summary of Coding of the Data from Phase 2

The focused coding of the seven in-depth interviews provided some initial verifiable ideas, thus introducing some additional codes as guidance for the next stage of the interviews. Many of these initial codes could be justified and categorised alongside those obtained from the relevant literature.

The codes identified during this stage were grouped into the six categories: 'Mobility', 'Simple and Friendly to Use', 'Wide Field of Services', 'Cost-Effectiveness', 'Data Security and Protection' and 'Infrastructure Compatibility' (see Table 12). The numbers, in brackets, again show how often the codes were used; "(three/seven)", for example, indicates that the code was used in three out of seven interviews. At a later stage these codes and categories guided the development of the final categories (see Section 4.5).

Table 12: Lists of further codes for the in-depth interviews from the 2nd interview phase

Mobility	Simple and Friendly to Use	Wide Field of Services	Cost-Effectivness	Infrastructure Compatibility	Data Security and Protection
• being mobile anywhere and anytime (seven/seven) • access to resources at any network on any device (five/seven) • being cost efficient by using network ressources (three/seven) • support WWAN and WLAN, WiMAX technologies (two/seven) • user's decision to switch to another network resource (two/seven) • having stable and reliable connections at anyplace (one/seven)	• easy to handle and use (six/seven) • support different types of enddevices (five/seven) • content has to be dynamic for different types of enddevices and displays (four/seven) • litte count of interactions to use the desired service or application (two/seven) • support of a broad range of smartphones (one/seven)	• ICT services should be available in a broad range, on a service provider SDP (five/seven) • provided services should be combined with others (two/seven) • services should be developed on standard technologies and offered for a broad range of use (two/seven) • SDPs will bring increasing benefit for service and application providers, in delivering a broad range of services to users (one/seven)	• has to be affordable for everyone (five/seven) • services have to be affordable for a broad range of users (two/seven) • automatic network switching mechanism has to be controlled in a cost efficient way for the users (two/seven)	• integrate existing environments (four/seven) • enddevice compatability and broad range of different devices (three/seven) • use of different network types (two/seven) • minor cost for integrating existing environments (two/seven) • standard technologies and components have to be used (one/seven)	• gain access to own data and services (four/seven) • protect users' data and information (three/seven) • offer reliable access to own services (three/seven) • personalise the portal with own services (two/seven) • being under surveilliance (one/seven)

The end-users' relationship to networks and end devices was highlighted by their attributes. This relation varied from user to user and seemed to be related to the ways in which the end device was used, particularly in terms of which kind of service was used by any given type of end device, and with which performance and availability. Some of the codes could be grouped together, as shown below in Table 13.

The attributes summarised in Table 13, for example, show some initial, then further developed attributes, as a result of the pilot and the in-depth interviews from interview phase 2, that were identified. These attributes were related to the challenges and design issues of SDPs and ICT systems.

Table 13: Some initial and further developed attributes for pilot- and in-depth interviews relating to challenges and design aspects of SDPs and ICT systems

Relationship User / End- Device	Relationship SDP / ICT System	Relationship User / Network	Relationship Network / SDP	Relationship End-Device / SDP
• mobility and Session stability is a must for enddevices and networks (five/seven) • personalised access to SDP and provided services anytime and anyplace (three/seven) • group and personalise own service package (three/seven)	• SDP as standard gatway for ICT service-related user interation (four/seven) • standard technologies and interfaces are a must for SDPs (three/seven) • web and IP based mechanisms to link an ICT system with an SDP (two/seven) • very important in addressing the challenges for users in SDPs as gatway to ICT systems (two/seven) • SDPs as standard communication technology for ICT systems (one/seven)	• users want to have high performance and available access to their services and applications (three/seven) • mechanism to control the cheapest network connection at the actual location of the user (two/seven) • users want to have their own selection possibility for selecting a performant or cost effective network connection (two/seven)	• different connections to standard network technologies is a must (WWAN, WLAN, Wimax, Bluetooth), (three/seven) • automatic interaction with user regarding the connection possibilities of the networks (two/seven) • IMS and SIP as IP-based standard technolgies for SDPs (one/seven)	• web-based SDP must support a broad range of enddevices (two/seven) • support in displaying different contents independent of display sizes (two/seven)

4.3.5   Justification of Further Codes and Categories from Phase 2 by Using Literature-Based Criteria Catalogue and the Mapping Process

All codes were once again justified, to ensure consistency, as described in Section 4.2.5 for the pilot interview data, whereby the data underwent a second colour coding process, to allow for comparisons between the two data sets and the literature-based data, in the criteria catalogue. The comparisons, described in Section 4.2.5, allowed the researcher to monitor the integrity of the data, taking into account the issue of theoretical sensitivity.

By looking to see if there was any overlap between the empirical data and the codes generated by mapping literature based data in the criteria catalogue, as described in Section 3.8, the researcher could validate and confirm the codes. Subsequently a set of codes could be devised, which captured, on a conceptual level, what had been expressed during the interviews, illustrated in Figure 35, below.

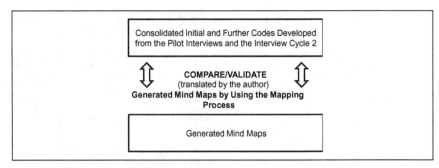

Figure 35:   Validation of initial and further codes and categories from pilot and in-depth
interviews from the second phase by using the Mapping Process

The outset of the Mapping Process began with the literature research. Aspects relating to SDP, NGN and ICT topics were grouped and structured to create general, and later more detailed, criteria catalogues with reference to the
academic literature. After that the literature-based aspects were transferred into a
Mind Map description as shown in Figure 35 and described in detail in the Section 4.1. These Mind Maps provide the basis for making comparisons and valida-
tions of the consolidated codes (see Figure 35) from the pilot and in-depth interview phase 2. These empirical codes have to be validated and justified to
complete the analysis and to fully justify the codes from phase 2. The consolidated codes are summarised in Section 10.6 - Appendix B.

At this stage it was already confirmed that the interweaving of literature-
based data to validate codes assists the researcher in providing a further possibility to justify empirical data by using the Mapping Process. Moreover, the generated aspects (literature-based categories) added an input to the focus coding as a
huge help and time saver within the scope of the data analysis.

After the analysis the colour-coded text passages were again transferred
into the Fact Finding Tool. The outcomes of this process were compared and
validated against empirical codes from the first and the second interview stages.
Based on this the initial model was updated with newly generated categories and
it was important for the researcher that the categories and sub-categories re-
mained stable and that no fundamental change in the models was necessary.

After the verification of the codes, focused codes and categories were developed. This process is discussed in detail in the following Section.

4.3.6 Development of Categories Based on Initial and Focused Codes

The second phase of interviews helped to develop initial codes (developed in interview phase 1) and later codes (developed in the following phases). This further development is called focused coding, as it is more directed and selective than the initial phase of open coding. These developed focused codes were not meticulously assigned to every single line of interview transcript, but the researcher made use of some initial concepts in order to focus on specific issues. These concepts were, for example, the respondents' relationship to their end devices and network connections, and their relationships to the SDP providing the services. To a large extent these focused codes influenced the development of categories.

The development of categories was facilitated by two inter-connected processes: firstly the iterative process of coding, which utilised different methods (open and focused coding by using a colour coding approach) to help to verify the codes, and secondly the process of reflecting on the codes, facilitated by memos, in order to establish links between codes and tentative categories. In order to offer an insight into this process and to illustrate how the researcher arrived from the interview transcripts to the final categories. The categories and memos are presented and explained in the following Sections.

4.3.7 Summary of Focused Codes after Phase 2

Table 14 below, shows a list of codes that were devised during the multi-staged coding process, described in the previous Section. More detailed descriptions and comments on each of the focused codes can be found in Appendix C, Section 10.6.

The focused codes listed below are based on codes developed with using Colour Coding, the mapping process, memos, and the literature-based criteria catalogue. After coding all transcripts, using open coding from one interview phase, each interview was re-coded with the Colour Coding method. By going through the process of coding, the colour-coded transcripts were transferred into the Fact Finding Tool. One colour represented one code and more colour zones within a colour code represented a developed category or sub-category. Section 3.4.4 (coding stages) provides an overview of the different coding phases.

Table 14: List of focused codes developed from the pilot and the in-depth interviews from the 2nd phase

A_Usability	B_Mobility	C_Field of Services	D_Data Security and Protection	E_Infrastructure Compatibility	F_Cost Effectiveness
A1_Handling • effective to use • Little clicks to operate A2_Types of Enddevices • support well-established devices • standardised interfaces • Different content according to display sizes A3_Access to Use • personalised • secured access • anytime and anyplace • any network on any device A4_Content Aware • dynamic contents A5_Interaction Decisions by the Users • switch to another network resource A6_Simple • quick and easy • self-explanatory	B1_Standards • WWAN, WLAN • WiMax • Bluetoth, Zigbee B2_Any Network on Any Device • Standard network technologies • Standard devices • Access to services and own resources B3_Stable and Reliable • Network connections B4_ Stable Sessions to Operate • stable and reliable connections B5_ High Availability • Being mobile anytime and anyplace B6_Broadband Resources • Service Roaming	C_1 Web based Service Control • Web- and cloud-based SDP • Support broad range of services • Benefit for operators C_2 Performance • performance • high availability C_3 User Control Mechanism • Mechanism to control • cheapest network connection at actual location C_4 Service Creation • possibility to select services • performance • cost effective C_5 Operator Usage • Broad usage for operators	D_1 Secured Access • Security standard mechanism • Personalised access • Assurance that different network technologies are secure • IMS and SIP security mechanism • Group and personalise own service packages D_2 Automatic interaction with user • connection possibilities D_3 Data Encryption • Protect and secure information and data	E_1 SDP Standard • standard gatway for ICT services • Standard technologies • Standard interfaces • Web and IP based mechanism to link lo an ICT system • very important to address challenges for users in SDPs as gatway to ICT systems E_2 Existing environments • has to be integrateable • SDPs standard communication technology for ICT systems E_3 Standard Technologies • Support state of the art ICT technologies • IMS, SIP, IP	F_1 Affordable for Everyone • Address a broad range of users F_2 Automatic mechanism has to be controlled • In a cost efficient way for the users • Being cost efficient by using network resources F_3 User want to have control • own control over selection • possibility to select a cost effective network connection

The final list of codes could be grouped into six topics that were of importance to participants, in relation to SDPs and ICT systems (see Section 5.9 - Summary of the Final Categories and the list of the Six Final Categories, and their relation to codes and theoretical memos, shown in link Table 35).

The focused codes listed below, are based on codes developed by grouping and structuring data. After adding comments and notes, each interview was re-coded by using Colour Coding again. By going through the process of coding the interviews on paper, and noting the codes in the Fact Finding Tool, the codes and categories were re-defined and re-affirmed. The next step 3, of the study was the additional collection and the analysis of a further four interviews and is described in the next Section.

Table 15: List of grouped focused codes and their description

Focused Codes Group	Description of Codes
A_Usability	• Handling – work in an simple way, with an SDP to control and administrate daily tasks using the ICT services from a cloud-based platform • Types of End-Devices – support a broad range of all state of the art enddevices • Access to Use – gain trusted acces to own information and data
B_Mobility	• Standards – Using state of the art mobile technologies as a standard to cover a potential high range of users • Any Network on Any Device – user has to be using data independently in an effective and efficent way, using existing networks and own enddevices anytime and anyplace • Stable and Reliable – users only will only develop trust, if a mobile sessions isn't interrupted
C_Field of Services	• Web-based service control : control a broad range of services by web-based portal and applications • Performance - High availability of services is a must • User Control Mechanism – users want to have the opportunity to control, because there is an impact to costs and or service quality
D_Data Security and Protection	• Secured Access - Secured access, account and data protection is a must for building trust • Automatic User Interaction – Network or client services, as well as application services, need to interact with user • Data Encryption – Standard level of internet data exchange
E_Infrastructure Compatibility	• SDP-Standard – Using standard technologies to address a broad range of potential users • Existing Environments – Cover existing environments at backend as wellas enddevice infrastructure
F_Cost Effectiveness	• Affordable for Everyone – SDP and provided servcies should be available and cost efficient for everyone • Users want to have control – control of the used services

4.4   Findings from Phase 3: In-Depth Interviews

The In-Depth Interviews in Phase 3, set out to conduct a third interview procedure with the SPICE-specialised groups of end-users, developers and architecture experts to deepen the participants impressions and to collect further data for
coding and analysis. Furthermore, a reliability check at the point of theoretical
saturation regarding new codes is the important reason why this methodology is
pursued with three data collection and analysis phases. The in-depth interviews
involved the same data collection methods used in phases 1 and 2. Four participants were interviewed, an end-user, a developer and two architecture experts
from the SPICE project. The detailed analysis and the findings from the interviews are presented in the following Sections.

4.4.1   Aims of the In-Depth Interviews from Phase 3

More in-depth interviews were provided to further deepen the participants' awareness of challenges related to the design aspects of SDPs and ICT systems. Moreover, it was necessary to conduct a reliable check of the developed codes and categories in the first and second interview steps, because it was necessary to check on a general level whether or not, found codes could be justified, or if new codes had been identified. In this study the codes could be justified, which led the researcher to conclude that three phases of data collection and analysis were sufficient for this qualitative study.

The data was analysed in the same way as before, by considering the outcomes from the seven in-depth interviews, focusing on the one hand on the experiences of the SPICE experts to support a realistic design of SDP for an ICT system of the future, whilst on the other hand, considering the personal feelings of the participants, from an end-user perspective. The interview aims were the same as those in the seven in-depth interviews, in phase two:

■   *Aim 1:* Awareness and attitudes towards design aspects of SDPs and ICT systems of the future

■   *Aim 2:* Participants' definitions of design aspects regarding SDPs

■   *Aim 3:* Potential features to help end-users of SDP-based ICT systems in making their lives easier

■   *Aim 4:* Identify challenges in relation to the three topics NGNs, SDPs and Ubiquitous Services

■   *Aim 5:* Participants' concerns regarding design aspects for addressing challenges in the areas of NGNs, SDPs and Ubiquitous Services

The data from the interviews were also arranged in content-analytic tabs, in an excel file named the Fact Finding Tool (described in Section 3.5). The complete Fact Finding Tool showing all interviews is shown on the DVD, see table of content in Section 11.1 - Appendix D – DVD with Data Sources and Raw Data.

4.4.2   Summary of the In-Depth Interviews from Phase 3

The four participants expressed similar thoughts during the interviews, and a range of SDP challenges and design aspect-related opinions could be noted again. All participants (p31_u, p32_ae, p33_ae and p34_d) echoed the opinions of the participants from the first and the second phase, that *mobility, usability, compatibility, security, a wide field of offered services* and *cost aspects* were very important in everyday life for ICT system users. The participants, p31_u and p33_ae, justified that the topics of *stability* and the *reliability of a platform such as an SDP* require for services to be highly available: *"The provided ser-vices, delivered by SDP to end-users, must support high availability. In this case, technology has to be chosen for the development, which can provide reliable and stable network connections, and, on the user side, support a very wide range of end devices [...] "* (translated by the author).

The participants, p32_ae and p34_d, were concerned with issues regarding the compatibility of existing components of operating infrastructures, as well as the aspect of protecting and securing users' data and resources: *"The technology cycle of ICT systems are getting shorter and shorter. This means that a new systems design with SDP as the general control system to provide and deliver services to end-users has to be considerate of existing environments operating in the field, that those environments are also compatible with a new standard. This means that SDPs must support state of the art technologies, as well as older technologies, and must support many different types of standards in different versions of up to 10-12 year old hard- and software"* (translated by the author).

The following extract (shown in Table 16), taken from the empirical data from the in-depth interviews of the third interview phase, shows, as an example, question Q38, with some answers given by the four participants, regarding the topic challenges of *security and data protection*.

In terms of the factors of *security* and *data protection*, everyone agreed that standard security technologies are important, but also enough to secure users' accounts and data on an SDP. All four participants stated that they saw chal-lenges in the topics *usability, mobility, security, range of services; such as com-patibility* and *cost effectiveness*. Their responses justified most of the issues raised in both the previous data collection and analysis phases. The Fact Finding Tool again proved to be useful in summarising the interview data, and could also be chosen to support an in-depth analysis.

Table 16: Extract taken from the empirical data from the in-depth interviews of phase 3 from Fact Finding tool (translated by the author)

Q38: Which security and data protection has to be applied on an SDP?			
p31_d	p32_ae	p33_ae	p34_d
I think an SDP should apply state of the art security mechanisms to protect access to the user account and the data and resources. From my point of view, standard data protection and security technologies using web security, wireless security standards as well as encryption technologies should be enough ...	The use of wireless and internet-based security technologies should achieve the goal here ... Important is the authentication mechanism. I would recommend a 2-factor authentication (e.g. token with pin or password) as a minimum standard ...	I think in the case of changing the delivery method of IT from operation centers to cloud-based operation services and the challenges, for instance, data compliance and data protection topics, etc., SDPs could help to move this new area of ICT a little bit faster, because an SDP is a cloud-based infrastructure, with a special focus on services and applications, and hosted by application and service providers with huge operation centers. Users don't know where physical data is stored, but they will get a Service Leve Agreement with a very good state of the art and compliant security and protection statement ...	I my opinion the protection of the users account is an important point, because we are living in a time with increasing cyber crime A user account, with personal information, files and data from protection as possible. This generates trust for the endusers and will help to make such systems more aware in different and a broad ranges of potential users ...

4.4.3   Analysis of the Interview Data from Phase 3

The analysis of the final four interviews served primarily as confirmation of the colour codes, categories and sub categories already identified, and so confirmed that theoretical saturation had been achieved by the second analysis phase, which indicated the final point in the development of grounded theory where after no further data can emerge.

4.4.4   Summary of Coding of the Data from Phase 3

The coding of the four in-depth interviews provided justified focused codes. Many initial codes could be justified and grouped together, and a number of new codes were also influenced by the relevant literature. The identified codes could be grouped into the six categories: *'Simple to Use', 'Mobility', 'Wide Range of Services', 'Cost-Control', 'Data Security and Protection'* and *'Infrastructure Compatibility'* (see Table 17). The numbers in brackets show again how often the codes were used, for example "(three/seven)" indicates that the code has been used in three out of seven interviews. These codes and categories later guided the development of the final categories (see Section 4.5).

Table 17: Lists of further codes for the in-depth interviews from the 3rd interview phase

Simple to Use	Mobility	Wide Range of Services	Cost-Control	Data Security and Protection	Infrastructure Compatibility
• simple to use (four/four) • user acceptance (four/four) • user friendly (two/four) • interaction controlled by the user (three/four) • SDP easy to administrate and personalisable (two/four) • support of a wide range of enddevices (one /four)	• being mobile on any network on any device and at anytime (three/four) • session control and stablility when user is moving (two/four) • support of mobile technologies (two/four) • high available network access and reliable connections (two/four) • stable broadband connection while moving (one/four)	• provides many different services (three/four) • service development and creation (two/four) • services must be deployable (two/four) • easy to operate, deploy and develop with no or very little donwntimes (two/four)	• managable costs for everyone (three/four) • affordable for a wide field of users (two/four) • good development of network coverage (one/four) • offer own created service groups also for other users (one/four)	• protected access to data and resources (three/four) • reliable access to user accounts (two/four) • personalise own account (one/four) • surveilliance and data security (one/four)	• integrate existing environments (three/four) • compatible enddevices (two/four) • integration of different network types (one/four)

As with the previous interview phases, end-users' relationships to their networks and end devices was highlighted by the further attributes. Again, this relationship varied from user to user, and seemed to be related to the ways in which way the end device was used, and for which kinds of services it was used, and with which level of performance and availability. Some attributes could be grouped together, shown in Table 18, below.

Table 18: Some initial and further attributes for pilot- and in-depth interviews, relating to challenges and design aspects of SDPs and ICT systems

Relationship User / End- Device	Relationship User / SDP	Relationship User / Network	Relationship End-Device / SDP	Relationship Network / SDP
• mobility and Session stability is a must for enddevices and networks (three/four) • personalised access to SDP and provided services anytime and anyplace (three/four) • group and personalise own service packages (three/four) • confidence in integrating more and more enddevices in daily working and leisure activities (two/four) • use applications and services reliably (two/four)	• SDP must be easy to handle and to administrate • a wide range of enddevices must be supported by the SDP (three/four) • mobile technology standards must be supported by SDP and enddevices (three/four) • confidence to store user data in cloud-based infrastructure SDP (two/four) • confidence to use services from application and services providers (one/four) • ability to support user needs with technologies and trust building activities (one/four)	• performance and highly available access to services and applications (three/four) • mechanism to control network connection at the actual location, from a cost and a quality service point of view (three/four) • users need possibility to select network type by themselves (two/four) • different standard network types with broadband capacity (one/four)	• SDP as standard gatway for ICT service-related user interation (three/four) • standard technologies and interfaces is a must for SDPs (two/four) • web and IP based mechanism to link an ICT system with an SDP (two/four) • very important to address challenges for users in SDPs as gatway to ICT systems (one/four) • SDPs as standard communication technology for ICT systems (one/four)	• different connections to standard network technologies is a must (WWAN, WLAN, Wimax, Bluetooth), (three/four) • automatic interaction with user regarding connection possibilities of the networks (one/four) • IMS and SIP as IP-based standard technolgies for SDPs (one/four)

The attributes summarised as an example in Table 18 show some initial and further developed attributes as a result of all interview phases identified. These attributes are related to the challenges and design issues of SDPs and ICT systems.

4.4.5 *Justification of Further Codes and Categories from Phase 3 by using Literature-Based Criteria Catalogue and the Mapping Process*

All codes were again justified to ensure consistency, described above in Section 4.2.5, for the pilot interview data, whereby the data underwent a second colour coding process, to allow for comparisons between the two data sets and the literature-based data in the criteria catalogue. These comparisons, described in Section 4.3.5, allowed the researcher to monitor the integrity of the data.

As with previous interview stages, the interview transcripts were coded with colour markers on paper, following the Colour Coding approach, and then the codes were transferred into the Fact Finding Tool, together with concise comments. The codes were summarised in groups, which helped to identify patterns in the data (see Chapter 3, and Appendix C, Section 10.6).

Comparisons between all the assigned codes afforded clarification on reliability and representativeness of the empirical data. The comparison showed that past and present codes were similar to one another. The benefit of a third-party researcher re-coding the interviews helped to reconfirm and check the reliability of the codes. Memos were used to reflect on the respondents' perspectives and the codes and categories developed from the empirical data at the stage of developing categories (see Section 4.5).

Additional justification of codes and categories was conducted, as described in previous Sections. In the third stage, after data collection and analysis, a verification of codes and categories was achieved by using the literature-based criteria catalogue again. The identified empirical data from the in-depth interviews of 3rd phase, was again compared with the literature-based data, to identify any overlap. In this case, only the codes from the empirical data were compared to the codes generated by mapping literature-based data in the criteria catalogue, as was described in Section 3.8 - Literature-based Study.

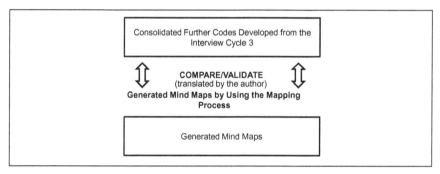

Figure 36: Validation of initial and further codes and categories from the in-depth interviews from the 3rd phase undertaken by using the Mapping Process

4.4.6 Further Development of Categories Based on the Focused Codes

The third phase of the interviews contributed to continuing development and verification of codes. As with previous interview phases, the developed, focused codes, made use of some initial concepts, in order to focus on specific issues, which were used to guide the development of the categories. The final development of categories was achieved using three interview stages. Each part used the iterative process of coding with different methods (open and focused coding by the use of the colour coding approach) and, in the final step, re-coding by a third party researcher, also based on these coding approach, for verification purposes.

The development of categories was facilitated by two inter-connected processes; first, the iterative process of coding, and then the process of reflecting on the codes, facilitated by memos, in order to establish links between codes and tentative categories.

In order to offer an insight into this process, and to illustrate how the researcher arrived from the interview transcripts, to the final categories. The categories and memos are presented and explained in the following Sections again.

4.4.7   Summary of Focused Codes after Phase 3

Table 19 below, shows a list of codes that were devised based on the multistaged coding process, described in the previous Section. More detailed descriptions and comments on each of the focused codes can be found in Appendix C, Section 10.6.

Table 19: List of focused codes developed from the pilot and in-depth interviews from the 3rd phase

A_Usability	B_Range of Services	C_Mobility	D_Data Security	E_Compatibility
A1_Handling • quick and easy • effective to use • Little clicks to operate **A2_Easy to Use** • support well-established devices • Different content for display sizes • anytime and anyplace • dynamic contents **A3_Simple** • Simple and easy to use **A4_User Friendliness** • self-explanatory **A5_User Acceptance** • Support users daily lives activities • Building trust **A6_ User Control** • user control regarding the selection of services, network and cost	**B1_Affordable for Everyone** • Address a broad range of users with broad range of services **B2_ Performance** • performance • high availability **B3_Control Mechanism** • Mechanism to control service • Control bandwith but also quality of the services • Control costs **B4_ Service Creation** • possibility to select services • performance • cost effective **B5_Operator Usage** • Broad use for operators	**C1_ High Availability** • Standard network technologies • Standard devices • Being mobile anytime and anyplace • Access to services and own resources, • stable and reliable connections **C2_Broadband Resources** • UMTS, HSPA, LTE • QoS **C3_Standards** • WWAN, WLAN • WiMax • Bluetooth, Zigbe **C4_Stable and Reliable** • Network connections • Service Roaming **C5_ Stable Sessions to Operate**	**D1_Secured Access** • Security standard mechanism • Personalised access **D2_Data Protection** • Protect data and information • Protect access to account • Encrypt data **D3_Preventive Data Security** • Secure data in a preventive way and form **D4_Account Protection** • Protect user account • Personalise user account	**E1_Support Existing Environments** • integrateable • standard communication technology • ICT Systems • Components • Interfactes • Hard and software **E2_Automatic Controlable Mechanism** • cost effective and efficient • Interatction with user is necessary **E3_Infrastructure reuse** • Reuse old operable environments and components

The focused codes listed in Table 14 and Table 19 are based on codes developed using the multi-staged coding procedure, and the mapping process, as well as written memos, and the literature-based criteria catalogue. After coding all transcripts using Colour Coding, the coded transcripts were transferred to the Fact Finding Tool and again one colour represented one category.

The final list of codes could be grouped into five topics that were of importance to participants in relation to SDPs and ICT systems. These are shown in the following table:

Table 20: List of grouped focused codes and their description

Focused Codes Group	Description of the Code
A_Usability	• Handling – work in an quick and easy way with an SDP on an daily basis, using the ICT services from an SDP • Easy to Use – support well established end devices • Simple – simple to use and administrate
B_Range of Services	• Affordable for everyone – a wide range of services will support a wide range of users • Performance – users have the possibility to use services with good performance and with high availability • Control Mechanism – users have the opportunity to control all interations of automatic system procedures
C_Mobility	• High Availability – Users need stable and reliable availability of their services • Broadband Resources – Stable and reliable high speed connections • Service Roaming – Session controlled by roaming services with high availability and comprehensible billing mechanism
D_Data Security	• Secured Access - Secured and personalised standard mechanism • Data Protection – User data and information must be protected • Preventive Data Security – Preventive mechanism to secure data and information
E_Compatibility	• Support Existing Environments – Integrate stamdard technologies to support existing environments • Automatic Controllable Mechanism – users must have the control if necessary • Infrastructure Reuse - Reuse of old operable environments and components

The focused codes listed above are based on codes developed by grouping and structuring data. After adding comments and notes, each interview was re-coded by using Colour Coding again. By going through the process of coding the interviews on paper, and noting the codes in the Fact Finding Tool, the codes and categories were re-defined and reaffirmed. Section 3.4.4 in Chapter Research Methodology provided an overview of the different coding phases.

4.5 Development of GT Categories Based on Focused Codes

This Section describes the development of the GT categories based on the focused codes generated in using selective coding in detail. Whilst conducting and analysing the interviews, it became apparent to the researcher that SDPs and ICT systems cannot be seen in isolation, but need to be placed within the wider technical and social context that the respondents were experiencing at the time. In addition, the study aimed at developing a substantive GT that interpreted and explained the subject area in a specific setting. In other words, to describe individuals' views of SDPs design aspects in relation to ICT systems of the future, within the context known to the participants of the study. In order to help to recognise the interviewees' micro and macro relationships, which may have shaped their perceptions of SDP challenges and design issues, a process with three stages was constructed (see described in Section 3.13, Table 7).

Coding data, using Colour Coding with a GT approach, was followed by a code reflection stage, in which connections between codes and the verification of codes were made. The last stage was to compare and validate the empirical data by the literature.

4.5.1   Category - Applicability

The final category *'Applicability'* is one of the results from the development of the final GT categories. It describes the ability of providing a wide range of services and applications on an SDP environment, which can be used by end-users using ICT systems to support their day-to-day lives. This category is a superior notation, which addresses the wide range and diversity of ICT services and applications that are provided for end-users on an SDP, in a contextually-aware manner, in order to support a broad range of possible end devices. Both sub-categories, *'Wide Field of Services'* and *'Context Awareness'*, support the main category *'Applicability'*, shown below in Figure 37:

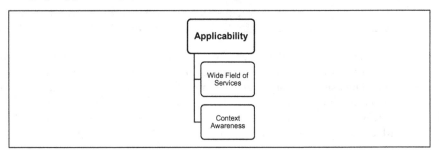

Figure 37:   Clustering of category "Applicability" with its sub-categories

The sub-category 'Wide Field of Services' addresses the potential services and service-categories provided on an SDP, to support users' daily needs, whilst the sub-category 'Context Awareness' addresses the flexibility of context provided in consideration of the wide range of user needs in different kinds of mobile environments. Each interview was initiated by inviting the participants to talk about possible fields of applications for SDPs, in terms of ICT systems in general. It quickly became apparent that the field of application is very broad, and according to the participants, that the potential of SDP platforms as a means of addressing challenges in the ICT mobile services is high.

The codes 'C_Field of Services' and 'B_Range of Services', and all their sub-codes summarised in Table 14 and Table 19, were applied to the followed Section, whereas p25_d, p27_ae and p32_ae describe the different application scenarios a potential end-user may encounter during a day:

p25_d: *"The possibilities of applications cover a broad range, but there are typical application scenarios which are the basis for defining application features, to address the challenges of ubiquity, with the help of an SDP, for example, Intelligent Portal: In this scenario, users are assisted by an 'intelligent portal' that proposes services adequate to the location, the context and the user preference. It mainly focuses on service roaming, seamless delivery, security and content adaptation (SPICE Project Deliverables 1.3, 2006). Another example would be emergency scenarios: elderly people and patients suffering from cardiovascular diseases use an innovative technology solution to monitor and process their critical biometric parameters, such as electrocardiogram, heartbeat, body temperature, blood pressure, physical activity, body position, etc. in real time, through a limited set of devices connected to their phone within a body area network (SPICE Project Deliverables 1.3, 2006).*

A third application could be E-Tourism: this scenario integrates the intelligent service enablers, user assistance and service creation, with different tourism scenarios (travel, event, at a hotel, going to the cinema), (SPICE Project Deliverables 1.3, 2006) [...]" (translated by the author).

In addition, the following three scenarios dealing with the requirement specifications of mixed-reality-driven add-on features were described by p27_ae: *"I want to describe three application scenarios, which have been fulfilling the requirements of SDP: Hiking Support: Users are supported by mixed reality services, in difficult situations, when they need essential support to find their hiking targets in the shortest and safest ways (e.g. in the event of poor weather conditions developing, etc.) and when using, a mobile, PDA or helmet set device with camera for showing the right way to the right position. This scenario includes device support, tracking, service roaming, and content displaying. E-Visiting: Many users are standing next to a physical advertising pillar, using only one device, a data glass. Different parts of the advertising pillar show different information content. Each user has to be authenticated, so as to customise the information on the data glass. Users have different personalised profiles, and can use this one data glass simultaneously. This scenario focuses mainly on profiling, user authentication, display, content and information adaptation, user assistance and inter-working. E-Windscreen: This scenario assists users when they are driving by their car and they drive through fog, for example. The driver can start a mixed-reality service application, which displays a sunny environment on the windscreen, and supports the driver in finding the way safely through the fog. The nearest hotels, food supermarkets and filling stations and the distance to them are also displayed. The E-Windscreen scenario refers to tracking, service roaming, seamless delivery, content display, inter-working, user profiling and authentication [...]"* (translated by the author).

At the same time, discussing applicable possibilities and linked challenges, p27_ae describes particular challenges related to an SDP in the context of an ICT system of the future solving the latest mobile challenges from a user's point of view:

P32_ae: *"I suppose the global vision of an SDP is to design, develop, evaluate, and prototype an extendable overlay architecture and framework that support the easy and quick service creation of intelligent and ambient-aware services, cooperation of multiple heterogeneous execution environments, and the seamless delivery of services across operator domains, networks and terminals. Moreover, it should provide ambient service enablers and explore issues of the seamless delivery of services at the service platform level. Furthermore, it has to facilitate easy and seamless access to electronic services and applications. Last but not least, it facilitates end-to-end communication, based on an open architecture, supporting fast service and content control and boosting end-user acceptance and confidence [...]"* (translated by the author).

Other interviewees' responses echoed some of the challenges described above. In summary, the respondents saw SDPs as being defined by the following approaches:

■ Platform-centric approach (SDP as a form of turntable between users and ICT services, independent of the networks or end devices used)

■ New service eco-system building (consisting of an ecological community and its ICT environment interacting as a system)

■ Open and controlled access to service providing capabilities (to support secured access, protected data and the personalisation of user access)

■ Multi-terminal and multi-access distributed communication sphere (to support end device and network autonomy)

The category *'Applicability'* was developed to capture the nature of these applicable scenarios. This category encapsulated the different codes relating to mobile applications scenarios. Different areas are relevant to the issue of *'Applicability'*. Participants' descriptions of *'Applicability'* varied, depending on the context, and became particularly evident when one of the interviewees talked about *'Applicability'* as being dependent on the different areas of a person's life. Following the constructive responses, the initial theoretical framework of SDPs, in terms of ICT systems, was developed and is depicted below in Table 21 below.

Table 21: Areas of "Applicability"

Category	Areas	Activities
Applicability	• Users (endusers, developers)	o communicate with family and friends o do commercial business o interact with government-related institutions o Setting to be controlled by the user
	• Operators	o inform customers and users o do commercial business o execute government-related procedures and regulations in a compliant way
	• End-Devices/Networks	o support all state of the art end-devices by using ICT standart technologies and interfaces
	• Features/Services	o application-related services, network-related services, location based services, etc.
	• ICT systems	o connect different types of ICT systems and components o support convergence (IT and mobile world)

The category *'Applicability'* has different areas, and these were presented to the participants in subsequent interviews, in order to obtain their comments (see for example Appendix B, interview p11_u in Section 10.1):

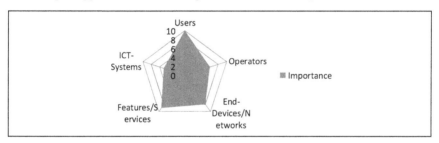

Figure 38: Different areas of "Applicability" and their scale according to participants' perceptions

These different scales of *'Applicability'* show the most important factors for those participants, using SDPs, and the services provided by them. This is followed by the connectivity possibilities of end devices and networks. The different areas of *'Applicability'* and their varying levels of importance inspired the researcher to write the following memo about *'Applicability'* with which to discuss the relationship between the named category and user needs, in terms of SDP:

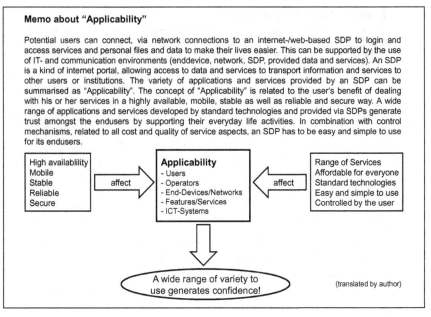

Memo about "Applicability"

Potential users can connect, via network connections to an internet-/web-based SDP to login and access services and personal files and data to make their lives easier. This can be supported by the use of IT- and communication environments (enddevice, network, SDP, provided data and services). An SDP is a kind of internet portal, allowing access to data and services to transport information and services to other users or institutions. The variety of applications and services provided by an SDP can be summarised as "Applicability". The concept of "Applicability" is related to the user's benefit of dealing with his or her services in a highly available, mobile, stable as well as reliable and secure way. A wide range of applications and services developed by standard technologies and provided via SDPs generate trust amongst the endusers by supporting their everyday life activities. In combination with control mechanisms, related to all cost and quality of service aspects, an SDP has to be easy and simple to use for its endusers.

Memo 1: Visual memo on the relationship between "Applicability" and users' needs, in terms of using an SDP

The SDP has the ability to generate confidence in its users. This was seen by some respondents as a good reason for creating a platform to support confidence-building activities amongst those who use ICT environments as a part of their daily lives.

The validation of the empirical data was achieved using the mapping process, by structuring literature-related aspects to *'Applicability'*, followed by a comparison of mapped literature-based data and the empirical data, as well as the categories, sub-categories and codes the researcher developed during this stage. In the following part, the mind maps displayed in Section 4.1 - Findings from the literature-based study, helped to compare and validate the empirical data (codes, categories and sub-categories) regarding the category "Applicability", based on the procedures shown in Sections 3.10.4 - Application of the Literature-Based Study and 4.5.7 - Justification of the Categories.

The participants' use of SDPs support their daily activities, in terms of them being more comfortable and independent of the location they want to work or spend their leisure time. The fact that this kind of an SDP environment has to offer the user a wide range of services and handle data and information in a broad way is very important to generate user confidence. In response to questions about performance, security and availability, participants raised the very important point, that generating confidence could help to bring about a greater level of acceptance of an SDP as a standardised platform in ICT environments.

Another important point was related to how those environments and activities, with direct influences on the costs incurred by users, could be controlled by the user, through the SDP, as single control instance. This point is discussed further in Section 4.5.2.

4.5.2 Category - Controllability

The final category *'Controllability'* is also the result of the development of the final GT categories. This category describes the control of SDP costs, and related systems and applications, from a user perspective, in terms of enabling end-users to enjoy good quality services whilst maintaining awareness and control of the associated costs. The three sub-categories of *'Controllability'* are *'Cost Awareness and Control'*, *'User Controls SDP'*, and *'Application and Service Control'*, as illustrated below in Figure 39:

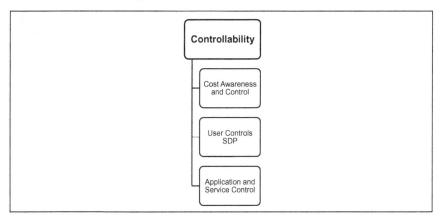

Figure 39: Clustering of category "Controllability" with its sub-categories

The identified category *'Controllability'* includes three sub-categories; *'Cost Awareness and Control'*, which helps to address the necessary cost issues from a user's point of view; *'User Controls SDP'*, which supports the idea that users need to maintain control of all SDP activities, and; *'Application and Service Control'*, which addresses the potential mechanisms for controlling services and applications.

In the interviews, participants discussed the importance of end-user control of different processes. It became apparent that the control procedures of SDP-related activities have to be controlled by end-users. Most of the codes and sub-codes summarised in Table 14 and Table 19 were applied to the following Sections, where p11_u, p14_d, p22_u, p26_d, and p31_u describe different scenarios, in terms of the control of SDP related activities from a user perspective:

p14_d: *"I believe that the concept of an SDP can increasingly improve the situation regarding offering users convergent services, whereby users need only operate by one device. What is important here is the fact that the user needs to have the control over the services used and their availability, and to be able to influence, directly and indirectly, the network bandwidth, quality of service and the costs of the services they use. To gain the acceptance of such a concept with a broad range of users it is necessary to implement control mechanisms, by which these issues can be addressed [...]"* (translated by the author).

Respondent p11_u mentioned that SDPs have to be affordable for everyone. *"More and more users will adopt SDP as a web-based ICT control and administration tool, if this becomes an affordable option for a broad range of users in society. The costs are the most important driver here. Additionally, users have to take over the control of services, network possibilities and service quality, because these drivers influence the level of costs [...]"* (translated by the author).

The aspect of secured access control was very important for participant p26_d: *"It has to be certain that access to the SDP account fulfils the requirements of secure and reliable access, with minimum 2-factor authentication process, because the end-user has the opportunity to store private data on the SDP as well. As such, data protection mechanisms must fulfil the state-of-the-art requirements of a web-based portal application with a 2-factor authentication procedure and data encryption mechanisms [...]"* (translated by the author).

p31_u: *"In my opinion the user has to assume full control responsibility, in terms of being able to influence the contracted costs, for instance service roaming outside the home domain environment. In this case the user must gain direct influence in selecting the desired network he or she wants, as well as the level of service quality, because this can have an impact on the costs he or she is willing to pay [...]"* (translated by the author).

Capturing the issues described by the different respondents above, it is clear that different areas are relevant to the developed category *'Controllability'*. Participants' description of this category varied, depending on the context, and became particularly evident when one of the interviewees talked about the concept of *'Controllability'* as varying depending on the different areas of control, as described in Table 22 below.

Table 22: Areas of "Controllability"

Category	Areas	Activities
Controllability	• End-user control	o service interaction - control acceptence has to be established by the end-user
	• Automatic control mechanisms/procedures	o control service selected and executed o control bandwidth used o control QoS selected o control own account o control application with wide range of end-devices o control costs
	• Controlled access to user information	o account access protection o data protection o secured and reliable access o web-based service control

This category encapsulated the different codes relating to control possibilities from a user perspective. These areas are relevant to the category *'Controllability'*. Following Strauss and Corbin's (1998) advice, properties and dimensions were developed for some of the tentative categories, to map their characteristics and to explore their meanings. Dimensions can be used to recognise variations of the final category. Table 23 below provides an illustration of the properties and dimensions of the category *'Controllability'*:

Table 23: Category "Controllability" and its properties and dimensions

Category	Properties	Dimensions
Controllability	• Service control settings	o QoS low o QoS middle o QoS high
	• Bandwidth control settings	o 1G guaranteed data rates o 2G guaranteed data rates o 3G guaranteed data rates o 4G guaranteed data rates
	• Account control settings	o low secured o middle secured o high secured
	• Cost control settings	o costs adequat to the actual contract o higer costs for higher QoS (user interaction)

The following memo helped to reflect on the category "Controllability" and its meaning:

Memo about "Controllability" (after Strauss and Corbin, 1988)   (translated by author)

Users want to control their activities related to their data, because these have an impact and influence on their personal commercial costs. SDPs have become part of modern communication platforms to provide the exchange of data and information from users in their everyday lives (in working and also leisure time activities). For this reason certain procedures have to be developed to give endusers control over end-devices, services, applications, networks and own accounts. Most users are willing to use a communication platform, such as an SDP when they have more control over the cost aspect. As one of the respondents describes:

p33_ae: "*I believe that the users of an SDP are in a discrepancy situation, because on the one hand they recognise that such platformas and cloud-based web technology will help to arrange some things more easily more in the future, but on the other hand they are afraid of losing control over the mechanism that influences their own costs, and they could lose money, because they oversee the use of a qualitatively higher service that costs more ...*".

Strauss and Corbin (1998) advocate the use of so-called relational statements to explore phenomenons:

A. **When** some users are bored, if they dont have direct influence to decisions they affect their own costs, an SDP won't build confidence by this group of users and won't be accepted (see p23_d). It enables the „normal" user (a user who isn't a „trekki") to influence on the own costs structure by thinking about the quality of a service or a network (direct related to the cost structure).

B. Using an SDP without deep technical know how brings users in the situation to **interact** with others on different communication channels and quality levels, because in this case they can direct influence their costs and they don't waste their money.

C. As a **consequence** automatic mechanisms, to interact with users (all level of users: normal users and power users), have to be implemented to interact with them (i.e. if there is a service available with a better data exchange rate and SLA; if a network with more bandwidth is available)

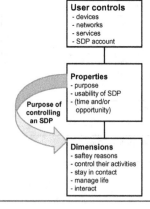

Memo 2: Memo about "Controllability" and its properties and dimensions

Memo 2 illustrates the category *'Controllability'*, its properties and dimensions. An SDP is seen as a multi-purpose communication platform that can be used, to structure a personalised service group for example, access different services, or simply to manage personal data and information. This seems to be more pertinent to the power-user generation, who have the knowledge, or to those who travel on a regular basis, and are thus without permanent Internet access.

The method of breaking down a category into its properties and dimensions, as advocated by Strauss and Corbin (1988), proved to be of limited use for the analysis. For some categories it was possible to devise a number of suitable properties. However, the researcher decided that, for most of the categories, it did not make sense to assign properties and dimensions, as this forced the qualitative data into a rigid framework without adding much value to the interpretation of data and analysis. Instead Charmaz' (2006) approach was adopted, which employs a less restrictive way of making comparisons between data. This was also achieved through the mapping process, comparing empirical and literature-based data, as previously stated and shown both in Sections 3.3.2 and 3.3.4.

The following Section, 4.5.3 – Category *'Interoperability'*, discusses the development of the compatibility aspects of an SDP to other related environments.

4.5.3 Category - Interoperability

The identified category *'Interoperability'* describes the compatibility of SDPs in relation to other environments, systems and technologies from a user perspective. Compatibility is the most important aspect of interoperable environments. This refers to how end-users' capabilities should not suffer when using additional platforms such as SDPs to support their daily lives. The four sub-categories, *'Compatibility to ICT-Systems, -Interfaces, and –Components'*, *'Compatibility to ICT-Standards'*, *'Infrastructure Reusability'* and *'Cost Effectiveness'* support the main category, as illustrated below in Figure 40.

The category *'Interoperability'* represents four sub-categories. The first sub-category, *'Compatibility to ICT-Systems, -Interfaces, and –Components'*, addresses the use of standard ICT environments in providing a wide range of applications for SDPs to provide the administrative and control functions of those environments.

The second sub-category *'Compatibility to ICT Standards'*, describes aspects of standardisation from a technological point of view, for instance, the fact that the technologies IMS, SIP, IP, SSL, UMTS and LTE are necessary standard technologies in order for SDP to be flexible enough to address a wide range of services by a broad range of users. The third sub-category, *'Infrastructure Usability'* describes a very important point for the compatibility of existing environments, given the vast amount of money invested in the last 10-15 years by network, service and application operators, on technological upgrades. In that case existing environments have to be considered, because it costs too much for completely new environments to be installed. The fourth sub-category *'Cost Effectiveness'* is the driver for compatibility and a sub-category of *'Interoperability'*, as all previously identified issues have been directly influenced by the issue of cost.

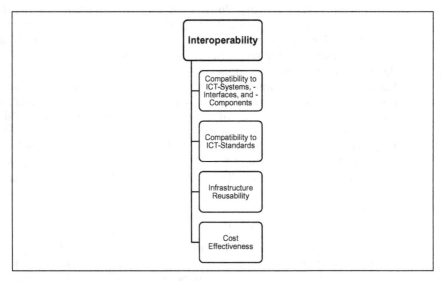

Figure 40: Clustering of the category "Interoperability" with its sub-categories

In all interviews, the participants were asked about compatibility aspects and their connection to other systems and users. It became apparent that the aspect of compatibility was very important and was seen as one of the key challenges in using SDPs in ICT environments, as a control system and communication tool. The codes 'E_Compatibility' and 'E_Infrastructure Compatibility', and all their sub-codes, summarised in Table 14 and Table 19, were applied to the following paragraphs, where p14_d, p22_u, p26_d and p34_d describe different aspects of compatibility in relation to other systems and technologies:

An SDP has the ability to act as a control system between users and the ICT environment. Of particular importance is the capability to enlarge and connect existing IT- and also CT- environments. p14_d: *"You know one of the reasons why I would like to engage SDP as a control and administration tool for ICT systems is that SDP is based on web 2.0 technologies and supports IT- as well as mobile communication standards. For example, the technologies IMS and SIP were part of the SPICE architecture. This could help us to find a common way of supporting the ongoing development of ICT technologies and the ICT standards behind this. Standard technologies are important in meeting the goal of linking existing and new systems quickly and easily [...]"* (translated by the author). Participants p26_d and p34_d had the feeling that standard technologies could help to drive SDP development, and acceptance amongst the users: p26_d: *"I believe that the wide range of heterogeneous IT systems will follow the rapid standardisation of mobile communication development over the last 10 years.*

For example, 10 years ago the development of WAP helped to achieve the first steps regarding end device-independent application execution. In terms of the fusion of IT and mobile environments, I think that the compatibility aspect of systems and technical standardisation is a very important point here, and it will come [...]" (translated by the author). The other respondent (p34_d) had the feeling that the upward and downward compatibility of systems would become increasingly important for the ICT industry. In this case, interoperable networks, devices, and certainly also application and services have to fulfil ICT standards, whilst meeting certain rules and requirements.

p22_u: *"Today's systems and software have to meet the standards of inter-operability. This is because the IT world and the mobile networks world are merging more and more. For example, 10 years ago we worked with a mobile and a PDA separately, to make phone calls and organise working appointments in outlook. In today's smart phones you can carry out both activities with one and the same device [...]"* (translated by the author). The category *'Interoperability'* was developed to encompass the issue of compatible scenarios. This category encapsulated the different codes relating to the scenarios of compatibility. The participants' descriptions of this category varied depending on the context, and became particularly evident when one of the interviewees talked about *'Interoperability'* as being dependent on different areas of existing environments. Following the constructive responses and the interview procedure, the researcher selected the theoretical framework of an SDP in terms of ICT systems. The following illustrations Table 24 shows different areas of "Interoperability".

The different areas of *'Interoperability'* show that the compatibility of SDP with other environments is an important factor from the participants' perspective. The compatibility of heterogeneous environments, software applications and services must fulfil a certain set of rules and requirements. These are environment specific and have to be defined and specified on a case-by-case basis. The most important factors are upward and downward compatibility with existing environments.

Table 24: Areas of "Interoperability"

Category	Areas	Activities

Interoperability	• Heterogeneous Environments
	  - systems
	  - interfaces
	  - organisations
	  - technologies
		o follow standard technologies
		o follow rules (compliance, risk, finance, government)
		o meet ICT standard requirements
		o meet requirements from older systems
		o meet basic requirements from new systems

	• Software
	  - programs
	  - data format
		o follow standard technologies
		o data format mapping
		o follow a common data format
		o meet requirements from older software
		o meet basic requirements from new software

	• Services
	  - communication services
	  - location base services
	  - network services
	  - data transport services
	  - application services
		o follow standard technologies
		o follow standard data exchange and communication formats
		o fulfill requirements of convergent service (ICT)
		o meet requirements from older developed services
		o meet basic requirements from newly developed services

The different areas of this category, and their importance factor, inspired the researcher to write the following memo about *'Interoperability'* in order to discuss the relationship between compatible environments and the user himself/herself:

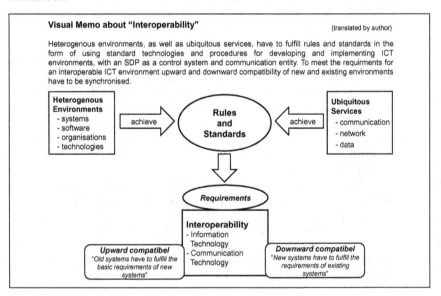

Memo 3: Visual memo on the relationship between compatible environments and users, in terms of using an SDP

The interoperability aspect of an SDP focuses on the ability to control new and existing ICT environments and generates trust in such environments from both operators and users, which was seen by some respondents as a positive factor. The validation of the empirical data was done using the mapping process, in terms of structuring literature-related aspects to "Interoperability", followed by a comparison of mapped literature-based data and empirical data, as well as the categories, sub-categories and codes the researcher developed during this stage. In the following, the mind maps displayed in Section 4.1 - Findings from the Literature-based Study as a result of the mapping process, helped to compare and validate the empirical data (codes, categories and sub-categories), with regard to the category "Interoperability", based on the procedures shown in the Section 3.10.4 - Application of the Literature-Based Study and Section 4.5.7 - Justification of the Categories.

The participants' use of an SDP supports their daily activities, in terms of allowing them to be more independent in the way they want to work or spend their leisure time. To offer the potential user an ICT platform environment, with a wide range of services, in a broad way, and to give the user possibilities to control which activities they engage in from a cost management perspective, there has to be the possibility to enlarge and expand existing environments and fulfil compatibility requirements, whilst encouraging operators up to push this new technology. In the following Section 4.5.4, the aspect of being mobile at all times is developed and discussed.

4.5.4 Category - Mobility

The developed category "Mobility" describes the possibility of being "always on". Users want to be online anytime and anyplace. One of the benefits that an SDP brings, from the participants' point of view, is that they can be online on any network and any device. From the user's perspective this is a very important aspect for an SDP in supporting their daily lives. The four supporting sub-categories are 'Availability', 'Stability and Session Control', 'Always on', and 'Any Network on any Device', as illustrated in Figure 41.

The sub-category 'Availability', addresses the proportion of time a system, or an ICT service, is in a functioning condition, while the user is on the move. The sub-category 'Stability and Session Control' describes the user's need to have a stable and session-controlled connection while he or she is on the move. The session control aspect addresses the service- and application-related functioning condition whilst the user is on the move. From the respondents' point of view, the sub-category 'Always On' describes the possibility of a service to be used continuously, online, and without interruptions.

The sub-category 'Any Network on Any Device' supports the other sub-categories to the extent that mechanisms have to be available to control services and applications over all available networks and at any device during the move from point A to B.

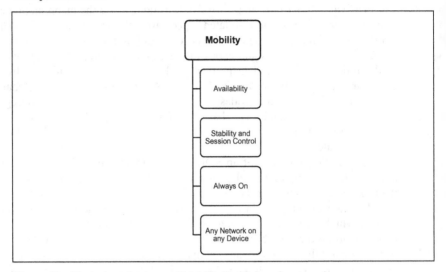

Figure 41: Clustering of category "Mobility" with its sub-categories

Three interactive coding and reflection stages (shown in Table 7) were necessary to develop the initial and focused codes. Based on these codes and the relationship between them, the category "Mobility" was generated. A verification of the codes was achieved by having a third party researcher intercode the empirical interview data, and by using previously written memos to establish links between codes and tentative categories, as carried out in the previous phases. Moreover, further categories were identified, which were further validated, by again using the Mapping Process.

During the interviews a few participants talked about the topic of ubiquitous services needing the capability to be online - and stay online - at all times. This brought up similar aspects regarding available services and infrastructure requirements. It became apparent that such mechanisms are a must in terms of an SDP, as the control system and communication instance for ICT environments, serves to maintain control over network bandwidth, service and application sessions and facilitates stable and reliable internet access even during periods of mobility. Most of the codes summarised in Table 14 and Table 19 were applied to the following paragraph, where p23_d, p32_ae, p33_ae describe different scenarios regarding mobility in SDP-related activities:

Individuals' descriptions of mobility varied, depending on the context. The perception of mobility became particularly evident when one of the interviewees talked about moving to different scales, with each scale having an impact on different areas of the availability of a ubiquitous service, as p23_d described:

"I personally believe that one of the most challenging aspects of today's ICT environments is always being on and mobile, because nowadays it doesn't matter if you are in your house, flat or at your desk at work. If you want to be competitive, then you must be reachable at all times for work, and if you want to fulfil an increasing number of daily activities you have to be available for your family and friends at all times. This has an impact on how we are supported by our ICT environments anytime and anyplace with stable and reliable applications. This is very challenging for the ICT environment, because a change in motion has to be controlled all the time by a network as well as by a service or application operator [...]" (translated by the author).

p32_ae: *"When a user is changing his or her location, four relevant aspects of the movement regarding mobility need to be addressed and controlled by the environment: 1. velocity, 2. acceleration, 3. displacement of movement from A to B, and 4. length of time of the motion. During this effect a connection to the user closed network during the movement as well as an existing and stable application or service session has to be controlled in a reliable way. The technological conditions for this exist today, by using IMS and SIP as convergent technologies. Developers and commercial companies have to make sure that such standardisation takes place [...]"* (translated by the author)

p33_ae's depiction of the aspects of motion, and the aspect of service roaming, summarises other interviewees' description of mobility. Most respondents distinguish the following definition of mobility, as a change in a position: *"Motion is a change in a position and is important for today's systems if they want to fulfil the requirements of a mobile convergent ICT system. If, for example, a person with a Smartphone is moving from point A to point B, there are several characteristics: time of a position change, displacement of a position change, velocity and acceleration in regard to the position change, which need to be addressed by controlled and stable connections. Broadband network implementation is concentrated in highly populated areas. The bottleneck is here, because network operators don't want to invest in countryside areas where they can't earn enough money to cover their investment costs [...]"*. *"Service Roaming is a very important aspect for an SDP. It has to control operator roaming mechanisms in terms of services, because it has to make sure that a potential user can also use services outside of the home domain [...]"* (translated by the author).

The following memo helped to reflect on the category "Mobility" and its meaning:

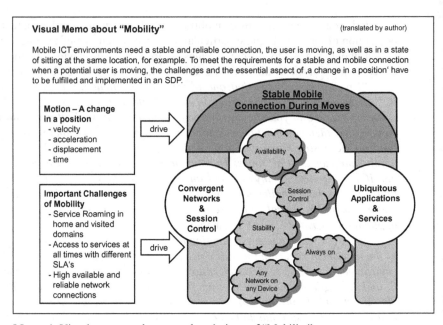

Visual Memo about "Mobility"   (translated by author)

Mobile ICT environments need a stable and reliable connection, the user is moving, as well as in a state of sitting at the same location, for example. To meet the requirements for a stable and mobile connection when a potential user is moving, the challenges and the essential aspect of „a change in a position' have to be fulfilled and implemented in an SDP.

Memo 4: Visual memo on the respondents' views of "Mobility"

The mobility aspect of an SDP is essential for a stable mobile connection between users, using their applications and services and networks. Some respondents saw this as a critical and important factor of an SDP, offering users a stable and reliable connection and controlling the network bandwidth and network availability, as well as the application and service sessions.

The validation of the empirical data was done using the mapping process, by structuring and mapping the literature-related aspects to "Mobility", and subsequently comparing them to the empirical data, as well as the categories, subcategories and codes the researcher developed during this stage. In the following, the mind-maps displayed in Section 4.1 - Findings from the Literature-Based Study from the mapping process, help to compare and validate the empirical data (codes, categories and sub-categories) with regard to the category "Mobility", based on the procedures shown in the Sections 3.10.4 - Application of the Literature-Based Study and 4.5.7 - Justification of the Categories.

The participants' views of the category "Mobility", were critical and can be seen as the most important aspect of all the challenges that exist in terms of SDPs for a standardised control system for ICT environments. The point is that mobility is essential for the 'always on' and the 'any network on any device' scenario. The respondents believed that both aspects will drive the progress of SDPs in ICT environments, but there are two critical arguments stemming from a technical and cost perspective. From the technical side, it has to be ensured by the network operators that an area-wide coverage of networks is possible and financially feasible for network operators, without resulting in high costs for the end consumers (end-users). The second aspect is one of cost. If operators have to invest more money in order to enlarge their basic infrastructure and to cover wider areas, they should not increase their costs, as users are unwilling to pay more to finance the operators' network infrastructures.

In the next Section 4.5.5 the aspect of security and reliability will be developed and discussed.

4.5.5 Category - Security and Reliability

The category "Security and Reliability" describes the security aspect of SDPs and related systems, to protect users' accounts and data from unauthorised access. The sub-categories 'Account and Data Protection', 'Data Security', and 'Authentication and Personalisation' support the main category "Security and Reliability", as shown in the following illustration Figure 42.

"Security and Reliability" dedicates the three sub-categories 'Account and Data Protection', which address the need for mechanisms to secure and protect data and access to user accounts. The sub-category 'Data Security' shows, that the SDP is also a form of storage for information and data. These data have to be secured and protected by appropriate mechanisms. From the respondents' point view, the sub-category 'Authentication and Personalisation' addresses the ability of users to gain access and personalise their user account and access their data.

Based on the codes shown in Table 7, the initial and focused codes for the category, "Security and Reliability" were developed, and a verification of these codes was achieved by intercoding of the empirical interview data by a third party researcher once again, and memos established links between codes and tentative categories as carried out in previous phases.

In the interviews, participants discussed the issue of SDP access and the need for a high level of protection of stored data. This brought up similar aspects regarding authentication mechanisms and data protection requirements. It became apparent that mechanisms to protect an SDP have to be implemented, in terms of building confidence, fulfilling compliance requirements, and data protection rules.

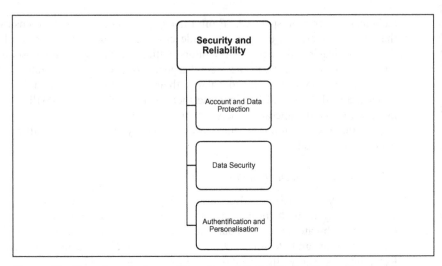

Figure 42: Clustering of category "Security and Reliability" with its sub-categories

Most of the codes summarised in Table 14 and Table 19 were applied to the following paragraphs, where p13_u, p22_u, p27_ae, and p34_d described aspects in terms of secure SDPs, to offer the users a reliable and protected platform from a SPICE users' perspective:

Participants' descriptions of "Security and Reliability" became particularly evident when three interviewees talked about service access control and trust management, each aspect having an impact on different areas of security, as described by p27_ae: *"The access control of services is an important issue as part of an SDP's implementation. I believe that one of the challenges here is to implement policy-based access control methods and a corresponding management control system. In terms of an implemented identity and privacy management system it could be assured that secure mediation functions are available to share information between stakeholders, i.e. user group accounts [...]"* (translated by the author).

The aspect of controlling secured access was very important for participant p34_d (it was also mentioned by p26_d before, see Section 4.5.2): *"It has to be certain, that access to the SDP account fulfils the requirements of secure and reliable access, with minimum 2-factor authentication process, because the end-user has the opportunity to store private data on the SDP as well. As such, data protection mechanisms must fulfil the state-of-the-art requirements of a web-based portal application with a 2-factor authentication procedure and data encryption mechanisms [...]"*.

p13_u: *"In terms of my data stored on an SDP, I prefer it being encrypted automatically. Furthermore, I think it could also help to standardise better account control with a pin and a password, for example [...]"* (translated by the author). p22_u: *"Reliable secured access is a must for an SDP user account. I think standard security algorithms must be implemented with the decision to go on webbased architecture. In terms of cloud solutions, the question of where the physical data is stored is also an important issue [...]"* (translated by the author).

Reflecting the phenomenon participants' descriptions of this category "Security and Reliability" varied, depending on the context, and became particularly evident when one of the interviewees talked about it as being related to different areas of controls, as illustrated in Table 25 below.

Table 25: Areas of "Security and Reliability"

Category	Areas	Activities
Security and Reliability	• Application Security	o set application policies o monitor development, deployment, upgrading and maintenance of an application o control the use of sources granted to application
	• Information Security	o protect information and information systems from unauthorized access, use, disclosure, disruption, modification, perusal, inspection, recording or destruction
	• Data Security	o backup and recovery data o encrypt disks and harddisk drives o protect data using hardware mechanisms (i.e. token, fingerprint reader, smartcards)
	• Network Security	o administrate network policies to prevent and check unauthorised access o Check access from and to other computer networks

This category encapsulated the different codes relating to control possibilities, from a user's perspective. These areas are relevant to the category "Security and Reliability".

Following Strauss and Corbin's (1998) advice once again, properties and dimensions were developed for some of the tentative categories in order to map characteristics and to explore their meanings. Dimensions can be used to recognise variations of the category and of the final category. The following, Table 26, provides an illustration of the properties and dimensions of the category "Security and Reliability":

Table 26: Category "Security and Reliability", and its properties and dimensions

Category	Properties	Dimensions
Security and Reliability	• Application settings	o low o middle o high
	• Data settings	o low o middle o high
	• Information settings	o low o middle o high
	• Mobile settings	o low bandwidth o middle bandwidth o high bandwidth
	• Network settings	o low o middle o high

The following memo (see Memo 5) facilitated reflection on the category "Security and Reliability" and its meaning. Memo 5 illustrates the category "Security and Reliability", and shows its properties and dimensions. An SDP is seen as a form of communication platform and can be used for various purposes, for example to structure individually personalised service groups using different services or only allowing access to personal stored data and information. In this case the user must experience the SDP as a reliable tool with secured activities, to protect accounts and data.

Memo about "Security and Relilability" (after Strauss and Corbin, 1988)

Users want to have their accounts and data secured when using an SDP, and store their services and data there. For this reason standard security has to be implemented, as well as additional procedures, to give the enduser the feeling that his or her data and information are safe. Most users are willing to use a communication platform such as an SDP when they have the feeling that their data is highly protected and secured, as one of the respondents described:

p22_u: *"Reliable secured access is a must for an SDP user account. I think standard security algorithms must be implemented with the decision to develop on web-based architecture. This decision included the consequence that the security mechanisms are selected with the selection of the architecture. In terms of cloud solutions, the question of where the physical data is stored is also an important issue. ..."*.

Strauss and Corbin (1998) advocate the use of so-called relational statements to explore phenomenon:

A. **When** some users are bored if they dont have direct influence over decisions which affect their secured data, an SDP won't gain trust amongst this group of users, neither will it be accepted (see p22_u).

B. Using an SDP without security activities puts users in the situation of **thinking about other ways (act)** to work and store their data, because otherwise they are afraid about their accounts and data.

C. As a **consequence** standard mechanisms to secure accounts and data have to be implemented as a minimum to enlarge the amount of users in using SDPs. (translated by the author)

Memo 5: Memo about "Security and Reliability" and the properties and dimensions

4.5.6 Category - Usability

The final category "Usability" is one of the results from the development of the final GT categories. It describes the ease of use and learnability of a human-made object to support end-users' daily lives and help to build user confidence. The three sub-categories 'User Acceptance', 'User Friendliness' and 'Simple and Easy to Use' support the main category"Usability", as shown in the illustration Figure 43: Clustering of category "Usability" with its sub-categories. The developed sub-category 'User Acceptance' addresses the aspect of accepting an SDP as a tool to work with the user's end devices, in daily life.

Very close to this aspect, the sub-category 'User Friendliness' describes the need for an effective and efficient way of working from the user perspective, and the sub-category 'Simple and easy to use' is one of the most important drivers for "Usability", because without an easy and simple look and feel to the user interface, it is not possible to generate trust and confidence amongst SDP users. This aspect is one of the most important challenges for the engagement of as many users as possible and for motivating them to use an SDP. It is necessary that the system be quick and effective, and provides easy communication and data operation in order to sufficiently fulfil the needs of users' daily lives.

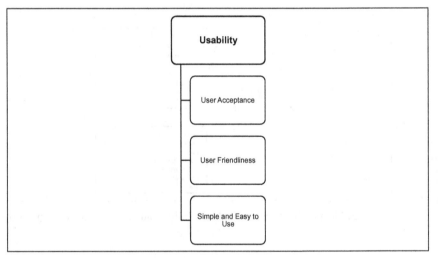

Figure 43: Clustering of category "Usability" with its sub-categories

Three interactive coding phases (shown in Table 7) as well as the three code reflection stages, brought about the initial and focused codes, which helped to develop the category "Usability". Based on the developed initial and focused codes, a verification of these codes was undertaken by intercoding the empirical interview data by another researcher, and facilitated memos to establish links between codes and tentative categories. Furthermore, initial categories and, in the phases two and three, further developed categories, were evolved. Moreover, to ensure that these made sense, in terms of a justification, the mapping process stages one to three helped to compare and validate codes and categories.

In the interviews the respondents were asked about aspects of using and interacting with a web-based communication and control portal, such as an SDP, for the purpose of communicating in their daily lives. It became apparent that the aspects of the look and feel of an SDP, effective communication, friendly to use, etc. were very important, and were seen as key factors in using SDPs in ICT environments as a control and communication tool. The codes 'A1_Handling', 'A2_Types of End devices', 'A6_Simple', 'A6_User Control' and 'A5_User Acceptance' and all their sub-codes, summarised in Table 14 and Table 19, were applied to the following paragraphs, where the participants p11_u, p13_u, p22_u, p24_u and p31_u described different aspects of usability.

SDPs can be used as a communication and control system for different types of ICT environments. To address a wide number of potential users, it is necessary that such a system has to be easy to use, understandable, very quick, and able to be administrated very simply by a wide range of users who are not experts in ICT. p11_u: *"I believe that a communication concept, with an SDP as communication and control system for ICT systems, can only be implemented if a broad range of users can be addressed and engaged. Standard technologies and systems are used to meet the aims of fulfilling the complex requirements for quick and easy implementation. On the other hand it isn't only technology that we can use to make our daily lives easier. It's also a question how we can create effective procedures; it's very important to motivate the end-users to change their daily procedures and address it also to people who don't want to use technology to support their daily activities. I think it's a question of clearly seeing the benefit for me as a user, of the willingness for users themselves to change and of operators establishing user confidence. Only then can users recognise SDP as a powerful and sustainable tool for supporting their everyday lives [...]"* (translated by the author).

Participant p22_u had the feeling that a broad use could help to make this concept and technology affordable for everyone. p22_u: *"Technology is in today's daily life. The interesting question is how we can provide technology and especially SDP technology in order to help our lives to be easier. For me it's a question of addressing a wide range of the population, as was done with the Internet in 1995. I think such platforms can help to make lives easier for everyone, if the operators act very carefully. If they invest in their infrastructures and find a way to offer a wide range of services on SDPs, which are easy and simple for everyone to use, they can influence this technology becoming the next 'speed-*

up', and they can also make lots of money by doing so. But they have to be very easy to handle and cheap systems [...]" (translated by the author).

p13_u and p24_u addressed the aspect of being user friendly and supporting as many standard end devices as are currently on the market: p13_u: *"In my opinion the aspect of end device independence is very important. I would like to use applications and services with any of my end devices. That means services have to support laptops, workstations, notebooks, tablets, Smartphone and mobile phones as well as PDAs or palmtops. This is a challenge for the operators, because a service must be developed in such a way that it renders and delivers contents for a huge amount of end devices, with different display sizes, and delivers the right content to the right device types (context awareness) ...".* p24_u: *"I think it's necessary that many end devices will be provided with the right context size for text, multimedia contents and graphics, by using the same application or service. This could be a great value-addition for end-users [...]"* (translated by the author).

p31_u described different aspects of usability: *"The issue of being able to use a complex environment in a simple way will be supported by the concept of an SDP as a control tool for ICT systems and components. The user doesn't want to take different web-based portals for using different services, because of different authentication procedures and different ways of working within the portals, or different ways of storing and using data. Users increasingly want to have one control, administration and working tool or environment to control and work, with a broad range of services for supporting daily work or leisure time activities. Furthermore, if operators would like to address a broad range of users, the many devices in the field have to be supported by using an SDP. Moreover, important decisions such as which network will be used, have to be controlled by the user themself, because this influences their costs. Additionally, the easier the procedure is to use, the more powerfully an SDP can establish the market. The best example for me is Apple with its own concept. Easy and simple way of use is one of the success factors and the reason why Apple has been penetrating the market over the last years [...]"* (translated by the author).

To capture the phenomenon of many applicable scenarios, the category "Usability" was developed, and encapsulated the different codes relating to usability scenarios and aspects. The different areas relevant to this core category were described by participants' views of "Usability". Following the constructive responses the theoretical framework of SDPs, in terms of ICT systems, were developed, and are depicted in the following illustration Table 27:

Table 27: Areas of "Usability"

Category	Areas	Activities
Usability	• Software Application or Service	o requirement analysis o user interacts with application or service o decisions to involve the user
	• SDP (website, portal) as a tool	o requirement analysis o user interacts with application or service o decisions to involve the user
	• Process of using SDP	o control application and services o control data and information o control settings
	• End-Device and SDP	o end-device support of SDP o context aware information o dynamic contents depend on display sizes

The category "Usability" has different areas, and these were presented to participants in subsequent interviews in order to obtain their viewpoints (see for example Appendix B, interview p11_u in Section 10.1).

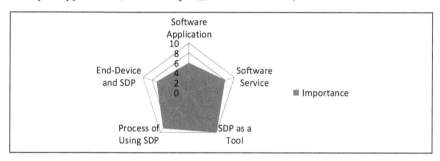

Figure 44: Different areas of "Usability" and the scale of importance according to participants' perceptions

These different scales of "Usability" show that the use of SDPs as tools, and the process of using SDPs are the most important factors for the participants, followed by the handling of software services as a response to their comments. The different areas of "Usability" and their importance factors inspired the researcher to write the following memo about "Usability" in order to discuss the relationship between this category and related environments.

The SDP has the ability to generate user confidence, to be acceptable and affordable for everyone. This is seen as a positive factor by some respondents in creating a platform to support confidence-building activities, amongst those who rely on ICT environments to assist them in their daily lives.

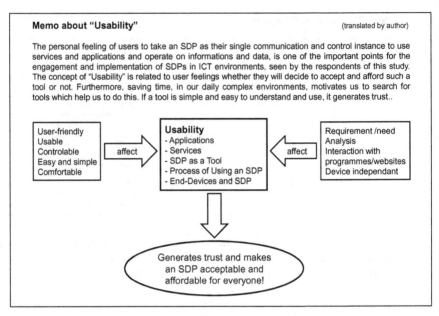

Memo 6: Visual memo on the relationship between "Usability" and its related environments

The validation of the empirical data was achieved using the mapping process, by structuring and mapping literature-related aspects to "Usability" and subsequently comparing them to empirical data, as well as the categories, subcategories and codes the researcher developed at this stage.

The participants' use of an SDP supports their daily activities, in terms of them being more comfortable and independent of the location at which they want to work or spend their leisure time. Such ICT platform environments have to be able to offer the user a wide range of services, in a broad way, in order to generate confidence amongst users.

The next Section illustrates the justification of the GT categories.

4.5.7 Justification of the Categories

The three interactive coding phases (shown in Table 7), and the three code reflection stages, led the researcher to the initial and focused codes, which facilitated in developing each of the categories. Based on these codes, attempts were made to verify the coding, through the intercoding of empirical interview data by a third party researcher, and through using the memos to establish links between codes and tentative categories. Furthermore, initial categories and - in phases two and three - further categories were developed. Moreover, to ensure that these results could be justified, the mapping process in stages one to three facilitated comparison and validation of the codes and categories.

The following table shows a detailed validation and classification of the categories that were developed from the interview- and literature-based data:

Table 28: Detailed validation and classification of categories developed from interview- and literature-based data[5]

Models	Categories developed from the Interview-based Data	Categories developed from the Literature-based Data
Challenges and Design Aspects for Service-Delivery-Platforms	• Applicability • Controllability • Interoperability • Mobility • Security and Reliability • Usability	• High Mobility • User Friendliness • Minor Energy Consumption • Security and Data Integrity • Multi Faculty of Speech • Context Awareness • Integration of Existing Environments • Minor Cost (Network Access, End-devices) • Centralisation of Net- and Client-Intelligence • Multimedia Applications

For the clarification of the column 'Models' in Table 28, the first column refers to the models, which were developed in this study and presented in Section 5.4.

The coded colour scheme used above reflects different colours and mixed colours in one category. The mixed colours imply several category affiliations, for example the category *'Security'* in the left column, which is in brown, is supported and validated by the literature-based data, on the basis of the categories covering the same colour portions in the right hand column; *'Multimedia Applications', 'Centralisation of Net- and Client-Intelligence', 'Integration of Existing Environments'* and *'Data Integrity'*.

This suggests that an ICT system of the future, using SDP, should address the generic challenges (categories) from a user-oriented point of view, as shown from the interviews with the SPICE experts. Besides this, a comparison and validation of the interview-based categories generated, shows that functionalities and services must be simply useable. The Security and Reliability of an ICT system are critical issues when it comes to the effectiveness of such a system and when considering security aspects. The questioned participants provided a consensus on the six final categories, which correlate well with the generic challenges from the literature.

---

[5] There could be limitations in reading the Colour-coded scheme in Table 28 for people with achromatopsia, depending, on the degree of colour vision deficiency.

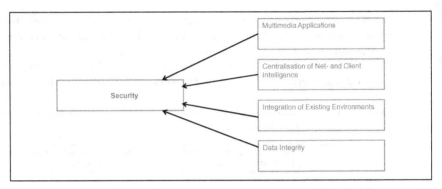

Figure 45: Example: Clustering of the Category "Security" with its sub-categories

Availability and usability correspond to mutual predictability and directability. The functionalities and mobility aspects go hand-in-hand with the generic challenges of signal interpretation, attention use and cost control. The confrontation of the challenges performed in this study and all of these underlying analyses show that the models are sensible, understandable and based on sound arguments. Therefore, from the researcher's point of view, the models have been appropriately justified and are easily comprehensible by third parties.

The following Section 4.5.8, summarises the final six categories and their sub-categories.

4.5.8   A Summary of the Final Six Categories and Sub-Categories

The data collection and analysis was guided by GTM and interview findings, illustrated and discussed in the previous paragraphs. In order to demonstrate how the final grounded theory categories were developed, interview codes, sub-codes, initial and further categories, as well as memos, were presented. The focused codes guided the development of the categories. The following, Table 29, provides a summary of the GT categories developed from the empirical data. The table lists all categories, and highlights how the focused codes have shaped each developed category.

The category "Applicability" referred to the way in which respondents identified a wide range of potential, universally affordable, applications and services. In the interviews participants described different scenarios in their lives, in which SDPs were important to them, and these were grouped into the GT category "Applicability" (Section 4.5.1).

Table 29: Summary of final categories and sub-categories

1. Applicability	2. Controlability	3. Interoperability	4. Mobility	5. Security and Reliability	6. Usability
11_Wide Field of Services 12_Context Awareness	21_Cost Awareness and Control 22_User Controls SDP 23_Application and Service Control	31_Compatibility to ICT-Systems, - Interfaces and - Components 32_Compatability to ICT Standards 33_Infrastructure Reusability 34_Cost Effectiveness	41_Availability 42_Stability and Session Control 43_Always on 44_Any Network on any Device	51_Account and Data Protection 52_Data Security 53_Authentication and Personalisation	61_User Acceptance 62_User Friendliness 63_Simple and Easy to Use

The demand to control cost and service quality, influences activities in the relationship between the user and an SDP, which are represented by the GT category "Controllability" (see 4.5.2). The respondents' descriptions of "Controllability" were closely related to those commonly discussed in the literature (Section 4.5.2). The category "Interoperability" is significant for the compatibility of systems and services for new and existing environments (see 4.5.3). "Mobility" is very important for SDPs to be able to fulfil the requirements of application and service users frequently when they are on the move (see 4.5.4). The category "Security and Reliability" was developed in response to interviewees' statements regarding the security of user accounts, data and information and their role in establishing user confidence (Section 4.5.5). The last category "Usability" discussed the very important aspect of user acceptance of technical environments, which have to be very simple and easy to operate (Section 4.5.6).

Individuals tend to develop particular routines in using their end devices. SDPs become an important tool for controlling, administrating and managing users' lives. Individuals belonging to the group of SPICE users (end-users and developers) feel that SDPs could help in making their lives easier with the support of ICT technology. This highlights the fact that SDPs can be used to single-handedly administer, control and manage daily ICT-supported activities. The six final categories will be revisited in Sections 5.4, 5.6, and 5.7, relating to findings from pilot interviews and interviews from phases two and three, as well as findings from relevant literature.

The following, Table 30, is a summary of the fifteen interviews showing how the attributes and codes occurred in the interviews in accordance to a relevant topic.

Table 30: Chain of evidence of attributes and codes (inspired by Urquhart, 2001)

Nr.	Topics and Attributes (interview coding phase stated)	Dominant GT Codes
1	Mobility; simple and to use; relationship user network and SDP; (interview coding phase 1)	Being mobile anytime and anywhere; easy to handle and use; support different types of enddevices; different connections to standard network technologies is a must.
2	Compatibility; relationship user-enddevice and SDP; (interview coding phase 1)	Integrate existing enironments; web-based SDP must support broad range of enddevices.
3	Data protection; relationship SDP and ICT system; (interview coding phase 1)	Gain access to own data and services; protection of user data and information; SDPs as standard gateway for ICT service-related user interaction.
4	Infrastructure compatibility; relationship user-enddevice and SDP; (interview coding phase 1)	Enddevice compatibility and broad range of different devices; support in displaying different content indipendently from display size.
5	Mobility; wide field of services; cost effectiveness; (interview coding phase 2)	Access to resources at any network on any device; ICT servcies should be available in a broad range, on a service provider SDP; has to be affordable for everyone.
6	Simple and friendly to use; relationship user and enddevice; (interview coding phase 2)	Easy to handle and use; content has to be dynamic for different types of enddevices and displays; mobility and session stability is a must for enddevices and networks.
7	Wide field of services; infrastructure compatibility; (interview coding phase 2)	Provided services should be combined with others; integrate existing environments;
8	Data security and protection; Mobility; (interview coding phase 2)	Gain acces to own data and services; protect users data and information; being cost efficient by using network resources;
9	Relationship user and network; relationship user and end-device; (interview coding phase 2)	Users want to habe high performance and available access to their applications and services; personalised access to SDP and provided services anytime and anyplace.
10	Cost effectiveness; infrastructure compatibility; (interview coding phase 2)	Has to be affordable for everyone; services have to be affordable for a broad range of users; enddevice compatibility and broad range of different devices.
11	Relationship SDP and ICT system; simple and friendly to use; (interview coding phase 2)	Standard technologies and interfaces are a must for SDPs; little count of interactions to use the desired service or application.
12	Cost control; mobility; infrastructure compatibility; (interview coding phase 3)	Manage costs for everyone; session control and stability when user is moving; compatible devices.
13	Relationship user and SDP; data security and protection; (interview coding phase 3)	SDP must be easy to handle and administrate; protect data and access to resources; reliable access to user accounts.
14	Simple to use; relationship user and network; (interview coding phase 3)	User acceptance; interaction controlled by the user; mechanism to control network connection at the actual location.
15	Relationship enddevice and SDP; wide range of services; (interview coding phase 3)	SDP as standard gateway for ICT service-related user interaction; provide many different services; service development and creation.

Table 30 summarises the topic-related adjustment of dominant codes, discovered and further developed, within the fifteen interviews using the empirical study described in detail in the Sections 4.2 to 4.5.

4.6   Chapter Summary and Conclusions

The views of individuals should have an influence on future policies regulating the design and development of ICT systems, using SDPs. Users should be central in debates on the administration, control and management of SDP-based ICT environments. This study has put considerable focus on the collection of empirical data. This Chapter has presented the empirical findings from all three data collection and analysis phases, which were aimed at learning about participants' awareness of SDPs and their impact on an individual when using SDP-based ICT technology, in terms of making their everyday lives easier.

Pilot and in-depth interviews were presented, and references to GT codes, attributes, theoretical memos and visual representations of ideas were made throughout this Chapter, in order to illustrate the process of developing the substantive GT in form of the six final GT categories: 1. Applicability; 2. Controllability; 3. Interoperability; 4. Mobility; 5. Security and Reliability; and 6. Usability. The first pilot interview phase provided an initial insight into the participants' views and was followed up with more in-depth, two stage interviews, which highlighted the challenges of SDPs in participants' daily activities when using these technologies. Furthermore, the interviews gave the researcher crucial insight into respondents' interpretations and perceptions of SDPs, in relation to ICT environments. The applications and services an SDP offers, are directly related to daily requirements of mobile environment users. It is therefore critical to consider the viewpoints of SDP end-users, developers and architecture experts, because they offer information about these requirements of mobile environment users, which are central in debates concerning design issues of SDPs for future-oriented services.

This Chapter has explained in detail, each of the data collection and analysis phases, including sampling and ethical considerations and provided a discussion of the findings obtained from all three data collection and analysis phases. Interpretations of the data are presented, together with a comparison of empirical findings from the relevant literature and the development of the categories based from the empirical data by using the EMPLIT framework with a GTM approach was shown and presented. The following, Chapter 5, presents and discusses the development of the models, based on developed GT categories. Moreover, the views of the respondents are presented in detail where the outcome and findings of the study are discussed.

5 Model Development and Discussion of the Results

Chapter 5 presents a description of the outcomes and findings from this qualitative study. This Chapter is divided into seven parts. After the introduction, Section 5.2 presents the theoretical integration of the empirical findings and reverts back to the literature. Section 5.3 explains the development of an exploratory framework for design issues of an SDP-based ICT system, from a users' perspective. This framework is representative of the six final GT categories, and their relationships, developed using theoretical coding, memos and integrative diagrams, presented in Chapter 4. A substantive theory diagram and description is presented as well within Chapter 5. The third part, Section 5.4, then discusses and presents the development of the interview-based model, based on the final GT categories and the literature-based model, based on the literature-based criteria catalogue.

The fourth part, Section 5.5, outlines a possible generic framework, represented through the functional requirements of an SPD-based ICT system of the future. This is done based on the viewpoints of individual experts and some design aspects taken from the empirical study. Section 5.6 describes a discussion of the respondents' views of the results of this study and illustrates the findings and outcomes of this study. Section 5.7 outlines interpretations regarding parallels and divergences from the interviewee's viewpoint to the academic literature and the theoretical integration of the six final GT categories in terms of the current literature. This Chapter concludes with Section 5.8, which presents a final discussion of user needs in terms of SDPs by, answering the four research questions (outlined in Paragraph 2.5.3.1 and Section 3.9.4) and the relation of the main findings to the requirements from Section 1.1, completing the Chapter.

5.1 Introduction

Firstly, the development of an exploratory framework for challenges and design issues for an SDP-based ICT system of the future, from a users' perspective is presented by employing theoretical coding to define relationships between the categories and their sub-categories presented in Section 4.5.

Additionally, an empirical and a literature-based model are presented, and the data from both studies is compared and discussed. The author generated two models: One was based on the categories developed in terms of the collected empirical data, and the other model was based on literature aspects, gathered, grouped and structured during the mapping process and presented in form of mind maps with their aspects and developed literature-based categories. Both models were compared to show correlations and differences, with respect to the interview and literature results, and to the challenges posed, of how they see the SPICE experts from a user's perspective.

Moreover, based on the results the development of a generic framework for an SDP-based ICT system of the future is described, and a correlation scheme for comparing the categories from both studies is illustrated. The following Sections describe the different results and the models that were developed. A discussion about the respondents' views of user needs in SDP-based ICT systems is also addressed. A diagram of the substantive theory based on the respondents' views (see Paragraph 5.3.4) is shown. Parallels and divergences to the academic literature regarding individuals' perceptions, is presented. A theoretical integration of the developed six GT categories is reflected by discussing each of the relevant categories in requirement engineering and design for testability of software architectures.

A discussion of user needs in terms of SDPs, when looking at the study results, implies the revisiting the research questions, which need to be answered. A discussion of the relationship of findings and the requirements outlined in Section 1.1 help to understand how the developed substantive GT contributes to user needs. The contribution of EMPLIT in terms of users needs is also discussed.

The next Section discusses and reflects the theoretical integration of the six GT categories, in terms of the relevant current literature.

5.2 Reflection and Discussion in Terms of the Relevant Literature

The empirical results in the form of the final six GT categories of this work were integrated into the literature to relate the emergent theory to other theories in similar fields of research. This was done, by undertaking another literature research and comparing the results of this study to the literature and related research from Sections 2.3 to 2.5, and additional current literature stated within this Section.

The relations between Outcomes, *SDP characteristics,* developed using EMPLIT, and those which were achieved, employing other methodologies for analysing user needs (especially requirement engineering and design for testability of software architectures), are addressed in the next Paragraphs.

5.2.1 Context of the Six Final Categories and the Current Literature

This Paragraph discusses the context of the final six GT categories and the active conclusions the author arrived at, in this study, based on academic literature. To reiterate, the results of this study were compared with the academic literature in terms of each of the presented six GT categories to ensure theoretical integration. This is presented by each of the six categories separately.

This research is a trans-disciplinary work and the next Paragraph illustrates the context of the six final GT categories in terms of terminology used with Requirement Engineering and design for testability of software architectures. All six final GT categories are evaluated with terms used with the methodologies requirement engineering and design for testability of software architectures. The terminology of the six final GT categories is analysed for consistencies and distinctions, regarding requirement engineering and design for testability.

GTM is generally used as an adapted methodology and part of EMPLIT, to make data analysis qualitative. It is also used for building a theory, and this developed emergent theory is related to the existing sets of literature. An emphasis on comparing the six categories to the literature on software quality characteristics is given.

Applicability

"Applicability", as defined from the respondents' feedback, ensures that a wide field of potential applications support the interoperability of applications and services, the context awareness of systems and devices, allowing for flexibility in use, for the users. The literature highlighted that applicability today, must be open and aware, to support of a broad range of existing and upcoming ICT software applications. For instance, different kinds of multimedia applications need to be supported by today's Internet and ICT applications. This was described in Paragraphs 5.4.4.1 and 5.4.4.2, and presented in Figure 49 and Figure 50.

Schilit et al. (1994), suggests a challenge of mobile distributed computing, is to exploit the changing environment with a new class of applications that are aware of the context in which they are run in. Such context-aware software adapts according to the location of use, the collection of nearby people, hosts, accessible devices, and to changes to such variables over time. A system with these capabilities can examine the computing environment and react to changes to the environment.

Schmidt (2011) suggests, that it is necessary for applications to learn what their users like, how they behave and how they want it to act. A certain mutual trust concerning privacy and the rights of the application is imperative. If the user cannot trust the assistant gadget then he will disable all these context-aware functions.

Killström *et al.* (2008), suggest that MobiLife service infrastructure fulfils the requirements for novel mobile services today, through providing a well-defined, extendable interface for mobile service provisioning. To be able to make use of the telecommunication infrastructure and to enable operators to introduce new services easily, the MobiLife service infrastructure specifies a mapping to the IP Multimedia Subsystem (IMS) components.

Krumenacher and Strang (2008), suggest that the use of ontologies in pervasive computing further improves ontology-based context models. The main contribution is a set of context modelling and ontology-engineering criteria that should assist in evaluating existing approaches and more importantly, that should serve as support for future deployments.

The term "Applicability" also exists in Requirement Engineering. The study of Sajjad and Hanif (2010), explores that applicability of method, or set of methods, depends on several factors (domain nature, budget, time). The edge point of multiple methods implication is that it reduces the chance of important requirements omission. If one method skips any important requirement then another will cover it.

Some of the following characteristics for method applicability shown by the study of Rottmann (2009), brought the following consolidated findings: 1. A large number of stakeholders should be involved, whose responsibilities cross traditional departments, or divisions boundaries. 2. First time project for organisation and considered critical to the future of the organisation. 3. Willing users should be involved. 4. Require more resources compared to traditional methods. 5. Best suit for complex and large projects.

The author is of the opinion that "Applicability" supports the use of SDP-based ICT systems in terms of the potential to reach a broad range of users supporting the acceptance on and the time to the market.

Controllability

The term "Controllability" described from the respondents perspective of this study, that one must have more control, via an SDP, to work with different ICT systems. Application and service control, in terms of the interoperability with different ICT systems, services and applications, is also required. This influences cost awareness in terms of applicability in a positive way as described in Paragraphs 5.4.4.1 and 5.4.4.2, and presented by Figure 49 and Figure 50.

Kantipudi (2002), suggests that circuits are becoming complex and they should be designed for testability, thus supporting need for accurate testability measures. Zhou *et al.* (2008) suggest, in a paper, that controllability, observability and stabilisation properties of a class of matrix linear systems need to be considered. For controllability and observability, necessary and sufficient conditions are derived. Based on these conditions the stabilisation of such class of matrix linear systems, from feedback, is also considered.

König and Nordström (2009), suggest that ICT system characteristics, and their impact on controllability and observability of future electricity distribution grids, needs to be investigated. The aspects of controllability and observability for active grids are key factors for guaranteeing safe, efficient and reliable network operations. An assessment framework for analysing the impact of ICT system quality on controllability and observability of the power distribution grid is also proposed.

The term "Controllability" is also used in Requirement Engineering, and Föhrenbach *et al.* (2007), defined controllability by suggesting that a user should be able to control the pace and sequence of an interaction. Maurino *et al.* (2003) argued, that PC's and PDA offer a wide level of controllability, where in fact, the controllable attributes are audio support, screen resolution, and number of colours, while the input device attribute, is only observable. The author is of the opinion, that a comparable level of controllability must exist for potential end-users, to control services and applications they use in the broad world of the Internet.

Testability can also be seen as a characteristic, or property, of a piece of software that makes it easier to test. Binder (1994) and Freedman (1991), adapt the notions of controllability and observability from hardware testing to a software context. Controllability is the ability to manipulate the software's input as well as to place this software into a particular state, while observability deals with the possibility to observe the outputs and state changes that occur in the software (Mulo, 2007). This was also outlined in Section 2.4.

From the author's perspective, "Controllability" of services and application, using SDPs, affords the user a chance to coordinate all their used services and applications in the complex world of the Internet when using a broad range of end-devices.

Interoperability

"Interoperability", presented from the respondents' perspective, is a critical aspect in developing new systems and integrating them into existing or other new systems, in the fastest growing innovative ICT market. Their compatibility with other ICT system interfaces and components is a must, when designing and developing new ICT systems to support applicability for services and applications. The support of ICT standards is also an important feature, described in Paragraphs 5.4.4.1 and 5.4.4.2, and presented in Figure 49 and Figure 50.

Cordier (2005), recommends that in existing SPICE architecture, challenges of the interoperability of terminals, networks, and distributed data have been addressed and developed. Gasser and Palfrey (2007), suggest that the issue of sustaining interoperability is a key area to focus attention on. Their case study points to concerns of the most informal arrangements, in the context of Web 2.0 functioning, similar to that of operating systems, may lead to problems in the future if not stabilised.

Gradmann (2009), suggests that interoperability is an essential feature for federated information architectures, to work overtime and in heterogeneous settings. However, use and understanding of the concept, are still very heterogeneous. Interoperability is perceived as an object-related or in a functional perspective, from a user's or an institutional perspective, in terms of multilingualism or of technical means and protocols. Moreover, interoperability is perceived on different abstraction levels: from the bit-stream layer up to semantic interoperability.

According to Hansen (1998), it is commonly agreed that software architecture of a system is concerned with overall composition and structure of computational elements, and their relations. Garlan and Shaw (1993), denote the computational elements, components and their relationship connectors. Buschmann et al. (1996), listed that interoperability is an important issue at the level of software architecture, with human factor properties as intelligibility of design and provision.

According to Scherbakov (2005), interoperability measures the ability of a group of parts, constituting a system, to work with another systems. Matinlassi and Eila (2002) argued, hardware, which engulfs other aspects of a system, has changed the role of software architecture. Quality attributes in particular, like modifiability, interoperability and reusability were sacrificed first, in the course of system development. Today, software-intensive systems are pervasive. The increasing complexity and size of software, the cost of software development and more mature software technologies, have changed the role of software architecture.

The author is of the opinion, that interoperability is important for the success of SDP-based ICT systems, when they have the possibility to address a broad range of Internet-based ICT systems, giving users of these systems an opportunity to control and communicate their environments, from a single instance.

Mobility

The term "Mobility" describes an always-on scenario from the respondents' point of view, meaning that a user is always connected and able to use their services and applications while getting information. To support such a scenario, any network on any device must be supported in terms of interoperable ICT environments. This must be done with stable and high connection availability, allowing users to control their services applications and environments all the time, described in Paragraphs 5.4.4.1 and 5.4.4.2, and presented in Figure 49 and Figure 50.

Umar (2004) suggested, that the network layer takes over tasks in connection with the spatial mobility of the user. Mobile users need to establish connections to different networks from various locations, without having to carry out extensive adaptations to a newly configured network. Mechanisms that accomplish the maintenance of the connection are described as handover and roaming.

Poiselka *et al.* (2004: pp. 49-51), suggest that IMS is based on the signalisation protocol Session Initial Protocol (SIP). The connection to diverse types of networks is created through Media Gateways. For the user it is irrelevant which network services or applications are accessed, because there is no longer any difference between mobile and wired networks. This can be described as "Seamless Mobility".

Tarkoma *et al.* (2007), suggest that people place great value both on professional and private mobility, as Information and Communication Technology (ICT) is ubiquitously available, everywhere, whether on business trips or during their leisure time. Accessibility has become necessary during travelling individuality and flexibility. The productivity of end-users is also rapidly increasing, in terms of mobile end-devices usage, such as, mobile phones, notebooks, tablet PCs, handheld or other small computers.

Cordier *et al.* (2006b: pp. 2-3), suggest enabling the use of mobility at any time, on every network, and at every location, by using telematic services on an SDP, SPICE integrates the connection between the IT and telecommunication worlds, with the IP multimedia subsystem (IMS).

Siegmund (2004), suggest that networks of collaborating smart objects, are extremely difficult to manage: some objects are mobile, often with distinct resource restrictions, communication is dynamic, takes place in a highly heterogeneous environment, and need not rely on a constantly available supporting background infrastructure.

The author is of the opinion that "Mobility" is a key factor for SDP-based ICT systems to support mobile ubiquitous environments, as well as mobile services and applications for today's end-user scenarios.

Security and Reliability

"Security and Reliability" in this study, refers to the participants' view of account and data protection of the users SDP access, and the ability to safely store the data and information on the SDP. Authentication and personalisation influence users activities with the SDP, in terms of usability and applicability, to keep stored information safe on the SDP. This is what respondents called "Reliability" and was described in Paragraphs 5.4.4.1 and 5.4.4.2, and presented by Figure 49 and Figure 50.

Honeyman *et al.* (2007), analysed manufacturer incentives to invest in software system reliability and security, when these failures, are caused by the same bugs. As a consequence, users cannot distinguish between security and reliability failures due to the prohibitive costs of differentiating them. The results suggest, that the presence of a hacker free-rider problem, might nullify some traditional policies recommended to alleviate manufacturer free-riding.

Noll (1994), suggests that modern telecommunication networks do not distinguish between signals, carried over the private and public networks of the past. Today's network is flexible and can be reconfigured dynamically, creating the virtual circuits needed to satisfy many users. The security and reliability of today's network is supported through alternative paths of high-capacity transmission routes and flexibility of sophisticated signalling. The technology behind a modern telecommunication network is described in this paper, with an emphasis on issues of security and reliability.

Pettichord (2002), argued that testability requests are sometimes met with concerns regarding security, as they could open back doors, that could then be open to hackers, compromising privacy of individuals. According to Jimenez *et al.* (2005), software testability, software testing, and formal verification are three pieces in a puzzle: the puzzle is whether the software we have has a high enough true reliability. They argued that every system has a true reliability, which is generally unknown.

The author considers that security of SDP-based ICT systems is very important to protect users privacy of information, which is stored on an SDP. Reliability from a security aspect is an important indicator to establish acceptance of such a system.

Usability

"Usability" described by the respondents, has a high potential of being accepted by users when an SDP is applicable in a broad range. Additionally, the software portal solution must be simple and easy to use, affording users more control when employing services and applications. In the literature, user-friendliness, multi-faculty of speech, context awareness and multimedia applications are often linked to usability. This was described in Paragraphs 5.4.4.1 and 5.4.4.2, and presented by Figure 49 and Figure 50.

Preece *et al.* (2002), focused on the creation of user experiences, enhances and extends the way people work, communicate and interact together. Dix *et al.* (2004) remarked, that users should no longer be seen as cogs in a machine, as it is not sufficient to use a system, arguing that users must want to use it. Weiss

(2002) pointed out, that there is a general lack of usability on most handheld devices. Nielsen's (2003), verdict on mobile usability in terms of mobile devices, is that they lack key usability features required for mainstream use.

Gloud and Lewis (1985), suggest that the principles of user interface design to provide a metric, are often expressed as a percentage. It is noteworthy to distinguish between usability testing and usability engineering. Usability testing is the measurement of easing the use of a product or piece of software. In contrast, usability engineering (UE) is the research and design process that ensures a product with good usability.

Shneiderman and Plaisant (2009), suggest that usability is often associated with the functionalities of the product, being solely a characteristic of user interface, separating usefulness into utility and usability. In the context of mainstream consumer products for example, an automobile lacking the reverse gear would be redundant according to the former view, and lacking in utility according to the latter.

Karwowski et al. (2011), suggests that a usability study may be conducted as a primary job function by a usability analyst, or as a secondary job function, by designers, technical writers, marketing personnel, and others. It is widely used in consumer electronics, communication and knowledge transfer objects (such as a cookbook, a document or online help) and mechanical objects such as a door handle or a hammer.

Usability is typically considered by users, as having issues or problems, where good usability entails solving these issues to then enable learning without obstacles and, which could be enhanced by certain features. According to Nielsen (1994), usability can be achieved by creating systems that are easy to understand, easy to remember, efficient to use and are subjectively pleasing. Finn (2005), mentioned that focus should be on planning-in, good usability features rather than eliminating bad ones, once they have occurred. The author is of the opinion that strong focus on usability at the onset of research, employing a user-based empirical study, can help minimise cost and complexity in the development process of SDP-based ICT systems, as it will facilitate focussing on what users really need.

5.2.2 Summary of the Theoretical Integration

According to the four types of analytical generalisation suggested by Walsham (1995) and presenting the literature (theoretical integration).

Table 31: Summary of the theoretical integration

GT-based investigation/ empirical study	Literature-based study	Systematic review of academic literature (examples)
Applicability	• Multimedia applications	o Context-aware software (Schilit *et al.*, 1999) o Trust concerning privacy & rights of applications (Schmidt, 2011) o Mobile service provisioning (Killström *et al.*, 2008) o Ontologies in context-aware apps (Krumenacher & Strang, 2008) o "Applicability" in comparison to RE method (Sajjad & Hanif, 2010) o Software characteristics (Rottmann, 2009)
Controllability	• Minor energy • Minor cost (network access, enddevices)	o Design for testibility (Kantipudi, 2002) o Controllability and observability (Zhou *et al.*, 2008) o ICT system characteristics (König & Nordström, 2009) o "Controllability" with RE method (Maurino *et al.* (2003) o "Controllability" with D4T method (Binder, 1994, Freedmann, 1991) o SW characteristics (Mulo, 2007)
Interoperability	• Multi Faculty of Speech • Context Awareness • Integration of Existing Environments • Minor Cost (Network Access, Enddevices) • Centralisation of Net- & Client Intelligence	o Challenges of interoperability in SPICE (Cordier, 2005) o Sustaining interoperability (Gasser and Palfrey, 2007) o Federated information architecture (Gradmann, 2009) o SW characteristics (Hansen,1998; Garlan & Shaw, 1993) o SW characteristics (Matinlassi and Eila, 2002))
Mobility	• High Mobility Centralisation of Net- & Client Intelligence	o Different networks from various locations (Umar, 2004) o Seamless mobility (Poiselka *et al.*, 2004) o Productivity and accessability is rapidly increasing (Tarkoma *et al.*, 2007) o Management of collaboration networks (Siegmund, 2004)
Security and Reliability	• Security & Data Integrity • Integration of Existing Environments • Centralisation of Net- & Client Intelligence • Multimedia Applications	o Software system reliability and security (Honeyman *et al.*, 2007) o High-capacity transmission routes (Noll, 1994) o "S&R" with D4T method (Pettichord, 2002) o "S&R" with D4T method (Jimenez *et al.*, 2005)
Usability	• User Friendliness • Multi Faculty of Speech • Context Awareness • Multimedia Applications	o Usability testing (Gloud and Lewis, 1985) o Usefulness into utility and usability (Shniderman and Plaisant, 2009) o Knowledge transfer objects (Karwowski et al., 2011) o SW characteristics (Nielsen, 1994; Finn, 2005)

Inspired by Sulayman *et al.* (2012), Table 31 summarises the GT-based investigation in form of the final six GT categories from a literature review perspective. It was created using the literature-based study and drawing on literature references to strengthen the theoretical integration of the GT categories presented in the Paragraph 5.2.1 above.

The following Section presents the development of an exploratory framework for design issues of an SDP-based ICT system from the user view.

5.3 Development of an Exploratory Framework for Design Issues of an SDP-based ICT System

The product of this study was an exploratory framework, for design issues of SDP-based ICT development from the perspective of users, that was done using the research methodology employed and presented in Chapter 3, and the qualitative analysis to reach the major categories and sub-categories, illustrated in Chapter 4.

5.3.1   Development of the Relations between the Categories

After completion of Selective Coding, shown in Section 4.5, Theoretical Coding was conducted helping to develop a coherent theoretical scheme - an exploratory framework for design issues of SDP-based ICT development from the perspective of users. With the help of memos generated during coding and the analysis phase (see Section 4.5, memos 1-6), relationships among the identified categories were formulated. The author analysed the interview transcripts to identify relationships between the categories based on the explanations of the interviewees.

The author also started to establish relations between categories with Colour Coding, however, as so many different colours were used in the interview transcripts, the author opted to look at the explanations given by the interviewees as a guide to relationships between categories and sub-categories for theoretical coding. On a flip chart, relations were identified and transferred to a graphical representation resulting in the presented graph (integrated diagram in Figure 46) below. This adopted approach of Theoretical Coding helped to relate categories and sub-categories that led to the theoretical model in Figure 46.

The major categories and their sub-categories were developed by applying open and focused coding as described within Sections 4.5.1 to 4.5.6. The key relationships between the categories were identified during Theoretical Coding added by theoretical memos outlined within Sections of 4.5. The relationships conceptualised the underlying data slices, with a set of categories and sub-categories.

5.3.2   An Exploratory Framework of Design Issues of SDP-based ICT Development from the Perspective of Users

Summarised, the six final categories were developed from the empirical findings are as follows:

- Applicability
- Controllability
- Interoperability
- Mobility
- Security and Reliability
- Usability

These categories, the sub-categories and their relations are presented by an integrative diagram (see 3.4.5) by the following Figure 46 and describes the relations of the six final categories with each other:

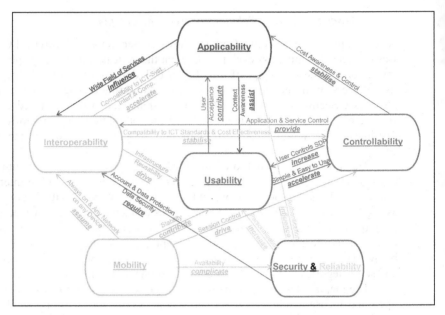

Figure 46: Theoretical model with final categories and their relations

The theoretical model shown above in Figure 46, is the result of this investigation, representing the challenges and design issues of SDP-based ICT systems, from the perspective of SPICE experts. This exploratory model shows the
major categories, the sub-categories and their relationships among them. The
categories and their relationship represented through the exploratory framework
is the main contribution of this investigation.

All final developed categories are related and connected to other categories.
This was because the user perspective is the focus perspective of this investigation and represented by the core category *"Usability"*. The same applies for the
major category *"Interoperability"*, which is also related to each other category,
because the respondents see this as one of the most critical issues when using an
SDP as a control and communication instance for ICT environments. Today's
ICT environments have to fulfil the upward and downward compatibility, as
there is an abundance of high-value ICT environments on the market. Any such
new concepts have to fulfil this requirement; otherwise there is no chance of
becoming established in an increasingly fast-paced high-tech market, with
shorter and shorter technological development phases.

The category *"Controllability"* has a variety of meanings and attributes for
the respondents. The most important aspects are summarised as the sub-
categories: Firstly, the cost awareness and control aspect specifies, that the user

has to have control of all service and application-related activities, which influences costs. Secondly, the aspect that the user controls the SDP means that the SDP is the single control and communication instance of the ICT environments being used for executing services and applications. Thirdly, the application and service control is also part of this category, as a single instance control system has to have the possibility to store and relate to applications and service activities too. There is a strong relation between this category and those of *"Usability"*, and *"Interoperability"*.

The category *"Mobility"* is related to the other categories *"Interoperability"*, *"Usability"*, "Security and Reliability" and *"Controllability"*. The respondents described a relationship of SDPs to other ICT environments for using standards to be compatible with, as well as to support, the user friendliness and the scenarios of being independent of networks and end devices. It is necessary that the user can maintain control of mobile support irrespective of time or location.

"Security and Reliability" is related to *"Interoperability"*, *"Usability"*, "Mobility" and *"Applicability"*. The aspect of security did not promote in-depth responses from the participants. Participants saw a greater need in making sure that the other categories exist, high availability and support when using an SDP to control and operate different kinds of ICT systems.

The following table gives an explanation of the developed relationships amongst the categories and a short description:

Table 32: Categories and relations amongst them

Category	Relationship	Category	Description
Applicability	*Influence*	Interoperability	More flexible applications needs more interoperable systems
Interoperability	*Accelerate*	Applicability	Compatible systems and interfaces impact a wide field of application
Controllability	*Stabilise*	Applicability	Cost control stabilise the impact of application fields
Applicability	*Assist*	Usability	Context aware applications help users in supporting daily tasks easily
Usability	*Contribute*	Applicability	Arrangements for user acceptance help to apply internet applications
Controllability	*Provide*	Interoperability	Applications and service control support convergent environments
Interoperability	*Stabilise*	Controllability	Compatible and cost-effective systems allow to control more simply
Controllability	*Increase*	Usability	User control of a broad range of apps and the SDP increase usability
Usability	*Accelerate*	Controllability	Easy to use applications support control activities for users
Interoperability	*Drive*	Usability	Reusable infrastructure help to increase usability activities
Security & Reliability	*Require*	Interoperability	Account and data portections require compatible environments
Mobility	*Assume*	Interoperability	Always-on is a must for convergent and interoperable systems
Mobility	*Contribute*	Usability	Stable mobile connections support users in daily procedures
Mobility	*Drive*	Controllability	Stable sessions for mobile applications are necessary for user control
Mobility	*Complicate*	Security & Reliability	High available systems need to secure reliable environments
Security & Reliability	*Increase*	Usability	Personalisation help to increase security and usability
Security & Reliability	*Influence*	Applicability	Authentication expect high requirements on applications and services

Table 32 shows a set of challenges and design issues for SDP-based ICT development representing the user view, which were identified. The theoretical integration was discussed in Section 5.2 with a discussion on the relationships, between the emerged GT categories, presented in the following Section.

5.3.3 Discussion of the Relationships between the GT Categories

Starting with a discussion on the relationships between the GT categories, it should be noted that challenges and design issues of SDP-based ICT systems from the user perspective, have not been reported in current literature, although, other studies that have had comparable results, in terms of the terminology used.

The six major categories shown with the help of the theoretical integration done in Paragraph 5.2.1 and summarised in Paragraph 5.2.2 were identified and also used in other more technically oriented methodologies to investigate gate systems for user needs such as: requirement engineering or design for testability of software architectures that were explained in Section 2.4.

Figure 46, in Section 5.3.2, illustrates the exploratory framework for design issues of SDP-based ICT systems, from the perspective of users. This theoretical model was integrated into six categories, where the core category is "Usability". Each of the major categories presents tailored sub-categories and relationships between them, that also contribute to this study. It was mentioned by all inter-viewees that there were benefits in achieving design issues for SDP-based ICT development, from the perspective of users. It was found in this investigation that:

■ More flexible applications influence the needs of more interoperable systems

■ Compatible systems and interfaces impact a wide field of applications

■ Cost control stabilise the impact of application fields

■ Context-aware applications help users in supporting daily tasks easily

■ Arrangements for user acceptance help to apply internet applications

■ Applications and services control support convergent environments

■ Compatible and cost-effective systems allow to control in a more simple way

■ User control of a broad range of applications and the SDP itself increase usability

■ Easy to use applications support control activities for users

■ Reusable infrastructure helps to increase usability activities

- Account and data protection requires compatible environments
- Always-on is a must for convergent and interoperable systems
- Stable mobile connections support users in daily procedures
- Stable sessions for mobile applications are necessary for user control
- High available systems need to secure reliable environments
- Personalisation help to increase security and usability
- Authentication expect high requirements on applications and services

Influence

On one hand, 'Applicability' influences 'Interoperability' in terms of, the more applications available in the field for users, the higher the percentage of interoperable systems, when using an SPD-based ICT system, will be. On the other hand, 'Applicability' is influenced by 'Security and Reliability' as authentication, in today's standards, makes high requirement demands on applications and services, to better protect user identity and data.

Accelerate

'Applicability' is accelerated by 'Interoperability'. Therefore, compatible systems and interfaces impact on a wide field of applications. 'Controllability' is accelerated by 'Usability', in terms of applications and services use, entails the ease of handling the support control of users, therefore more users would then be willing to use SDP-based ICT systems.

Stabilise

'Controllability' stabilises 'Applicability' in terms of cost control that impacts the fields of applications. 'Controllability' is stabilised by 'Interoperability' which allows compatible and cost-effictive systems control in a simpler way.

Assist

'Applicability' facilitates 'Usability', in terms of context-aware applications, which in turn assists users in supporting and easing their daily activities and tasks.

Contribute

'Usability' contributes to 'Applicability' by applying arrangements for user acceptance, in terms of Internet applications. 'Mobility' contributes to 'Usability' for a more stable mobile connection supporting users in their daily working procedures.

Provide

'Interoperability' is provided by 'Controllability' to support convergent environments for applications and service control.

Increase

'Controllability' increases 'Usability' by helping users control a broad range of applications and SDPs. 'Security and Reliability' increase 'Usability' in a simple way, to control and protect user's personalised access to an SDP which facilitate increased levels of security.

Drive

'Interoperability' drives 'Usability' by reusing infrastructures. 'Mobility' drives 'Controllability' when stable sessions for mobile aapplications are necessary for user control.

Require

'Security and Reliability' require 'Interoperability' when account and data protection are used, in compatible environments.

Assume

'Mobility' assumes 'Interoperability' when always-on senario is able to support convergent and interoperable systems.

Complicate

'Security and Reliability'is complicated by 'Mobility' when high availability systems need to secure reliable environments.

The author reviewed the existing literature in order to take a closer look and identify partial equal and partial comparable results when looking at the technical-driven approaches, mentioned. Due to the terminology of the identified categories, it is interesting that the results provided by this study and those reported in the existing literature are comparable and use similar terminology in "Usability", "Mobility" or "Security". This was highlighted in the comparison of interview-based and literature based categories in Figure 50 and Table 33, Paragraph 5.4.4.1. A comparison of the six GT major categories and the academic literature, especially from requirement engineering and design for testability of software architectures was done within the theoretical integration part of this study, in Section 5.2. Table 31 in Section 5.2.2 gives a good overview of the identified six GT major categories and their relation to the literature-based study and to broader factors of the literature review.

The major categories and their sub-categories relate to each shown with theoretical coding. Relating categories and relationships to factors from the systematic review were shown in Chapter 4, specifically in Sections 4.5.1 to 4.5.8 where the interview excerpts were presented. Relating the six major categories to the literature was done with the literature-based study (see Figure 50 and Table 33) and the theoretical integration by relating six major categories to factors from a broader literature review (see Table 31 and the entire Section 5.2).

5.3.4   Substantive Theory Diagram of this Investigation

According to Reid (2006), theories have relationships between the constructs. One possibility to depict these relationships, is by using a substantive theory diagram. The researcher used this type of diagram to present the emergent substantive theory of this investigation. This scaling-up process shows that the emergent substantive GT of this investigation is able to contribute positively and benefit a potential researcher. It is an abstract form of Figure 46 in Section 5.3, showing the relationship between the technical and user perspective of SDPs as a single control and communication instance for ICT systems:

Theme 1 represents a more abstract view of the challenges and design issues of SPICE. This could be seen as the contribution of the SPICE project - the SPICE architecture, which represents a technical viewpoint. Theme 2 represents the exploratory framework (six GT categories and their relations) of the respondents' view in this investigation. Theme 3 represents the user needs and perspective, when designing ICT systems.

Figure 47 shows three core themes. These themes should be viewed as larger than the categories and give instances from the data, of the relationship between those core themes:

■ *Theme 1 - Challenges and design issues of SDPs (SPICE) - the technical perspective:* Theme 1 is influenced by Theme 3, in the outcomes of a user study, with the help of specific user groups (in this study SPICE experts are described in Section 2.3.4.3). This can help to focus on specific technical implementation activities and affecting Theme 2 by pushing the acceptance of potential users of an ICT system and therefore be quicker on the market (see also Finding 2 and 4). The outcome will either influence Theme 2 in a positive or negative way.

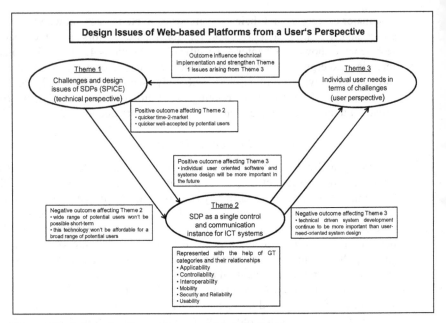

Figure 47: Substantive theory diagram of this investigation

- *Theme 2 - Individual user needs in terms of challenges - the user perspective:* If the six final developed GT categories are representative issues to legitimise a user specific empirical study before starting with a technical implementation development, then a positive or negative outcome will influence whether innovative ICT system development, will or will not be developed further, by a technical-driven approach, or influenced to start with a user needs analysis before jumping in, to develop an ICT system (see also Finding 1).

- *Theme 3 - SDP as a single control and communication instance for ICT systems - the user perspective:* Theme 3 could help strengthen a technical study using an individual's views to prioritise technical features and the implementation of those (see also Finding 3).

Theme 1 represents the technical view, based on SPICE outcomes. Themes 2 and 3 are based on findings of this qualitative study and represent the perspective of users. Concluding the substantive theory diagram of this study the author considered, that a combination of user-oriented and technical-oriented guidelines, in combination, would be highly beneficial to design and development of SDP-based ICT systems.

5.4   Development of Category-based Models for the Empirical and Literature-based Study

This Section discusses the category-based model development, regarding the six final categories from the empirical study, as well as the aspects of the literature-based criteria catalogue which represents firstly the respondents' views of challenges and design issues in terms of SDPs as a communication and control instance for ICT systems and secondly those commonly presented in the literature.

5.4.1   Preconditions for the Development of both Models

The structure of the developed models shows in both internal circles the preconditioned terms that were clearly presented in this investigation. These consist of two main characteristics and four base requirements and the concepts used, were taken from the literature described by Christoffersen and Woods (2001), illustrated in Paragraph 2.5.1.1. Derivation is carried out with the respective models for the purpose of better understanding. The categories generated, by means of GT analysis, are shown in different colours in the external ring highlighted in "grey" and also presented in Figure 48 and Figure 49.

5.4.2   GT Categories and the Interview-Based Model

The interview-based model that was created from the collected data of the empirical study with SPICE experts, in three phases, is illustrated in Figure 48. Six final GT categories were developed, within the scope of the analysis, with relevance to the interviewed groups, represented by SPICE end-users, developers, and architecture experts. The model concerns the range of challenges that exist if innovative technologies, such as SDPs, are used for the profitable improvement of ICT systems. The six categories can be summarised as follows:

- Usability
- Mobility
- Security and Reliability
- Applicability
- Interoperability
- Controllability

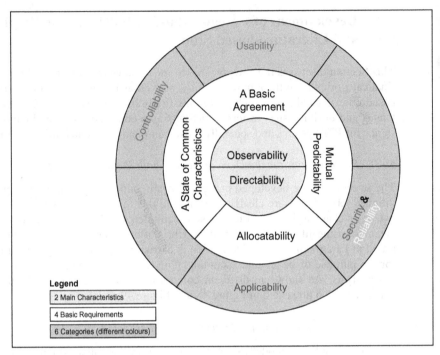

Figure 48: Interview-based model from this investigation

Both inner circles of Figure 48, described in Paragraphs 2.5.1.1 and 2.5.1.2, are preconditions for the models developed in this study. These are based on the works of Christoffersen and Woods (2002: pp. 4-10; see also Paragraph 2.5.1.1), and Klein *et al.* (2004: pp. 91-94). From the analysis of the SDP and NGs litera-ture, six final categories were developed and shown in this investigation, where the categories are developed as final results from the analysis. They had to fulfil the requirements outlined in the preconditions outlined in Paragraph 2.5.1.2. The six final categories are described in detail, in the following Section, with refer-ences to the respondents' views.

The next six Paragraphs detail the selective categories of design issues for SDP-based ICT systems. The categories identified in Chapter 4 and the resulting initial exploratory framework of SDP-based ICT development, constitutes the main contribution of this investigation. The description for each of the six GT categories also includes the respective sub-categories, properties and important relationships, was presented in the Section 4.5. The data source of each category is the interview, conducted for this research, and thus the categories represent the true perspective of a set of practitioners, based on their experiences of working with SPICE, and on projects specific to SDPs and SDP-based ICT developments. According to Sulayman *et al.* (2012), the chain of evidence is provided for each category in the form of quotes from interviews.

Usability

The category "Usability" describes the quick, and easy-to-use, possibilities for developers and end-users, with regard to end device access of an SDP. Context awareness as part of usability describes the need to make information available in different display dimensions, independent of the type and size of the end device used.

SPICE expert opinion, from a development perspective, and also an end-user perspective, concerning the *User Friendliness and Context Awareness* of an SDP, state the essential core aspects as being: the configuration of the SDP, the usability of executable services, and the use of a very large number of different end devices: *"SDPs are applicable on a wide scale and it must be guaranteed that a large number of services and applications can be deposited, and can also be used simply, anytime, from anyplace. It is important that the platform can be used. I mean, in detail, that the right content is indicated from the type of use of the end device, independently"* (interviews p14_d; translated by the author). *"The selected services can be made available quickly and easily, in an uncomplicated manner.*

Besides this, I would like to point out the fact that the connection to different networks (e.g. Wi-Max, Bluetooth or WAN) has been released immediately. The control and administration to network accesses must be easily guaranteed in a simple way for every user, because not every user is an IT expert, but the decision to select has got on a direct impact of the costs [...]" (interviews p12_d and p26_d; translated by the author).

Dealing with information and enhancing awareness of context differentiation between different end devices is decisive: *"One should be clear, that in using different end devices, which gain access to services on an SDP, the right content has to be generated depending on the accessing end device type [...]"* (interview p11_u; translated by the author). *"If I receive a Smartphone from my employer as a working device, the official information must be processed and displayed in a different form than that which I can provide with a notebook"* (interview p23_e and p34_d; translated by the author). Besides, it is important to show information on the display, independent of the type of end device used (e.g. Smartphone, tablet, workstation, etc.).

That means, that it is absolutely relevant which display size is available to present graphical information for instance at one page on display for a used end device: *"Used content creation engines are specialised on the different types of end devices. These engines provide content information dynamically, to the rele-*

vant end device, whereby content is displayed and ready to use [...]" (interview p25_d; translated by the author).

For the application of an SDP in an ICT system, easy administration and the configuration management of end devices has to be offered, as well as usable services. Furthermore, preferred services, and also usable end devices, can be simply configured on an SDP, e.g., for a specific group of people, such as SPICE experts, and can also be provided for mobile use on any network on any device. The possibility to access, above all, is enhanced by mobile end devices, which bring a large degree of freedom and flexibility.

Mobility

By "Mobility" it is understood, in the context of an SDP, that access to services may occur independently of place and time. This is of importance for developers and also for end-users.

"Mobility" is a core functionality within an SDP, which is hallmarked by suitable connectivity and mobility technologies: *"The advantage of services, which are offered to end-users with an SDP is, that these services are available independently of the end device used and the place at which the end-user is at that moment"* (interview p12_u; translated by the author). *"You can figure it out as a kind of 'Software as a Service', which has to be equalised with an SDP, and is offered to potential customers with an accommodate suitable service level, in a public cloud environment"* (interview p26_d; translated by the author). This identifies the clear desire of the users for very independent, reliable access possibilities, for professional or private use: *"For me it is only an added value if I'm able to switch on my mobile phone or my laptop independently of the place where I am. In this case I already need a stable Internet connection too [...]"* (interview p31_u; translated by the author).

The mobility of an SDP, and the services available on this platform, are seen by the respondent as necessary criteria to be able to use it in a sensory-like way. Besides, access to networks and the stable use of a typically well-chosen service with this high level of availability are necessary in order to build user confidence and acceptance: *"Implementation and rollout of B3G technologies, such as IMS and SIP, are the preconditions for guaranteeing high availability and stable coverage, at least in areas with concentrated populations [...]"* (interview p23_d; translated by the author). *"For the acceptance of SPICE services by their end-users, the easy use of these services, and a well functioning infrastructure, are necessary main conditions - you know [...]"* (interview p34_d; translated by the author).

Nowadays, for ICT systems, the high mobility of an SDP or that of the service offered on this platform are indispensable, as the constant movement of the end-user has to be taken into consideration.

Security and Reliability

"Security and reliability" are imperative for protecting an SDP, and the services located on it. Additionally, it is necessary to provide specifically required groups, e.g., the groups of developers and end-users, with different security policies, to access different types of networks, services, applications, end devices and web-contents.

Security on an SDP is an important criterion in ensuring that no misuse of services can happen. Authentication, as well as personal access to the platform, protect services from abuse: *"It is important that an SDP provides access for the end-users, for example, an end-user name and password with an authentication procedure are absolutely necessary [...]"* (interview p32_ae; translated by the author). *"The provision of IP-based data has the advantage of wide diffusion the disadvantage is that big attention is to be paid to the broad topic of data security. Internet hackers are constantly active, and therefore access to the SDP must be protected accordingly, for example, with LDAP (Lightweight Directory Access Protocol) or PAM (Pluggable Authentication Module) mechanisms [...]"* (interview p25_d; translated by the author). *"The standard authentication methods by using passwords are no longer sufficient, because it is easy to hack them. Alternatively, to achieve better and safer results regarding security, alternative authentication measures, such as the use of keys or maps, biometric fingerprint readers or a host authentication can be applied [...]"* (interview p34_d; translated by the author).

An SDP must also operate reliably and ensure that the provided services are available all the time: *"A high degree of standardisation contributes to the network area, with the use of standardised network access, UMTS and IP-based technology, as well as standardised interfaces for many terminals and end devices [...]"* (interview p11_u; translated by the author). *"SPICE offers the advantage that new services can be brought in an easy way onto the Service Creation Environment (SCE) in the SDP, without compromising the operation. Existing and new services can be combined on the SCE. They can be stored as a group of services on the SDP, and can also be used by other users[...]"* (interview p14_d; translated by the author).

For the purposes of security in terms of ICT systems, user authentication is indispensable to protect the users identity, data and service provision with the help of an SDP.

Applicability

Services provided on an SDP are to be understood as a Spectrum of Services from a general perspective.

The Spectrum of Services offered on the SDP are multi-faceted: *"The carrier services, for example Location Based Services (LBSs), which are used, for example, on Smartphones or PDAs, can be offered here"* (interview p23_d; translated by the author). *"Different services are basis network services, such as, mobility management and the support of end-user mobility, for example. Moreover, end-user supported services, such as, for example, end-user-support for Samsung tablets are offered for the support of a large number of different features in terms of a Nokia Smartphone for instance, to encourage the end-user with the ability to use as many end device specific services as possible [...]"* (interview p33_ae; translated by the author). Services provided on an SDP should be concentrated in different groups of services, offering users as many possibilities to operate with single or multiple groups of services as they choose to use: *"On SDPs, provided services can be combined with other existing or newly developed services. This useful procedure to orchestrate a new type or class of service uses existing services in combination. Basically, we distinguish basic services, for example location-based services, and m-commerce services, such as, for example, the mobile phone parking ticket, or GPS services. These services are already to be understood as a use which can be also coupled with other services"* (interview p24_d; translated by the author).

Interoperability

"Interoperability" describes the 'usability', above all, of the available technical infrastructures currently available in different networks, as well as state-of-the-art network connections, for example GSM-, GPRS-core networks, UMTS and LTE networks, etc.

The existing infrastructure located in companies, and networks located with operators, has to be suitable, and operational compatibility must be guaranteed. From an economic sense this goes without saying: *"The network operators have invested a lot of money in mobile radio networks and in wired network infrastructures. These infrastructures were technically available and prepared to deliver services and applications to end-users, and were based on the most modern state-of-the-art technologies.*

A lot of money has currently been invested in the removal of old technologies in order to renew these with fibreglass technology. Therefore, it must be certain that SDPs and web 2.0 technology can be linked, and can use existing infrastructures within the scope of the mobilisation of the Internet" (interview p13_u; translated by the author). *"It is necessary to make sure that existing infrastructure is still compatible, for example, to GSM-, GPRS-, and UMTS-based infrastructures with new convergent technologies. Systems must be technically prepared in order to fulfil the requirements of making real implementations a feasible reality, particularly as operators have invested a lot of money over the last 20 years in the reorganisation of their networks"* (interview p23_d; translated by the author).

For Sdps in future-oriented ICT systems, this means that prepared and complex B3G technologies, such as UMTS and LTE, have to be available for a broad range of ICT systems and components. Furthermore, high-quality services need UMTS components, which must be highly mobile, within the scope of the availability of an SDP infrastructure.

Controllability

"Controllability" refers to the preconditions that services, offered on the SDP, perform for end-users, and show an appealing possibility for conversion, within the scope of suitable business models, for companies.

Engaging new ways through innovative ICT systems, as an example, the provision of different kinds of mobile applications and services to support daily life of end-users anywhere at any place, and any network on any device, is motivation to put web-based platforms such as SDPs, on the market immediately, and then to make this technology available for a broad range of services and users from the onset: *"The added value generated by SDPs, with provided standardised services, is also to be reviewed from a cost perspective. As the past has already shown us, the supply of 3G services were a flop at the beginning [...]"* *(interview p22_u; translated by the author). "The payment model for the services on an SDP must make sure that this system is easily accessible for every citizen. Therefore, it is necessary to offer services at affordable costs, otherwise it will not be able to assert itself"* (interview p26_d; translated by the author). With respect to ICT systems and components, the cost aspect will become more essential. Besides this fact, the risk linked to costs will play an important role, and any suitable sales argument needs to also include consideration of the added value.

5.4.3 Literature-based Categories and the Literature-Based Model

Ten categories, of relevance for the SPICE experts group, taken from the literature, were developed, within the scope of the mapping process in the analysis. The literature search - with reference to NGNs and SDPs - revealed ten generic categories (shown in Figure 49), in three phases of validated empirical data, and can be summarised in the following categories:

- Multimedia Applications
- High Mobility
- Centralisation of Net- and Client-Intelligence
- Integration of Existing Environments
- Minor Energy Consumption
- Multi Faculty of Speech

- Security and Data Integrity

- Context Awareness

- User Friendliness

- Minor Cost (Network Access, End devices)

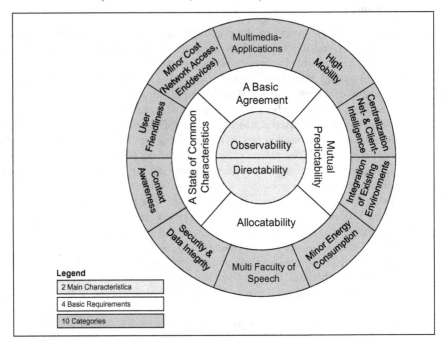

Figure 49: Literature-based model from this investigation

Both inner rings in Figure 49 were extracted from the literature model (see Paragraph 2.5.1.1), and show preconditions for the purposes of human-computer interaction, as described in the works of Christoffersen and Woods (in 2002: pp. 4-10; see also Paragraph 2.5.1.2 and Klein *et al.*, (in 2004: pp. 91-94). The ten generic categories are derived from the results (aspects and requirements), of the Mapping Process, and must be fulfilled based on the references of the preconditions shown in Paragraphs 2.5.1.1 and 2.5.1.2 above, in order to gain a better understanding of the ten challenges for the development of an SDP, concerning the application of an ICT system. These are briefly described and illustrated:

The next ten Paragraphs summarise the literature-based aspects of design issues for SDP-based ICT systems collected from the literature to illustrate a comparative literature-based model, similarly with the interview-based model.

The literature-based categories refer to the literature-based criteria catalogue and succession to a reference from the original literature (Section 10.3 and Chapter 11).

Multimedia Applications

Multimedia applications are applications where the content of digital media is displayed. This includes complex animation, video files and high definition television (HDTV) streams. These applications need a broadband data connection, in order to guarantee stable interaction with data contents. Applications in this context are served by SDP services. Standardised SIP- and IP-based data transfer becomes necessary, so that an existing user session is not interrupted. This means, in the context of ICT systems or components, that the use of SIP- or IP-based technologies allows the engagement of the Internet for all of these ICT systems and components. Furthermore, higher ranges and more stable connections, with higher availability of existing services, are possible with the use of convergent network technologies. SIP technology, as part of an SDP, has a very high impact when used in multimedia applications. It can be concluded that both preventative IT-based control and security can be improved in ICT systems. Details are given in the Sections 4.1 and 10.3.

High Mobility

By High Mobility it is to be understood in the context of an SDP that access to services may occur independently of place and time. This core aspect demands the requirement of possibly independent and reliable access to services and applications. The mobility of provided services on an SDP has already been mentioned. A necessary criterion is to be able to use SDPs nowadays. Stable network access possibility and easy configuration, within the scope of an ad-hoc-network, are also necessary, in order to guarantee acceptance with potential users. In the ICT field, the mobility of any SDP is extremely necessary, as services have to be available at all times (see Sections 4.1 and 10.3).

Centralisation of Net- and Client-Intelligence

A service-oriented system, that touches onto on a physical network, for example a telephone network, is understood to be an intelligent network. This network extends physically due to intelligent components, which bring additional performance characteristics, such as value-added services, mobile radio, fax etc. The term intelligent client can be understood to mean an expansion of components within a client, for example standardised interfaces, Location-Based-Service or email.

The centralisation of many network and client services, and centralised paging on the SDP, are necessary for such a connection, for example on the interface that is nowadays extensively standardised in the network area, as well as in the client area. A centralisation of network and client intelligence makes sense in terms of ICT systems, because, for example, the UMTS-network technology adjusts very well to the services provided on an SDP, thus enabling quick and effective administration (see Sections 4.1 and 10.3).

Integration of Existing Environments

SDP and ICT-systems' respective components have to be compatible with existing infrastructures, such as existing networks located in companies (for instance GPRS or UMTS), as well as other ICT infrastructures. The need arises for an existing ICT system to be simply transferable, without a completely new ICT system immediately having to be developed and introduced. This is in line with Pan-European and other standards, such as GPRS, UMTS and LTE-based ICT infrastructure. It is also necessary to be able to use the existing components of ICT system environments (see Sections 4.1 and 10.3).

Minor Energy Consumption

"Minor Energy Consumption" is an essential point, and must be addressed on both network and ICT system sides, as well as on the mobile end devices. It has to be considered for the control of an ICT system (see Sections 4.1 and 10.3).

Multi Faculty of Speech

Multi-linguistic ability and its ease of use within an ICT system is another important point, which can be controlled through an SDP for network components, and ICT systems, through the terminals or end devices used (see Sections 4.1 and 10.3).

Security and Data Protection

Security and data protection describes the need to protect services and information. Authentication is necessary for the purposes of security in an ICT system and therefore ensures access for the user of an ICT system (see Sections 4.1 and 10.3).

Context Awareness

Context awareness describes the need to generate information dynamically, based on the content and in relation to the end-user, their devices and their different display dimensions. In addition to this information, data must be provided in a conscious and sensitive way on different end devices, as a function of the display and its resolution (see Sections 4.1 and 10.3).

User Friendliness

User friendliness permits the end-user of an ICT system to operate in a simple and easy way, not only for the administrators of an SDP, but also for the users of end devices who want to have access to the platform. The configuration of an SDP and use of the services are to be guaranteed for the support of a large number of end devices (see Sections 4.1 and 10.3).

Minor Costs (Network Access, End devices)

Costs are an important aspect with regard to an ICT system of the future. They must be computed with the help of a cost-benefit analysis tool. The costs for the purchase and application of such a system would have to be taken into account (see Sections 4.1 and 10.3).

   The following Section discusses the relationship of the six final GT categories, their relationships and the literature-based criteria of design issues, for SDP-based ICT-systems is illustrated.

5.4.4 Reflection and Discussion

Klein *et al.* (2004: p. 94) exactly represent the focal point, the four basic requirements described in 2.5.1.2 that was identified for this investigation. Together with Christoffersen and Woods (2002: pp. 4-10) the main characteristics (described in Paragraph 2.5.1.1) are defined, and they pointed out that team play between automated systems such as SDPs and ICT systems and users can be improved. These generic aspects shown in Paragraphs 2.5.1.1 and 2.5.1.2 post a valid consistent possibility to describe the improvement of human computer interaction between SDP-based ICT systems and their end-users again.

   According to the focus of this work, an ICT system should, in the future, be able to achieve at least some form of collaborative interaction with the human user. In the future, computer agents could become better team members. Today they can already be seen, as being like a young child in a team of adults, or a novice in an already well-functioning mature team. Research has indicated that with this system, security and human computer interaction can be improved.

5.4.4.1   Relationship between GT Categories and Literature-Based Categories

A comparison of all categories, from the data collected, from the interviews (six final categories), and those gathered from the literature (10 final categories), proves that similar challenges are to be considered. These challenges are shown in the following Table 33.

Table 33: Comparison of categories developed from interview and literature-based data

Models	Categories developed from the Interview-based Data	Categories developed from the Literature-based Data
Challenges and Design Aspects for Service-Delivery-Platforms	• Applicability • Controllability • Interoperability • Mobility • Security and Reliability *direct relations* • Usability	• High Mobility • User Friendliness • Minor Energy Consumption • Security and Data Integrity • Multi Faculty of Speech • Context Awareness • Integration of Existing Environments • Minor Cost (Network Access, Enddevices) • Centralisation of Net- and Client-Intelligence • Multimedia Applications

Table 33 shows that the categories *'Mobility'*, *'High Mobility'*, *'Usability'*, *'User Friendliness'*, and *'Security'*, shown in green, were frequently identified by the participants in the empirical study, and are comparable to the categories developed by the literature-based studies on NGN and SDP topics. Interestingly, the categories marked with arrows, in the left column (categories developed from the interview-based data) were almost identical to, and confirmed by, the categories developed from the literature-based data (in the right column) in a direct relation.

5.4.4.2 Comparison of GT Categories, their Relations and the Literature-Based Categories

A comparison of all GT categories and their relations (described in Section 5.3) with the issues gathered from the literature (10 final categories), are related with the following Figure 50.

Figure 50 visually represents the six GT categories and their relationship, based on selective codes, described in Section 5.3.3. The small tables coded with the colours of the GT categories, show the relation of the ten literature-based categories to the final GT categories.

The next Section details the development of a generic framework for an SDP-based ICT system of the future, by describing the functional requirements of such a system.

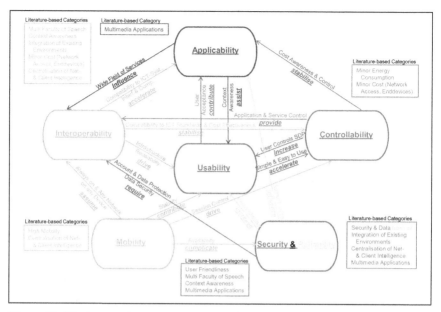

Figure 50: Final categories, their relations and the connection to literature-based data

5.5 Development of a Generic Framework for a SDP-based ICT System of the Future

This Section deals with the generation of a framework, based on the final categories and developed models, and is supported by the results from the application of EMPLIT, within this special study setup. The aim is to generate a theoretical construct, which serves as an explanation for the developed final categories, by means of GT, with the help of the well-chosen investigation criteria shown in Sections 1.1 (challenges and design issues) and 0 (problem finding). The functional requirements, derived from the results of the study, are described in detail, enabling other researchers to have further development and more deeply detailed studies, in the future.

A generic delivery model for an SDP of a future-oriented ICT system, is described in Figure 51, as a result of the development of categories from the empirical data shown in Chapter 4, Table 7 and Table 35. This generic model focuses on the final six categories developed in the empirical study.

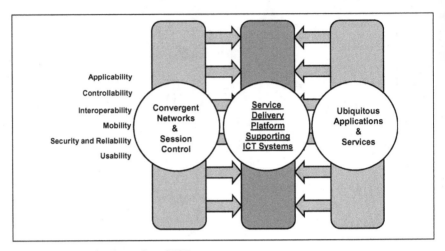

Figure 51: SDP for future-based ICT systems

The following functional requirements for an ICT system of the future are to be understood as a consolidation of the results of this study, and a recommendation for future research projects. What follows is a discussion of the results, as an example, looking at how modern communication technologies could help support end-users of ICT systems in their everyday lives, and exploring the potential uses connected with this.

5.5.1 Functional Requirements of the Generic ICT Systems

In the following, the development of the functional requirements for an ICT system of the future, using an SDP, is described. The Mind Map representations in the following two illustrations, Figure 52 and Figure 53, are based on the empirical findings, and depict the relevant requirements of an ICT system of the future.

5.5.1.1   General Requirements of an ICT System

An ICT system of the future is one that uses an SDP for the provision, operation and development of ubiquitous services. This kind of system is based on functional architecture. This model of functional architecture describes the functions and dependencies that the system should provide. The description concentrates on the perspective of individuals, based on the developed categories. The functional framework concentrates on the description of functions, independently of their integration and logical or technical architecture.

5.5.1.2   Functional Requirements of an ICT System

Based on the concept represented in Figure 51, and the developed categories shown in Table 28 and Table 33, general functional requirements were developed, propelled by the results of the mapping process. The functional requirements for each of the categories are shown in Figure 52.

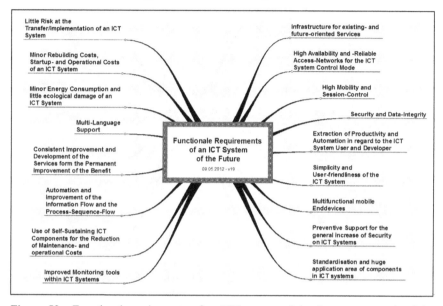

Figure 52:   Functional requirements of an ICT system of the future, as a result of the literature-based study and the mapping process, and seen from a generic level

Current or existing infrastructure should be used, and should ideally be compatible with this generic level of functional requirements. The new system should support the existing services of ICT systems and enable the implementation of future services. Highly available and reliable access networks are necessary and form the basis of control of these ICT systems. High mobility and the control of stable application and services sessions are also a must. On the one hand a reliable connection between the user and applications or services must be available. On the other hand, access to the account, data and information of the end-user of the SDP, has to be securely protected. Security and data protection are guaranteed by suitable access and encoding mechanisms. The productivity of the duties of an SDP, such as SPICE, becomes multifunctional, mobile terminals, quickly adaptable services and a high standardisation degree. The simplicity of ICT systems and their user-friendliness is another requirement.

5.5.1.3 Functional Requirements of an SDP for an ICT System

The following Figure 52 shows the functional requirements of the service creation platform, and execution platform (SDP), of an ICT system of the future.

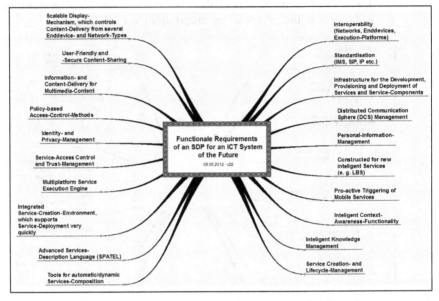

Figure 53: Functional requirements of an SDP for an ICT System of the future as a result
of the Mapping Process, and seen from a meta-level

The functional requirements described, concerning an SDP for an ICT system of the Future (Figure 53), are the final results of the codes gathered from the
interview data, which relate to the codes gathered from the literature-based data.

Standardisation and a high adaptation percentage of IT- and web-based services, to support the precaution, to fulfil the requirements of future-based ICT
systems, have to be controlled and operated by an SDP. The cost aspect for the
company, and the servicing, can be improved by the application of self-sufficient
ICT system components. Steady improvement of services is promoted by the
high standardisation degree (IMS, SIP, IP) on the SDP. Low conversion costs, as
well as a low risk, are guaranteed by the integration of existing technologies and
ICT system components.

5.5.2 Correlation of GT Categories and Functional Requirements

According to the requirements of SDP and ICT systems, it is essential to have a
correlation between developed categories and functional requirements, and then

to compare these with literature-based data, so that both SDP users, and developers, ultimately profit from innovations. Table 34 below shows the correlation of the functional requirements (right column), the developed categories (left column), and their mapping.

Table 34: Correlation of the aspects (developed categories), with the functional requirements of future-oriented ICT systems

Aspects from the empirical study	Derived, dedicated functional requirements
Usability	• Simplicity • User friendliness of ICT systems • Multi faculty of speech • Context awareness
Mobility	• High availability of services and network access • Session Control • Multi-functional mobile end-devices
Security and Reliabilty	• Security and Data Protection • Support of preventive provision (general increase of security in regard to ICT systems) • Monitoring of ICT processes • Minimized energy consumption and ecological damage
Applicability	• Spectrum of services • Standardised services and ICT systems • Wide field of application for ICT systems • Continuous improvement • Simple enlargement of services (improvement of benefit for the users)
Interoperability	• Infrastructure must support existing and also future-oriented services
Controllability	• Controlled by end-users • Cost Awareness • Use of self-sustaining ICT systems for the reduction of maintenance- and operational costs • Low rebuilding costs • Low startup- and operational costs • Little implementation and tranfer risk

Table 34 shows the correlation of the developed categories, with the functional requirements of a future-oriented ICT system, developed as a result of applying EMPLIT. The comparison of the developed categories from the literature-based study with those developed by means of the empirical study, is described.

The category "User Friendliness" is linked to the functional requirements 'Simplicity', 'User Friendliness of ICT systems' and 'Multi Faculty of Speech'. The category "High Mobility" consists of 'High Availability of Services and Network Access', 'Session Control' and 'Multi-functional Mobile End devices'. The category "Security and Reliability" is linked to the functional requirements, 'Security and Data Protection', 'Support of the Preventive Provision (general increase of security in regard to ICT systems)', 'Monitoring of ICT processes' and 'Minor Energy Consumption and Ecological Damage'. The category "Spectrum of Services" is linked to the functional requirements, 'Standardised Services and ICT Systems', 'Wide Field of Application of ICT Systems', 'Continuous Improvement' and 'Simple Enlargement of Services'. "Infrastructure Usability" is linked to the concept 'Infrastructure must support existing and also future-oriented services'.

The last category, "Cost Awareness", is linked to the dedicated functional requirements, 'Use of Self-Sustaining ICT Systems for the reduction of Maintenance and Operational Cost', 'Low Rebuilding Cost', 'Low Start-up and Operational Cost', and 'Low Implementation and Transfer Risk'. The following Section points out a comparison of categories, developed from the interview-based data and "categories/aspects" developed in terms of the literature review, by using the Mapping Process, with references to the academic literature.

The next Section describes the researcher's interpretation of the empirical findings within this study, and discusses the relationship between the developed six final categories, among themselves, and highlights the outcomes and findings of this study, based on the respondents' views.

5.6   Interpretation and Discussion of the Empirical Findings

This Section hones in on the relationships and connections between the developed GT categories presented in the previous Sections. The categories and their relationships form the basis of the GT, and offer an explanation about the phenomenon under study: User needs by using individuals' perceptions of design aspects of SDPs. Each GT category is related to findings from the pilot and interview phases, and this triangulation of empirical data and comparison to the relevant literature has helped verify and strengthen the theory. Moreover, this Section presents four main findings relevant to the relationship between challenges and design issues of SDPs, and related ICT environments, and respondents' perceptions. These originated from the categories and the connections that have been established between them.

5.6.1   Respondents' Perspectives of Challenges and Design Issues on SDPs and ICT environments

The six final developed GT categories represent the views of the interviewees in terms of SDP-based ICT development. These categories were developed from the empirical data. To highlight the respondents' perspective, the researcher starts summarising the categories again and discusses each category separately:

■ Applicability

■ Controllability

■ Interoperability

■ Mobility

■ Security and Reliability

■ Usability

Applicability

Two different areas of the GT category *"Applicability"* were identified in the descriptions of the respondents, and those have been structured in GT sub-categories *'Wide Field of Services'* and *'Context Awareness'*. Some statements of the interview respondents can be categorised in different areas, such as users, operators, end devices/networks, features/services, ICT systems, etc.

Respondents pointed out that *"Applicability"* is affected by different attributes and a wide range and variety of services and applications, that makes users everyday lives easier, and helps generate user confidence within their community and gives them a good feeling while using (as shown in Sections 4.5.1 and 5.4.2).

Controllability

Respondents identified three different areas of the GT category *"Controllability"* in their descriptions. These were structured in GT sub-categories *'Cost Awareness and Control'*, *'User Controls SDP'* and *'Application and Service Control'*. Participants' statements are shown in Sections 4.5.2 and 5.4.2 in detail.

Respondents commented that *"Controllability"* refers to users wanting to control activities related to their data, as this control can have an impact and influence on their own costs. SDPs have become part of modern communication platforms for providing the exchange of data and information from users in their everyday lives (as shown in Sections 4.5.2 and 5.4.2).

Interoperability

Four different areas of the GT category *"Interoperability"* were identified in the description of the respondents and those have been structured into the GT sub-categories *'Compatibility to ICT-Systems, - Interfaces, and – Components'*, *'Compatibility to ICT Standard'*, *'Infrastructure Re-usability'*, and *'Cost Effectiveness'*. The respondent views can be categorised in the following areas: heterogeneous environments, software, and services. The participants' pointed out in their statements that *"Interoperability"* even can be achieved if different rules and standards are required. They have to be upwardly and downwardly compatible (as described in Sections 4.5.3 and 5.4.2).

Mobility

The respondents identified three different areas of the GT category *"Mobility"* in their descriptions. These have been structured into the GT sub-categories *'Availability'*, *'Stability and Session Control'*, *'Always On'* and *'Any Network on any Device'*. In Section 4.5.4 the statements of participants are presented in detail. The respondents see *"Mobility"* in terms of users needing a stable mobile connection whilst on the move.

When the user is between wired locations, mobile ICT environments need a stable and reliable connection. What was important, from the respondents' point of view were the following challenges: service roaming in home and visited domains, access to services at all times with different service levels, and a highly available and reliable connections to networks (presented in Sections 4.5.4 and 5.4.2).

Security and Reliability

Three different areas of the GT category *"Security and Reliability"* were identified in the description of the respondents and these have been structured in the GT sub-categories *'Account and Data Protection'*, *'Data Security'*, and *'Authentication and Personalisation'*. The comments of the respondents can be categorised in the following areas: application settings, data setting, information settings, mobile setting and network setting. The participants' pointed out, that users want to have their accounts and data secured, when using an SDP, because they want to be able to store their data and services on such platforms (as described in Sections 4.5.5 and 5.4.2).

Usability

Three different areas of the GT category *"Usability"* were identified in the description of the respondents. These areas have been structured in the GT sub-categories *'User Acceptance'*, *'User Friendliness'*, and *'Simple and Easy to Use'*. The respondent's statements can be categorised in the following areas: software application or service, SDP (web-site, portal) as a tool, process of using SDP, and end-device and SDP. Respondents pointed out that *"Usability"* is affected by different attributes, generates trust and makes an SDP acceptable and affordable for everyone (as shown in Sections 4.5.6 and 5.4.2).

5.6.2 Respondents' Views and the Findings and Outcomes of this Study

This Section provides further interpretation of the empirical data and focuses on four main findings, which encapsulate the relationship between perceptions of challenges and design issues for SDP-based ICT systems. The findings are based on the GT categories and their relationships, developed from pilot and in-depth interviews, illustrated previously. The comparison between findings from this study and the SDP and ICT-system related academic literature leads to the development of the main argument of this study. The difference between findings and outcomes is that outcomes correspond to the aim of the study, and the findings to the objectives in more detail.

Finding 1: Need for a single instance control and communication platform (SDP) represented with the explanatory framework of design issues for SDP-based development from the perspective of users.

There is a need to have a single instance control and communication platform in the form of an SDP, to control and communicate with different ICT environments, and to provide and operate services and applications on different end devices, within different ICT environments. This study has developed an explanatory framework of design issues for SDP-based ICT development from a users' perspective to represent the views of the respondents by the qualitative, user-oriented study.

Finding 2: SPICE is a representative model for an SDP in order to control and communicate with ICT systems.

SPICE is a representative model for an SDP as a control and communication instance for ICT systems of the future seen from a user's perspective. The actual SPICE views are only focused on the technical perspective, and the findings of this study can help address aspects from the user's perspective. What is important is that the technology is able to fulfil the requirements of the technical features, and that users and their daily activities, are the focus of this technological support.

This study indicated and discussed that, from a user's perspective, the SPICE platform and the design and development process, focusing strongly on the technical perspective. From the researcher's point of view, SPICE has to meet the requirements of different user groups to have a chance to become well-accepted, quickly, by the community.

Finding 3: Located and related challenges and design issues of SDPs in terms of ICT environments for the future.

The located and related challenges and design issues of SDPs in terms of ICT environments for the future, seen by the respondents of the empirical study are summarised as functional requirements:

- Interview and literature based models (Figure 48 and Figure 49 in Section 5.4).

- Functional requirements of an ICT system of the future (Figure 52 in Section 5.5.1)

- Functional requirements of an SDP for an ICT system of the future (Figure 53 in Section 5.5.1)

- Correlation of categories and functional requirements (Table 34 in Section 5.5.1)

Finding 4: Enlarging guidelines to design SDPs from a technical point of view with guidelines from a user's perspective will support user activities represented a substantive theory diagram.

SDPs have to meet the requirements of end-users, to have a chance of becoming well and truly accepted by users, as a single instance to control and to communicate with different ICT environments, thus making user's lives easier. Everyday life is supported using SDP-based ICT environments and is influenced by the need for a broad range of potential users. SDP technology concepts have to be affordable for everyone to fulfil the quick-time-to-market principal in order to be successful in supporting this broad range of end-users. This investigation conceptualised a substantive theory diagram for design issues of web-based platforms, from a user's perspective, inspired by Reid (2006), described in Paragraph 5.3.4.

To enlarge technically driven design and development guidelines with the results, taken from user specific analysis, such as the application of EMPLIT within this study, the researcher is of the opinion that this is beneficial for ICT system development as, starting a system design, and development process with a user-based analysis, strongly supports user-oriented development. SDPs, as a control and communication instance for ICT-systems, could be engaged to support end-users' daily lives by providing services to operate. The researcher isolated the three most important outcomes of this investigation, which have been summarised as follows:

Outcome 1: Expansion of design and development guidelines to such a process with a users-based analysis.

The enlargement of design and development guidelines with the results from a target user-specific analysis, is beneficial in ICT system development. To start a system design and development process with a user-based analysis, strongly supports user-oriented development (Figure 61).

Outcome 2: EMPLIT is an unexpected finding of this investigation. The final results were justified by applying EMPLIT methodology and the dual-layered justification process.

The EMPLIT methodology is an unexpected finding of this study. Based on the validated and justified results using EMPLIT, the mapping process related user needs, challenges and design issues, to literature-based categories (shown in Chapters 4 and 5). Empirical codes and categories were validated in multiple ways:

▪ Confirmed codes (3rd-party researcher)

▪ Reflected respondent views (theoretical memos)

▪ Compared codes with literature-based criteria catalogue

▪ Thesis results in context with other research (related research)

▪ Validated research questions presented in Section 3.9.4

▪ Validated results by presenting these to interview participants and received their feedback

The validated and justified results, using dual-layered justification and the mapping process, were described in the Chapters 4 and 5 respectively, particularly in Section 5.5.1 (literature-based categories: aspects, requirements from the mind maps) in detail.

Outcome 3: Recommendations for design guidelines for an SDP-based ICT system of the future, based on the developed six final GT categories, and the derived functional requirements, shown in Section 5.5.

Based on the developed six final GT categories, and the literature-based categories developed using the literature-based study, a generic category-based framework was developed in Section 5.5. This generic framework consolidates the categories coming from the empirical study, with those created based on the literature, and outlines dedicated functional requirements for an SDP-based ICT system, of the future. These aspects are presented in 5.5 (Figure 48 and Table 34 describe a recommendation for an SDP-based ICT system of the future) by concluding and sorting codes from empirical and literature-based findings, in a grouping and structuring procedure, again using a mind map representation. They are revisited and described in detail in the Section 5.5.

The researcher supports the complementary approach of this study as being of great benefit for user-oriented SDP-based ICT development. This conclusion was arrived at by a user focused study, before developing and implementing technical features, as the researcher strongly focused on individual user needs and the priorities of features can be defined by users.

5.6.3 Reflection and Discussion of the Respondent Views

According to the aims and objectives (shown in 1.3) of this work, the researcher discusses the relationship between aim, objectives, findings and outcomes to summarise the results of this qualitative study. Additionally, the author concludes, depicting the results in a substantive theory diagram presented in Figure 47.

5.6.3.1 Relations between Findings and Objectives

The objectives of the study (see also Section 1.3) were met as follows: Chapter 4 presented the findings and showed how the analysis was done by the application of EMPLIT in order to investigate the relationship between users and an SDP to administrate ICT systems (Objective 1) and Chapter 5 presented the results from an empirical study. The current technological situation supporting user tasks for SDPs, particularly SPICE, was addressed in the literature review. In Chapter 2, the relevant literature regarding SDP-related technologies was presented and its relationship to other research, discussed (Objective 2). The location and relation, of user needs and design issues of SDPs, to support user tasks, was addressed by interviewing experts from the SPICE project. In Section 1.3, the location and relation of user needs and design issues of SDPs was set out in terms of supporting daily user tasks (Objective 3).

A model and framework explaining the challenges and design issues to support daily user tasks were presented in Chapter 5 (Objective 4). The four main findings of this study are related to the objectives as shown in Figure 54.

Objective 1: To investigate the relationship between users and SDPs to control and operate ICT environments from an individual's perspective.

The identified needs of different groups of individuals, (end-users, developers, and architecture experts) in terms of the technological influences on SDPs, have an effect on the challenges and design issues to regulate future-based ICT infrastructure, from a user's perspective. This was shown by the respondents' views. To summarise, SDPs have to meet the requirements of end-users; this is a key success factor for implementation of SDPs in an ICT environment. This is because there is definitely a need, driven by the perspective of the users, to have a single-instance control and communication system, such as an SDP, to engage in all communications, using the ICT environment, as a control system.

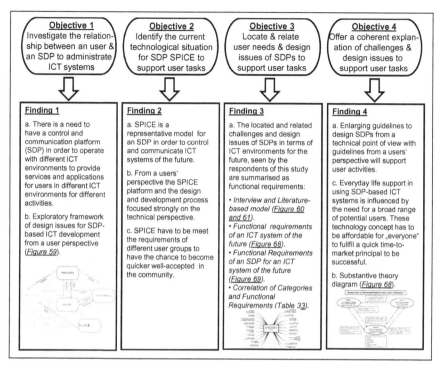

Figure 54: Objectives and main findings of this study

The benefit of selecting an SDP as a control and communication instance for ICT environments could be increased if the aspects of applicability, controllability, interoperability, mobility, security, reliability and usability of the SDP control instance, as well as the controlled ICT environment, can be fulfilled. What needs to be emphasised is that all end-user related aspects are increasingly more important for the acceptance of new environments and technologies on the market. All respondent groups (end-users, developers, architecture experts) have seen a clear improvement potential in general development principals, if the focus can be put, on the user perspective (Finding 1).

Generally, the availability of ICT services is increased by the introduction of SDPs from the point of a communication single instance to control ICT systems, services and applications. The essential aspect lies in the supply of broadband network access, standardised IP services and system use, which allows for any number of services and applications for ICT systems of the future, by using technologies like SIP, IP and IMS. The respondents (SPICE experts) see the introduction of standard technologies with SIP, IP and IMS, as having a clear advantage in the improvement of both availability and reliability of ICT environments.

Objective 2: To identify the current situation regarding challenges and design issues for SDPs (SPICE) in terms of supporting users' everyday lives from a technological perspective. The second objective was necessary to identify and discuss the current technological background regarding the SDP SPICE, observed from the perspective of various groups of individuals (end-users, developers, and architecture experts).

The review of relevant developments in the SDP environment, as well as the representation of general requirements in the literature, was carried out and shown in Chapters 2, 4 and 5. An extensive review of the relevant literature (SDPs, SPICE, NGNs, etc.) was done in Chapter 2. The objective was to paint a picture of the dynamics involved in developing a general framework for ICT infrastructure, whilst considering the viewpoints of the various people involved.

SPICE is representative for SDPs as a control and communication instance for ICT systems of the future, seen from a user's perspective. SPICE focuses more on the technical architectural perspective and the associated technical potential. The respondents argued that the user perspective is of greater importance to focus on (Finding 2).

Objective 3: To locate and relate user needs and design issues in terms of web-based platforms such as an SDP to support user needs from an individual's perspective. The empirical findings were related to the relevant literature and a limited number of interviews with SPICE experts, which served to supplement the review of the literature. The findings and results of this were illustrated in a meta-model based on the categories discovered in Chapter 5. The challenges and design issues are summarised in Chapter 5, in Figure 52, Figure 53 and Table 34, as outcomes of the Mapping Process showing the results of the validated empirical aspects/codes. The located and related challenges and design issues of SDPs in terms of ICT environments for the future as seen by the respondents of this study are summarised (Finding 3).

Objective 4: To offer a coherent explanation of the individuals' views of challenges and design issues in relation to SDP and ICT technologies of the future to support users' everyday lives. The final objective addressed, was achieved through the development of a theoretical model, which mapped out the relationships between SPICE SDP parameters of information and communication infrastructure design aspects. SDPs have to meet the requirements of end-users to have the chance of becoming better accepted by users as a single instance to control and communicate within different ICT environments (Finding 4). Everyday support in using ICT environments is influenced by the need for a broad range of potential users.

As such, this technology has to be affordable to everyone to fulfil a quick time-to-market principal, in order to achieve successful implementation. The SPICE experts can well assess which information is essential for the end-users of SDPs, and can additionally make a distinction between what they would like to see in SDP and what is irrelevant. It is important from their point of view, that ICT systems make data and information highly available. They see a clear use if the current gaps in information access, can be filled.

5.6.3.2   Relations between Findings and Outcomes

The three main outcomes of this study are related to the findings, which is shown in Figure 55. The aim of this investigation was to identify challenges and design issues and develop a model/framework from the perspective of users, to make everyday tasks easier. Figure 55 relates Outcome 1 to Findings 1 and 2, and illustrates the author's argument, that the enlargement of design and development guidelines as a result of this study is beneficial in SDP-based ICT development. Starting a system design and development process by employing a user-based analysis strongly supports user-centred design and development. Outcome 2, illustrates the unexpected finding of this study, the EMPLIT framework, as a methodological contribution. Outcome 2 was connected to Findings 1 and 4 and assisted the justification of the research results by the application of EMPLIT and the dual-layered justification process at this specific study setup. Outcome 3 derived from Findings 1, 3 and 4 and recommend derived functional requirements for design guidelines from the perspective of users representing the respondent views.

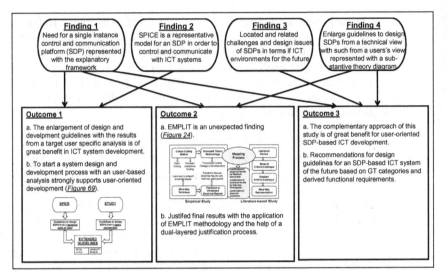

Figure 55: Findings and outcomes of this investigation

5.6.3.3   Summary of Challenges in SDP development from this Study

The challenges from the perspective of the potential web-based platform user were derived from the empirical interview data and identified through focused coding. These findings were then collected, structured and grouped, and are presented in Chapter 4, in form of functional requirements from the perspective of web-based platform users (such as SDPs), as represented by the respondents of the interviews.

The final categories, their relationships and functional design aspects obtained from the interview data, are related to aspects from the literature, which were generated through the mapping process to provide the literature-based criteria. Developer and user perceptions of design aspects for SDPs, within the framework of ICT systems, are relevant because of the divergent perspectives of individuals and literature, regarding aspects of designing ICT systems. The viewpoint of developers and users has an effect on future policies regulating the use of services, over the Internet for example, and addresses the implications of increasing the use of SDPs, with respect to ICT systems, and the impact of SDPs and ICT systems on people's everyday lives. Hence, it is important to represent the needs of those ordinary citizens who use ICT technologies in their everyday lives. The selected research methods are based on applied research, using the abductive approach employing the EMPLIT methodology for the development of a theory and the EMPLIT methodology for the dual-layered justification process, for the justification of the theory. The knowledge acquired will facilitate the creation of a common model for the operation and development of SDP-based ICT systems from a user's perspective.

Based on the challenges identified, a substantive GT was developed. The final categories that were created helped to map and identify a generic framework in the form of a functional meta-model. These functional aspects specified the design aspects for web-based platforms (SDPs) with regard to the use of this technology in ICT environments as indicated from users' perspectives. From these design aspects, it was possible to derive recommendations regarding SDPs as control and communication instances, for future-oriented ICT systems.

Free services on the Internet and the "opening" of the Internet and IP based data processing with the inclusion of an SDP, such as SPICE, in an ICT system of the future, leads to potentially boundless possibilities which need to be controlled. However, guidelines on how to protect the security level and how to avoid an explosive increase of services on SDPs need to be addressed. This is due to performance, availability and the execution of commercial processes, which should remain possibilities for end-users. Suppliers can offer customers different packages of services with a commercial leasing model.

The essential functional components of that are audio, video, route planning (navigation) and IT end-devices, such as via notebooks, PDAs and Smartphones. Through the interoperability enabled by the introduction of new communication possibilities, it is possible to guarantee international fee systems. This requires the use of standards and norms, at least throughout Europe, but preferably internationally. The research undertaken in this study has shown that SDPs can be highly improved for profitable interaction with the ICT system users. Even if no quantum leaps are made, it could still be possible to develop ICT systems in the future by linking them with innovative SDPs.

The following Section finalises the whole phase and reverts back to the literature discussing parallels and divergences, of the empirical findings of this study, against the academic literature.

5.7   Individuals' Perceptions - Parallels and Divergences from the Academic Literature

This Section discusses parallels and divergences between the participants' views of challenges and design issues, regarding user needs of SDP-based ICT systems, with those commonly presented in the literature. It illustrates similarities and variances between individuals' perceptions and those predominantly expressed in the literature.

5.7.1 Scope of SDP definition

The study identified that the perspectives of individuals facing challenges within the area of acceptance, and coverage of the population, are essential. To be successful in applying the concept of SDPs to administrate ICT environments, the user's view is essential (see Section 5.6.2, Findings 1 and 4). According to Cordier (2005), technical consultants believe user's demand that many requirements are met, often having little to do with the operating features of a technical system. However, the predominant views in the literature read, are driven and dominated by technical consultants and technological hypes, to shorten technology cycles and drive innovation. The overachieving goal is to launch a product before competitors can place their product in the market.

Another perspective is that usability becomes increasingly important in driving the development of technological environments, to stay ahead of competitors. This is another area where development differentiates between competitors. Psychologists believe that individuals will always decontextualise data back into an individually defined whole, or context, in order to interpret it. This may explain the behaviour of the respondents in this study. Individuals describe the impact of 'being simple to use' as a necessary success factor to become a quick and well-accepted technology, moreover, addressing a broad range of potential customers, with time constraints, is also a contributing success factor. For example, individual definitions of an SDP relate to a potential administration tool to operate a broad-range of ICT environments. This is due to the support of the end-users to make their lives easier, when the use of technology and not the technologies themselves, drive and execute scenarios, which are not necessary for a broad range of potential users (Karwowski et. al, 2011).

This may provide an explanation why participants do not comprehend the impact of technology-driven ICT environments, for a broad range of people. There must be a need to handle everyday-life scenarios, to quickly become more widely accepted. Finding 4 supports this argument, as individuals see user acceptance is a must, and the need of increasing affordability for using and getting this technology, to better support everyday things (Nielsen, 2004).

In contrast to the views of the respondents of this study, other academic literature predominantly focused on the impacts of technologically driven developments, such as SPICE. The retention of ICT systems users, has an impact on a wider, potential of users and ultimately society, allowing for homogenous environments, and thus making it easier for people who are not experts, or technically minded, to handle such systems (see Section 3.9.4, Research question 1: Explosion of applications on ubiquitous technologies versus the need of the end-user to support their everyday lives and Finding 4, Section 5.6.2).

5.7.2 SDP influenced by technologies

The respondents' definitions of using SDPs relate to the views of SDPs represented in the academic literature, and tend to be independent of technological influences. For the respondents of this study, SDPs are about to interoperate in the convergent worlds of mobile communication and information technology, with applications and services, anytime and anyplace. Furthermore, they consider it as being independent of which network access exists, at the actual location, and independent of which end device they are going to use. According to Karwowski et al. (2011), and Nielsen (2004), this is also identified in the academic literature. More importantly however, is focussing on the technological part and how it can be implemented (Cordier et al., 2006). Respondents are not focussing solely on the technology, but the focus is on the end-user of SDPs and ICT environments. This is illustrated by the GT category "Usability" and also their relationship to the other GT categories developed (see Sections 4.5.6 and 5.4.2).

When respondents gave their views of SDPs it seemed that technologies were not the focal part. They were of the opinion of supporting the users' daily activities (see Finding 2). What seemed most relevant is the role of the end-user of SDPs and their daily activities respectively. The SDP is a control tool that stores data and services, to communicate and control the operation of the user's end device as a single instance (see Finding 1).

However, there is a need to offer as much of the services and applications of everyday-life support as possible, to increase acceptance and also to successfully launch on the market, from a commercial point of view (see GT category "Applicability" and Finding 4 as well).

The literature takes on different views of SDPs compared to those of the individuals taking part in this study. SDP published literature, focussed on the role of technology in relation to the convergence of mobile communication systems and information technology as well as a cloud based communication platform providing ICT services. Particularly the potential of technologies to drive the development of individual customer and human needs is argued to have an impact on society as a whole (see Research questions 1 and 2, Section 3.9.4).

To summarise, two different views of SDPs can be identified – one is the prevailing SDP definition by the respondents of this study, which can be interpreted as corresponding to the traditional views of SDPs, as postulated by Ahson and Ilyas (2011). This is the definition that will be referred to, in the following, as 'individual view of SDPs', and respondents describe the needs from an end-user's perspective.

In contrast the 'collective view of SDPs' that can be identified in recent literature is very technically oriented. This view of SDPs relates to the impact of technologies and the implication of these influences on society as a whole. These two distinct views of SDPs developed from the analysis of empirical evidence, and its comparison to the literature, leads to the following claim: A fundamental rift can be identified between the views and definitions of challenges and design issues with SDPs and ICT systems, between individuals and the academic literature. These are:

■ Individual views postulate that, a user-orientated study makes sense, before starting a technical analysis and implementation.

■ Common views represented by the academic literature, postulate a strong technology driven development, as innovation is strongly related to technical feasibility. However, the ongoing importance of more user-oriented development in terms of software and ICT development is also presented in the literature.

The depiction and recognition of this divergence is relevant, as it can affect future aspects, challenges and policies, to control and operate ICT environments. This discrepancy between individual and collective views, represented by the academic literature, of SDPs is to some extent recognised by the participants of this study, and also within the literature, as explained in the following Sections.

5.7.3 Respondents' Views Regarding SDP, ICT Systems, Society and Technology

During the interviews, respondents frequently referred to the SPICE project and the technological aspects of SDPs in terms of ICT systems. This is related to challenges and aspects considered by a technological perspective of an SDP to fulfil technical features and requirements. Many respondents referred to the user-centred view of technological environments.

The interesting point here is that some of the developers and architectural experts, representing the more technical view, grappled with the user-focused view of technical systems and pointed out, that technical systems should exist to support the users' daily tasks and activities. This is related to a more user-focused view of an SDP to support a broad range of potential users. Society is going to be influenced by technology with a strong development-driven approach geared towards an end-user.

Parallels exist, in that potential use of an SDP as a control and communication instance for ICT systems, which gives mobile end device users the feeling that they are constantly in control for example, and that they can operate their services, data and applications with different devices anytime and anywhere. However, individuals are often either unaware of SDPs, as they do not know their potential or they do not want to invest time and energy in learning new environments or changing current processes.

The respondents saw a clear need for a single instance to control and operate ICT environments, and from their perspective, an SDP can be an instrument to execute this. However, there are two important challenges they argued in the interviews: 1. The SDP technology has to become well-accepted, by a wide range of users, this implies usability aspects, such as easy to handle, user-friendly and so forth, to generate confidence among the end-users. 2. This kind of technology has to become affordable for everyone. In this way a rapid, successful change and quick time-to-market principal can drive this concept.

5.7.4   Individual and Collective Views of SDPs in the Literature

Voorsluys et al. (2011), describe three forms of SDP concepts in relation to delivering services and functionalities. These are the IaaS, PaaS and SaaS concepts of delivering different kinds of ICT functionalities (see 0). IaaS is related to delivering infrastructure as a service, PaaS platform as a service and Saas software and application as a service. Individual, as well as, the collective view, see an ICT-related paradigm change moving ICT services to the cloud-computing model in the three dimensions IaaS, Paas and SaaS. Research questions 1 and 4 in Section 3.9.4, support the facts that the current cost pressure on CIO's in companies, and the need to focus more on the user needs, not on technically driven development, will bring a fundamental change and rebuilding of current ICT infrastructures, because the shift to the cloud reduces high investment costs. This will be totally equal both on the individual and collective views.

Pagani's (2005) analysis, encapsulates SDPs concerns articulated in other publications about personal space, mass data collection and private versus public data. Firstly, Talukder and Yavagal (2010) recognise, an invasion of personal storage for information, which makes SDPs a matter of end-user data and information storage systems. Secondly, the authors Ahson and Ilyas (2011) identify, that many different types of ICT systems have to be controlled and standardised concerning the more and more complex world of IT and mobile communication environments. This can result in SDPs only being used by technically oriented people, because not all potential end-users can afford these environments.

Furthermore, Hevner et al. (2004) argue that, the focus of ICT system design has shifted in the 21st century, towards the personal front, due to the increased use of mobile end devices that are carried by, and assigned to, one person. Hevner's account, and those of others support this study's outcome, that user-centred ICT system design can be divided into two distinct categories: firstly, SDPs as an individual control and operation instance and secondly SDPs on a collective level. Respondents of this study perceive SDPs as a control and operation single instance for ICT environments as an individual matter, independent of technology, whereas scholarly authors, such as Agarwal and Lucas (2005), March and Smith (1998), or Paas (2008), focus on the impacts of technology driven developments of such systems, and tend to take into account wider social impacts of developing such system's use of technology.

5.7.5 GT Categories and the Different Notations of Individual and Collective Views of SDPs

The distinction between two differing views of SDPs as identified by this study and in the literature, leads to the following argument. Whilst individuals still hold a rather traditional picture of SDPs, not influenced by technology and solely related to their own personal lives, 'individual view of SDPs', scholars paint a picture of SDPs that is affected by technology and relates to society as a whole, 'collective view of SDPs'. This observation is supported by the notion brought forward by Stalder (2002), proclaiming that many authors see recent developments in information and communication technologies, as shifting the notion of SDPs away from a view focused on the individual, towards a social concern on a wider scale.

The study supports Stalder's view, but simultaneously acknowledges, that citizens' interpretations of SDPs do not match-up with this shifted concept of SDPs. The GT categories developed in this study (see Sections 4.3.6 and 5.4.2) and the findings based on these categories (see 5.6) support the idea of a changing notion of SDPs.

5.7.5.1   Final Six GT Categories

The GT categories, derived from empirical findings, support the arguments described above as follows: SDP, as defined by respondents, corresponds to the traditional views of SDPs that are related to simplicity and user-friendliness for the end-users. The support of context awareness and multiple languages for the respondents are also important (see GT Category *"Usability"*). Individuals' views of the availability of SDPs are predominantly related to the idea of being mobile regardless of time and location. Availability, and control of services and applications, are important aspects and challenges, as well as the support of end devices and multimedia applications (see GT Category *"Mobility"*). The mobile end device is a communication technology that can be used to communicate by using services and applications from an SDP.

Respondents explain that data and account protection as well as process monitoring are important challenges of SDP-based ICT environments (GT Category *"Security and Reliability"*). Respondents explained that the actual process of using many different instances to control ICT systems is of relevance for SDPs - whether facilitated by technology or not - the control of cost-related aspects has to be fully controlled by the end-user of an SDP (GT Category *"Controllability"*).

The spectrum of services offered and provided by an SDP to support the end-users' daily lives activities as well as the support of a wide field of applications and the ability to enlarge and deploy new services, in a simple and quick way, which was described by the respondents (GT Category *"Applicability"*). It is of particular importance that users have the need to communicate by using new and existing ICT environments. Respondents argue that the support of existing and future-oriented environments and services is a must (GT *Category "Interoperability"*).

5.7.5.2   Four Main Findings

To summarise, participants see a need for a single instance communication platform, such as an SDP, operating different ICT systems from a single point, due to its benefits in making ICT-related activities easier to control (Finding 1). SPICE is a technical representative Service Delivery Platform, supporting the daily procedures and tasks from a user perspective. SDPs, are thus perceived to be related, from a user-benefit perspective (Finding 2). Challenges and design issues for SDPs in terms of ICT systems, that were uncovered in this study, are summarised as functional requirements from a user's perspective, in Mind Maps shown in Section 5.5.1 and represented in Figure 52, Figure 53 and Table 34 (Finding 3). SDPs have to be embraced by their potential users, as a single instance to control and operate ICT environments, as this technology will only be implemented if operators can reach a broad range of potential users. Additionally, this implementation is correlated with cost-intensive technological change (Finding 4). However, individuals can imagine beneficial uses of SDPs in ICT environments, and therefore SDPs have to be affordable for everyone to use. This is one of the most critical indicators to bring about successful change and fulfil a quick time-to-market concept.

5.7.6   Respondents Views on the Results Presented and Discussed in the Re-Validation Phase

In the last stage of this study the author referred back to ten participants and conducted a workshop with all of them, to validate the results that came out of this research. A presentation with all relevant results was given and in the workshop the results were discussed. The outcome of phase 4 was that all ten participants were satisfied, with the outcomes of this study. The following, Section 5.5, describes the development of a generic framework for an SDP-based ICT system of the future, based on the generic empirical codes and categories and the outcomes and findings from this study, as described above.

In a workshop the researcher presented the results of this study to the respondents and discussed their views and comments on the results. Eight of the SPICE experts confirmed that, from a general point of view, a user-oriented study could actually help to focus on the user perspective by classifying the design and implementation criteria. This helps to focus on user relevant parts when designing and implementing a technical solution. The six GT categories were not new, but outline the current challenges when designing web-based systems and they are comparable and confirmable with the results taken from other approaches, like requirement engineering method or design for testability.

The next Section discusses SDP user needs in terms of SDPs.

5.8   Discussion of User Needs in Terms of SDPs

This Section discusses the user needs in terms of SDPs from a user's perspective. This empirical investigation used EMPLIT to follow a user-based study, to analyse user needs when designing information systems, especially when designing SDPs. To validate the research outcomes a number of research questions defined in Section 3.9.4, are revisited and answered. The relation of the four main findings of this study, as well as the six GT categories, is discussed in terms of the challenges shown in Section 1.1. In the last Section the contribution of EMPLIT to understand user needs for information systems, is illustrated.

5.8.1   Answering the Research Questions of this Investigation

The research questions defined in Section 3.9.4 are summarised and answered as follows.

Answer to Research Question 1: Can SDPs be used to support people's everyday activities when using innovative ICT technologies?

To recapitulate the research question shown, Paragraph 2.5.3.1 highlights the use of SDPs supporting everyday activities of potential users in term of ICT technologies. The objective was to gain a deeper understanding of whether today's technology-driven aspects could meet the goal of future-oriented ICT environments.

Today's ICT environments are very technology-driven, as innovation is an important factor, generally driving development of information system. Unfortunately, the complexity of technical environments is increasing constantly. To implement and establish SDP-based ICT systems on the market, the importance of usability and handling of different systems over one single control and communication instance when using information systems is growing. If control units such as for example an SDP to control ICT systems can help to reduce complexity and address a broad range of potential users. In terms of the results of this study, respondents saw that employing SDPs helps support common tasks in ICT environments. Participants see a need for SDPs in operating different ICT systems, due to the ease of control in ICT-related activities. This is shown and discussed in Sections 5.6 and 5.7.

Answer to Research Question 2: Where are the difficulties in engaging an optimal interaction between technical environments and end-users?

Paragraph 2.5.3.1 highlights that the exponential growth of ICT makes it necessary, but very difficult, to provide services and applications that engage an optimal interaction between technical environments and end-users

The next generation of applications and services must be extremely user-friendly, as ICT systems and their related services, cannot be observed independently from those who use them. The ICT development is strongly technology-focussed. With the aid of user-based studies from the beginning of the system development process, in the conceptual phase, a user-focused study facilitates analysis and focuses exclusively on the perspective of users and setting the scene for the technology-based conception. This is shown and discussed in Sections 0 to 0.

Answer to Research Question 3: Why are the purposes of Internet Platforms changing when users want more support in their daily lives?

This research question highlights, that the needs of Internet platforms are changing, due to an individual's increased dependence on other technologies, in their daily lives. Internet application development has increased in importance in today's software development, due to the web's rapid growth (see Paragraph 2.5.3.1).

The Internet is growing faster and increasingly more users are going online, in our information society. Today, a typical user is not a technical professional, but is instead focussed on the use of applications and services and IT knowledge is average. It is therefore important that Internet platforms, especially SDPs, become well-accepted, by their potential users, as a single instance to control and operate in ICT environments. This technology will only be implemented if operators can reach a broad range of potential users. This implies that it has to be both easy to use, and affordable, for everyone. This is shown and discussed in Sections 5.6 and 5.7.

Answer to research Question 4: What is the impact of rebuilding today's ICT infrastructure in terms of using new ubiquitous services? What extent of SDPs (with the example of SPICE) can be integrated to the sphere of existing ICT systems, in order to achieve maximum usability for the single user of the ICT system?

It highlights the fact of high cost in relation to rebuilding ICT infrastructures, to use new ubiquitous services as an important point to rebuild and use existing ICT systems today. What are the important enlargements of existing SDPs and ICT systems to be prepared for new ubiquitous services, from the users point of view, to achieve maximum usability (see Paragraph 2.5.3.1)?

Strategies and costs increasingly impact on today's ICT systems when enlarging, developing or building new systems, as ICT systems are used to support more business processes today, than in the past. Companies have therefore invested heavily in ICT with extensive and long-term projects. However, once systems are implemented they are already outdated as the next generation of systems is already available on the market. Companies carefully consider their ICT investments, highlighting the point of how significant it is, that their old and new system components fit together, and can support new generations of services and applications.

Design issues for SDPs in terms of ICT systems uncovered in this study, are summarised as functional requirements in Section 5.5.1, and complement design guidelines with the perspective of users. SPICE is a technical representative SDP. SPICE is able to support the daily procedures and tasks with a user-based study. This is shown and discussed in Sections 5.5, 5.6 and 5.7 respectively.

The next Section relates and discusses the four main findings of this study, to the requirements outlined in Section 1.1.

5.8.2 Relation of the Four Main Findings and the GT Categories to the Requirements from Section 1.1.

The four main findings are illustrated in Paragraph 5.7.5.2 and the six final GT categories are presented in Paragraph 5.7.5.1.

The participants' view of a need for a clear single instance communication platform, such as an SDP, to operate different ICT systems from a single point, was specifically argued with the benefits in making ICT-related activities, easier to control. This is illustrated in Finding 1. From the author's point of view, Trick and Weber's, and Ahson and Ilya's, requirements, presented within Section 1.1, correspond and support the possibility of universal access to public infrastructures for a broad range of potential users, enabling the integration of many different social groups as well. Moreover, productivity and automation of a variety of services and applications, simply and easily, was supported for these different groups of users. Furthermore, the integration of existing ICT environments and the support of future-oriented services, especially in making these services mobile, are crucial, from the participants' point of view and correspond to Trick and Weber's challenges.

Finding 2 highlighted, that SPICE is a technical representative Service Delivery Platform, and also supports daily procedures and tasks, from a user perspective. The empirical study showed that the 15 interviewees from the SPICE
project, were intimate with the SPICE environment and argued, that from a
user's perspective, the alternative way shown in this investigation, facilitates in
sharpening user needs, outlining a realistic set of priorities of what users need
when designing information systems like SDPs. They were also adamant that
usability is an important factor in designing ICT systems.

The challenges and design issues for SDPs, in terms of ICT systems that
were uncovered in this study with Finding 3, and are summarised as functional
requirements from a user's perspective, depicted in the Mind Maps in Section
5.5.1 and represented in Figure 52, Figure 53 and Section 5.5.2 in Table 34. The
author showed the relation in terms of the developed GT categories and the challenges presented in Section 1.1.

Finding 4 illustrated that SDPs have to be well-accepted by their potential
users as a single instance to control and operate ICT environments, as this technology can only be implemented if operators can reach a broad range of potential
users, corresponding to Trick and Weber's points.

5.8.3 Substantive GT to Contribute the Understanding of User Needs

This research investigates SDP-based ICT development from a user's view by
using a qualitative empirical study leveraging the principles of Grounded Theory
within the EMPLIT research framework. The major categories and their relationships were integrated into an exploratory framework of design issues of SDP-
based ICT systems, from the perspective of users as the main contribution of this
research study. The developed substantive GT employing EMPLIT is an alternative to investigating user needs, and it was the first time, that this methodology
has been applied to the stated research topic.

There is a difference in undertaking a user study focussing on technical aspects, and a technical study focusing on user aspects. An existing technical concept or system is therefore needed to investigate user needs, based on the parameters of this system. When researching a user study from a technical aspect
no technical concept or system is needed when starting the research. This affords
an early start for the research and the researcher is objective of technical parameters from the onset.

5.8.4 EMPLIT to Contribute the Understanding of User Needs

EMPLIT helps contribute to user needs, from the researcher's point of view, in
designing information system such as SDPs when doing an empirical user study,
to analyse real user needs before starting the technical feasibility of information

systems. EMPLIT is a complementary approach regarding Requirement Engineering, or Testing for Testability, as it focusses only on a user-based study and it needs no existing technical concept or system to start with.

The author is of the opinion that the research findings of this study, extend the current literature by starting the design phase of an information system (especially an SDP-based ICT system) with the help of a user-based study, by interviewing groups of experts who are experienced in using or developing within the focussed study field.

EMPLIT is a research methodology, showing an alternative view to classical user-focussed processes, such as requirement engineering, or design for testability, to design a system for user needs employing a qualitative empirical study. The author also feels that this alternative way expands design guidelines from a users perspective.

From the researcher's perspective, EMPLIT helps methodologically, to improve the design of SDP-based ICT systems, as it extends the consolidated findings from technical methodologies and feasibility studies (e.g. Requirement Engineering and Design for Testability for software architectures) with additional expertise from the user-based study to design guidelines. This can be seen in everyday situations as an example, with support in using SDPs being influenced by the need for a broad range of potential users. This implies that this system has to be user_friendly and have an easy design.

Looking back to the research problem outlined in Section 1.1 this study investigates the development of a model, based on Grounded Theory categories and represents the perspective of the SPICE experts. Derived from the model (see Section 5.4.2) a framework of functional requirements of the respondents, was defined, and presented in Section 5.5, which illustrated design issues from a user's perspective and recommended guidelines.

There are two ways to look at: 1. It is irrelevant if a technical concept/system exists, if EMPLIT or other methodologies for analysing user needs (e.g. requirement engineering or design for testability) are used. Both allow one to discover similar comparable results. 2. If no technical concept or system exits, then EMPLIT can help start research very early without prior technical information.

The next Section summarises the final GT categories and references this to the relevant parts presented within this study. Moreover, the contribution of knowledge of this study is presented.

5.9 Summary of the Substantive GT of This Study

GTM has guided the data collection, as illustrated in the previous Sections, where findings from the qualitative investigation were discussed. In order to demonstrate how the final substantive GT categories were developed, the related codes and memos are presented in Table 35:

Table 35: List of six final categories, and their relation to codes and theoretical memos

Category	Related topic of focused codes	Development illustrated in section
Usability	• Simplicity and User-friendliness • Support of context awareness and multi languages • Context awareness	• Chapters 4.5.6, 5.4.2 • Figure 43, 44 • Table 27, Memo 6
Mobility	• Availability and Control • Multi-functional mode • Support of enddevices and multimedia applications	• Chapters 4.5.4, 5.4.2 • Figure 41 • Memo 4
Security and Reliability	• Data protection • Monitoring of processes • Network Intelligence centralisation • Client Intelligence centralisation • Integration of existing environments	• Chapters 4.5.5, 5.4.2 • Figure 42 • Table 25, 26 • Memo 5
Applicability	• Spectrum of standardised Services • Simple enlargement with additional services • Wide field of application	• Chapters 4.5.1, 5.4.2 • Figure 37, 38 • Table 21, Memo 1
Interoperability	• Infrastructure compatability • Support of existing services and future-oriented services • Centralisation • Integration of existing environments • Cost awareness	• Chapters 4.5.3, 5.4.2 • Figure 40 • Table 24 • Memo 3
Controllability	• Controlled by end-users • Low startup-, rebuilding and operational costs • Low implementation and transfer risk	• Chapters 4.5.2, 5.4.2 • Figure 39 • Table 22, 23, Memo 2

In order to demonstrate how the final six GT categories were developed, interview codes and theoretical memos are presented. The focussed codes guided the development of the categories in the empirical study. The literature based criteria catalogue guided the literature-based study, where Tony Buzan's *Mind Maps* (see Section 3.6) helped identify literature based aspects, to validate and justify codes, categories and sub-categories. The categories, "Usability" and "Interoperability", were identified by the participants.

It is very important to design and implement, an SDP-based ICT system, that is simple for everyone to use and which corresponds with a large amount of existing systems and environments, as time-to-market is one of the current key aspects bringing innovative technology successfully onto the market.

Additionally, to get the support of the different user groups, masses and potential users, it is viable to address a wide range of potential users, fulfilling user acceptance, by focusing on prioritising user needs before going into technical conceptualisation and implementation. In order to be mobile anytime and anywhere, SDP-based ICT systems have to be consistently available and controllable, and must offer strong support for multiple languages, end-devices and multimedia applications. Respondents described "Security and Reliability" as being very important, in order to protect data and to control the process of protection monitoring.

The participants' descriptions of the "Spectrum of Services" were closely related to a wide range of standardised applications and services. These are also extensively discussed in the literature. The category "Infrastructure Usability" is important for the compatibility of new SDP based infrastructure with based on existing ICT environments and components. The category "Cost Awareness" was also very important for the respondents, due to the issues of rebuilding, start-up, transfer of data and operational costs. Costs should not explode as a result of the issues previously mentioned.

The researcher has identified six GT categories in an empirical user-specific study. This represents an alternative to identifying user needs of SDP-based ICT systems, when no technical concept or ICT system existed. This contributes to the research in starting with a user-based study, instantly, without having that technical information.

The last Section summarises and concludes the presented results.

5.10 Chapter Summary and Conclusions

This Chapter has provided the development of an explanatory framework and based on the conceptual framework outlined in Section 2.5 and introduced research methodology presented in Chapter 3, based on the EMPLIT framework. This explanatory framework to develop SDP-based ICT systems from a user's perspective represented the final six GT categories (developed in Chapter 4 by applying open and selective coding) and the relationships between the categories (defined in Section 5.3 by applying theoretical coding). Models for the interview-based and literature-based study were introduced based on the work of Christoffersen and Woods (2002), and Klein *et al.* (2004), presenting categories in comparison to Human-computing interaction characteristics.

This Chapter has discussed generic framework, which represents the functional requirements of an SDP-based ICT system from the users' perspective. This framework developed was created based on the results of empirical and conceptual aspects, identified from the data. From the perspective of the empirical study, each of the categories has its own properties and behaviours, which bring specific aspects and relations to each of the categories, so that each of them conceptually denotes a specific paradigm. An interpretation and discussion of the empirical findings from interviews were presented. GTM was utilised, to illustrate patterns and themes useful in understanding the broader discourses concerning SDPs as single instance to control ICT environments. The three data collection phases were at the centre of the study, as it was imperative to identify the perceptions and views of respondents, whose experience of SDP-based control of ICT system was being developed over a longer continuous period. The GT categories have been used to connect the empirical reality to the theory, so as to create a substantive theory from the empirical data.

The first part of the Chapter presented the GT categories and the relationships between them, to offer an explanation of the phenomenon under study: individual views of challenges and design issues on SDPs to control and operate ICT environments of the future. A triangulation of empirical findings was successfully executed in a pilot and two in-depth interview phases, which confirmed the GT categories developed during the interview phases. Findings from the empirical data were compared to the relevant literature, in order to provide a holistic interpretation and theoretical integration of the research objectives. The categories, relationships and comparisons with the relevant literature have resulted in the development of five findings, which were presented and discussed in the second part.

The third part of this Chapter, drew attention to the discrepancies between the respondents' views and those predominantly depicted in the literature. The researcher argued that the concept of SDPs to administrate ICT environments is changing, with the need to support user's daily needs, when they are using many different types of communication technologies. End-users tend to hold a rather traditional view of SDPs in supporting their administrative and control tasks of many different services and applications, influenced by their own personal daily lives and not by technology. Developers and scholars depict a picture of an SDP-related ICT-system development that is affected by technology and relates to the different groups of users.

The final Section provides a set of broad conclusions and demonstrates how the aim and the objectives, as introduced in the first Chapter have been addressed throughout the thesis. Contributions to the field of studies and ideas for future research are presented and discussed.

6 Conclusions

This final Chapter presents the contribution of the author's research investigation to the field a user's perspective of SDPs, with respect to ICT systems. The final categories and their relationships, developed in Chapters 4 and 5 are illustrated. Moreover, the main contributions of this research are presented. Additionally, the findings and outcomes of this study, presented in the previous Chapter, are revisited to address the aim and the objectives, introduced in Chapter 1. Discussions on the completion of the Grounded Theory criteria (outlined in Section 3.4.3) and methods, as well as the study itself, are illustrated. Furthermore, specific scenarios of SDP and ICT technology applications are given, based on the concepts of the developed generic framework, in this study. This Chapter provides conclusions on the overall research, considers the study's limitations, presents lessons learned from the process, and offers suggestions for further research.

6.1 Main Contributions of this Research Study

This study, investigated the use of web-based platforms, such as SDPs, for the administration of Information and Communication Technology (ICT) systems and resulted in two main contributions: The substantive GT and the EMPLIT methodology outlined in Section 1.5. The major contribution of this investigation is the development of a substantive Grounded Theory (GT) for web-based platform related ICT systems, based on empirical data gathered from interviews with participants from the SPICE project. This theory is specific to a particular area, as it maps the relationship between the design aspects and the perceptions of challenges within technology independent web-based platforms from the respondents' viewpoints. The theory establishes links between concepts, such as definitions of design aspects, both from a technical and a user perspective, and the process of developing SDP-based ICT systems. It explains how individuals view the benefits of using web-based ICT technology to assist them in their day-to-day activities. Six final GT categories were found and are directly based on empirical data. The categories are summarised as follows:

- *Usability:* The need to design an SDP in terms of ICT environments, which is simple and easy to handle, thus being very user-friendly. Moreover, support of context-aware content must be fulfilled in various languages.

■ *Mobility:* High availability of services and applications in multifunctional modes is a must as well as the support of a broad range of end devices and multimedia applications.

■ *Security and Reliability:* Account and data protection and a transparent monitoring are important as new ICT environments must be protected to secure the data of users and increase the reliability of such systems. Additionally, these environments have to have the ability to work together with existing, older environments and keep those secure as well.

■ *Applicability:* The need of a wide field of services and applications for the users must have the ability to support standards and offer a simple possibility to enlarge the services portfolio.

■ *Interoperability:* The need for infrastructure compatibility is a must for new and older environments.

■ *Controllability:* Procedures with direct impact to costs must be controlled by the end-users.

The developed result categories were summarised in the interview-based model, which was developed based on the work of Christoffersen and Woods (2002), and Klein *et al.* (2004), and was described in detail, in Section 5.4.2.

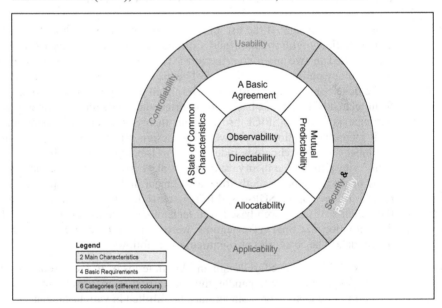

Figure 56: Interview-based model representing the six GT categories

The justification of the empirical data was done in six different stages and activities (see also 3.12):

■ A third-party researcher colour-coded the whole data source from the interviews to confirm and check the reliability of the codes developed by the researcher (see Paragraph 3.12.1.1 and Section 3.11.4).

■ The author reflected his interpretation of the respondents' view on SDPs, in terms of the category development, based on recorded memos (see Section 4.5).

■ Empirical codes and categories were compared, justified and validated with literature-based data with the using the developed literature criteria catalogue (see Chapters 4 and 5).

■ Related research was shown in Chapters 2 and 5, and this thesis developed in context of what other researchers have done (see Sections 2.3 to 2.5 and 5.2).

■ Research questions were defined in Section 3.9.4 then validated and discussed in Section 5.8.1.

■ After the three interview phases and the development of the final categories, the author reverted to the interviewees to present, discuss, and validate, the results with them (described in Sections 3.7 and 4.5.7).

A theory about the phenomenon being studied, was developed through consideration of the relationships between these categories, summarised in Figure 57 (see Section 5.3) below. The theory points out, that users are predominantly aware of the existence of services anytime and at anyplace and can envisage suitable applications. Findings from this PhD thesis support the argument that the design aspects and needs of SDPs are changing due to individuals' increased dependence on ICT technologies in their daily lives. This argument highlights the divergence between the viewpoints on and about designing SDPs, based on literature, and those expressed by the respondents of this study.

In 5.4.4, the relations between the GT categories were presented. The colour codes of the connections represent the associated category and symbolise a relation to other categories. A detailed description of the development of the categories and their relations, is given in Chapters 4 and 5.

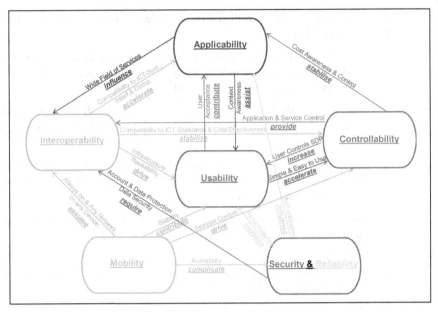

Figure 57: The theoretical contribution of this research (6 GT categories and their relations)

Literature describes many challenges related to technology-driven aspects. In comparison to this, individuals express a higher daily benefit-driven viewpoint of the challenges of such a system, which is related to their own personal lives, and tends to define these challenges independently of technological influences. This also indicates that individuals' views are less likely to become obsolete by continuing technical progress, than with views taken from literature.

The contribution to knowledge of this thesis is the development of a substantive GT, in empirical data, taken from interviews. This theory is specific to a particular area, as it maps the relationship design issues of SDPs from a users perspective to technical -driven guidelines. The theory establishes links between concepts, such as challenges for future-based ICT systems using SDP. This study provides an alternative way to start a research study with a technical content and contributes to design guidelines.

The Colour Coding method, which was developed a short time ago (Stottok, 2010a: p. 7-10), could be successfully applied in this study. It has been proved as a GT method, as the analysis was carried out very effectively, and without the investment of a great deal of time spent on studying alternative coding tools such as NUDIST or NVIVO. Colour Coding is a pragmatic approach that supports effective data analysis and processing which the researcher found easy to use. The process of Colour Coding could be used in any form of inter-view coding and not is restricted to Grounded Theory Methodology.

Mapping procedures for the justification of empirical results as well as the structuralisation and grouping of literature-based data are concentrated on very early in the analysis process to structure large and complex sets of data, so fo-cused coding therefore started at an early stage. The developed EMPLIT meth-odology was generally applicable for mapping empirical data by literature-researched, structured and grouped data in qualitative research studies, summa-rised in the following Figure 58 (see also Sections 3.3 and 3.10).

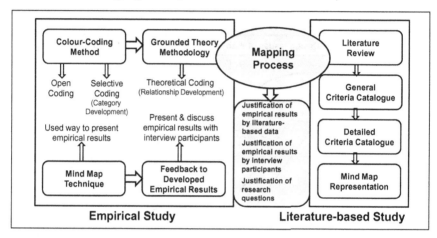

Figure 58: The methodological contribution of this research (EMPLIT framework)

The EMPLIT methodology, and its application, supported this study in re-searching SDP-based ICT development, through employing a qualitative ap-proach, which resulted in an unforeseen (unexpected) finding. The literature-based study facilitated in comparing empirical interview-based data taken from the literature, and was grouped and structured using mind-mapping techniques. This methodology helped justify codes and the collected and analysed data was validated using the dual-layered justification process (six different stages), (see Chapters 3 and 4), allowing the researcher to start the research early, as no tech-nical parameters or concepts of a system should exist before thwarting the re-search. This was described in Section 5.8.4.

The described mapping technique supports researchers in understanding different topics of which they need not necessarily be experts. It also supports the visualisation of literature-based data in mind maps, to help compare and validate empirical data in research justification phases. The process supports the validation of large amounts of data through different researchers, as the resultant maps that are generated are set out in a transparent manner for all those involved. It is possible to validate the data derived from an empirical study with the categories generated via the mapping process. The following Section relates the aim and the objectives to the outcomes and findings, and discusses the criteria shown in Chapter 3, in terms of the empirical findings in Chapter 4 and 5.

Scaling up the developed GT, the researcher used a substantive diagram to present the emergent substantive theory of this investigation, on a higher level (see Paragraphs 3.4.2 and 5.3.4). It represents the relationship between the technical and user perspective of SDPs, as a single control and communication instance, for ICT systems:

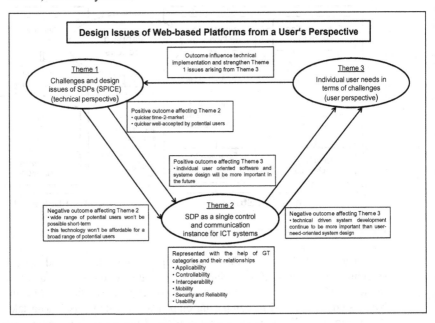

Figure 59: Substantive theory diagram of this investigation

A description of this substantive theory diagram is given in Paragrah 5.3.4 in detail.

6.2   Findings and Outcomes of this Investigation

ICT manufacturers play an important role in the development and spreading of multimedia services. Nowadays, technical development creates a higher demand on hardware, software, service architecture, electronics, security and environmental protection. Computer and software technologies are responsible for innovative ICT systems for communication and navigation, as well as for multimedia services. They provide extensive multimedia uses. There is an increasing demand for data transfer, in particular for online, but also for offline, use. Hence, from the perspective of the empire of SDPs and NGNs today, ICT technologies such as UMTS, LTE and IMS, also web and Internet technologies, play an essential role in the ICT sphere.

This study researched challenges and design issues for SDP-based ICT systems of the future, and discussed challenges from a usability point of view by developing a conceptual model representing these challenges and issues as guideline for the implementation of such a system, from an individual's perspective. The central point in this study was to focus on SDPs as single control and administration instance for ICT systems to improve the everyday work of users when using such environments. Based on the empirical categories presented in the previous Section 6.1, the findings and outcomes, as presented in Section 5.6 of this research study, are briefly summarised as follows:

6.2.1 Brief Summary

To summarise, SDPs as a control and communication instance for ICT-systems to support the end-users' daily tasks, are a couple of results and consolidated insights came out of this study. For this purpose the aim and the objectives presented in the Section 1.3 are represented again and linked to the findings and outcomes. To clarify, the results including findings and outcomes of this study, are briefly summarised here:

Findings of this Investigation

- ▣ *Finding 1:* Need for a single control and communication platform (SDP). This is represented with the explanatory framework of design issues for SDP-based development, from the perspective of users. Broadening design and development guidelines benefits ICT system development, starting with a user-based analysis, and strongly supports user-oriented development.

- ▣ *Finding 2:* SPICE is a representative model of an SDP in order to control and communicate with ICT systems, focussed strongly on the technical perspective. SPICE has to meet the requirement demands of different user groups to effectively become well-accepted, in the community.

- ▣ *Finding 3:* Located and related challenges and design issues of SDPs in terms of ICT environments for the future (see Figure 52 and Figure 53, and Table 34).

■   *Finding 4:* Broader guidelines to design SDPs, from a technical point, with
    guidelines from a user's perspective. This was represented using a substan-
    tive theory diagram in Paragraph 5.3.4. The complementary approach of
    this study in terms of those described in the literature, is of significant bene-
    fit to user-oriented SDP development. SDPs have to be affordable for eve-
    ryone, to fulfil a quick time-to-market principal, in order for success.

A detailed description of the findings was done in Section 5.6.2.

Outcomes of this study

■   *Outcome 1:* Explanation of design and development guidelines to such a
    process with a user-based analysis. Challenges and aspects to develop SDP-
    based ICT systems from the perspective of users were identified (see Chap-
    ters 4 and 5)

■   *Outcome 2:* EMPLIT is an unexpected finding of this study. The final re-
    sults were justified with the application of EMPLIT methodology and the
    dual-layered justification process, illustrated in Chapters 3, 4, and 5.

■   *Outcome 3:* Recommendations for design guidelines of an SDP-based ICT
    system for the future, based on the developed six final categories and the
    derived functional requirements shown in Chapter 5.

The next Section discusses concrete and abstract experiences in context, with the
findings and outcomes of this study, relating to the methodology in general, and
the study setup described in Section 3.9.

6.2.2 *Relationship between Aim, Objective, Findings and Outcomes of the Study*

The relationship between the aim, the objectives, findings and the outcomes of
this study are related and summarised, and shown in Figure 60 below.

Figure 60 overviews the relations of the study aim, the concrete four
objectives, the four findings and the three outcomes of this study. What is vital,
is the direct relation of four objectives to the four findings of this investigation.

The three outcomes can be interpreted as findings from a higher
perspective, which are ideas and recommendations from the author, and that
reflect the interpretations of the author in terms of the findings. A detailed
presentation of the relation between objectives and findings is given in
Paragraphs 5.6.3.1 and 5.6.3.2.

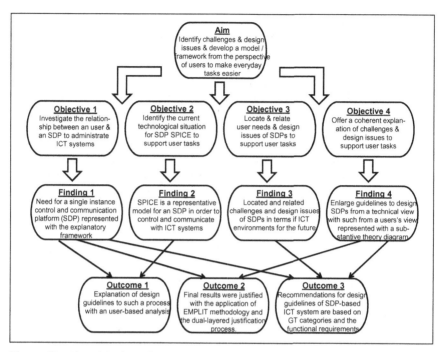

Figure 60: Aim, objectives, findings and outcomes of this investigation

The author is of the opinion that an alternative way, focusing only on user needs, can bring significant contributions by undertaking a user-focused study to investigate how users perceive information systems, such as SDPs. Based on that additional guideline to those described in the academic literature, user-specific needs can be sharpened and be an alternative in designing a system, for their needs.

6.2.3 Confirmation, Extensions and Contradictions of Final GT Categories to the Current Literature

In the following Section the author states what his research has done to confirm, extend and contradict current literature. The findings of this study have extended current literature in that usability becomes increasingly important in driving the development of technological environments, to stay ahead of competitors, by focussing on a user study, completely technically-oriented with individual data, derived directly from user groups compiled of experts in the topic. The ability to implement this technology in an easy and simple way, to be well-accepted is vital, and was discussed in Section 5.7.1.

Furthermore, the impact of technology-driven ICT environments supports today's investments in technology-driven research. Certainly, there are other methodologies (Requirement Engineering or Design for Testability) to support user need analysis, but only from a technical point of view. This entails that those methodologies can only support user needs analysis, when a concept or technical system already exists. If no system exists then this alternative way of doing a qualitative user-based study, enlarges users views and supports other methodologies: for example, to address a broad range of potential users when designing a system, illustrated in Section 5.7.1.

The role of end-users of SDPs is more important than that, that the academic literature describes, as in terms of ubiquitous computing services and applications, they support increasingly more daily activities of ICT users. Using an SDP as a control tool to communicate and control the operation of the user's end device, as a single instance, implies a stronger focus on user-based design and development (described in Section 5.7.2).

Summarising the confirmation, contradiction, and extensions of the findings of this study, Table 31, outlined in Section 5.2.2, was extended with the addition of the column 'Confirmation, extention or contradiction of the current academic literature' stating the relation of each of the six GT categories, to the current academic literature, and is depicted below.

Table 36 above, summarises the theoretical integration of each of the six final GT categories by representing related literature-based categories, with examples of related academic literature, using a systematic review, described in detail in Section 5.2.2. Additionally, the researcher stated how the findings confirmed, extended or contradicted the current academic literature.

Comparing the findings of this study, with the current literature in terms of the point that, academic literature predominantly focusses on the impacts of technologically driven developments, shown using SPICE. This has an impact on a wider potential of users and ultimately society, allowing for homogenous environments, and thus making it easier for people who are not experts or technically minded, to handle such systems, discussed in Section 5.7.1. Additionally, two different views of SDPs were identified, in Section 5.7.2. Respondents of this study supported that a user-oriented study, prior to starting a technical analysis and implementation, is sensible. Academic literature postulates strong technology driven development.

Table 36: Presentation how research findings confirm, extend or contradict current literature

GT-based investigation/ empirical study	Literature-based study	Systematic review of academic literature (examples)	Confirmation, extention or contradiction of the current academic literature
Applicability	• Multimedia applications	o Context-aware software (Schilit *et al.*, 1999) o Trust concerning privacy & rights of applications (Schmidt, 2011) o Mobile service provisioning (Killström *et al.*, 2008) o Ontologies in context-aware apps (Krumenacher & Strang, 2008) o "Applicability" in comparison to RE method (Sajjad & Hanif, 2010) o Software characteristics (Rottmann, 2009)	• Extends current literature in comparison to RE and D4T methodologies (systematic review) as well as literature-based aspects (literature-based study)
Controllability	• Minor energy • Minor cost (network access, enddevices)	o Design for testibility (Kantipudi, 2002) o Controllability and observability (Zhou *et al.*, 2008) o ICT system characteristics (König & Nordström, 2009) o "Controllability" with RE method (Maurino *et al.* (2003) o "Controllability" with D4T method (Binder, 1994, Freedmann, 1991) o SW characteristics (Mulo, 2007)	• Partly strong confirmation on current literature in terms of RE and D4T • Contradictions in terms of the main focus on Controllability – respondents focused on capabilities to focus on single control of Internet apps opportunities because of acceptance, coverage, needs, and costs)
Interoperability	• Multi Faculty of Speech • Context Awareness • Integration of Existing Environments • Minor Cost (Network Access, Enddevices) • Centralisation of Net- & Client Intelligence	o Challenges of interoperability in SPICE (Cordier, 2005) o Sustaining interoperability (Gasser and Palfrey, 2007) o Federated information architecture (Gradmann, 2009) o SW characteristics (Hansen,1998; Garlan & Shaw, 1993) o SW characteristics (Matinlassi and Eila, 2002))	• Confirms current literature in comparison with RE and D4T as well as literature-based aspects
Mobility	• High Mobility • Centralisation of Net- & Client Intelligence	o Different networks from various locations (Umar, 2004) o Seamless mobility (Poiselka *et al.*, 2004) o Productivity and accessability is rapidly increasing (Tarkoma *et al.*, 2007) o Management of collaboration networks (Siegmund, 2004)	• Strongly confirms current literature in terms of RE and D4T shown in the systematic review as well as literature-based aspects
Security and Reliability	• Security & Data Integrity • Integration of Existing Environments • Centralisation of Net- & Client Intelligence • Multimedia Applications	o Software system reliability and security (Honeyman *et al.*, 2007) o High-capacity transmission routes (Noll, 1994) o "S&R" with D4T method (Pettichord, 2002) o "S&R" with D4T method (Jimenez *et al.*, 2005)	• Confirms current literature in comparison with RE and D4T regarding Security • Extends current literature in terms of Reliability strongly recommended by the interview participants)
Usability	• User Friendliness • Multi Faculty of Speech • Context Awareness • Multimedia Applications	o Usability testing (Gloud and Lewis, 1985) o Usefulness into utility and usability (Shniderman and Plaisant, 2009) o Knowledge transfer objects (Karwowski et al., 2011) o SW characteristics (Nielsen, 1994; Finn, 2005)	• Confirms current literature in terms of RE and D4T as well as literature-based aspects

6.3 Meeting Grounded Theory Criteria

The findings of this research are specific to design issues of SDP-based ICT development from the perspective of users (Section 5.3), and have led to the development of a substantive GT, which is specific for a particular context and a particular area. The following section revisits the criteria for GT studies, presented in Section 3.4.3.

Credibility

The criterion of credibility describes the links between theory and data, such as links between the empirical data and the main argument of the study. For this investigation, a range of empirical data in form of pilot and in-depth interviews was collected to develop a substantive GT. Open and focused codes were devised for the interviews and the categories and sub-categories were developed based on the focused codes (see Chapter 4). Relationships between categories were shown using theoretical coding and formed the basis for the substantive GT presented in Chapters 4 and 5. A comparison of the developed theory to the literature assisted to develop the outcomes of this investigation, described in Chapter 5.

Originality

The criterion of originality assesses whether the categories developed in the study offer new insights into the area of research. This study claims to be of theoretical significance, as the development of SDP-based ICT system has not been researched by applying a user-based study, representing the perspective of user's using GTM within the EMPLIT framework.

The finding, that everyday life support, when using SDP-based ICT systems, is influenced by the need for a broad range of potential users connected to everyday life. It highlights that these technology concepts should be affordable for everyone to fulfil a quick time-to-market principal to be successful when launching an SDP-based ICT product on the market (see Section 5.6.3). Moreover, to enlarge existing development guidelines to design SDPs, from a technical point of view, with guidelines based on a user study representing the perspective of users, contributes user-centred ICT development, as the user's view is deeply integrated from the very beginning.

Resonance

The substantive GT developed in this study presents the experiences of individuals with design issues, of SDP-based ICT development from a user's perspective. The criterion of resonance aims at assessing whether the GT categories developed from the data relate to the studied experience of participants, and whether the categories make sense to them. Data collection and analysis for this study was conducted in alternating sequences in order to verify early findings and to shape further data collection. In addition, the presentation and feedback session (see Section 3.7) was used to present the final GT categories and their relations to the participants, to evaluate how participants interpreted them.

Usefulness

The criterion of usefulness evaluates whether the analysis is related to individuals' day-to-day lives and whether it can be transferred to other areas, other than the one under study. A particular motivation for using GT within the EMPLIT framework was to learn how individuals perceive system design for user needs, in relation to SDPs. For this reason, the empirical data collection for this study was aimed at capturing participants' feelings and opinions about the subject area, and to let them express what was important to them within this context. Further research would be necessary to develop a more general GT that would be transferable to other subject areas (see Section 6.6).

6.4   Discussion

A possible limitation of this investigation is that the findings are based on a small sample of fifteen interviews, based on three essential groups of SPICE experts - SPICE end-users, developers and architecture experts. The findings were developed based on this limited sample, and hence cannot be generalised across large populations. It should be pointed out that it was not the goal of this research to conduct an entirely quantitative study with statistical validity. GTM was used to develop criteria, to explain the phenomenon of individuals' views of challenges and design issues on SDPs and ICT systems of the future. The limitations of GTM were considered in Section 3.4.7.

GTM has not been applied to the topic of SDPs before. This study highlights the fact that GTM can be a useful tool with which to study individuals' perceptions about the specific subject areas of ICT in an inductive (in this investigation, an abductive) way. This study is an example that the 'traditional' GTM research areas, nursing and general health care could be enlarged by other areas of research, in this case the information system research area. However, from the researcher's point of view it can be very helpful when using GTM to ensure the possibility of reliability checks, as was the case in this study. It is not easy to find the right way to balance enough empirical data without changing stable results of codes and a good, but limited, number of interview participants. In this investigation the researcher conducted three phases to check the reliability of the empirical results between each stage of interviews and to carry out data validation exercises using literature-based data generated by the mapping process.

There is a further limitation if researchers want to follow the classical Glaserian way of using GTM, i.e. with the Mapping-Process approach, to validate collected empirical data by literature-based data, before the completion of the analysis. This approach worked by using the Charmaz (2006) approach to GTM, which enables the researcher to apply theoretical sensitivity to the conduct of the literature review parallel in the analysis phase. However, in this investigation, the researcher decided to start the literature review and the Mapping Process in interview phase two, after the colour-coded analysis of the empirical data had been done. Because of the issue of theoretical sensitivity, it was found necessary to avoid being influenced by the literature in both the pilot interviews and the second interview phase prior to the analysis of the data.

Limitations in using the Colour Coding Method may exist for people with achromatopsia. Depending on the degree of the colour vision deficiency, the affected analyst can only restrictedly, or not at all, use some colours and tones, as these may only be observed as contrasts. Similar restrictions have to be considered for researchers who suffer from a colour abnormality like Daltonism (Stottok *et al.*, 2011).

According to Bergaus *et al.* (2012), there are certain limitations regarding the Mapping Process and the use of Mind Maps in this study. Extensive literature cannot usually be displayed in one map alone. Normally, it is not possible to use only single terms in the maps, as they do not reflect meaningful content. Instead, parts of a sentence have to be shown. Experts of the respective subject compile maps from their field of research independently, within the scope of this mapping process, and make them available to others. This offers researchers the possibility to gain an overview of new topics in areas they are not well versed in. Furthermore, a mind map can also be split into two parts, in order to present several hierarchy levels. Challenges and problems occurred when grouping aspects on the first hierarchical level, as in this case it was often necessary to provide synonyms or short descriptions for the topics addressed. In the next lower hierarchical level, all aspects that could have been allocated to such a topic, were collected. The same principle was used for all further hierarchical levels (Bergaus *et al.*, 2012).

Within the scope of this study, the author acquired additional knowledge and new expertise:

■ The definition of a saturation mark to estimate the interview phases before the start. For example, how many interviews and interview phases will probably be necessary, even if this shows a rather typical, yet still pragmatic activity in GTM, to reach saturation, and stable (reliable) results.

■ An expansion of the potential circle of participants to be interviewed, within the sphere of European research projects, who are connected to SPICE, and the sphere of network-based, or application-based, research content, would allow for a discovery of additional aspects or challenges, for new innovative ICT systems which are also using SDPs.

■ A concluded literature-based study offers the possibility to start quickly with focused coding. Therefore, speedy completion of the literature-based analysis would permit more efficient analysis of the data.

The researcher was able to acquire additional knowledge and understanding, and could gain new experience during the research project. The mapping technique supports researchers in understanding different topics for which they do not necessarily need to be experts. The process, as described in this paper, supports the validation of large amounts of data through different researchers, as the resultant maps that are generated are set out in a transparent manner for all those involved. It is possible to validate the data derived from the empirical study with those categories generated via the mapping process.

This mapping process has proven its practical usability. Relevant aspects can be systematically derived from extensive literature. Hierarchies and correlation are, at the same time, graphically reprocessed. Assimilating structured information trees from literature-based data, in the form of maps, enables the possibility of rapid acquisition of previously unknown topics for the researcher. Complex topics can be understood quickly, and at the same time they are structured. It should be noted that the creation of these maps is a time consuming process (see Sections 3.6.3, 3.3.4, 3.11.3 and 3.11.6).

When using a Grounded Theory approach, it is feasible as per the concept of theoretical sensitivity (including pre-acquired knowledge about a topic) to use the aspects taken from a map to validate empirical data, if the latter has already been coded independently, and as long as the data analysis process is not manipulated or influenced by information gained from literature.

From the perspective of the author, one of the main advantages is that one only needs two files for the complete analysis of all interview data, which makes it quite simple for the researcher to edit and to even analyse large sets of interview transcription data.

The first file is the text file, which contains all colour coded interview texts at the end of the analysis process; the second file is the analysis tool that was named the Fact Finding Tool (see Section 3.5.2).

The Fact Finding Tool displays all the processes of one GTM analysis step, including coding, interpretation and memo-taking. Furthermore, this tool facilitates other researchers in tracking all the necessary steps of the analysis process (Bergaus and Stottok, 2010: p 131). An additional feature is that the coded text passages are easily, visually identified in the transcribed interviews. Consistently using the same colour, for coding, each of the categories in all interviews could then be identified, which allows for all categories to be consistently coded and compared.

Due to the standardised width of the columns in the Fact Finding Tool the analyst can compare the number of cells, i.e. text passages assigned to a category, giving an indication of how important the different categories were for each interviewee. Some parts of text are suitable for more than only one category, which means that such text passages have to be colour coded repeatedly, which proved time-consuming. However, this obvious disadvantage can sometimes also develop into an advantage, for the following reason. Using the Colour Coding Method becomes more difficult, the larger the sets of codes are, as the colours that can be used for coding are limited by the number of words of the analysed text passage. If there is a colour coded text passage with too many colours, for example five or more colours, then the researcher would have to reconsider combining some of them.

If a category only consists of text passages that never appear coded alone but always in combination with other colours, then these text passages could probably also be subordinated to other categories, and should be reviewed as well. Such findings might be an indication that not enough attention has been spent on the possibility that some of these categories could be the sub-categories of a new superior category.

The analyst must also be aware that there is a risk of trying to simplify and minimise the number of codes per sentence, especially when several colours have to be used within the same sentence. An analysis using the Colour Coding Method can thus be considered to be very time-consuming.

The author is of the opinion, that the interviewees of this study were able to understand technically related aspects of SDP-based ICT development. Primarily, the SPICE developer's group and the group of the architecture experts were very experienced with strong technical know-how. It should be noted that this is the most important point, why the used and discussed terminology, is equal and comparable to those used in the literature.

What is beneficial of the exploratory framework and the methodology used? The author contends that the categories and exploratory framework of the design issues for SDP-based ICT development from a users' perspective would probably support user-focused SDP and ICT development and contribute research in information systems when no technical concepts or systems are available, as researchers are able to start immediately with a user-specific study on SDP or ICT related topics. However, technically-oriented methodologies of design systems for user needs, are powerful and can also be selected and used, when a technical concept or systems exist, because technical parameters to research on user aspects from a technical point of view, is a necessary requirement.

The exploratory framework proposed in this research extends design aspects of SDP-based ICT development published in existing literature, in terms of the user perspective of SDP-based ICT development, and the procedure (EMPLIT framework) of how the findings were realised, by employing a user-centred study. An advantage of the depicted framework is that research can start immediately without any technical concept or system. Fundamentally, SDP-based ICT development can start from the beginning with a user-centred development where users focus on what is, or should be, important for end-users, when designing and developing a system for user needs.

Interviewee's reflected, that there are also drawbacks when investigating an exploratory framework for design issues of SDP-based ICT systems from the user view:

▣ Participants must be highly experienced and familiar with a technical topic when deciding to start such a development process with a user-centred study.

▣ Time-to-market of a technical product can influence the time and willingness in doing a user-based study, before any technical design and development activity. This implies that enough implementation time must be required.

▣ Focusing on the user view implies additional documentation to focus on technical parameters, for the next stage of system design, which can influence the development budget and time.

The respondents were clear, that the benefits, of the theoretical model, is higher in designing and developing with a focus SDP-based ICT system, and include the user perspective at the very beginning of researching in information systems.

6.5 Lessons Learned and Recommendations

Innovative technologies are considered future-oriented if they support lasting dialogue between the sender of a message and receivers, e.g. intelligent software which systematically supports the dialogue. Great opportunity lies in knowing and understanding customers. It is important, particularly in terms of mobile devices, that one does not simply dispatch a message by SMS, but that one transmits personalised, needs-based and context-oriented content. Very small and portable devices connect to the periphery and to networks.

The future new business scenario could be characterised by a differentiation between access and service provision. User access to services will be achieved through different networks. The user's communication environment will be generally composed of various terminals (e.g., PDA, Laptop, PC, mobile, embedded computers in vehicles, communicating objects), which may vary dynamically, depending on the user's context. This will create new challenges, not only for the interface and user end devices, but also for SDPs. Developers speak of Ubiquitous Computing as the new phase of the technology of information, and speak of background assistance or even intelligence, namely from sensors and engines, calculators, transmitters and receivers which work as independently as possible and are either almost or completely non-recognisable.

As a precondition for this development, the exhaustive interlinking of persons and computers, rooms and objects, has to be addressed. User acceptance, a series of positive scenarios is available such as vehicle control systems, health care, and intelligent budgetary systems. There are also a large number of negative scenarios, for example: uncontrollable systems that do not function properly, false controls, and collective device failure, to mention but a few. UMTS and LTE telephony is widespread. In the following, some possible scenarios are briefly outlined.

Scenario "Intelligent Portal"

In this scenario, the users of ICT system surroundings, is supported by an intelligent portal that offers services in connection with localisation, context generation (independently of the terminal being used or of a potential user), and suitable user preferences. This intelligent portal focuses on services such as service roaming, seamless delivery, security and content adaptation.

Scenario "Emergency"

In this scenario, the user is assisted by innovative technologies while an emergency case is initiated. In this case the user is constantly supervised and supported by an emergency service, used on a PDA and accessed, in this case, from an SDP. In addition, sensors and technology components are used, which are linked up to each other.

Scenario "Electronic Windscreen"

This scenario supports the user in controlling and driving a car and supplies him with information. Control information is visually displayed on the windscreen of the car, for example the distance to the next critical point or the next petrol station. The scenario, "Electronic Windscreen", is supported by the functionalities position, regulation, roaming, dynamic content announcement, interoperability, and user profiling and authentication.

Scenario "Intelligent Environments"

In the near future, intelligent environments (Smart Environments) will link up all the devices with which a person is surrounded by. Services can be customised to suit the end-user, and can be offered in different versions. These include, for example, in the area of passenger traffic stations, information within the train about train journey and plans, purchase and validation of tickets. Moreover, the use of office services, such as broadband access, NextGenTV (personalised TV services), sensor nets, community services and content management functions, is included. New hardware and software solutions will integrate the heterogeneous device networks, making comfortable interfaces for the control of these networks available, and enable adaptive services.

In this case, a communication platform, such as SPICE, will support quick adaptation, and the supply of new and combined services of every description.

Scenario "Interactive Advertising Surfaces – Placards"

Interactive advertising surfaces address the mobile human being, and are already considered to be the future of marketing. The placards do not only address humans, but also "invite" a dialogue. These technologies are being used in projects where advertising messages find their way to the end-customers via mobile phones.

Placards that address passers-by are no longer unusual. The current new medium is the mobile phone. A connection between mobile phone users and placard surfaces can be established by using radio technology, via Bluetooth or RFID/NFC (radio frequency identification/near field communication), by SMS, pattern recognition and 2-D-Cooler. Companies have been experimenting for several years with this combination of external advertisement and mobile marketing, in order to connect the mobile phones for example via Bluetooth. Whoever answers an SMS receives, for example, MP3-Songs, video tie clips, etc., or can directly buy concert or cinema tickets over mobile Internet. However, such "Push services", are open to the danger of spam floods and data protection concerns. This can be off-putting for the customer. With "Pull technologies" the user is able to decide on the application used, and must take the first step. He is therefore not overridden which greatly increases user acceptance.

Since August 2010, 600 placards and 200 City lights, showing the "Venus of Willendorf", have been positioned in and around Vienna. They carry out four different forms of interactivity. Via the City Light showcases, data can be downloaded onto mobile phones using Bluetooth. A classical SMS lottery is offered on a placard series, or passers-by can photograph the Venus by mobile phone, and then receive further information about it. The software developed by EVOLARIS recognises 5,000 different terminals and supplies the information either as a text, or as a link, to the mobile Internet.

A quick response code (QR) is shown on the placards of the third series. This is a square with a "pixeled" pattern. If photographed, this pattern will open a link on the mobile Internet. The software required can be downloaded free of charge, and QR scanners are preinstalled on almost all modern phones. All interactions are completed, noted and analysed by a system developed by EVOLARIS with the goal of developing personalised dialogues with the potential customer.

In a further project, tested by Vita TV, a television format for waiting rooms, it is possible to send an SMS, with an email address, during a cookery show, and then to immediately receive cookery advice on the PC, plus a purchase list on a mobile phone. Thus three media forms are linked to one another, and used in the most efficient and effective way. In the future, archives could be provided with this technology. For example, articles in newspapers will not have to be cut out anymore, but could be stored and assigned by photographing the Quick Response Coolers.

Closing, with these kinds of cases and scenarios, with which we are confronted in the 21st Century, the technologically-driven development of ICT environments is, and will continue to be, in our lives. The importance is to focus more on user needs when designing and developing ICT systems, and it becomes increasingly important to develop more end-user centred support which enhances our everyday lives making life better and easier, when using ICT environments.

The author recommends combining existing guidelines to design SDPs from a technical viewpoint with those designed from a user viewpoint, as investigated in this study. This complements the approach, in using a user-oriented study, defining specific user needs when designing a web-based ICT system, then designing and implementing such a system, by checking the technical feasibility. Guidelines for the design, based on the technical perspective, together with guidelines resulting from the empirical user study, benefit the design of a technical ICT system, from the researchers' perspective.

The following, Figure 61, is a recommendation of the author's view, on how a user-based study contributes to broadening design guidelines.

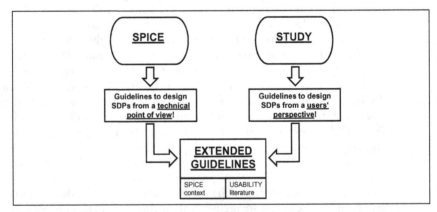

Figure 61: Recommendation for 'extended' design guidelines contributed by this thesis

Figure 61 outlines the author's recommendations in terms of enlarging guidelines, which offers a potential designer, and developer team of an SDP, the possibility to access, with the help of a user-based study, the perspectives of users when no technical concept or system is present. This could help such a team to start very early on, in the research of user perspectives and which could be used when starting to think about technical design principles, as this could help to focus on very specific user needs.

6.6   Further Research

By creating technical guidelines, in terms of technical oriented study, together with user-based guidelines, could generate enormous benefits for designing and developing SDP-based architecture and ICT systems in the future. This study showed an alternative to starting a design process for an SDP, based on the user perspective. EMPLIT methodology helps to improve on SDP-based ICT development. The goal for future research on this topic is to apply and prove the EMPLIT methodology in developing design guidelines for users, before starting a technical design and proof of concept. In this case it can be validated if SDP based ICT development can be improved.

In the author's opinion, this general procedure could also be adapted to other design and development procedures in ICT relevant topics, whereby further research could focus on comparing and justifying EMPLIT, in terms of other research procedures in developing user guidelines, and to apply EMPLIT to other areas of information systems to validate this methodology in other research areas. In this case it would be critical to replicate the results from this study and apply those results to other scenarios.

The thesis findings could enrich future research on SDPs by providing and supporting an alternative way to investigate this research field, in applying the user perspective, employing a user-based study to investigate user needs, when designing and developing SDP-based ICT systems. The user perspective of experts in the field of research helps initiate research in complex SDP environments, expediently without having prior technical concepts or pilot environments, by using qualitative analysis of empirical data.

EMPLIT is a framework for abduction research, a prototype, and was only compared to the methodologies, Requirement Engineering and Design for testability, in this investigation. It has to be proved by additional research, making further comparisons to other methodologies, described in the literature, and applying it to other fields of research as well.

7 References

3G Americas (2005). *Convergence – An outlook on device, service, network and technology trends.* white paper, July 2005.

3GPP-*The Mobile Broadband Standard.* http://www.3gpp.org/ [Accessed: May 15, 2011].

Agarwal, R. and Lucas, H. (2005). *The information systems identity crisis: focusing on high- visibility and high-impact research.* MIS Quarterly, 29 (3), pp. 381-398.

Ahson, Syed A. and Ilyas, Mohammad (2011). *Service Delivery Platforms – Developing and Deploying Converged Multimedia Services.* Taylor and Francis Group, LLC, 2011.

Alexander, I. F. and Stevens, R. (2002). *Writing Better Requirements.* Reading, MA: Addison-Wesley.

Almeida, João Paulo; Baravaglio, Alberto ; Belaunde, Mariano; Falcarin, Paolo; Kovacs, Ernö. (2008). *Service Creation in the SPICE Service Platform.* SPICE paper.

An SDP Alliance White Paper. (2006). *A Service Delivery Platform for End-to-End Value Web Enablement.* http://www.TheSDPAllicance.com.

Armbrust, M., Fox, A., Griffith, R., Joseph, A., Katz, R., Konwinski, A., Lee, G., Patterson, D., Rabkin, A., Zaharia (2010). *A view of cloud computing - Communication of the ACM (4).* pp. 50–58. http://dl.acm.org/citation.cfm?doid=1721654.1721672. [Accessed: August 11, 2012].

Arnaud, Julien; Negru, Daniel; Sidibe, Mamadou; et. al. (2011). *Adaptive IPTV services based on a novel IP Multimedia Subsystem.* Multimedia tools and applications Volume 55 (2) pp. 333-352, published Nov 2011.

Asimov, Issac (1990). *Meine Roboter. Essay, in: Robotervisionen.* Bastei Band 21 201, Bastei Lübbe by Byron Preiss Visual Publications Inc.

Bailey, K. D. (1994). *Sociology and the New Systems Theory: Toward a Theoretical Synthesis.* New York: State of New York Press.

Baldoni, R.; Di Ciccio, C.; Mecella, M; et al. (2009). *An Embedded Middleware Platform for Pervasive and Immersive Environments for-All.* 6th Annual

IEEE-Communications-Society Conference on Sensor, Mesh and Ad-hoc Communications and Network (SECON 2009), Rome, Italy, Jun 22-26, 2009.

Ballon, Pieter; Walravens, Nils; Spedalieri, Antonietta; Venezia, Claudio. (2008). *An Advertisement-based Platform Business Model for Mobile Operators*. IBBT SMIT, Vrije Universiteit Brussel, Belgium. 12th International ICIN Conference, Bordeaux, France, 20-23 October 2008.

Bartlett, D. and Payne, S. (1997). *Grounded Theory - It's Basis, Rational and Procedures*. In: McKenzie, G., Powell, J., Usher, R. ed. Understanding Social Research: Perspectives on Methodology and Practice. Falmer Press, London.

Bassey, M. (1990). *On the Nature of Research in Education*. Part 2, Research Intelligence (37) Summer.

Begic, Z.; Bolic, M.; Secerbegovis, E. (2009). *Active Networking Support for Group Communication*. 22nd International Symposium on Information Communication and Automation Technologies, Sarajevo, Bosnia & Hercegovina, Oct 29-31, 2009.

Belaunde, M. *et al.* (2006). *Advanced Language for Value added services composition and creation*. IST Spice Project Deliverable D5.1, August 2006.

Benbasat, I., Zmud, R. (2003). *The identity crisis within the IS discipline: defining and communicating the discipline's core properties*. MIS Quarterly, 27 (2), pp. 183-194.

Bergaus, Martin (2005). *PhD Research Proposal*. PhD Research Programme. Danube University/Leeds Metropolitan University.

Bergaus, Martin (2006). *Architecture Model for a Service Delivery Platform supporting mobile distributed services in interoperability networks, shown by the example of mixed reality applications*. Faculty Research Conference, Leeds Metropolitan University, Leeds.

Bergaus, Martin (2007). *Service Roaming in Interoperable Networks*. Faculty Research Conference, Leeds Metropolitan University, Leeds.

Bergaus, Martin (2010a). *Mind- and concept mapping method for literature based criteria catalogue*. Grounded Theory Research Salon, 18 January 2010, Leeds Metropolitan University.

Bergaus, Martin (2010b). *Design aspects on service delivery platforms by analysing perception of ubiquitous services – Data collection and methodology*.

Grounded Theory Research Salon, 18 January 2010, Leeds Metropolitan University.

Bergaus, Martin N. and Stottok, Bernd O. (2010). *Verbesserter Nutzen von Telematiksystemen im Schienenverkehr durch Bereitstellung innovativer Service-Delivery-Plattformen.* Master Thesis, Danube University Krems.

Bergaus, Martin N., Stottok, Bernd O., Gorra, Andrea (2012). *Validation of Grounded Theory Based Data by Means of Analytical Mapping Techniques.* ECRM article, published and presented at the 11th European Conference on research Methodology (ECRM) for Business and Management Studies 2012, 28-29 June, University of Bolton, UK, Leeds Metropoletan University.

Bergaus, Martin N., Stottok, Bernd O., Gorra, Andrea (2012b). *Validierung Grounded-Theory-basierter Daten mittels Mapping Techniken'.* at the Forum Qualitative Social Research (FQS) (under consideration).

Bertin, Emmanuel and Crespi, Noel (2009). *Service business processes for the next generation of services: a required step to achieve service convergence.* Vol. 64, 3-4, pp. 187-196, Institut Telecom and Springer-Verlag France 2008.

Bieberstein, N.; Bose, S.; Walker, L.; Lynch, A. (2005). *Impact of Service-Oriented Architecture (SOA) on Enterprise Systems, Organisational Structures, and Individuals.* IBM Syst. J., 44, pp. 691-708.

Beck, Kent and Andres, Cynthia (2004). *Extreme Programming Explained: Embrace Change.* (2nd Edition). Addison-Wesley Professional.

Binder, Robert V. (1994). *Design for testability in object-oriented systems.* Commun. ACM, 37(9):87–101.

Binder, Robert V. (1999). *Testing object-oriented systems: models, patterns, and tools.* Addison-Wesley Longman Publishing Co., Inc.

Black, Rex (2007). *Pragmatic Software Testing: Becoming an Effective and Efficient Test Professional.* John Wiley & Sons, Inc.

Blackman, C.R. (1998). *Convergence between telecommunications and other media: how should regulation adapt?.* Telecommunications Policy, Vol. 22, No. 3, pp. 163-170.

Blaxter, Loraine, Hughes, Christina, Tight, Malcolm (2001). *How to Research.* Second Edition, New York Open University Press.

Blum, Niklas (2010). *Formalization of a Convergent Internet and Telecommunication Service Environment.* Dissertation, University Potsdam, Germany.

Bores *et al.* (2001). *Technological convergence: a strategic perspective.* Working Paper, Department of Economics, University of Girona, Spain.

Botha, Adele; Makitla, Ismael; Tolmay, JP; Ford, Merryl; Seetharam, Dhiren; Butgereit, Laurie; Ogunleye, Olalekan; Abouchabki, Colin. (2010). *Mobile4D Platform.* IST-Africa 2010 Conference Proceedings.

Brown, A. (1995). *Managing understandings: politics, symbolism, niche marketing and the quest for legitimacy in IT implementation*, Organization Studies, Vol. 16 No. 6, pp. 951-69.

Brown, Scott C.; Stevens, Richard A.; Troiano, Jr. Peter F.; Schneider, Mary Kay (2002). *Exploring Complex Phenomena: Grounded Theory in Student Affairs Research.* Vol 43 No. 2, Journal of College Student Development.

Brühlmann, Marina (2007) *Sind Mind Mapping und Concept Mapping effektive Lernstrategien?* Department for Psychology, University Freiburg, German.

Bryant, Antony (2009). *Grounded theory and pragmatism: The curious case of Anselm Strauss.* Forum Qualitative Sozialforschung / Forum: Qualitative Social Research, *10*(3), Art. 2, http://nbn-resolving.de/urn:nbn:de:0114-fqs090325 [Accessed: Oct. 15, 2009].

Burkhardt, Jochen, Henn, Horst, Hepper, Stefan, Rinkdorff, Klaus, Schaeck, Thomas (2001). *Pervasive Computing*, Addison Weseley.

Buschmann, F., Menuier, R., Rohnert, H., Sommerlad, P., Stal, M. (1996). *Pattern-Oriented Software Architecture: A System of Patterns*, Wiley, 1996.

Bhushan, B.; Tarlano, A.; Fischer, G.; Hendriks, J. (2007). *Development and Publication of Generic Middleware Components for the Next Generation Mobile Service Platform.* In the Proceedings of 3rd IEEE SAINT 2007 Workshop on Next Generation Service Platforms for Future Mobile Systems (SPMS 2007), Hiroshima, JAPAN, January 15-19, 2007.

Bushnesll, W. (2004) *IMS Based Converged Wireline-Wireless Services.* Proc. 9th Int'l. Conf. Intelligence in Service Delivery Networks, Bordeaux, France, pp. 18–21.

Buzan, T. and North, V. (1999). *Business Mind Mapping.* Vienna, Wirtschaftsverlag Ueberreuter.

Buzan, T. (2003). *How to Mind Map: Make the most of your mind and learn to create, organize and plan.* Thorsons, London.

Carter, Stacy M.; and Little, Miles. (2011). *Qualitative Health Research - Methods in Qualitative Research Justifying*. *Qual Health Res* 2007 17: 1316.

Chappell, Caroline and Finnie, Graham (2009). *The Agile Service Provider: A New Model For Service Delivery*. www.heavyreading.com. On behalf of Cisco Systems, Inc., May 2009.

Charmaz, Kathy (2006). *Constructing Grounded Theory: A Practical Guide Through Qualitative Analysis*. SAGE Publications, London.

Christian, Rolan (2011). *Service Delivery Platform for the Next-Generation Network*. published in Ahson and Ilyas (2011). CRC Press Taylor and Francis Group.

Christoffersen, K., & Woods, D. (2002). *How to make automated systems team players*. In E. Salas (Ed.), Advances in human performance and cognitive engineering research (Vol. 2): JAI Press/Elsevier.

Cordier, Christophe (2005). *Service Platform perspective: Overview of the Service Platform for Innovative Communication Environment proposal*. WWI Workshop, Mobile IST Forum, Dresden.

Cordier, Christophe, Carrez, François, Van Kranenburg, Herma, Licciardi, Carlo, Van der Meer, Jan, Zoric, Josip, Spedalieri, Antonietta and Le Rouzic, Jean-Pierre (2006a). *Advanced Beyond 3G service delivery environment: the SPICE service platform design principles*. Wireless World, Research Formum, IST.

Cordier, Christophe, Carrez, François, Van Kranenburg, Herma, Licciardi, Carlo, Van der Meer, Jan, Zoric, Josip, Spedalieri, Antonietta and Le Rouzic, Jean-Pierre (2006b) *Addressing the challenges of Beyond 3G service delivery: the SPICE service platform*. Wireless World, Research Formum, IST.

Cockpit Voice Recorder Database (1991). *A database containing CVR transcripts of aviation accidents and incidents*. 26 May 1991 - Lauda 004, http://www.tailstrike.com/260591.htm [Accessed: 06.09.2012].

CORDIS – Report from the Information Society Technologies Advisory Group (ISTAG). *(2006). Shaping Europe's Future Through ICT*. http://www.cordis.lu/ist/istag.htm, March 2006.

CTIT - Centre for Telematics and Information Technology (2011). *Progress Report 2010-2011*. University of Twente, Netherland.

Creswell, J. W., (1994). *Research Design: Qualitative and Quantitative Approaches*. Thousand Oaks, CA: Sage Publications.

Creswell, J. W. (2012). *Educational research: Planning, conducting, and evaluating quantitative and qualitative research*. Upper Saddle River, NJ: Prentice Hall.

DeBellis, M. and Haapala, C. (1995). *User-centric software engineering*. IEEE Expert, 34-41.

Deitel, H. M., Deitel, P. J., Nieto, T. R., Steinbuhler, K. (2002). *Wireless Internet & Mobile Business - How to Program*. New Jersey, Prentice-Hall, Inc.

Deppermann, Arnulf (2003). *Argumentieren in Gesprächen – gesprächsanalytische Studien*. Stauffenburg Verlag, Tübingen.

Demeter, Hunor (2008). *Mobile Service Platforms Cluster White Paper: Mobile Service Platforms – Architecture Whitepaper*. Date delivered: 11 March 2008.

Devine, A. (2001). *Mobile Internet Content Providers and their Business Models*. Master's thesis, Dept. of Elec. Eng. and Mgmt., Royal Inst. Technology, Stockholm, Sweden.

Dey, I. (1993). *Qualitative Data Analysis: A user-friendly guide for social scientists*. London: Routledge.

Dilger, Martin und Wulf, Christoph (2000). *Grounded Theory – Ein Überblick über ihre charakteristischen Merkmale*. Freie Universität Berlin.

Dix, A., Finlay, J., Abowd, G. D., & Beale, R. (2004). *Human-Computer-Interaction*. 3rd edition. Harlow, UK.: Prentice-Hall.

Domingue, John; Fensel, Dieter; Davies3, John; González-Cabero, Rafael; Pedrinaci1 Carlos (2010). *The Service Web: a Web of Billions of Services. Towards the Future Internet G. Tselentis et al. (Eds.), IOS Press, 2010.*

Donaghy, W. C. (1990). *The Interview – Skills and Applications*. Sheffield Publishing Company, Salem, WI.

D'Roza, T. and Bilchev, G. (2003). *An overview of location-based services. BT Technology Journal*. Vol. 21, No. 1 January 2003, pp. 20-27.

Dubey, Sanjay Kumar and Rana, Ajay (2010). *Analytical Roadmap to Usability Definitions and Decompositions*. Department of Computer Science and Engineering Amity University, India.

Eisenhardt, K.M. (1989). *Building theories from case study research*. Academy of Management Review, vol. 14, no. 4, pp. 532-550.

Esteves, Jose, Ramos, Isabel, Carvalho, João (2002). *Use of Grounded Theory in Information Systems Area: An Exploratory Analysis.* Barcelona, Spain, 2002.

Farrero, J. M. Castán und Argüelles, M. J. Martínez (2005). *Using the critical incident technique to evaluate the service quality perceptions of virtual higher education students: An exploratory study.* Publication of the EADTU Working Conference "Towards Lisbon 2010", Rom.

Fendt, J. and Sachs, W. (2008). *Grounded Theory Method in Management Research: User's Perspective.* Organizational Research Methods, Vol. 11 (3), pp. 430-455.

Fielding, N. (1998). *Computer analysis and qualitative research.* London: SAGE.

Fink, J.; Kobsa, A.; Nill, A. (1998). *Adaptable and adaptive information provision for all users, including disabled and elderly people.* New Rev Hypermedia Multimed 4:163–188.

Fireball - Project Report (2012). *D2.1 - Landscape and Roadmap of Future Internet and Smart Cities.* (M24). Report. FP7-ICT-2009-5.

Fitts, P.M. (1954). *The information capacity of the human motor system in controlling the amplitude of movement. Journal of Experimental Psychology, 47,* 381-391.

Flanagan, John C. (1954). *The Critical Incident Technique.* Psychological Bulletin, Vol. 51, pp. 327-359.

Flick, U. (1996). *Qualitative Forschung: Theorie, Methoden, Anwendung in Psychologie und Sozialwissenschaften.* Rowohlt Taschenbuch Verlag, Reinbek b. Hamburg.

Frattasi, S.; Olsen, RL; De Sanctis, m.; *et al.* (2005). *Heterogeneous services and architectures for next-generation wireless networks.* 2nd International Symposium on Wireless Communications Systems (ISWCS 2005), Siena, Italy, Sep 05-07, 2005.

Freedman, R. S. (1991). *Testability of software components.* IEEE Transactions on Software Engineering, 17(6):553–564.

Föhrenbach, Stephanie; Geyer, Florian; Rinn, Johannes; Samad, Kerstin (2007). *Term Paper - Visual Requirements Engineering;* Department of Computer & Information Science, University of Konstanz, Germany.

Funk, J. L. (2000) *The Mobile Internet Market: Lessons from Japan's i-mode System*. The E-Business Transformation: Sector Developments and Policy Implications, Washington DC.

Gao, Jerry and Shih, Ming-Chih (2005). *A component testability model for verification and measurement*. 29th Annual International Computer Software and Applications Conference (COMPSAC '05), pages 211–218. IEEE Computer Society.

Garlan, D. and Shaw, M. (1993). *An Introduction to Software Architecture, Advances in Software Engineering and Knowledge Engineering*, Volume I (Eds. Ambriola, V. & Tortora, G.), World Scientific Publishing Company, 1993.

Gasser, Urs and Palfrey, John (2007). *Breaking down digital barriers - When and how ICT interoperability drives innovation*. Berkman Publication Series.

Gibbs, G. (2002). *Qualitative data analysis: Explorations in NVivo*. Technical Report, Buckingham, UK: Open University.

Gilb, T. (2003). *Competitive Engineering*. Addison-Wesley.

Glaser, Barney G. and Strauss, Anselm L. (1967). *The Discovery of Grounded Theory: Strategies for Qualitative Research*. Aldine de Gruyter, Hawthorne, New York.

Glaser, B. (1978). *Theoretical sensitivity: advances in the methodology of grounded theory*. Sociology Press, Mill Valley.

Glaser, B. (1992). *Basics of Grounded Theory Analysis: Emergence vs. forcing*. Mill Valley, Sociology Press.

Glaser, B. ed. (1994). *More Grounded Theory Methodology: A Reader*. Mill Valley, Sociology Press.

Glesne, C. (1999). *Becoming qualitative researchers: An introduction* (2nd ed.). New York: Longman.

Gould, J.D. and Lewis, C. (1985). *Designing for Usability: Key Principles and What Designers Think*. Communications of the ACM, 28 (3), March 1985.

Goulding, Christina (1998). *Grounded theory: the missing methodology on the interpretivist agenda*. Qualitative Market Research: An International Journal, 1 (1), pp.50 – 57.

Glouding, Christina (2002). *An Exploratory Study of Age Related Vicarious Nostalgia and Aesthetic Consumption.* Advances in Consumer Research Vol. 29, 2002, pp. 542-546, University of Wolverhampton.

Goncalves da Silva, E. M. and Ferreira Pires, L. and van Sinderen, M. J. (2007). *An Algorithim for Automatic Service Composition.* In: 1st International Workshop on Architectures, Concepts and Technologies for Service Oriented Computing, ICSOFT 2007, 22 July 2007, Barclona, Spain. pp. 65-74. INSTICC Press. ISBN 978-989-8111-08-1.

Gorra, Andrea (2007). *An analysis of the relationship between individuals' perceptions of privacy and mobile phone location data: a grounded theory study.* PhD Thesis, Leeds Metropolitan University.

Gorra, Andrea (2008). *Implications of mobile phone location data on individuals' perceptions of privacy - a Grounded Theory study.* School of Information Management, Leeds Metropolitan University.

Gorra, Andrea (2009). *Qualitative Data Collection & Analysis.* Workshop presentation at the Danube-University Krems, 4 December 2009.

Gradmann, Stefan (2009) *Interoperability - A key concept for large scale, persistent digital libraries.* Digital Preservation Europe, Humboldt University, Berlin.

Grech, MLF; Torabi, M.; Unmehopa, MR. (2002). *Service control architecture in the UMTS IP multimedia core network subsystem.* IEEE Conference publications. 3rd International Conference on 3G Mobile Communication Technologies. London, May 8-10, 2002.

Greenbaum, Joan and Kyng, Morten (1991). *Design At Work - Cooperative design of Computer Systems,* Lawrence Erlbaum.

Griffin, A., and Hauser, J. R. (1993). *The voice of the customer.* Marketing Science, 12(1), 1-27.

Hackos, J.T., and Redish, J.C. (1998). *User and Task Analysis for Interface Design.* John Wiley & Sons, New York.

Hamlet, Dick (1994). *What is software reliability?* In Proceedings of the 9th Annual Conference on Computer Assurance (COMPASS '94) 'Safety, Reliability, Fault Tolerance, Concurrency and Real Time, Security',* pages 169–170, July 1994.

Hansen, Klaus Marius (1998). *Exploiting Architecture in Experimental System Development.* Department of Computer Science, University of Aarhus, Åbogade 34, DK-8200 Aarhus N, Denmark.

Harper, Richard; Rodden, Tom; Rogers, Yvonne; and Sellen, Abigail (2008). *Being Human – Human-Computing Interaction in the Year 2020*. ISBN: 978-0-9554761-1-2, Publisher: Microsoft Research Ltd., Cambridge, England.

Haythornthwaite, Caroline and Wellman, Barry (2002). *The Internet in Everyday Life: An Introduction*. Oxford, Blackwell Publisher.

Heeks, Richard (2009). *The ICT4D 2.0 Manifesto: Where Next for ICTs and International Development?* Working Paper Series, Development Informatics Group, University of Manchester.

Hevner, March, Park and Ram (2004). *Design Science in Information Systems Research*. MIS Quarterly, *28(1), pp. 75-105.*

Hilbert, Martin (2011). *When is Cheap, Cheap Enough to Bridge the Digital Divide? Modelling Income Related Structural Challenges of Technology Diffusion in Latin America*. World Development. Volume 38, issue 5, pp. 756–770.

Hjelm, Johan (2005) *User Centric Services Without the Guesswork: The MobiLife Approach*. Ericsson Research.

Holland, JH, Holyoak KJ, Nisbett RE, Thagard PR (1989). *Induction: Processes of Inference, Learning, and Discovery*. Cambridge, MA, USA: MIT Press

Holm, Ivar (2006). *Ideas and Beliefs in Architecture and Industrial design: How attitudes, orientations, and underlying assumptions shape the built environment*. Oslo School of Architecture and Design.

Holyoak, K. and Morrison R. (2005). *The Cambridge Handbook of Thinking and Reasoning*. New York: Cambridge University Press.

Honeyman, Peter; Schwartz, Galina A.; Van Assche, Ari (2007). *Interdependence of Reliability and Security*. Research paper.

Huber, G. L. and Mandl, H. (1994) *Verbale Daten*. 2. Auflage, Beltz Psychologie Verlags Union, Weinheim, Basel.

Hull, Elizabeth; Kenneth Jackson; and Jeremy Dick (2005). *Requirements Engineering*, London: Springer.

Hutchins, Edwin (1995) *Cognition in the wild*. MIT Press, Cambridge, MA.

ICTs for e-Environment - Final Report (2008). *Guidelines for Developing Countries with a Focus on Climate Change*. ICT Application and Cyber security Division, Policies and Strategies Department. ITU.

IEEE. (1990). *IEEE glossary of software engineering terminology*, IEEE standard 610.12. Technical report, IEEE.

IEEE Std 1149.1 (JTAG) Testability Primer (1997). *A technical presentation on Design-for-Test centered on JTAG and Boundary Scan*, Texas Instruments.

INDENICA Research Project (2010). *Engineering Virtual Domain-Specific Service Platforms*. Specific Targeted Research Project: FP7-ICT-2009-5 / 257483.

Information Society Technologies Research (IST in FP6), http://cordis.europa.eu/ist/ [Accessed: November 22, 2011].

IST-MOTIVE Deliverable D2.2 - MOTIVE system architecture, http://www.cn.ntua.gr/ist-motive. [Accessed: 22.09.2013].

Jeon, Taewoong; Seung, Hyon Woo; and Lee, Sungyoung (2002). *Embedding built-in tests in hot spots of an object-oriented framework*. ACM SIGPLAN Notices, 37(8), pp. 25–34.

Jimenez, Guillermo; Taj, Shahram; Weaver, Jonathan. (2005). *Design For Testability*. University of Detroit Mercy. The NCIIA 9th Annual Meeting, March 17-19, 2005, San Diego, CA.

Jin, Li; Wen, Zhigang; Gough, Norman. (2010). *Social virtual worlds for technology-enhanced learning on an augmented learning platform*. Learning media and technology, Volume 35 (2) pp. 139-153; published 24. Aug. 2010.

Johnston, A.; Gabrielsson, J.; Christopoulos, Ch.; Huysmans, M.; Olsson, U. (2007). *Evolution of service delivery platforms*. Ericson Review No. 1.

Johnson-Laird, Philip and Byrne, Ruth M. J. (1991). *Deduction*. Psychology Press 1991.

Karwowski, W.; Soares, M. M.; Stanton, N. A. (2011). *Human Factors and Ergonomics in Consumer Product Design: Methods and Techniques (Handbook of Human Factors in Consumer Product Design): Needs Analysis: Or, How Do You Capture, Represent, and Validate User Requirements in a Formal Manner/Notation before Design*. CRC Press. 2011.

Kantipudi, Kalyana R. (2002). *Controllability and Observability*.Department of Electrical & Computer Engineering, Auburn University, Australia.

Kelle, Udo (1994). *Empirisch begründete Theoriebildung*. Weinheim, Deutscher Studienverlag.

Kelle, Udo (2005). *"Emergence" vs. "forcing" of empirical data? A crucial problem of "grounded theory" reconsidered.* Forum Qualitative Sozialforschung / Forum: Qualitative Social Research, 6(2), Art. 27, http://nbn-resolving.de/urn:nbn:de:0114-fqs0502275 [Accessed: August 20, 2006].

Kerlinger, F.N. (1986). *Foundations of behavioural research.* 3rd ed. New York: Holt, Rinehart, and Winston.

Killström, Ulla; Mrohs, Bernd; Immonen, Olli; Pitkänen, Olli; Galli, Luca; de Reuver, Mark; Haaker, Timber (2008). *A new mobile service architecture addresses future mobile business environments.* paper.

Klein, Gary, Woods, David D., Bradshaw, Jeffrey M., Hoffmann, Robert R. and Feltovich, Paul J. (2004) *Ten Challenges for Making Automation a "Team Player" in Joint Human-Agent Activity.* IEEE Intelligent Systems, Vol. 19, (6), pp. 91-95.

Klemettinen, M. and Salo, J. T. (2005). *MobiLife – Project overview and highlights,* June 2005.

Klockner, K., Pankoke-Babatz, U., and Prinz, W. (1999). *Experiences with a cooperative design process in developing a telecooperation system for collaborative document production.* Behavior and Information Technology, 18(5), 373-383.

Kolb, Ronny and Muthig, Dirk (2006). *Making testing product lines more efficient by improving the testability of product line architectures.* ISSTA 2006 workshop on Role of Software Architecture for Testing and Analysis (ROSATEA '06), pages 22–27. ACM Press.

Korpipää, P., Häkkilä, J., Kela, J., Ronkainen, S., Känsälä I. (2004). *Utilising context ontology in mobile device application personalization.* ACM International Conference Proceeding Series, Vol. 83 (pp. 133-140).

Kotonya, G, and Somerville, I. (1998). *Requirements Engineering - Processes and Techniques.* Chichester, UK: John Wiley & Sons.

König, J. and Nordström, L. (2009). *Assessing Impact of ICT System Quality on Operation of Active Distribution Grids.* paper IEEE Bucharest Power Tech Conference, Romania.

Krummenacher, Reto and Strang, Thomas (2008). *Ontology-Based Context Modelling.* Digital Enterprise Research Institute, University of Innsbruck, Austria.

Lamont-Mills, Andrea (2004). *Computer aided qualitative research - A NUD*IST 6 approach.* Department of Psychology, University of Southern Queensland, Toowoomba, Australia.

Latour, Bruno (2006) in Belliger, Andrea and Krieger, David J. (Ed.). *ANthology. Ein einführendes Handbuch zur Akteur-Netzwerk-Theorie.* Transcript, Bielefeld.

Lécué, F., Goncalves da Silva, E.M., Ferreira Pires, L. (2007). *A Framework for Dynamic Web Services Composition. In: 2nd ECOWS Workshop on Emerging Web Services Technology.* (WEWST07) 26 Nov 2007, Halle, Germany. CEUR Workshop Proceedings. ISSN 1613-0073.

Lee, A. S. (1991). *Architecture as a Reference Discipline for MIS, in Information Systems Research: Contemporary Approaches and Emergent Traditions.* H.-E. Nisen, H. K. Klein, and R. A. Hirschheim (Eds.), North-Holland, Amsterdam, pp. 573-592.

Lee, I. *et al.* (2006). *A Study on Architecture and Performance of Service Delivery Platform in Home Networks.* Int'l. Assn. Sci. and Tech. for Development, Proc. 24th IASTED Int'l. Conf. Parallel and Distrib. Comp. and Networks, pp. 244–49.

Lehmann, Hans (2012). *Grounded Theory and Information Systems: Are We Missing the Point?.* Information Systems Theory: Explaining and Predicting Our Digital Society, Vol. 2, Integrated Series in Information Systems 29, Springer Science Business Media, LLC 2012.

Levin, D. M. (1988). *The opening of vision: Nihilism and the postmodern situation.* London: Routledge.

Leffingwell, Dean and Widrig, Don (2003). *Managing Software Requirements: A Use Case Approach,* Second Edition, Boston, MA: Addison-Wesley.

Leyden, J. (2005). *MEPs vote for mandatory data retention. The Register.* [Internet]   Available   from http://www.theregister.co.uk/2005/12/14/eu_data_retention_vote/   [Accessed 21 August 2012].

Liberal, Fidel; Fajardo, Jose-Oscar and Koumaras, Harilaos (2009). *QoE and *-awareness in the Future Internet.* Towards the Future Internet G. Tselentis et al. (Eds.), IOS Press, 2009.

Lu, R., Jin, Z., and Wan, R. (1995). *Requirement specification in pseudo-natural language in PROMIS.* Paper presented at the Proceedings of COMPSAC, USA.

Lundqvist, Henrik; Despotovic, Zoran; Frtunikj, Jelena; Kunzmann, Gerald; Kellerer, Wolfgang (2006). *Service Program Mobility Architecture.* DOCOMO Communications Laboratories Europe.

Lyon, D., Marmura, S. and Peroff, P. (2005). *Location Technologies: Mobility, Surveillance and Privacy - Report to the Office of the Privacy Commissioner of Canada.* March 2005. [Internet] Available from http://www.queensu.ca/sociology/Surveillance/files/loctech.pdf [Accessed: 3 January 2005].

Magedanz, T., Witaszek, D., Knuettel, K. (2005) *The IMS Playground @ Fokus - An Open Testbed for Next Generation Network Multimedia Services.* Proc. 1st Int'l. Conf. Testbeds and Research Infrastructures for the Development of Networks and Communities, IEEE Comp. Soc., pp. 2–11.

Magedanz, T. and Sher, Muhammad (2007). *IT-based Open Service Delivery Platforms for Mobile Networks From CAMEL to the IP Multimedia System.* Technical University Berlin/Fokus, Fraunhofer Institute Berlin, Germany.

March, S. and Smith G. (1995). *Design and natural science in Information Technology (IT), Decision Support Systems.* Vol. 15, pp. 251- 266.

Maurino, Andrea; Pernici, Barbara; Schreiber, Fabio A. (2003). *Adaptive channel behaviour in financial information systems.* Politecnico di Milano, Dipartimento di Elettronica e Informazione Piazza Leonardo da Vinci, 32 I-1033 Milan, Italy.

McAllister, Chad A. (2006). *Requirements determination of information system: User and developers perceptions of factors contributing to misunderstandings.* Dissertation.

MacDonald, D. J. (2003) *NTT DoCoMo's i-mode: Developing Win-Win Relationships for Mobile Commerce* Mobile Commerce: Technology, Theory, and Applications, Idea Publishing Group, pp. 1–25.

Matinlassi, Mari and Niemelä, Eila (2002). *Designing High Quality Architectures.* VTT Electronics, Embedded software. Software Architectures Group. Oulu, Finland.

McKaughan, Daniel J. (2008). *From Ugly Duckling to Swan: C. S. Peirce, Abduction, and the Pursuit of Scientific Theories.* Transactions of the Charles S. Peirce Society, v. 44, no. 3 (summer), pp. 446–468.

McLean, E. R., Kappelman, L. A., & Thompson, J. P. (1993). *Converging end-user and corporate computing.* Communications of the ACM, 36(12), 79-92.

McNamara, Kerry S. (2003). *Information and Communication Technologies, Poverty and Development: Learning from Experience.* World Bank, Washington D.C., USA. http://www.infodev.org/en/Document.19.aspx. [Retrieved 2007-04-08].

Mell, Peter and Grance, Timothy (2011). *The NIST Definition of Cloud Computing.* Special Publication 800-145; Recommendations of the National Institute of Standards and Technology.

Melody, William *et al.,* (1991). *Information and Communication Technologies: Social Sciences Research and Training.* A Report by the ESRC Programme on Information and Communication Technologies, ISBN 0-86226-179-1, 1986. Roger Silverstone et al., "Listening to a long conversation: an ethnographic approach to the study of information and communication technologies in the home", Cultural Studies, 5(2), pp. 204-227.

Menzies, T. (1996). *Applications of Abduction: Knowledge-Level Modelling.* International Journal of Human-Computer Studies, 45.3, pp. 305-335.

Michaelides, Panayotis G. and Milios, John G. (2008). *Joseph Schumpeter and the German Historical School.* Cambridge Journal of Economics 2009, 33, 495–516, Advance Access publication 18 November 2008.

Miles, M., Huberman, A. (1994). *An Expanded Sourcebook - Qualitative Data Analysis.* 2nd ed. Thousand Oaks, California, SAGE Publications, Inc.

Mobile Future Report (2004). *Mobile Ability - The Transformation of Wireless Innovation for People with Disabilities.*

Morse, J. M. and Richards, L. (2002). *Readme First for a User's Guide to Qualitative. Methods.* Thousand Oaks, CA: SAGE.

Moskvitch, Katia (2010). Glonass: *Has Russia's sat-nav system come of age?* BBC News. http://news.bbc.co.uk/2/hi/8595704.stm. [Accessed: 18 July 2012].

Mueller, Milton (1999). *Digital Convergence and its Consequences.* Vol. 6 (1999), 3, pp. 11-28, the public, Futurelab Series.

Müller, Benjamin and Olbrich, Sebastian (2012). *Developing Theories in Information Systems Research: The Grounded Theory Method Applied.* Information Systems Theory: Explaining and Predicting Our Digital Society, Vol. 2, Springer Science Business Media, LLC 2012.

Mulo, Emmanuel (2007). *Design for Testability in Software Systems - A Software Engineering Research Group Literature Study,* Software Engineering

Research Group, Department of Software Technology, Faculty EEMCS, Delft University of Technology, Delft, Netherlands.

Namoun, Abdallah; Wajid, Usman; Mehandjiev, Nikolay (2010). *A Comparative Study: Service-Based Application Development by Ordinary End Users and IT Professionals.* Manchester Business School, The University of Manchester, Manchester, M13 9SS, UK

Naismith, L., Lonsdale, P., Vavoula, G., Sharples, M. (2004). *Mobile technologies and learning' in Futurelab Literature Review Series*, Technical Report, University of Birmingham, UK.

Narros, Leena and Savioja, Paula (2004). *Usability Evaluation of Complex Systems – A Literature Review.* STUK-YTO-TR 204, VTT Industrial Systems, Finland.

National Academy of Public Administration (1995). *The Global Positioning System: A Shared Nations Asset: Recommendations for Technical Improvements and Enhancements.* National Academy Press. ISBN 0309052831, 9780309052832.

Neuendorf, K. A. (2002). *The Content Analysis Guidebook.* Thousand Oaks, CA., Sage Publication Inc.

NFC Forum (2001). *What is NFC?.* http://www.nfc-forum.org/aboutnfc/. [Retrieved 14 June 2011].

Niculescu, Cristina; and Pana, Laura (2010). *Architecture of a Multi-Framework set for Collaborative Knowledge Generation.* 11th European Conference on Knowledge Management, Famalicao, Portugal, Sep 02-03, 2010.

Nielsen, Jakob (1993). *Usability Engineering.* academic press.

Nielsen, J. (2003, August 18). *Mobile Devices: One generation from useful. Alertbox posting on useit.com: Jakob Nielsen's Website.* Retrieved February 14, 2007 from: http://www.useit.com/alertbox/20030818.html.

Nielsen, Jakob (2004). *Designing Web Usability,* German edition. Markt und Technik. ISBN 3-8272-6846-X.

Nissenbaum (1998). *Protecting Privacy in an Information Age: The Problem of Privacy in Public.* Law and Philosophy, 17 pp. 559-596.

Noll, Michael (1994*). Network Security And Reliability - Emergencies In Decentralized Networks.* University of Southern California.

Novak, J. D.; Gowin, D. B. (1984). *Learning how to learn,* Cambridge University Press, New York.

Nguyen, L. and P. Swatman (2000). *Managing the Requirements Engineering Process.*2003.

Osorio Luis, A.; Afsarmanesh, Hamideh; Camarinha-Matos, Luis M. (2010). *A Service Integration Platform for Collaborative Networks.* Conference: 9th IFIP International Conference on Information Technology for Balanced Automation Systems (BASYS 10). Valencia, Spain, Jun 21-23.

Orlikowski, W. J.; and Baroudi, J. J. (1991). *Studying Information Technology in Organizations: Research Approaches and Assumptions.* Information Systems Research, 2(1), 1-28.

Paas, Leslie (2008). *How Information and Communication technologies can Support Education for Sustainable Development.* Information Institute for Sustainable Development, Manitobes, Canada, http://www.iisd.org. [Accessed: July 17, 2012].

Pagani, M. (2005). *Mobile and Wireless Systems Beyond 3G - Managing New Business Opportunities,* IRM Press.

Pandey, Dhirendra; Suman, U.; and Ramani, A. K. (2010). *An Effective Requirement Engineering Process Model for Software Development and Requirements Management.* International Conference on Advances in Recent Technologies in Communication and Computing.

Pannevis, Martijn (2007). *I'm bored! Where is Everybody? Location Based Systems for Mobile Phones.* Master Thesis, Business Information Systems, University of Amsterdam.

Paris, Rubert and Hürzeler, Peter (2008). *Was versteht man unter Grounded Theory?.* Institute for Technology Management, University St. Gallen, St. Gallen.

Pastuszka, S.; Vergnault, S.; Betgé-Brezetz, S.; Aghasaryan, A.; and Lopes, P. (2008). *Mitigating Risk in the New Economy - Addressing changing user needs and market trends.* enriching communications, volume 2, issue 2, 2008, http://www.alcatel-lucent.com/enrich.

Patel, Chetankumer and Ramachandran, Mutu (2010). *Best Practices Guidelines for Agile Requirements Engineering Practices.* IGI Global.

Patrício, L., Cunha, J.F., Fisk, R.P., and Nunes, N.J. (2003) *Addressing Marketing Requirements in User-Interface Design for Multiple Platforms.* DSV-IS 2003 - the Tenth Workshop on the Design, Specification and Verification of Interactive Systems, Springer Verlag, Funchal, pp. 331-345.

Patton, M.Q. (1987). *How to Use Qualitative Methods in Evaluation.* California: Sage Publications Inc.

Pavlovski, C. J. (2002) *Reference Architecture for Mobile Internet Service Platform.* Proc. 2nd Asian Int'l. Mobile Comp. Conf., Langkawi, Malaysia, pp. 114–23.

Pavlovski, C. J. (2007). *Service Delivery Platforms in Practice.* IEEE Communications Magazine • March 2007.

Pavlovski, C. J. and Staes-Polet, Q. (2005) *Digital Media and Entertainment Service Delivery Platform.* Proc. 1st ACM Int'l Wksp. Multimedia Service Composition, Singapore, pp. 47–54.

Pavlovski, C. J.; and Plant, L. (2007). *Service Delivery Platforms in Mobile Convergence.* Service Computing. Idea Group Inc.

Peirce, Charles Sanders (1931-1935). *The collected papers of Charles S. Peirce (8 Vol.).* Cambridge, Harvard University Press.

Peirce, Charles S. (1955). *Deduction, Induction and Hypothesis.* In: Peirce, Charles S.: Collected Papers Vol. II, Harvard University Press, Cambridge, pp 619-644.

Peirce, Charles Sanders (1992). *Reasoning and the Logic of Things.* Edited by K.L. Ketner. Cambridge, Harvard University Press.

Peirce, Charles Sanders (1997). *Pragmatism as a Principle and Method of Right Thinking.* Edited by P. A. Turrisi. New York: State University of New York Press.

Perez, Carlota (2005). *Respecialisation and the deployment of the ICT paradigm - An essay on the present challenges of globalisation.* Cambridge and Sussex universities, U.K. Paper for the IPTS FISTERA Project November 2005.

Pescovitz, David (2008). *Roy Amara, forecaster, RIP.* http://boingboing.net/2008/01/03/roy-amara-forecaster.html, [Date of access: 3. August 2012].

Pettichord, Bret (2002). *Design for Testability.* To be presented at the Pacific Northwest Software Quality Conference, Portland, Oregon, October 2002.

Pfoser, D., Pitoura, E., and Tryfona, N. (2002). *Metadata modelling in a global computing environment.* In The 10th ACM International Symposium on Advances in Geographic Information Systems.

Plagemann, Thomas; Munthe-Kaas, Ellen; Skjelsvik, Katrine S.; Puzar, Matija; Goebel, Vera; Johansen, Ulrik; Gorman, Joe; and Marin, Santiago Perez. (2007). *A Data Sharing Facility for Mobile Ad-Hoc Emergency and Rescue Applications*, The First International Workshop on Specialized Ad Hoc Networks and Systems (SAHNS 2007).

Poikselkä, Miikka, Mayer, Georg, Khartabil, Hisham and Niemi, Aki (2004). *The IMS – IP Multimedia Concepts and Services in the Mobile Domain.* John Wiley & Sons, Ltd, West Sussex.

Popper, Karl R. (1959). *The logic of scientific discovery.* London: Hutchison.

Preece, J., Rogers, Y., & Sharp, H. (2002). *Interaction Design: Beyond human-computer interaction.* New York: John Wiley.

Qiao, Xiuquan; Li, Xiaofeng; and Junliang Chen; (2008). *Telecommunications Service Domain Ontology: Semantic Interoperation Foundation of Intelligent Integrated Services.* State Key Laboratory of Networking and Switching Technology. Beijing University of Posts and Telecommunications. China.

OSR International. *"What is qualitative research?"*. http://www.qsrinternational.com/what-is-qualitative-research.aspx [Retrieved on 15th of July 2012].

QSR International. *"About NVivo 10"*. http://www.qsrinternational.com/products_nvivo.aspx [Retrieved 16th of July 2012].

Rajendra, Singh and Siddhartha, Raja (2010). *Convergence in information and communication technology: strategic and regulatory considerations.* Washington, D.C.: World Bank.

Ramachandran, M. And De Carvalho, R. A. (2010). *Software Engineering and Productivity Technologies.* Engineering Science Reference, Hershey, U.S.

Ramamoorthy, C. V. and Ho, S. F. (1975). *Testing large software with automated software evaluation systems.* In Proceedings of the international conference on Reliable software, pages 382–394. ACM Press.

Reichertz, Jo (1993). *Abduktives Schlußfolgern und Typen(re)konstruktion.* In: D. Jung/St. Müller-Doohm (Ed.): 'Wirklichkeit' im Deutungsprozeß. Ffm. pp. 258 - 282.

Renkl, A. and Nückles, M. (2006). *Lernstrategien der externen Visualisierung.* Mandl, H. and Friedrich, H. F. (Hrsg.), Handbuch Lernstrategien, pages 135-147, Hogrefe, Göttingen.

Rescher, N. (1978). *Scientific Progress: A Philosophical Essay on the Economics of Research in Natural Science*. Oxford: Blackwell.

Research Ethics Policy (2012). Leeds Metropolitan University, August 2012, http://www.leedsmet.ac.uk/about/files/Research_Ethics_Policy_2012.pdf [Accessed: 02.09.2012].

Reid, G. (2006). *Non-ICT executive perceptions of, and attitudes towards, ICT infrastructure projects*. Unpublished PhD thesis. Information systems and operations management, University of Auckland.

Richter, K. F., Dara-Abrams, D., and Raubal, M. (2010). *Navigating and Learning with Location Based Services: A User-Centric Design*. in: Gartner, G. / Li (Eds.), Y.: Proceedings of the 7th International Symposium on LBS and Telecartog-raphy,   pp.   261-276,   http://cindy.informatik.uni-bremen.de/cosy/staff/richter/pubs/richterdaraabramsraubal-lbs2010.pdf [Accessed: August 2, 2012].

Rolan, Christian and Hu, Hanrahan (2008). *Defining a Service Delivery Platform Architecture by Reusing Intelligent Network Concepts*. Centre for Telecommunications Access and Services, School of Electrical and Information Engineering, University of the Witwatersrand, Johannesburg.

Ron, Oliver (2002). *The Role of ICT in Higher Education for the 21st Century: ICT as a Change Agent for Education. University*. Perth, Western Australia, 2002. http://elrond.scam.ecu.edu.au/oliver/2002/he21.pdf. [Accessed: August 3, 2012].

Rossman, G. B. and Rallis, S. F. (2003). *Learning in the field: An introduction to qualitative research*. (2nd ed.). Newbury Park, CA: Sage Publications.

Roth, Jörg (2005) *Mobile Computing – Grundlagen, Technik, Konzepte*. 2. Auflage, dpunkt Verlag GmbH, Heidelberg.

Rottmann,   D.   (2009).   Joint   Application   Development http://www.umsl.edu/~sauterv/analysis/488_f01_papers/rottman.htm. [Accessed: 11 August, 2013].

Roy, Jeffrey and Langford, John. (2008). *Integrating Service Delivery Across Levels of Government: Case Studies of Canada and Other Countries*. Collaboration: Networks and Partnerships series. IBM Centre for the Business of the Government.

El Saghir, Bassam and Crespi, Noel (2006). *A New Framework for Indicating Terminal Capabilities in the IP Multimedia Subsystem*. GET / Institut National des Telecommunications, France.

Saiedian, H. and Dale, R. (1999). *Requirements engineering: making the connection between the software developer and customer*. Information and Software Technology 42 (2000) 419–428.

Santaella, Lucia (1997). *The Development of Peirce's Three Types of Reasoning: Abduction, Deduction, and Induction*. 6th Congress of the IASS. Eprint.

Sajjad, umar and Hanif, Muhammad Quaisar. (2010). *Issues and Challenges of Requirement Elicitation in Large Web Projects*. Master Thesis, School of Computing Blekinge Institute of Technolog, Sweden.

Schaefer, Josef; and Haeffner, Walter (2006). *Paving the Way for a Next Generation Business Model for Carriers; How the paradigm shift culminating in separated IP-transport and service layers topsy-turvifies the traditional telecommunications industry and how NGN and IMS could help carriers and telcos to reach new terra firma*. 12th International Telecommunications Network Strategy and Planning Symposium, New Delhi, India, Nov 06-09, 2006.

Scheffer, Louis.; Lavagno, Luciano; Grant, Martin (2006). *Electronic Design Automation for IC System Design, Verification, and Testing*. Taylor & Francis Group, LLC, U.S.

Scherbakov, Nick V. (2005). *Software Architecture*. Presentation, Technical University of St. Petersburg.

Schilit, Bill N.; Adams, Norman; and Want, Roy (1994). *Context-Aware Computing Applications*. IEEE Workshop on Mobile Computing Systems and Applications.

Schmidt, Constantin (2011) *Context-Aware Computing*. Berlin Institute of Technology, Germany.

Schülke, Anett; Abbadessa, Daniele; Winkler, Florian (2006). *Service Delivery Platform: Critical Enabler to Service Providers' New Revenue Streams*. World Telecommunications Congress 2006

Schülke, Anett and Misu, Toshiyuki (2011). *Enabling Service Delivery in Next-Generation Networks towards Service Clouds*. published in Ahson and Ilyas (2011). CRC Press Taylor and Francis Group.

Sears, A., and Jacko, Julie A. (2007). *Human-Computer Interaction Handbook*. 2nd Edition, CRC Press. ISBN 0-8058-5870-9.

Selwyn, Neil (2011). *Web 2.0 applications as alternative environments for informal learning - a critical review*. Institute of Education, University of London, UK.

Semiawan, Transmissia (2006). *Grounded Theory in Practice – the Use of Object-Oriented Concept*. Post graduated conference "Methodological issues and ethical considerations", Leeds Metropolitan University, Leeds.

Shams-Ul-Arfif, Khan, Qadeem, and Gayyyur, S. A. K. (2010). *Requirements Engineering Processes, Tools/Technologies, & Methodologies*. International Journal of Reviews in Computing.

Shannak, Rifat O., and Aldhmour, Fairouz M. (2009). *Grounded Theory as a Methodology for Theory Generation in Information Systems Research*. European Journal of Economics, Finance and Administrative Sciences ISSN 1450-2275 Issue 15 (2009) © EuroJournals, Inc. 2009. http://www.eurojournals.com/EJEFAS.htm.

Sherman, R., and Webb, R. (1988). *Qualitative Research in Education: Forms and Methods*. Lewes, Falmer Press.

Shiaa, M., Falcarin, P., Pastor, A., Lécué, F., Goncalves da Silva, E.M., and Ferreira Pires, L. (2008). *Towards the automation of the service composition process: case study and prototype implementations*. In: ICT-MobileSummit 2008 Conference Proceedings, 10-12 June 2008, Stockholm, Sweden. pp. 1-8. IIMC International Information Management Corporation. ISBN 978-1-905824-08-3.

Shneiderman, B. and Plaisant, C. (2009). *Designing the user interface*. 5th edition. Boston: Addison-Wesley.

Siegemund, Frank (2004). *A Context-Aware Communication Platform for Smart Objects*. Proc. 2nd International Conference on Pervasive Computing, Springer-Verlag Berlin Heidelberg.

Silver, Mark S., Markus, Lynne M., and Beath, Cynthia Mathis (1995). *The Information Technology Interaction Model: A Foundation for the MBA Core Course. MIS Quarterly*, Vol. 19, No. 3, Special Issue on IS Curricula and Pedagogy (Sep., 1995), pp. 361-390.

Simmons, Odis E., and Gregory, Toni A. (2003). *Grounded Action: Achieving Optimal and Sustainable Change*. Volume 4, No.3, Art 27., published in FQS, September 2003.

Smartcities Project (2010). ICT architecture - supporting daily life in the smart cities - An introduction to ICT architecture for city managers and policy makers. Technical Report.

Smit, J. and Bryant, A. (2000). *Grounded theory method in IS research: Glaser vs. Strauss*, Working Paper, Leeds Metropolitan University, www.leedsmet.ac.uk/inn/2000-7.pdf. [Accessed: January 19, 2010].

SPICE deliverable 1.2 (2006). *Scenarios for the representative next generation communication and information services*. EU IST SPICE IP deliverable (D1.2), June 2006.

SPICE Project Deliverables 1.3 (2006). *Service Platform for Innovative Communication Environment – Functional Architecture.* FP6 Integrated Project. http://www.ist-spice.org/ [Accessed: 27.10.2011].

Stalder, F. (2002). *Privacy is not the antidote to surveillance.* Surveillance & Society, Vol. 1, issue 1, pp. 120-124.

Starner, T., Mann, S., and Rhodes, B. (1995). *The MIT wearable computing web page.* http://wearables.www.media.mit.edu/projects/wearables. [Accessed: 22 July 2012].

Steininger, S., Neun, M., and Edwardes, A. (2006). *Foundations of Location Based Services, Lecture Notes on LBS.* 1. Version, source: http://www.spatial.cs.umn.edu/Courses/Spring10/8715/papers/IM7_steinige r.pdf [Accessed: 17. August 2012].

Stottok, Bernd O., Bergaus, Martin N., and Gorra, Andrea (2011). *Colour Coding: an Alternative to Analyse Empirical Data via Grounded Theory.* ECRM article, published and presented at the 10th European Conference on Research Methodology (ECRM) for Business and Management Studies 2011, 20-21 at Normandie Business School, University of Caen, France, Leeds Metropoletan University, stottok.rollsport-nuernberg.de/.

Stottok, Bernd O. (2010a). *Colour Coding – A Grounded Theory Method to Analyse Data.* Grounded Theory Research Salon, 18 January, Leeds Metropolitan University.

Stottok, Bernd O. (2010b). *Towards True Team Play in Railway Telematics.* 4th EurailTelematics Conference, Berlin.

Strauss, Anselm (1987). *Qualitative Analysis for Social Scientists*, Cambridge: Cambridge University Press.

Strauss, Anselm (1991). *Grundlagen qualitativer Sozialforschung.* München: Fink Verlag. (Orig. 1987).

Strauss, Anselm L. and Corbin, Juliet (1990). *Basics of Qualitative Research: Grounded Theory Procedures and Techniques.* Newbury Park, CA and London, SAGE Publications.

Strauss, Anselm L. and Corbin, Juliet (1996). *Basics of Qualitative Research: Grounded Theory Procedures and Techniques.* Second Edition, SAGE Publications, Thousand Oaks, California.

Strohbach, Martin; Kovacs, Ernö; and Goix, Laurent-Walter. (2006). *Integration IMS Presence in a Service-Oriented Architecture.* SPICE paper.

Stuart, K., Moran, Thomas P., and Newell, Allen (1983). *The Psychology of Human Computer Interaction.* Erlbaum, Hillsadale 1983. ISBN 0-89859-243-7.

Strübing, Jörg (2004). *Grounded Theory.* Wiesbaden. VS-Verlag.

Strübing, Jörg (2005). *Pragmatistische Wissenschafts- und Technikforschung. Theorie und Methode.* Frankfurt/New York: Campus.

Sulayman, M.; Urquhart, C.; Mendes, E.; and Seidel, S. (2012). *Software Process Improvement Success Factors for Small and Medium Web Companies: A Qualitative Study.* Information and Software Technology, 54, 5, May 2012, Pages 479-500.

Sutinen, Erkki, and Tedre, Matti (2010). *ICT4D: A Computer Science Perspective. Algorithms and Applications.* Lecture Notes in Computer Science. Springer-Verlag.   pp.   221–231. http://www.springerlink.com/content/j7j5n6731k616075/?p=4b1e36801fc3 478ea9fd2ee59a42f2e3&pi=1 [Accessed: August 7, 2012].

Talukder, Asoke K. and Yavagal, Roopa R. (2005). *Mobile Computing – Technology, Applications, and Service Creation.* McGraw-Hill Communications Engineering, India.

Tarkoma, Sarsu, Prehofer, Christian, Kovacs, Ernö, Moessner, Klaus and Zhdanova, Anna V. (2007a) *SPICE – Evolving IMS to Next Generation Service Platforms.* IEEE paper.

Tarkoma, Sarsu; Bhushan, Bharat; Kovacs, Ernö; van Kranenburg, Herma; Postmann, Erwin; Seidl, Robert; and Zhdanova, Anna V. (2007b) *SPICE: A Service Platform for Future Mobile IMS Services.* IEEE paper.

Tatnall, Arthur and Gilding, Antony (1999). *Actor-Network Theory and Information Systems Research.* Department of Information Systems. Centre for Educational Development and Support, Victoria University of Technology, Melbourne, Australia.

The SPICE Project: http://www.ist-spice.org/ [Accessed: 7 April 2012]. *The MIDAS* *Project:* http://equ.tele.pw.edu.pl/www/index.php/MIDAS#Project_Objectives [Accessed: 25 May 2013].

Trick, Ulrich (2002). *Infrastruktur der Informationsgesellschaft - Weg zur öko-nomische effizienten, sozial gerechten und ökologischen verträglichen Fort-entwicklung der Informations- und Kommunikationsgesellschaft.* In the con-text of the "Reimut-Jochimsen-Preis der Landeszentralbank Nordrhein-Westfalen" distinguished essay. September 2002.

Trick, Ulrich and Weber, Frank (2009). *SIP, TCP/IP und Telekommunikations-netze – Next Generation Networks und VoIP.* 4. Auflage, Oldenbourg Wis-senschaftsverlag GmbH, 2009.

Trochim, William M. (2000). *The Research Methods Knowledge Base.* 2nd Edi-tion. Atomic Dog Publishing, Cincinnati, OH.

Turner, B. (1983). *The Use of Grounded Theory for the Qualitative Analysis of Organisational Behaviour.* Journal of Management Studies, vol. 20, pp. 333-348.

Umar, Amjad (2004). *Mobile Computing and Wireless Communications – Appli-cations, Networks, Platforms, Architectures, and Security.* NGE Solutions, Inc.

Unwin, Tim (2009). *ICT4D: Information and Communication Technology for Development.* Cambridge University Press. ISBN 978-0-521-71236-1.

Urquhart, Cathy (2001). *An Encounter with Grounded Theory: Tackling the Practical and Philosophical Issues.* in Trauth E (Ed) Qualitative Research in Information Systems: Issues and Trends. Ide Group Pubilshing, pp 104-140, 2001.

Urquhart, Cathy (2007). *The Evolving Nature of Grounded Theory Method: The Case of the Information Systems Discipline.* In: The SAGE Handbook of Grounded Theory 2007, edited by Antony Bryant and Kathy Charmaz SAGE Publications Ltd.. pp. 339-360. .

Urquhart, C., Lehmann, H., Myers, M. (2009). *Putting the 'theory' back into grounded theory: guidelines for grounded theory studies in information sys-tems.* Info Systems Journal (2010) 20, 357-381, Blackwell Publishing Ldt., 2009.

Urquhart, C. (2012). *Grounded Theory for Qualitative Research; A Practical Guide.* Sage Publications, published November 2012.

Urquhart, C.; and Fernandez, W. (2013). *Grounded Theory Method: The Researcher as Blank Slate and other Myths.* Journal of Information Technology.

Valipour, Hadi M., Zafari, Bavar Amir, Maleki, Niki, and Daneshpour, Negin (2009). *A Brief Survey of Software Architecture Concepts and Service Oriented Architecture.* in Proceedings of 2nd IEEE International Conference on Computer Science and Information Technology, ICCSIT'09, pp 34-38, Aug 2009.

Van Bossuyt, Michaël; Ballon, Pieter; Galli, Luca; Spedalieri, Antonietta; Rovira, Jordi. (2008). *Cross-Case Analysis of the User Value Proposition for Next-Generation Mobile Service Platforms.* SPICE paper.

Verdot, Vincent; Bumside, Gerard; Bouche, Nicholas; (2011). *An Adaptive and Personalized Web Telecommunication Model.* Bell Labs Technical Journal, Volume 16 (1) pp. 3-17, published Jun 2011.

Vickers, John (2010). *The Problem of Induction.* Section 2.1, Stanford Encyclopaedia of Philosophy. 21 June 2010.

Villalonga, Claudia; Strohbach, Martin; Snoeck, Niels; Sutterer, Michael; Belaunde, Mariano; Kovacs, Ernö; Zhdanova, Anna V.; Goix, Laurent Walter, Droegehorn, Olaf. (2007). *Mobile Ontology: Towards a Standardized Semantic - Model for the Mobile Domain.* SPICE paper.

Villegas, David; Bobroff, Norman; Rodero, Ivan; et al. (2012). *Cloud Federation in a Layered Service Model.* Journal of Computer and Systems Science Volume 78 (5) pp. 1330-1344; published Sep 2012.

Voorsluys, William, Broberg, James, and Buyya, Rajkumar (2011). *Introduction to Cloud Computing.* In R. Buyya, J. Broberg, A.Goscinski. *Cloud Computing: Principles and Paradigms.* New York, USA: Wiley Press. pp. 1–44. ISBN 978-0-470-88799-8.

Voas, Jeffrey M. (1992). *A dynamic failure-based technique.* IEEE Trans. Software Eng., 18(8):717–727.

Voas, Jeffrey M. and Miller, Keith W. (1995). *Software testability: The new verification.* IEEE Software, 12 (3):17–28.

Walker, C., and Akdeniz, Yaman (2003). *Northern Ireland Legal Quarterly.* 54(2) Summer edition, pp 159-182.

Walsham, G. (1995). *Interpretive Case Studies in Information Systems Research: Nature and Method.* European Journal of Information Systems, 4, pp74-81.

Wang, Ning; Zhang, Yan; Serrat, Joan; *et al.* (2012). *A Two-Dimensional Architecture for End-to-End Resource Management in Virtual Network Environments.* IEEE Network Volume 26 (5):8-14; published Sept-Oct 2012.

Weber, R. (2003). *Editor's comments: theoretically speaking.* MIS Quarterly 27(3): iii-xii.

webinos Project Deliverables (2012). *Phase II architecture and components.* http://www.webinos.org/. [Accessed: 21.09.2013].

Weinberg, Gerald (1975). *An Introduction to General Systems Thinking.* 1975 ed., Wiley-Interscience, (2001 ed. Dorset House.

Weiss, S. (2002). *Handheld Usability.* Chichester, UK.: John Wiley.

Weis, Stephen A. (2007). *RFID (Radio Frequency Identification): Principles and* *Applications,* MIT CSAIL. http://citeseerx.ist.psu.edu/viewdoc/summary?doi=10.1.1.182.5224. [Accessed: December 7, 2011].

Weiser, Marc (1991). *The computer of the 21st Century.* Scientific American, Vol. 265, (3), pp. 94-100.

What *is* *Galileo* (2010). http://www.esa.int/esaNA/GGGMX650NDC_galileo_0.html. 2010-04-11. [Retrieved 2012-07-21].

Williamson, K., and Healy, M. (2000). *Deriving engineering software from requirements.* Journal of Intelligent Manufacturing, 11(1), 3.

Winter, Marie-Anne (2005). *A-GPS soll Navigations- und Ortungsdienste erleichtern.* Teltarif.de, 18. März 2005. http://www.teltarif.de/arch/2005/kw16/s16847.html. [Accessed: June. 3, 2012].

Wohltorf, Jens (2004). *Enhanced User Interface and Pervasive Computing – Technical Report des DAI-Labors der technischen Universität Berlin.* DAI-Labor der Technischen Universität Berlin, Berlin.

wwiteware™ (2010). *Service Delivery Platform - A Directory Service Evolution.* V1.5 – October 2010.

Yeh, Q.-J., and Tsai, C.-L. (2001). *Two conflict potentials during IS development.* Information & Management, 39(2), 135-149.

Zaidman, Andy; Van Rompaey, Bart; Demeyer, Serge; and van Deursen, Arie (2007). *On how developers test open source software systems.* Technical

Report TUD-SERG-2007-012, Delft University of Technology, Software Engineering Research Group.

Zarefsky, David (2002). *The Study of Effective Reasoning Parts I and II*. The Teaching Company 2002.

Zarnekow, Ruediger and Brenner, Walter (2002). A Product-based Information Management Approach. University of St. Gallen; Institute for Information Management; paper; *Product-based Information Management*.

Zhang, Ping; Carey, Jane; Te'eni, Dov; and Tremaine, Marilyn (2004). *Integrating Human-Computer Interaction Development into SDLC: A Methodology*. Proceedings of the Americas Conference on Information Systems, New York, New York, August 2004.

Zhdanova, Anna V., Zoric, Josip, Marengo, Marco, Van Kranenburg, Herma, Snoeck, Niels, Sutterer, Michael, Räck, Christian, Droegehorn, Olaf, and Arbanowski, Stefan (2006). *Context Acquisition, Representation and Employment in Mobile Service Platforms*. the SPICE service platform. Wireless World, Research Formum, IST.

Zhdanova, Anna V.; Du, Ying; and Moessner, Klaus (2007). *Mobile Experience Enhancement by Ontology-Enabled Interoperation in a Service Platform*. SPICE paper.

Zhou, Bin; Duan, Guang-Ren; and Zhong, Zhen (2008). *Controllability, observability and stabilisability of a class of matrix linear systems*. Centre for Control Theory and Guidance Technology, Harbin Institute of Technology, China.

Zoric, J. *et al.* (2006). *Service and information roaming – architecture and design aspects*. WWRF17, November 2006.

8 Appendix A – Theoretical Background

8.1 Essentials in Mobile Communication Technologies

This Section describes the essential materials of technologies used and applied to SDPs and facilitate the reader in acquiring more information about SDP related technologies in terms of their complexity.

According to Roth (2005: p. 29), the challenges of wireless i.e.: mobile - communication can be well illustrated, in a simple form, using the seven layered, Open Systems Interconnection (OSI) Reference Model (see Figure 62 below)

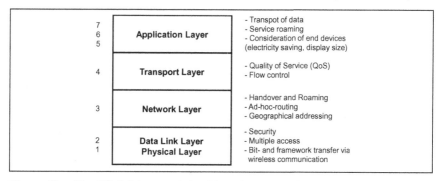

7 6 5	**Application Layer**	- Transpot of data - Service roaming - Consideration of end devices (electricity saving, display size)
4	**Transport Layer**	- Quality of Service (QoS) - Flow control
3	**Network Layer**	- Handover and Roaming - Ad-hoc-routing - Geographical addressing
2 1	**Data Link Layer** **Physical Layer**	- Security - Multiple access - Bit- and framework transfer via wireless communication

Figure 62: Simplified 7 layers of the OSI reference model and dedicated aspects of mobility (Roth, 2005: p. 29)

In the following, the aspects of mobility are presented in relation to the different layers of the OSI reference model.

8.1.1 Aspects of Mobility in relation to OSI Layers

8.1.1.1 Physical and Data Link Layer

In the first two layers of the OSI reference model (see Figure 62), requirements are addressed by the wireless interface. Bit transference, which concerns the areas of hardware development, electronics, electrical engineering and physics, along with the physical and data-link layer, presents significant differences when comparing wireless and wired communication. In particular, the bit transference associated with radio communication must follow, and pay detailed attention to a series of basic conditions.

In the case of radio communication, in comparison to wired communication, the risk of disturbance is considerably higher due to the absence of cables to provide resistance to areas of disturbance (Roth, 2005).

Radio media reacts to every electromagnetic disturbance, which, in turn, has a profound effect on the data to be transmitted. Furthermore, radio communication only allows a considerably lower rate of data in comparison to wired forms of communication. This is due to the low frequency bands used, along with the high numbers of users sharing a limited bandwidth (Roth, 2005: p. 30-31).

Wired networks are, according to Roth (2005: p. 31), well protected against listening in, whilst wireless networks require appropriate security mechanisms. These cannot prevent listening in, but restrict it considerably, because a person who listens in cannot interpret the encoded user data. In order for the command medium to be used by multiple participants, access has to be regulated by multiplex procedures. Roth (2005) described in detail today's most common and important procedures with multiple use of a command medium.

8.1.1.2   Network Layer

According to Umar (2004), the network layer takes over tasks in connection to the spatial mobility of the user. Mobile users need to establish connections to different networks from various locations, without having to carry out extensive adaptations to a newly configured network.

Mechanisms that accomplish the maintenance of the connection are described as handover and roaming. In terms of mobility, spontaneous integration of end devices with different net access, known as ad-hoc networks, is also important. Both of these terms will now be looked at in more detail.

Handover

According to Talukder and Yavagal (2005: p. 156-157), should a mobile participant move with their end-device out of the existing cell area into the area of a new cell, the communication connection must be newly configured and re-aligned. This new configuration is called the handover. Equally, it could also be necessary to release a new configuration if the signal receiving quality becomes worse, even though the participant has not necessary moved spatially.

In this case, a handover to another set of frequencies within the network of a mobile radio operator, takes place. A handover between the cells of different mobile radio operators is not possible.

Roaming

The term roaming is connected to handover and basically has two meanings. It describes the characteristics of making a call or being called from a preferred location within a mobile radio network. In this case, the mobile participants do not have to explicitly reveal their locations, as the network automatically determines it. Furthermore, the term roaming describes the possibility the participant, has to use networks for which they have no contract. Should different mobile radio operators have a roaming agreement, they are able to exchange details with each other regarding access to information such as data relevant for bills. Therefore it is possible, for example, to access mobile telephones abroad (Talukder and Yavagal, 2005: p. 318).

Ad-hoc Networking

In case of ad-hoc networking, also known as ad-hoc routing, an attempt is made to connect computers to one another without having to employ a permanent network infrastructure. For this purpose other mobile end devices are used as a form of temporary station between stations, with the purpose of increasing the communication possibilities for every mobile device.

Examples of ad-hoc networks are sensor networks, formed from a variety of sensor nodes, which are placed in the area of application, so they can gather information and pass it on, to other sensor nodes. This also contributes, for example, to increasing the entrance area of the radio cell of a mobile network through ad-hoc networks.

Basically ad-hoc networks share the following characteristics (Roth, 2005: p. 164):

■   There is no access and no wired network infrastructure.

■   Computer addresses are not mirrored within the topology of the network, and therefore the routing problem can, unfortunately, not be simplified, as is the case with traditional networks through the choice of addresses.

■   Routing assignments are implemented through the end-user's infrastructure and therefore there is no decisive router, as is the case with traditional networks.

Ad-hoc routing, described by Rolan and Hu (2008), has the capability to build up a connection via many steps. For this purpose, many special precautions are necessary. In terms of networks with a high rate of change, structured starting points for the choice of route, are not realistic. A high administrative effort would be necessary in the event of topological change, i.e. when a user wishes to change nodes. In this case, a dynamic network is often the only efficient solution for spreading all user data to all nodes.

8.1.1.3   Transport Layer

Once the challenges in relation to the wireless connections and the mobility of end-user in the bit transference, security/protection and network layer have been solved, the existing transport control, without changes, must also be employable for wireless communication (see Figure 62). In fact, existing transport protocols function principally in wireless scenarios, although with insufficient performance. The reason for this is that during the development of some transport controls, wired networks were thought of. On the service level, IP is mostly used (with this protocol it is possible to address mobile nodes), along with cellular IP. Both mechanisms enable the mobility of computers in the Internet. Problems caused by the mobility of computers have an effect on the transport layer. Internet applications, therefore, mostly use the Transport Control Protocol (TCP) to communicate outside of the network borders (Roth, 2005: p. 29, 224).

According to Trick and Weber (2009), TCP creates a reliable end-to-end connection, where comfortable data can be exchanged, thus securing user data being sent whilst a connection has been established. If a wireless transmission is supported by the protocol IP (Internet Protocol), then it is principally possible, with wireless transmissions, to apply the TCP protocol. TCP guarantees that the receiver properly receives every message. In the event that the order of the IP packets becomes mixed up, it assures that the messages in the applications will be delivered in the correct order. TCP was developed for transmission media. There are hardly ever any mistakes between two nodes directly connected together, whereas with two indirectly connected nodes on the routine route, data can go missing, due to router overload.

Therefore the TCP protocol makes provision for a process for overload control, which, through the reduction of the volume of packets, attempts to deal with narrow passes. The User Datagram Protocol (UDP) provides connection-free transport and increases the IP with the capacity to administrate applications connected in particular port numbers, and therefore can be identified externally. UDP neither guarantees that a packet will arrive, nor that the order of the packets will remain the same (Talukder and Yavagal, 2005: p. 34, 104).

Mobile IP

With the Dynamic Host Configuration Protocol (DHCP), a computer that is connected to a network automatically gets an IP address. Additionally it receives specific information about the network (subnet information for the address area of the subnet, address of the domain name server (DNS) and the router). Additionally, a set of optional information can be transferred to the computer, i.e.

which computers are in the web server network and which in the email server. A user carries out the transmission of information such as the settings of the parameters on the computer without manual configuration. The mobile computer that is connected on the network can, therefore, use the services of the local network, for example, for printing or storing data in a central location. A problem is created when the computer has to provide services. The IP address changes in every network that the mobile computer is connected to, as it has received an IP address from the respective DHCP server. A potential service user, therefore, cannot find the mobile computer when it moves to another network. There is a similar problem when the IP address changes within an existing TCP connection and when an interruption of the connection takes places without preventative measures (Talukder and Yavagal, 2009).

With mobile IP, the mobile computer is given an IP address that it also retains in other networks, and therefore remains reachable under a fixed address. Mobile IP differentiates, therefore, the following computer types (Roth, 2005: p. 215):

■   *Mobile computer:* This is a computer, which can be moved between different sub networks and can therefore be identified by a specific IP address.

■   *Communication partner:* This is a computer that makes contact to a mobile computer.

■   *Home agent:* This is the representative of the mobile computer, as long as it does not remain in its original sub network. It is constantly informed as to the location of the mobile computer.

■   *Foreign agent:* This is to be found in the sub networks in which the mobile computer is moving and sends incoming packets to the mobile computer.

8.1.1.4   Application Layer

Further circular problems can be assigned to the application layer (see Figure 62). The service operation in mobile environments is responsible for the services in new environments being automatically found and used. The transmission of data in mobile scenarios often destroys heterogeneous systems. To be able to exchange data with others there has to be a process, which allows for platform exchanges. The consideration of end device capacity implies higher protocols, which take into account the reduced capacities of end devices (Trick und Weber, 2009).

Should application data be transferred onto a mobile network, the presentation of the data gains the meaning of the use. Applications do not, ideally, communicate directly over a transport protocol; rather, they use higher protocols, which offer more comfortable services for the transport of data. In the case of data transfer in mobile environments, the connection is often built spontaneously and terminated after a short period of use. The devices involved should automatically adjust to one another and communicate with one another the necessary parameters for the data transference. It is important that devices from different manufacturers communicate. Therefore, no proprietary data format or protocols should be used. It is precisely the mobile sector that is distinguished by a wide variety of devices, operating systems and application software (Roth, 2005: p. 359).

Complicated configurations or interventions, which are often customary in association with traditional software, are not welcomed in the mobile environment. The special characteristic of mobile end devices, regarding hardware and software, is to be considered here. Security aspects are of particular importance in the mobile scenario. Ideally security mechanisms are integrated in protocols for data transmission (Umar, 2004). The following Paragraph describes the possible modes of mobility.

8.1.1.5 Mobility Modes

One of the most important features a mobile network has to offer is the support of mobility, including roaming and handover capability. Handover means the capacity to continue an ongoing session, even in the case of a point of access change (e.g. different cells, base stations, access networks) to a telecommunication network. By use of the roaming service, the mobile subscriber is able to gain access to a telecommunication network in visited networks, outside of his home service provider domain.

In order to provide the subscriber access to, and support of, the subscribed services in the home network/service provider domain, different concepts and approaches have been proposed, discussed, defined and also standardised. The following types of mobility can be distinguished (see also ITU Draft Q.1706, WWRF Vision of System Concepts for Wireless world):

■ *Terminal Mobility:* Availability of a terminal to access (telecommunication) services from different locations (access networks), and whilst in motion. It also includes the capability of the network to identify and locate the terminal.

■ *Network Mobility:* Availability of a network, where a set of wired or mobile network nodes are connected to each other.

■ *Personal Mobility:* Possibility of a user to access (telecommunication) services at any terminal, on the basis of a personal identifier (e.g. stored on the USIM), and the capability of the network to provide these services.

■ *Service Mobility:* This is mobility applied for a specific service, i.e. the ability of a moving object (e.g. terminal/user) to use the particular (subscribed) service, irrespective of the location (access network) of the user, and the terminal that is being used for this purpose. A user can obtain subscribed and personalised services consistently, even if connected to a foreign network service provider - for this purpose it is required that access to a service is guaranteed (anywhere, anytime, anyplace).

■ *Profile Mobility:* This is the ability to access the user's profile information on different devices and in different access networks.

■ *Session Mobility:* Session mobility is the support of the transfer of active sessions between different devices, and possibly across different access networks. Using different devices with diverse characteristics, whilst maintaining state, is called session mobility. For example: planning a journey on a PC (Large screen, mobile connectivity), continuing the journey on a tablet computer and finishing it on a Smartphone by using different steps.

Some of these types of mobility, such as terminal and personal mobility are already fully available within existing networks, whereas others are standardised, and have been only partly introduced within commercially available networks and in some cases not at all. In order to provide a service platform, capable of providing services within NGNs, the support of all these types of mobility, as well as any combination of these types, is required.

In addition to the different types of mobility, an improvement of the service provision, of the service delivery, and especially of the dynamic service composition within one domain (e.g. home domain), in domains being visited, or even across domains, will be required. Therefore, location-based services are necessary to combine positioning and the actual location with an application or service.

Based on the challenges in the area of mobile communications that were introduced, the most important technologies are defined and explained in the following Sections.

8.1.2 Mobile Telecommunication Network Systems

The following Paragraphs look at the most important mobile telecommunication network systems which are relevant to SDPs and ICT systems.

8.1.2.1 Global System for Mobile Communications (GSM)

Fundamentals of GSM

In the last few years, data transference alongside, speech transference, has become more feasible. It is, for example, possible to use a combination of notebook and mobile telephone, to be connected to the Internet whilst travelling, and through this, use a variety of applications. Special protocols allow for the transference of data without extra equipment. Therefore, particular Internet sites can be presented directly on the mobile phone. Roth (2005: p.49) divided mobile radio systems into the following generations:

■ Mobile radio first generation, with analogue networks (A-, B-and C- networks).

■ Mobile radio second generation with digital GSM networks (D- and E-networks).

■ The UMTS network belongs to the mobile radio third generation.

■ The mobile radio fourth generation enables entry to different networks, like for example the Wireless Personal Area Networks (WPANs), and wireless local networks. This generation allows for very high data rates and the integration of IP- technology.

Unlike analogue networks, the GSM is laid out in a way that the needs of millions of customers per network, can be taken care of. GSM allows many mobile radio operators to cover the same area without disturbing each another. The striving within one network to achieve complete area coverage enables participants to telephone without restriction. Should a participant move, a handover (see Paragraph 8.1.1.2) ensures that the next base station becomes responsible for the participant, also during an ongoing connection without discontinuity. Through roaming (see Paragraph 8.1.1.2) it can be ensured that a participant remains reachable when leaving his or her network (Roth 2005: p. 48-49).

Through roaming agreements between network operators, the possibility exists that participants are reachable on the same number in other networks, and that their bill can cross country borders. GSM networks offer, along with speech transference, a row of additional services. Therefore small text messages (SMS) can be sent between mobile telephones. Information pages similar to those in the World Wide Web can be called up and represented on the mobile telephone using the Wireless Application Protocol (Roth 2005: p. 48-49). From third Generation (3rd Generation) of mobile communications systems on full Internet access is possibly using Smartphones, notebooks or tablet computers. Roth (2005), presents the GSM architecture in detail.

Further Developments with regard to GSM

The data rate of 9.600 bit/s for data, which GSM offers, is no longer sufficient when mobile radio technology is used for the transfer of data. The resulting further development of GSM technology will now be briefly presented and explained.

High Speed Circuit Switched Data (HSCSD)

HSCSD involves a procedure that hardly causes any change to the existing GSM infrastructure. An increase of the rate of data can be achieved in two different ways. By using an improved coding procedure, it is possible to maintain 14.400 bit/s instead of 9.600 bit/s. Furthermore, through the bundling of a number of channels together the data rate can be multiplied. HSCSD is an intermediatory transference procedure, and theoretically speaking, allows for data rates of 115.2 kbit/s (Trick and Weber, 2009).

General Packing Radio Service (GPRS)

GPRS works-packet provides, and allows, a considerably better exploitation of existing transfer capacities for applications with changing communication needs. GPRS is not only intended as a network. It allows for theoretical data rates of 171.2 kbit/s (Roth, 2005: pp. 64-65).

Enhanced Data Rates for GSM Evolution (EDGE)

With EDGE, through a new modulation procedure, an increase in the data rate is achieved. Instead of the Gaussian Minimum Shift Keying (GMSK) procedure used in GSM, EDGE uses the procedure 8-phases Shift Keying (8-PSK) modulation procedure. This theoretically allows 473.6 kbit/s and is viewed as a bridge to the mobile radio third generation UMTS (Roth, 2005: p. 66).

8.1.2.2   Universal Mobile Telephone System (UMTS)

The mobile radio technology of the third generation maintains, above all, the vision of meeting the high requirements of future mobile applications. UMTS is represented by the standards, Terrestrial Radio Access Frequency Division Duplex (UTRAFDD) and UMTS Terrestrial Radio Access Time Division Duplex (UTRA TDD). In any case, through the decision of the International Telecommunication Union (ITU), the desired standardisation did not take place, whereby the mobile participant still had the choice to support one or more air interfaces (Pagani, 2007).

Fundamentals of UMTS

The new mobile radio standard should not only offer fundamentally higher bandwidth, but should also provide architecture for different use scenarios. Therefore, UMTS is not only conceptualised as an air interface, but also as the accomplishment of the following requirements (Roth, 2005: p. 68):

■   Different variants of air connections are possible with this mobile radio standard (wireless technology, cellular mobile radio based on GSM or GSM-further development standards, or UMTS or satellite/GPS technology).

■   UMTS is not only thought of as being relevant for speech, but also for data transfer, and for access to the Internet.

■   Transfer rates up to 2 Mbit/s are possible.

■   Connections are configurable for different scenarios.

■   Access to further networks via ISDN and TCP/IP is possible. Through Virtual Home Environments (VHE) a user, irrespective of his position in the network, can always have access to the same services.

■   Roaming and handover should be possible between providers, and different radio station connections. Handover should also function with the mobile radio system of the second generation.

With the development and introduction of UMTS the following applications and services were kept in mind (Roth, 2005: p. 69):

■   *Internet/Information services:* World Wide Web, reservations, ticket booking, news ticker, weather reports.

■   *Entertainment:* E-books, music on demand, video clips, network games.

■   *Location Based Services:* Navigation, researching local information, logistics and fleet management.

■   *Financial Services:* Online banking, micro- and macro-payment, home shopping, questions regarding stock market courses.

■   *Communication:* Voice telephony, video telephony, e-mail and SMS, Instant Messaging, video postcards.

UMTS uses the following frequency bands:

■   *UTRA FDD:* 1.920 up to 1.980 MHz (Uplink); 2.110 up to 2.170 MHz (Downlink)

■   *UTRA TDD:* 1.900 up to 1.920 MHz (Uplink); 2.010 up to 2.025 MHz (Downlink)

In order to increase the data rates, two protocol options have been designed and introduced: High Speed Downlink Packet Access (HSDPA) and High Speed Uplink Packet Access (HSUPA). Similar to EDGE (see Paragraph 8.1.2.1), the increase of data rates has been achieved through a new modulation procedure, the Quadrature-Amplitude-Modulation (16-QAM). HSDPA reached downlink rates up to 14.4 Mbit/s. HSUPA reached uplink rates up to 5.8 Mbit/s on the uplink channel (Roth, 2005: p. 72).

The Architecture of UMTS

Figure 63shows the architecture of the UMTS networks. There are many similarities to the GSM network in the area of the access networks. Therefore, a Radio Network Controller (RNC) corresponds to a BSC, and NodeB to a BTS. Next to the actual UMTS Access Network UTRAN, the GMS access network, named GSM Edge Radio Access Network (GERAN) can be used (Roth, 2005: p. 75.)

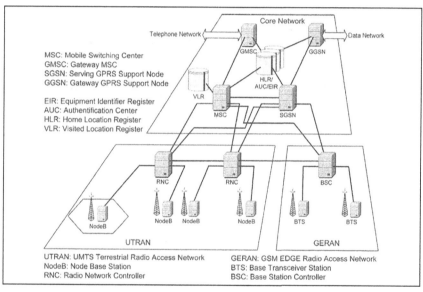

Figure 63: Architecture of the UMTS network (Roth, 2005: p. 75)

The core network consists of the data banks VLR, HLR, AUC and EIR, known from the GSM network (see Paragraph 8.1.2.1). The components MSC and GMSC serve the wired-oriented communication, in particular speech telephony. The component serving GPRS System Nodes (SGNs) and Gateway GPRS Support Nodes (GGSNs) are exclusively for packet-oriented data traffic (Roth, 2005: p. 75). The UMTS specification Release 99 provided for two separate core networks, by the time of Release 2000, later called Release 4, only one single IP based core network (All IP Network) existed. Thereby, all speech, data and multimedia services are dealt with over IPv6.

Further Developments of UMTS

The investment needed to set up a UMTS network, is, in accordance with Roth (2005: p. 76), extremely high, because large areas of network infrastructure must be re-worked. For example, costs for the radio network licenses must be bought before the construction of the infrastructure can begin.

A challenge when introducing UMTS is that an already fully functioning mobile radio network with GSM is available, that is sufficient for pure speech telephony, so that with UMTS, the rapid extension of data can be concentrated on.

The end-user will be provided with an easy way to switch from GSM to UMTS. Therefore, it is possible with a dual-mode mobile phone to telephone in both networks, and even a change between the networks is possible, without an interruption to the connection. Along with higher data rates, UMTS is attractive due to its offered services. Part of the UMTS specification deals not only with the technical aspect, but also areas such as area-specific services (Location Based Services), or flexible billing models. These topics are dealt with under the collective term Customised Applications for Mobile Network Enhanced Logic (CAMEL), (Talkuder and Yavagal, 2005: p. 290).

Technology, such as Long Term Evolution (LTE), is a new high-speed wireless data communication technology standard based on GSM/EDGE and UMTS/HSPA network technologies. This is described in the next Paragraph.

8.1.2.3   Next Generation Networks (NGNs)

In the case of UMTS, it is not only a direct migration path from GSM/GPRs to UMTS that is necessary; migration paths have to be implemented for a variety of UMTS versions. UMTS Release 99, based on a GSM/GPRS core network, has been improved due to the more powerful access network UTRAN. Networks today already operate using UMTS Release 99. UMTS Release 4 separates the connection management of user data transport. This can be observed in practical implementation changes, through the splitting of the monolithically MSC server, for dealing with signalisation, and the Media Gateways (MGWs), for user data transport (Trick and Weber, 2009).

UMTS 5 applies the NGN concept most far-reaching, the introduction of Session Initial Protocol- (SIP)-based IP Multimedia Systems (IMS) for multimedia communication. It also offers, through expansion with HSDPA, considerable improvements for the downstream bit rates (up to 14.4 Mbit/s) in access networks (Talkuder and Yavagal, 2009: pp. 30-31, 417).

The most notable functions of UMTS Release 6 are multimedia broadcast and multimedia services. These involve WLAN access network support in terms of HUSPA with upstream bit rates up to 5.8 Mbit/s in the UTRAN. Furthermore, in comparison to Release 5, normal phone calls are not conducted over MSCs, i.e. MSC server, and MGWs. These calls can also be carried out via IP Multimedia Subsystem (Voice over IMS). Release 7's most important feature is to accomplish the connection to wired networks. Here, the necessary IMS expansions (IMS services on broadband, wired network, connections), as well as the complete or partial Public Switched Telephone Network (PSTN), i.e. Integrated Service Digital Network (ISDN), are replaced. Through this, IMS is also made accessible for wired and convergent networks. Furthermore, an IMS expansion for Packet Cable Based Hybrid Fibre Coax- (HFC-) networks has been inserted. Along with this, with the High Speed Packet Access Plus (HSPA+), the bit rates have once again increased, reaching a maximum of 42 Mbit/s for down streams, and 22 Mbit/s for up streams (Trick and Weber, 2009: pp. 417-418).

With its standardisation Long Term Evolution (LTE), UMTS Release 8 represents future UMTS access networks. Due to evolved-UTRAN (E-UTRAN), bit transfer rates up to 100 Mbit/s in downlink, and 50 Mbit/s in uplink-direction are possible. The target of the newly applied core network architecture is to connect different radio access networks, for example E-UTRAN, and other wired participant connections, as simply as possible, and without the inclusion of GPRS in the UMTS core network. The most important goal of LTE has been to increase the speed rate and the capacity of wireless data by using new Digital Signal Processing (DSP) techniques and modulations that had been developed in the meantime. Moreover, one of the goals was the redesign and simplification of the network architecture to an IP-based system with significantly reduced transfer latency compared to the UMTS and HSPA architectures. The wireless interface of LTE is incompatible with 2G and 3G networks, means, it has to be operated on a separate wireless spectrum (3GPP, http://www.3gpp.org/LTE).

The LTE standard specification was developed by the 3GPP, in its Release 8 documents. It provides downlink peak rates of 300 Mbit/s and uplink peak rates of 75 Mbit/s, as well as Quality of Services (QoS refers to several related aspects of IT and telecommunication networks that allow the transport of data with special requirements) provisions permitting a transfer latency of less than 5 ms in the radio access network. LTE has the ability to manage fast-moving mobiles and supports multi-cast and broadcast streams.

LTE supports Frequency Division Duplexing (FDD means that the transmitter and receiver operate at different carrier frequencies) and Time Division Duplexing (TDD is the application of Time Division Multiplexing, or TDM, to separate outward and return signals). The Evolved Packet Core (EPC) is the IP-based network architecture in LTE and it has been designed to replace the GPRS core network. EPC supports seamless handovers for voice and data to cell towers with older network technologies such as GSM, UMTS and also CDMA2000. The simpler IP-based architecture provides lower operating costs (3GPP, http://www.3gpp.org/LTE).

UMTS Release 9 offers, as an interesting development, the support of Personal Area Networks (PANs). It also offers, as a step in the direction of active networks, self-optimising and curative networks or Self Organising Networks, SON, (Trick and Weber, 2009: p. 418). While Release 9 to 99 places human mobile communication at the centre, Release 10 focuses, among other things, on the communication between machines and equipment, for example in terms of car manufacture and delivered vehicles, or for long distance control of heating and alarm systems in the household (Trick and Weber, 2009: p. 418).

The future vision of bringing mobile speech, data communication, and Internet technology together, and of bringing under the control of the user, different Internet applications and services and their controls, represents the challenge of today's computer age. The deployment of IP-based multimedia services allows Person-to-Person real-time services. IMS enables IP interoperability for real-time services between wired and mobile networks, and thereby solves the current challenge of the seamless exchange of convergent speech and data services. The IP Multimedia Subsystem offers two fundamental key features. One is the IP based transport for real-time and non real-time data, and the other is a multimedia call model, based on the Session Initial Protocol (SIP). The development of an IP-based infrastructure drives the application-related development of Voice over IP (VoIP) services.

With a possible implementation and introduction of the next IP generation (IPv6), all IP addresses will be increased from 32-bit length to 128-bit length, which will enable the future growth of the Internet, whether in terms of wired or mobile devices (Trick and Weber, 2009: pp. 419-420).

8.1.3   Location-based Systems

There are several ways to determine the position of an end-user, based on a location-based system. This technology will depend on the required characteristics of the service. Variables between different technologies include: accuracy, price, availability and size of the area that needs to be covered. Investment for the type of coverage, whether it is (indoor or outdoor) power consumption or the physical size (Pannevis, 2007). In the following the relevant location determination possibilities for mobile end devices are presented.

8.1.3.1   Satellite-based Systems

Global Positioning System (GPS)

From as early as the 1960s, a satellite-supported position tracking system was being worked on, as the old navigation system was no longer meeting the demands. From the early 1970s, the American Defence Ministry was working on the concept of a system called NAVSTAR GPS (Navigational Satellite Timing and Ranging-Global Positioning System), described as GPS. In 1984 the first GPS satellite was launched. This offered global coverage from the equator to the poles of the earth, with 4 satellites in 6 circulation cycles. Therefore, a total of 24 satellites were in the circulation of the earth. Each satellite circled the earth with a distance of about 20.100 km. In order to circle the earth each satellite took approximately half a day. The satellites were arranged so that from every point of the earth, at least five, and a maximum of eleven, satellites were visible above the horizon. Each satellite was expected to last for 7.5 years, and demanded a high level of operational readiness. As a result, there was often more than the required number of satellites in orbit. Sometimes the number was extended to 28 (National Academy of Public Administration, 1995).

GPS Services

Users who wish to determine their position with the help of GPS, can use one of the signals sent out by the satellites, and in this case do not incur any costs. The determination procedure is based on one-way communication from the satellite to the user. This means that the user does not need to send any data to the satellite to determine their position. The relevant service existing for position determination (Roth, 2005: p. 286) is the Precise Positioning Service (PPS).

This service, also named P-Code in the past, allows a position determination with a precision of 22 m horizontally and 27.7 m vertically. This service was, for a long time, encoded and could only be used by USA military and NATO but since 2000, is available to everyone. Roth (2005) provides in detail information regarding GPS satellite signals and architecture respectively.

Assisted GPS (A-GPS, aGPS)

Assisted GPS is a system that pinpoints location and can improve the initial performance of a GPS-based positioning system, under optimum conditions. This system is used extensively with GPS enabled mobile phones so that emergency rescue workers can locate at caller. A-GPS uses network resources to detect and utilise the satellites in poor signal conditions, for example in cities, where signals suffer multipath propagation because signals bounce off buildings, or are slowed when passing through the atmosphere, or are hampered by trees cover. When first switched on under these conditions, some standalone GPS devices are unable to determine position because of fragmentary signal, and they are thus unable to function until a clear signal is received continuously, for a specified period, of up to 12 minutes (Winter, 2005).

According to Winter (2005), an A-GPS system can address these problems by using data available from a network. Two categories of assistance are supported:

■ Information to locate satellites quicker

■ Server calculating position by using information from the GPS receiver

Typically, a receiver that is A-GPS-enabled uses a data connection, such as the Internet, to contact the assistance server for positioning information. Additionally if it has autonomous GPS, it then uses standalone GPS, which albeit slower, does not depend on the network, and works beyond network range, without additional data fees being incurred. Some aGPS devices do not have the option of falling back onto standalone or autonomous GPS. Many mobile phones combine A-GPS and other location services, for example WLAN or WiFi positioning system (see Paragraph 8.1.3.3).

Other Satellite-based Systems

Galileo

With the European Satellite Navigation System, Galileo, 30 satellites, on 30 cycles, with 3 frequencies and GPS compatibility, with improved precision and 5 basic services (more open, more commercial, more secure and more regulated, along with search and rescue service) will soon become available. Between 2001 and 2014 the system will be up and running even with limited service capability. By 2020, Galileo should achieve complete extension level and be fully operable. Within the confines of the secure basic service, air and railway traffic should be controlled, therefore guaranteeing continual accessibility (What is Galileo, 2010).

Glonass

Globalnaya Sputnikovaya Sistema or Global Navigation Satellite System, is a radio-based system for satellite navigation. It is operated by the Russian Aerospace Defense Forces, to support the Russian government and provides an alternative to the U.S. GPS. Glonass is currently the only alternative satellite navigation system with a global coverage and a comparable precision to GPS. By 2010 it achieved 100% coverage of the Russian territory and in the end of 2011 24 satellites were installed to enable full global coverage (Moskvitch, 2010).

8.1.3.2 Network-based Positioning Systems

The implementation of a positioning system implies investment costs to build up the technical infrastructure. One approach is to reduce costs by using possible existing networks for the positioning using cellular networks, because of the disposition of the radio cell a rough positioning is thought possible. There are two fundamental network-based positioning methods (GSM Positioning, WLAN Localisation) that are presented in the following.

According to Steininger *et al.* (2006), there are network-based and device-based localisation methods. Cell of Origin, Time of Arrival, and Time Difference of Arrival are examples for networked-based methods. Accuracy values between 100 m up to 1 km are possible. A device-based local regulation can occur, e.g., using GPS with the place of the location regulated by means of cell-ID. GPS and the use of cell-IDs are the most current methods of the positioning of the actual location.

GPS requires after the positioning of the actual location, and the device receives information about the position data of satellites, with an accuracy of up to 5 metres. For "Indoor location based service", WLAN, Bluetooth or Infrared, are referred to as possible tools for capturing position. In the following, the most important network-based mobile phone positioning technologies will be briefly described:

GSM-based Positioning Methods

Cell of Origin

The simplest technique for identifying the location of a mobile handset is based on cell-ID, and is also known as the cell of origin. Since a mobile phone can be situated anywhere within a cell, the accuracy of these methods depends on cell size, which can vary from a few hundred metres to several kilometres. This method of locating a mobile phone is the least accurate, but the cheapest, as it does not require the alteration of individual handsets or network infrastructure. It takes approximately three seconds to locate the mobile phone cell (Lyon *et al.*, 2005). The accuracy of the cell-ID method can be improved by specifying the cell sector, as each base station typically has multiple antennas, each covering a sector of the cell.

For example, a base station with three antennas will produce a cell with three 120-degree sectors. By detecting the antenna with which the handset does a registration, the location can be narrowed down to a sector of the cell (D'Roza and Bilchev, 2003).

Angle of Arrival

A technique known as Angle of Arrival determines a user's location. It works by measuring the angles from where a mobile phone signal is received, by two, or more, base stations. This method is not particularly precise due to movement of the mobile device (Steiniger *et al.*, 2006). Base stations need Angle of Arrival equipment, in order to identify the direction of the phone's signal. This equipment compares the angle between the caller and various receiving base stations, and uses triangulation to determine the caller's longitude and latitude.

The Angle of Arrival technique is limited because of reduced accuracy, i.e., when various forms of signal interference occur. This phenomenon is known as signal bouncing, and is caused by tall buildings. The result of this is different forms are of signal weakness or even a loss of signal. Angle of Arrival is known to work best in less populated areas, as there is a lower likelihood of interference (Deitel *et al.*, 2002; Lyon *et al.*, 2005).

Time Difference of Arrival

The Time Difference of Arrival technique, measures the time it takes a mobile phone signal to reach the receiving tower and two additional towers. The signal's travel time allows user's distance to be determined from each tower. This makes it possible to work out the user's position. By calculating the user's distance from the receiving tower and two adjacent towers, a (virtual) set of arcs (a closed segment of a differentiable curve) is created, whose intersection indicates the handset's location. Handsets do not need to be modified to utilise this location technique, as the calculation of the position is done by the network provider (Deitel *et al.*, 2002).

Enhanced Observed Time Difference

Enhanced Observed Time Difference uses triangulation between at least three different base stations, to provide more accurate location identification than Cell-ID. The distance between handset and base station is calculated based on the different times it takes a signal, to arrive at the base station, once it leaves the handset.

Accuracy can theoretically reach 30 metres, but in reality, it lies between 50 and 125 metres (Lyon, 2005). Enhanced Observed Time Difference only works in GSM and GPRS networks. It requires an upgrade to the level of the mobile network infrastructure, and an uploading of software to base stations, in order to ensure compatibility.

Base stations need to be enhanced with location measurement units, and by measuring the signal from the mobile phone. The measurement units triangulate the user's position. This technique offers greater precision than that of cell of origin and the speed of the response takes around 5 seconds. The calculation of the position differs from Time Difference of Arrival and is done by the mobile phone handset. For this reason an update for the handset is necessary in form of software modification (Steiniger *et al.*, 2006; Deitel *et al.*, 2002).

8.1.3.3   WiFi-based Positioning Method

Another development is using WiFi networks. Originally WiFi was intended for computer users, it is increasingly integrated into pricey handsets, to access the Internet faster and cheaper, either at home or the office. Some handsets are equipped with features that enable VoIP phone calls using a WiFi connection. As WiFi networks increase in numbers city dwellers can often receive several networks at once. Seattle, for example, has got a WiFi access point density of 1,200 access points per square km.

WiFi has got a limited transmission power range of 100 mW – in cities this is further exacerbated and the range is limited to a few hundred metres. Each network device has got a unique MAC address that can be received, even if the network is secured. Thus the network reception in a specified location can be used to uniquely identify the place. Once this place and its respective network are indexed, it can then be used to determine the location of the user (Pannevis, 2007).

One advantage of using this method is that only a WiFi receiver in the handset is required to determine the location, and this is now included in higher-end handsets. Also this method works optimally in cities, where satellite based solutions are at their weakest. Accuracy in cities is between 13 to 20 metres and 40 metres in less populated areas, enough for most LBS applications. However, this method only works if there are enough WiFi base stations in range - at least one is needed to determine a location.

This makes this technique unsuitable for sparsely populated areas where WiFi reception is minimal. A solution in combining WiFi with other techniques such as GPS, has been proposed (Pannevis, 2007).

In addition reception of WiFi signals alone does not suffice, since WiFi networks themselves do not include geographical references. The location of the network needs to be determined before a combination of MAC addresses can be translated to location parameters. Groups such as wiggle.net are working on a database for this translation. These databases of WiFi networks are generally built by war-driving (or war-walking) an area. War driving is the process of driving around with a WiFi receiver and a GPS, recording the reception of networks in different places. This leads to an estimate of the beacon location, which can be used to locate the receiver. However the estimation of the beacon introduces an error in the locating, and the usage of GPS also adds a small further error (Pannevis, 2007).

Since WiFi locating is based on uncontrolled infrastructure, the mapping of beacons changes over time, as users replace their hardware. The areas will then need to be occasionally re-scanned an example is a student campus, where 50% of the beacons changed within a couple of months, as students, switched areas intermittently. Fielding *et al.* (2006), show that war-drive based location collections are not as reliable in showing users location, as using real access point locations.

They prove that an accurate map of access points increases the accuracy of WiFi-based location techniques up to 70% (Pannevis, 2007). To resolve this issue of uncontrolled infrastructure, it is also possible to use systems of commercial vendors that are using special purpose hardware or software and a precise calibration of a limited area. While this is accurate, it only works in a limited space. Alternatively, Wi-Max localisation uses ready systems, integrated in most Smartphones provided by the mobile phone software platform providers.

8.1.3.4   Near Field Communication (NFC) and Radio-Frequency Identification (RFID) Localisation Method

Near Field Communication (NFC) is a set of standards for Smartphones and similar devices to establish radio communication by bringing them into close proximity of one another. Current and future applications include contactless transactions, data exchange, and simplified setup of more complex communications such as Wi-Fi communication. This technology offers a possible connection between an NFC device and an unpowered NFC tag or chip (NFC Forum, 2011). NFC standards cover communications protocols and data exchange formats, and are based on existing Radio-Frequency Identification (RFID) standards.

This technology builds on RFID systems by allowing two-way communication between endpoints. Older systems such as contactless smart cards were one-way only. Since unpowered NFC "tags", can also be read by NFC devices, they are also capable of replacing older one-way applications (NFC Forum, 2011).

RFID is the use of a wireless non-contact system based on radio-frequency electromagnetic fields to transfer data from a tag attached to an object, for the purpose of automatic identification and tracking. Some tags require no battery and are powered by the electromagnetic fields used to read them. Others use a local power source and emit radio waves. The tag contains electronically stored information which can be read from up to several metres away. Unlike a bar code, the tag does not need to be within line of sight of the reader and may be embedded in the tracked object.

RFID tags are used in many industries. An RFID tag attached to a car during production can be used to track its progress through the assembly line. Pharmaceuticals can be tracked in warehouses. Since RFID tags can be attached to clothing, possessions, or even implanted in people, the possibility of reading personally-linked information without the individual's consent has raised privacy concerns (Weis, 2007).

Another possibility to do positioning is to use the systems offered by the commercial vendors that work within a broad/wide range of areas of high population density, because the vendors invest in the towns due to potential customers and there is a high density of access points, installed and working.

Location data was conducted by those vendors, years ago, and this supported the advantage, that the hotspots should not be measured, and trained, users could start their Wi-Fi access immediately. An additional advantage of Wi-Fi is, that today's commercial mobile phone vendors sell their phones with this technology.

8.1.4   IP Multimedia Subsystem (IMS)

The IP Multimedia Subsystem (IMS) is extremely relevant for future mobile radio networks, beginning with UMTS Release 5, and including NGN wired networks and convergent networks. IMS is a purely IP-based service that can make use of various services simultaneously, i.e. while telephoning, gaining access to documents, and offers communications concept that support differing communication worlds. Therefore, homogeneous protocols for service and access network administration are in place.

The most important IP Multimedia Subsystems are (Poikselka *et al.*, 2004: pp. 3-5; Trick and Weber, 2009: p. 432):

- IP-based initialisation of communication services in real time, for example speech and video telephoning, games and automation.

- Initialisation of interactive services such as presence communication or Instant Messaging.

- Connecting of multimedia communication, for example chat and live streaming.

- Individualisation, personalisation of life style applications.

- Diverse provider functions.

- Shortening of the implementation time for new releases of products and services already on the market.

Regarding IMS, 3rd Generation Partnership Project (3GPP) defined an IP multimedia overlay for a Next Generation Network (NGN). This not only specifies session administration and management, but also Quality of Service (QoS) preparation (QoS refers to resource reservation control mechanisms in computer network traffic) and all necessary functions for security authentication, access administration and collection of billing data.

Due to this, access to Internet protocols, such as Session Initial Protocol (SIP) Session Description Protocol (SDP), Megaco/h.248, Command Open Policy Service and Diameter is possible. Current user data transport does not support IMS. Principally SIP does not distinguish between telephoning and multimedia services. The result of this is that the introduction of new services is easy. Also, the IP transport platform offers an excellent basis for combined speech and data services, for example convergent services. The advantage, in terms of service availability, is that a separate SDP can be applied (Trick and Weber, 2009: pp. 433-434).

According to Poiselka *et al.* (2004: pp. 49-51), as well as to Trick and Weber (2009: p. 432-433), IMS is based on the signalisation protocol Session Initial Protocol (SIP). Through Media Gateways, the connection to diverse types of networks is created. For the user it is of no importance from which network services or applications are accessed because there is no longer any difference between mobile and wired networks. This can be described as "Seamless Mobility". In this situation it is irrelevant which end device delivers contents. Modern location determination or Location Based Services can recognise when a participant from the telephone book is nearby.

Through Instant Messaging the user is informed when his acquaintances are online. IMS based end devices are as important factors for success as is the infrastructure. SIP is highly relevant, both for mobile radio operators, and wired operators, and for prospective providers, and possibly also Internet Service Providers. In a technical environment, IMS can be applied in telecommunication, in Internet/VoIP, or in Multimedia-over-IP. At IMS user level, clients, media and application servers can be connected. User identity, security, and QoS are further important aspects, which should be taken into consideration.

8.1.5 Session Initial Protocol (SIP)

This architecture supports mobile devices with differently configurable formats, by the use of device controlling mechanisms, which manage all devices within a given area. Presence and Instant Messaging are the most important IMS applications. The Session Initial Protocol (SIP) is a VoIP and multimedia communications protocol. Viewed practically, and in relation to VoIP, it fills the same purpose as a signalisation protocol in the conventional telecommunications world.

Firstly, SIP enables the transmission of signalisation messages, for the establishment of communication relationships, called "Sessions", in the field of Multimedia-over-IP. SIP provides a few supportive protocols, for example, Session Description Protocol (SDP), the entire communication basis for construction and deconstruction, as well as control of an existing communications relationship (Trick and Weber, 2009: p. 133).

In terms of NGNs, according to Trick and Weber (2009: pp. 36-37), SIP enables the required QoS to assure VoIP multimedia. SIP has been specified as the standard for UMTS's Release 5. In comparison to the ITU-T specified H.323 protocol collection, SIP offers, amongst other things, the advantage of being a correspondingly simple architecture, orientated on typical IP applications. In SIP based communication, standard processes, for example connectivity, are clearly more easily realised. Along with the function session operation, SIP offers a large, relatively easy to expand, basis for further communication mechanisms, such as the session independent exchange of short messages, as well as retrieval of state-related events concerning the communication readiness of a participant.

Session Initial Protocol (SIP) can alternatively be transported over UDP, TCP, and Stream Control Transmission Protocol (SCTP). SIP, as a connectivity and signalisation protocol, is able to employ handshakes, repetition, and timeout procedures, as measures for communication security. It therefore works in a connection orientated way and it is not necessary to use connection-oriented, functioning, transport protocols. Due to this, the connectionless UDP is used as a transport protocol for SIP.

This offers, in comparison to the connection-oriented functioning protocols TCP and SCTP, the advantage that neither an extra connection construction before the signalisation data exchange must take place. Due to this the use of the protocol saves time, and it offers much better performances regarding data traffic by using the UDP, as a transport protocol on SIP. For the purpose of communication with SIP, two forms of SIP messages exist. These are requests (SIP Requests), and status information (SIP Responses). Principally, one differentiates between two levels of connection-orientated communication relationships, between SIP network elements: SIP dialogues and SIP transactions (Trick and Weber, 2009: p. 134).

8.1.6 Summary

Related research in terms of Information and Communication Technology (ICT), essential challenges, aspects and technologies in mobile communications regarding the dedicated aspects of mobility, was presented and discussed. Mobility was illustrated with the simplified seven OSI-layers. This Section described the technologies of Global System of Mobile Communications (GSM), Universal Mobile Telephone System (UMTS), Long Term Evolution (LTE), IP-Multimedia Subsystem (IMS), Session Initial Protocol (SIP), Global Positioning System (GPS), Near Field Communication (NFC) and Radio-Frequency Identification (RFID) as well as some of their important further developments. It discussed these developments, along with several positioning systems and methods such as GSM positioning, Wi-FI location and RFID tagging, and has also pointed out some important definitions.

All essential technologies and methods described are relevant for applications and the Information and Telecommunication Infrastructure of today, and the future. The next Section outlines some applications of the systems and technologies presented in the previous Sections.

8.2   Applications and the ICT Infrastructure of the Future

This Section provides background information to the application of the relevant topic areas and gives explanations in the field of research, by presenting application scenarios and possibilities.

Nowadays, people place great value on professional, and private mobility, as Information and Communication Technology (ICT) is ubiquitously available, everywhere, whilst on official, work-related trips,or during leisure time. Accessibility is particularly necessary during journeys, and in times of heightened individuality and flexibility. Furthermore, in terms of the use of mobile end devices, such as, mobile phones, notebooks, tablet PCs, handhelds or other small computers, the productivity of end-users is rapidly increasing (Umar, 2004).

8.2.1   Challenges for Today's Infrastructures

Convergence between different types of user devices and core network systems is not ubiquitous, in terms of the operation and the development of mobile services, on any network, or any device. Applications supporting users have become a part of everyday life, and the challenge now lies in how to use them, in order to make people's everyday lives easier (Klemettinen, 2004). Currently, there are no available systems for supporting and connecting different types of ubiquitous services to the correct backend system, and none with which to offer the operation and development of these services together. At present various architectural models are available for dealing with Information and Communication Technologies (ICT), and mobile communication aspects, based on a common platform (Trick and Weber, 2009).

In a basic sense, existing server architectures are used for establishing the conceptual framework of new service architectures, such as a Service Delivery Platform (SDP). An SDP is an intelligent platform that supports the communication of mobile users on converging technologies. The idea behind this is to bring client-related intelligence and Operation Support Systems (OSS) and Business Support Systems (BSS) intelligence onto an SDP (Ahson and Ilyas, 2011).

Availability, mobility, performance, and usability are today's basic driving forces behind the use of ubiquitous and mobile computing technologies, in technical communication environments, because applications and services have the task of supporting users in their everyday lives, at any time and any place. Through the introduction of these technologies a further beneficial enhancement of, for example, telematic systems can be gained, and also improved access and functionality, such as the faster allocation of services for specific user groups (Bergaus and Stottok, 2010: p. 3-4). SDPs are important for ICT systems as they offer huge potential for various improvements through the power of mobile communication and internet-based technologies. This Section describes the initial situation, the telecommunication infrastructure of the future, and the requirements for communication infrastructure in line with the user perspective. Moreover, the problem statement is described (Talukder and Yavagal, 2005, Umar, 2004).

Ubiquitous computing, introduced earlier, refers to the ubiquity of computer systems that are not immediately recognisable to the user. The progressive development of this technology brings about new possibilities for computer systems, and therefore for ICT systems themselves. ICT systems support individuals by means of personalised services. They are widely universal, facing the challenge of having to be interoperable always and everywhere. Due to the provision and application of new technologies, such as, for example, Internet Protocol Multimedia Subsystem (IMS) and Long Term Evolution (LTE), these technologies can be integrated into telecommunication provider's private clouds in a simple way (Wohltorf, 2004).

IMS (Internet Protocol (IP) Multimedia Subsystem) is the reference technology for dealing with convergence between IT and mobile communication networks. IMS specifies a common control layer for session construction, based on IP (Internet Protocol) technology, and is seen as the future-oriented technology for IP-based communication. The location of new architecture extensions for developing (deploying) and operating services, from a user-centred point of view, is currently not supported by existing architecture technologies (Poikselkä et al., 2004). To focus on the perspective of users the drivers for ICT environments of the future are presented in form of at triple layered architecture described in the following Section.

8.2.2 Drivers for the Communication Infrastructure based on the User Perspective

ICT systems are continuously gaining ground. Nowadays, it is essential to offer a practical communication platform for everyone, and therefore, the method of accessing information and knowledge, has to be ubiquitous. The vision is based on the idea that everybody has the possibility of gaining affordable access to the infrastructure of information and communication, from their location. The drivers of the requirements for a telecommunication infrastructure of the future are shown, within the framework of an SDP based approach. This is illustrated by a triple-layered architecture, based on the network, the Internet-based platform itself, and the services and application aspects, detailed in the following illustration (Ahson and Ilyas, 2011; Bergaus and Stottok, 2010):

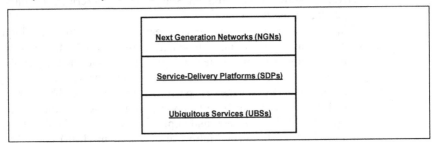

Figure 64: 3-layer architecture of ICT infrastructure of the future (Ahson and Ilyas, 2011; Bergaus and Stottok, 2010: p. 6 and 7)

Next Generation Networks (NGNs)

Packet-oriented network infrastructures and network architectures, which are compatible with older telecommunication networks, are brought together under the NGN concept. This concept also includes convergent networks. These networks illustrate the fusion of wired and mobile network infrastructures. NGNs possess an adjustment to packet-oriented infrastructure, a convergence of the different networks, with management and packet-oriented switching infrastructure, as well as wired and mobile connections, voice and multimedia communication via Internet Protocol (IP), along with UMTS functionality. NGNs support the system beyond the third generation (3G)/fourth generation (4G) of mobile telecommunication systems (Trick and Weber, 2009).

Service Delivery Platforms

The term Service Delivery Platform (SDP) refers to an intelligent infrastructure platform for the support of communication between mobile users and converging technologies, as well as the support of service development, and the execution of services in a simple way. Technologies such as UMTS, LTE and IMS are used to support "Anytime, Anywhere, Anyplace" (AAA) or "Any Network on Any Device" (ANAD) paradigms, for the purpose of enabling the interoperability of IT and telecommunication environments. These technologies are basis technologies for SDPs and as such are able to support services and applications, which are "always on" and must always be available, e.g. SPICE (Ahson and Ilyas, 2011; Cordier *et al.*, 2006a).

SDPs are made available for the development and supply of services, and offer a limited number of specified, complex, as well as combined, services. They show high performance and good scalability. This facilitates the quick and easy development of those services, which are offered on the platform. Usability and high availability are further essential aspects. SDPs are characterised by their independence from operating system and hardware. The costs for these systems must be affordable for everyone (Bergaus and Stottok, 2010: p. 7). SDPs, more specifically SPICE, are described in detail, in Section 2.3.

Mobile Applications and Ubiquitous Services from a User-Centred Point of View

Mobile applications and ubiquitous services stand apart as they offer a high privacy sphere level, and customisation for the user. Reliability and checkability, together with security and trust, are critical for the users of such services. Regarding these applications, it is important to create potential access possibilities everywhere, and for every user. This calls for cost control and personal customisation of the applications and services. Along with this, identity verification, filter possibilities for information, and the supply of suitable context information are necessary (Hjelm, 2005; Klemettinen, 2005).

However, the problem is that today's existing systems have to handle a wide range of systems, applications and services and the users lose their overview because of many different versions of systems. Additionally, the aspect of mobility described in Section 8.1.1 drives the need for location-based services that allows positioning, everywhere and at anytime, to process location data, with services and applications.

8.2.3 Location-Based Services (LBS)

Location-Based Services (LBS) are applied to mobile terminals and end devices, and they accordingly function in the same way as the devices found in the user's permanent environment. According to Richter *et al.* (2010), a network connection and mechanism to regulate the position, is named as a pre-suspension for a mobile terminal around LBS so as to be of use. Below is an illustration of LBS required architecture:

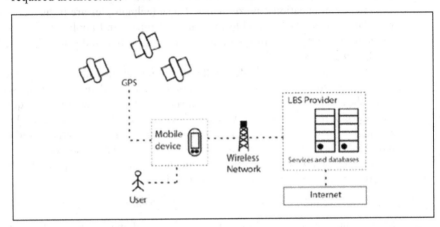

Figure 65: LBS architecture illustrating 2 possibilities for position regulation according to Richter *et al.* (2010: p. 3)

Richter *et al.* (2010), differentiate between active and passive position regulations. GPS is used for the active regulation of the position, whilst, a mobile radio or WiFi network can be used for passive regulation. On this network, users are connected to the respective LBS supplier. The connection to the Internet allows contents to be generated by the LBS provider as well as functioning as a distribution channel. Steininger *et al.* (2006) claim, that there are five necessary named components for the use of LSB. Richter *et al.* (2010) describe, the architecture similarly:

- Mobile terminal (e.g. PDAs, mobile phones, laptops, navigation systems)

- Communication network: provides the connection with the LBS supplier

- Component for position regulation (e.g., mobile radio network or GPS, WLAN for "Indoor-LBS")

- Service provider: providing services and uses for the LBS

- Content provider: providing content for the service providers

Using LBS and several other solutions for the development of value-added services based on the network level, ubiquitous applications and services can be designed, developed and delivered. The following Section describes some possible solutions.

8.2.4 Possible Solutions for the Development and Availability of Value-Added Services

According to Trick and Weber (2009: pp. 485-488), the following solutions for the development and availability of value-added services in NGNs exist:

Process Automation: For the implementation of new services, provider support automation of end-to-end configurations within the network.

Combination of known solutions: Many different technical solutions can be combined with one another over three different starting points:

- The initial starting point uses the logical network element service capability interaction manager. This provides a form of service-broker, which can combine services that are provided on application servers, in order to offer them as new services. Technical solutions have to be able to support SIP in this case.

- The second starting point uses a combination of different solutions through gateways.

- The third starting point involves using different solutions within one or more SIP-application servers.

Application-Router: An Application-Router organises the combination of different services into a new value-added service. The AS makes it possible to organise and execute different SIP-Servlets in service chains.

Web 2.0: The Web 2.0 confirms the approach that the service user himself can appear as service provider. Transmission onto future-oriented communication networks would mean that the user would increasingly develop new services, in NGNs.

Peer-to-Peer Network: Decentralised availability of value-added services through peers is driven by the increase of peer-to-peer communication, particularly in the field of multimedia real-time communication. This Web-2.0 development leads to new value-added services, and to centralised and de-centralised solutions, within integrated network architecture.

Semantic Web Services: These possess the capacity to re-compose themselves or to combine. Through this technology it is possible for a provider to offer new value-added services, without having to precisely specify them beforehand. This means that new Web Services are created through the automatic combination of those already available. For this purpose an expansion of Web Services is necessary.

Automatic Development of Value-added Services: Proceeding automatically from a simple textual description, the desired value-added service is made available on a "Jain Slee AS", (this specifies a universal Java based, components supported and scalable execution environment for the implementation of telecommunications services). The named environment is formally described through Business Process Execution Language.

8.2.5   User-Centred/Ubiquitous Services (UbS)

User-centred services (Context Awareness Services) focus, as the name suggests, on momentary context in connection to the user's location. Users play different roles and are involved in different situations during the day, and should be supported with user-centred services. These services make content available according to the user situation (Hjelm, 2005: pp. 1-2).

The research project "MobiLife", part of an EU research programme, followed the target of developing concepts for the further development and organisation of mobile infrastructure, taking into consideration the habits and needs of human beings (Klemettinen, 2004: pp. 5-10). Solutions are striven for, in connection with the integration of mechanisms for security; end devices, data protection, personalisation and content information, i.e. different user-centred interactive models.

8.2.6 Summary

This Section has described today's challenges and the drivers for the communication infrastructure of the future, based on the user's perspective. Furthermore, several applications including location-based services and some possible solutions for the development and availability of value-added services in NGS, were discussed, and where user-centred services were illustrated.

8.3   Service Delivery Platforms

This Section provides background information on Service Delivery Platforms and gives explanations about the theoretical background of the field of research, in the form of defining and introducing terms and definitions.

In general, an SDP as a web-based platform and mobile application describes a combination of components, which offer the availability of public or private service performances, through, the creation of services, session control and the support of various protocols (Roland and Hu, 2008: pp. 1-2). An SDP provides standardised and scalable software architecture for the development, administration, management, operation and integration of value-added services. It is part of the application layer and is connected, over the abstraction interface, with the underlying call control and transport level. As a result, the complexity of this layer is hidden, and simple access to network functions, such as the basis services of third-party providers, also realised with IMS, is made possible.

8.3.1 Fundamentals and the Architecture of SDPs

An SDP provides standard interfaces to Service Creation Environment (SCE), A-A-A servers, networks, i.e. service management (Operations Support Network-OSS), and management of business processes (Business Support System-BSS), (Trick and Weber, 2009: p. 474). The following graph (Figure 66) illustrates the abstract, general architecture of an SDP. The platform functions are represented as services (Roland and Hu, 2008: pp. 2-3).

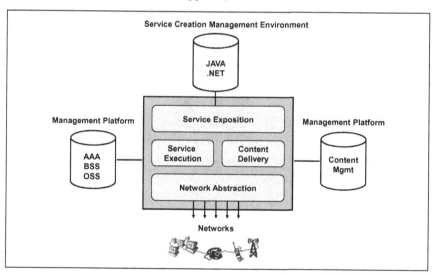

Figure 66: General representation of an SDP (Roland and Hu, 2008: p. 2)

The Management Platform connects the functionality of management services for Business Support Systems and Operation Support Systems. The SDP has the task of deploying, managing, and implementing already available, and newly developed, telecommunication applications. The Service Expositions Platform makes available services with which external developers (who are neither employees of a given telecommunication company nor operators) can have easy access to all functions of Service Delivery Platforms (Roland and Hu, 2008; pp. 2-3; Pagani, 2005).

According to Trick and Weber (2009: p. 475), the specific SDP environment is completed by the Service Creation Environment (SCE). An SCE provides a developmental environment through which new and existing services can be developed, deployed and configured. As a result of this, developers are supported with graphic tools. As a result of the connection of SCE to SDP, value-added services in networks are immediately available.

This procedure is called deployment. Figure 67 clearly illustrates that the media server is part of the user data process, and likewise part of the SDP, which means that parts of the SDP in the call and transport layer are also available.

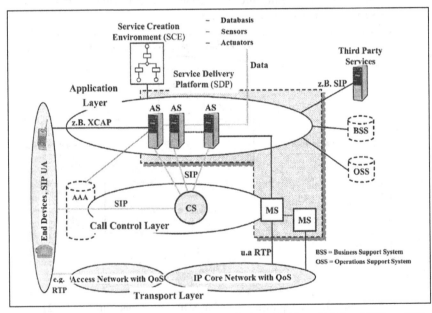

Figure 67: Architecture of a Service Delivery Platform (Trick and Weber, 2009: p. 475)

The actual SDP core elements for provision of services are:

▪ SIP interface to NGN and call server

▪ Initiation and termination of SIP and RTP sessions (SIP UA, SIP B2BUA)

▪ Dial switching of SIP sessions (SIP proxy, SIP redirect server)

▪ Modification of SDP media-session parameters

▪ Control of one or more media servers

▪ Data interface, e.g. web interface

▪ Application Programming Interface (API) for the development of services

▪ Software platform for service development and service execution

▪ Calling up of other SIP application services, in order to carry out complex services

▪ Support of the protocols SIP, HTTP, XML, Diameter, and so forth

▪ Interfaces for systems authentication, access control, and registration of billing data (accounting, billing), e.g. to an AAA server with Diameter protocol

Figure 68 illustrates the functions of an SIP Applications Server, including the possible functions of the Media Server. Tremendous possibilities, in terms of the service development and availability that an SIP-/IP-based SDP is able to offer, become clearly available when considering this figure. There are various solutions for service development and availability, through SCE and SDP. By means of the available programme interfaces, these can be subdivided into two groups. Each technology, which is directly implemented into servers, is characterised by "Low Level API", whereas "High Level API" is based on middleware. This is an additional hidden software layer, which consolidates the attributes and complexity of a network and applications (Trick and Weber, 2009: p. 475-476).

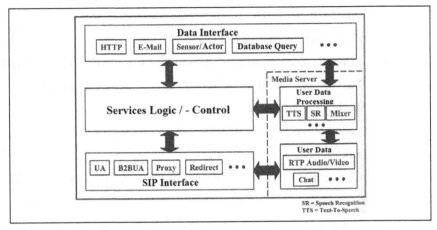

Figure 68: Functions of an SIP application server (Trick and Weber, 2009: p. 476)

8.3.2 Functional Architecture of SPICE and the Functional Components

Distributed Communication Sphere Management (DCSM) supports multiple access technologies, varying end devices, the use of diverse communication channels, and offers optimal configuration and combination of the available communication capacities, for end devices. Selection possibility, for appropriately desired access networks, and end device support for service implementation, are made available over the Communication Decision Engine.

The Distributed Communication Sphere possesses the following functions (Cordier *et al.*, 2006b; Zhdanova *et al.*, 2006): Widget-based interface (Widget: Components such as graphic window systems, which can be used for interaction with users or other widgets. It is not an independent programme, i.e. window or event management or plug-in) for mobile end devices, with a search procedure and service access. This interface is also called Dynamic Desktop (Cordier *et al.*, 2006a, The SPICE Project: http://www.ist-spice.org/).

- Technical Manager and Resource Discovery System, for the recognition and administration of mobile services within a user's environment.

- Group Management System and Terminal User Engine: This is used for the administration of user roles.

- Multi-modal Delivery and Control System: Content must be offered, in different interactive forms, between human beings and computers, whereby many modes, such as, sight, hearing and touch, are available.

Intelligent Service Enablers: These have the task of supporting services with corresponding Context Awareness functions: in this case, Service Platform Profiles for User Profile and Context Information Management, such as middleware functions, are available. This means, on the one hand, that the user has access to knowledge, and, according to his situation, context-sensitive information, and intelligent service mechanisms are made available, which are pre-selected according to user situation on the other.

Thereby, a set of specific and varying intelligent Service Enablers is offered, and the field is constantly expanding (Shiaa *et al.*, 2008):

- Knowledge Discovery, as well as Exchange and Interpretations Enabler

- Personal Information and attentive Service Enabler

Service Creation and Lifestyle Management: Easy service creation, deployment and administration, which must be secure within the confines of the SDP. The aim here is to keep the delivery time to a minimum, so that services can be immediately available, without major standstills, breakdowns or waiting time.

Tools are necessary to enable users to assemble and combine easily, with minimal programming effort involved. Therefore, tools for service composition are made available (The SPICE Project: http://www.ist-spice.org/):

- Service Description Language (SDL): SDL is a platform, programme and protocol independent description language for network services, for the exchange of messages, on the basis of XML. In SPICE, this SDL is described as SPICE Advanced Description Language for Telecommunications Services (SPATEL).

- Service Creation Environment: This is a development environment, or an end-user studio, which includes an automatic Service Composition Engine, and a deployment tool for the quick adaptation of services.

- Distributed Service Execution Environment: This is an execution platform that contains and supports different execution machines.

Mobile Service Ontology: Ontologies are used to exchange digital information and knowledge between user programmes and services. They contain rules and conclusions.

- Service Roaming: Service roaming serves to make services stable, and thereby to enable access to the mobile radio technology of the 3rd generation, and its features.

■   Adaptive Information and Content Delivery: The pre- and post-preparation
     of multimedia content is a very important function, in combined with the in-
     teroperability and use of SDPs. The context types, texts, images, graphics,
     video and audio, can be made available for different end devices, in varying
     formats, over different network paths.

Simply, SPICE can be integrated into the Service Delivery Platforms of a telecommunications provider, and is tasked with improving the service offered, i.e.
to make better use of technical possibilities, and the availability, development
and deployment of services. The target is to identify the technological challenges
for a universally usable architecture model, which supports services and interfaces over differing technology platforms, with particular focus on the development, deployment and operation of those services.

       SPICE should, therefore, offer the combined possibility of data transfer,
without media interruption, and support this through diverse implementation
platforms, terminals and networks. The services offered can be made available to
users quickly, effectively, and efficiently, through personalisation and customisation suitability. A natural result of this is that a generation of completely new
business models is made possible. Customers should be able to make use of the
services offered, for example, in the whole of Europe (Cordier, 2005: pp. 1-2).

8.3.3   The SPICE Architecture

In the existing SPICE architecture the challenges of the interoperability of terminals, networks, and distributed data have been addressed and developed. Therefore, the European Research Project has been of a great importance for large
telecommunication companies, operators and universities. This is because SPICE
represents a new architecture, whose services were made available for operation
within a short period of development time. Users gain independence from their
end devices by using the services they choose. Such embedded systems are head-
ing in the direction of Ubiquitous Computing. Devices become increasingly
smaller and more mobile, and people use them without being aware of this. Proceeding from NGNs and SDPs, services are called for, which support the user in
his daily working life and everyday tasks, and which are omnipresently available
to him (Cordier 2005; Cordier et. al., 2005; SPICE Project Deliverables 1.3,
2006).

       The SPICE architecture (Figure 69) is built on a layer-based design, on a
terminal and a Service Execution Environment. SPICE makes possible the availability of services based on these layers, through IMS and Value Added Services, a heterogeneous Service Running Time Environment. SPICE middleware
is represented in blue on the graph below, and is made up of four layers (Tarkoma et al. 2007a: pp. 1-2):

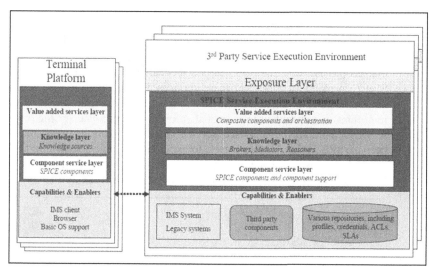

Figure 69: Functional SPICE architecture (Tarkoma *et al.*, 2007a: p. 2)

In the following, the individual layers are presented and explained (Tarkoma *et al.*, 2007a: p. 2 and Demeter, 2008):

▪ Capabilities and Enabler Layer: This layer is made up of the services and enablers that are used by the SPICE platform.

▪ Component Services Layer: This enables the establishment of deployment and management of fundamental SPICE components and adaptor resources. The adaptor resources activate the layer function and export this onto the SPICE platform.

▪ Knowledge Layer: The Knowledge Layer is concerned with the discovery of services and resources, and information transfer.

▪ Value Added Services Layer: The Value Added Services Layer (VAS Layer) is based on a Service Orientated Architecture (SOA), it is responsible for the hosting of value added components, such as, for example, the service logic of a new service component.

Exposure Layer: This layer allows for communication between the different SPICE platforms in different areas of organisation. 3rd party service providers can publish and offer their services on this platform.

The next Section presents how service and information transfer is done using SPICE.

8.3.4   Service and Information Transfer in SPICE

A user must be able to use services seamlessly. Services should be available anytime and everywhere at the same capacity and functionality. As the services that people use are composite, certain mechanisms are needed in order to allow SPICE to maintain control of these services. For this reason, service and information transfer is an important issue. Besides service transfer, it is somehow important to transmit users personal information (personal profile/preferences) so as to maintain personalised service deliveries. This is important precisely because SPICE should enable users to experience seamless transition and service consistency despite changes at operator, network, terminal or service provider level (SPICE Project Deliverables 1.3, 2006; da Silva *et al.*, 2007).

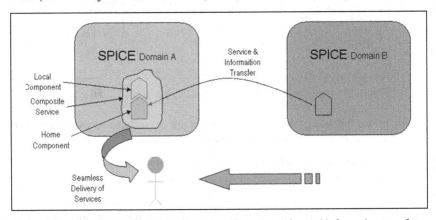

Figure 70: Accessing home and local services through service and information transfer

Thus, SPICE users in a roaming situation, for instance people visiting other countries, are able to combine both local and home services, in order to have a high experience at their location, as long as this combination can be carried out optimally in the local domain, either by being charged for it, or by it being an integral part of a global service performance (SLA, QoS, etc.) Moreover, it is very important to be able to effectively import user profile information into the local domain, so as to ensure that users can continue to enjoy customised services regardless of the local domain or operator (Cordier, 2005).

8.3.5   Service Composition with SPICE

Inter-Domain Service Composition

Another way of providing people with a seamless delivery experience is by using the inter-domain service composition technique. Here, the user is consuming a composite service, and there are no SLA's, QoS's, charging issues, etc. that force the transmission of components onto the local platform. Thus, a new composite service is created between different SPICE platforms, and the new service logic can be hosted, both by the local and the home SPICE platform. The following illustration shows, how the user, on the local platform, creates a new travel service when he/she is travelling to another country.

The new service logic will be hosted on the home platform, and be responsible for coordinating the optimum performance of the whole service. Normally, this technique is used by services that do not need a great deal of message exchange between the different platforms (Lecue *et al.*, 2007).

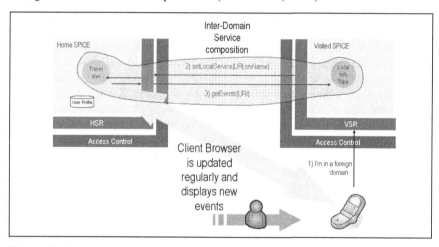

Figure 71: Inter-domain service composition

Automatic Service Re-Composition - The Basic Idea of a Communication Sphere

Mobile environments and the web converge, forming a shared communication sphere. This causes the appearance of new settings that must be supported, e.g. when the user utilises mobile and wired devices in order to interact with systems. Interaction and connectivity of mobile applications with the Internet are increasing. To ensure the interoperation of mobile web applications and tools, running on heterogeneous service platforms, developers need to have a shared specification of the objects belonging to the sphere and their roles. Certain ontologies have already been developed for the mobile communications domain, by employing Semantic Web formalisms (Korpipää *et al.*, 2004; Pfoser *et al.*, 2002). However, widespread and global adoption of such ontologies remains a challenge.

8.3.6 Service Roaming in SPICE

The worlds of Telecommunications and Information Technology are converging in a direction that will allow people to have permanent access to their services, regardless of networks, terminal types or administrative domains. Service Roaming is more highly focussed on the latter aspect, and it enables users to enjoy their personal services, even when they are in a different country and using a foreign operator. In terms of the typical roaming situation, it seems that this scenario has been partially solved by IMS, since signalling can reach and trigger services on the home domain.

However, the problem has become more complex, due to the fact that currently, SPICE deals with composite services made up of other components. These components are brought together under different operator domains and service providers. For this reason, the Service Roaming Manager will make it possible for users to enjoy services wherever the domains user access is located. In short, people wish to have the possibility of using their services irrespective of the circumstances they find themselves in. They do not want to deal with problems that arise due to an expired component of the composite service, or complications that could arise if the service is composed of components from different domains, or if components have to be transferred for reasons of efficiency or economic gain. The impact of service and information roaming within SPICE is multiple: When a user enters a Foreign Service domain, he/she must be able to have (da Silva *et al.*, 2007):

■ *Access to the chosen set of home services and information:* This functionality is already available within currently 2nd and 3rd generation networks while SPICE focused on the enhancement and improvement of existing solutions.

■ *Access to suitable services and information from a foreign domain:* The possibility of access to local services from the visited domain is only partly supported within existing networks, and is mainly only possible via the home domain. The discovery of local services corresponding to user profile, preferences and service context information, or only partly supported or not at all. Another issue, which has not yet been addressed, is the personalisation of these local services according to the as required by the user. Therefore the provision of appropriate access to local services is an important aspect of service and information roaming related work within SPICE.

■ *The possibility of combining home services/service enablers with services/services enablers from the visited domain:* This possibility is presently not available within the networks that are currently allocatable, and is also not yet addressed in telecommunication related standardisation bodies. To provide the roaming user the possibility to personalise local services (e.g. access a user interface in his language) or to combine/enhance existing home services with additional, locally available service components, a (dynamic) composition of home and local services will be needed. This challenge provides a good basis for research activities, and the defining of novel mechanisms. It is therefore included within the scope of SPICE's service and information roaming.

Another aspect to consider, concerning service and information roaming, is the situation at which roaming applies at the Service/Service Enabler/Service Components level:

■ *Total roaming,* during which a subscribed/used service from one service provider is entirely provided by another service provider. This service provider can, for example, be a service provider within the visited service domain.

■ *Roaming of a composite service,* i.e. the parts/components of a composite service offered by one service provider may need to be replaced by a respective service component offered by another service provider.

■ *Dynamic re-composition* of a service offered by one service provider with an equivalent/similar service offered by the same or another service provider.

Service roaming can be divided into several different functionalities, having implications on the overall SPICE architecture. As already stated in the previous Section, the following functionalities need to be covered by the architecture:

■ Consuming services from the home domain in the visited domain. This scenario is called "Total Roaming".

■ Consuming home services from the home domain in the visited domain, where one / or more service components are taken from the visited domain. This scenario is called "Dynamic Service Re-Composition".

■ Consuming home services in the home domain, where one of the service components is no longer available and therefore needs to be replaced by a similar component from another domain. This is known as "Roaming of a Composite Service".

The architecture should make a distinction between Service Roaming Control and Service Roaming Transport. Service Roaming Control deals with aspects such as access control, SLAs, AAA, etc. Service Roaming Transport deals with routing aspects, and transporting the service data to the end-user in the most efficient way (i.e., with least resource consumption).

Consuming Home Services in Visiting Domain

The intention of SPICE is to enable end-users, who are connected in the visited domain, to consume services from the home domain. In general, this is the case for "Total Roaming" from the Service Roaming Scope. For this to happen, the following information has to be available in the visited domain (The SPICE Project: http://www.ist-spice.org/):

■   The user profile, which includes information about the preferences of the end-user and what service subscription(s) he/she has in the home domain.

■   The service specification for the service that will be accessed in the visited domain.

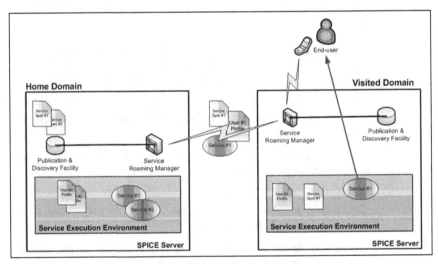

Figure 72: Functional architecture for consuming home services in the visited domain (according to the SPICE Project: http://www.ist-spice.org/)

Consuming Local Services in Visited Domain

The intention of SPICE is also to enable end-users, who are connected in the visited domain, to consume services from the visited domain. In general, this covers items 1 and 2 from the Service Roaming Scope. For this to be realised, the following information has to be available in the visited domain:

■ The user profile, which includes information about the preferences of the end-user and which service subscription(s) he/she has in the home domain.

■ The service specifications of the subscription(s) an end-user has in the home domain. The service specification(s) are used in order to find service(s) in the visited domain. This includes any generic, user-group specific, service tailoring or business logic.

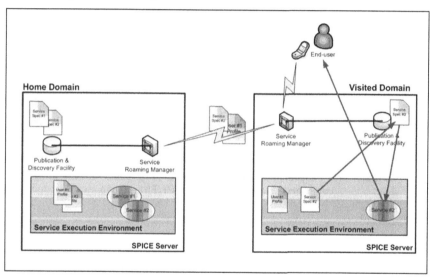

Figure 73: Functional architecture for consuming local services in the visited domain (according to the SPICE Project: http://www.ist-spice.org/)

Consuming Composite Services

The intention of SPICE is to enable end-users, who are connected in the visited domain, to consume services from the home domain, using local components from the visited domain. Essentially, to enable the use of the service "Dynamic Service Composition" from the Service Roaming Scope, the following information has to be available in the visited domain (The SPICE Project: http://www.ist-spice.org/):

■   The user profile, which includes information about the preferences of the end-user and which service subscription(s) they have in their home domain.

■   The service specifications of the subscription(s) an end-user has in the home domain. The service specifications, are used to find service components in the visited domain. This includes any generic or user-group specific service tailoring or business logic.

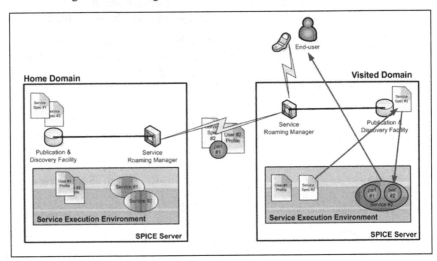

Figure 74:   Functional architecture for consuming home services using local service components (according to the SPICE Project: http://www.ist-spice.org/)

8.4   General Research Approaches

The following Sections describe the theoretical background of the deductive, inductive and abductive approaches, for doing research studies.

8.4.1 Deductive and Inductive Research Approach

Concerning research, two methods of reasoning - the deductive and inductive approaches - are often employed in people-focused research. Formal logic has been described as the science of deduction, as illustrated in Figure 75. The study of inductive reasoning is generally carried out within the field known as informal logic or critical thinking. The inductive approach, also named the bottom-up approach works by moving informally from specific observations to broader generalisations and theories (Trochim, 2000), as illustrated in Figure 76. The phases of both research approaches are shown in the following graphics:

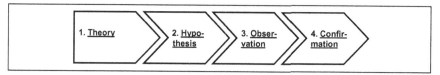

Figure 75: Phases of the deductive research approach

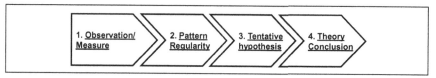

Figure 76: Phases of the inductive research approach

The deductive research approach starts with the field of study of a given theory. The researcher then develops a verifiable hypothesis, before observing and verifying the hypothesis in question, thus confirming the relevant theoretical aspects, and drawing relevant conclusions related to the theory.

Without theory deductive research cannot be applied, as nothing exists with which to derive research questions from (Trochim, 2000; Holyoak and Morrison, 2005).

The deduction theorem can be seen from a mathematical or logical point of view, as a meta-theorem of a formal logical system. This is a statement about a formal system proven in a meta language, and it is a formalisation of the common proof technique in which an implication is proved by assuming A, and then producing B out of this assumption (Johnson-Laird and Byrne, 1991; Holyoak and Morrison, 2005).

$$A \to B$$

More precisely, the deduction theorem states whether formula B is deductible from a set of assumptions where A is a closed formula, then the implication $A \to B$ is deducible from Δ (whereas Δ is a set of assumptions)

$$\Delta \cup \{A\}$$

Using mathematical formulae

$$\Delta \cup \{A\} \vdash B$$

implies $\Delta \vdash A \rightarrow B$. In the unique case where Δ is the empty set, the deduction theorem shows that $A \vdash B$ implies $\vdash A \rightarrow B$.

Alternatively, the inductive research approach (Figure 76), begins with specific observations and measures, to detect certain patterns and regularities. Furthermore, the formulation of certain tentative hypotheses, and their exploration, is undertaken. The last step is to develop some general conclusions or theories. Inductive research is only possible when there are generalised findings (or in fact any findings) from which to draw conclusions (Trochim, 2000; Zarefsky, 2002).

The axiom, also called basic assumption of induction, can be shown in logical symbols (Holyoak and Morrison, 2005; Zarefsky, 2002):

$$(\forall P)[P(0) \wedge (\forall k \in \mathbb{N})(P(k) \Rightarrow P(k+1))] \Rightarrow (\forall n \in \mathbb{N})[P(n)]$$

where P is a proposition, and k and n are both natural numbers. The basis $P(0)$ being true along with the inductive case, the '' ($"P(k)$) being true implies $P(k+1)$ is true" for all natural (k) being true together imply that $P(n)$ is true for any natural number n. Proof by induction is that these two conditions hold, thus implying the required conclusion. This works because k is used to represent an arbitrary natural number. Applying the inductive hypothesis, i.e. that $P(k)$ is true, shows that $P(k+1)$ is also true. This implies that $P(0)$ is true and that $P(1)$ is also true, and carries $P(1)$ to $P(2)$, etc., thus proving that $P(n)$ holds for every natural number n (Vickers, 2010; Holland et. all, 1989).

This following inductive step shows that $P(n)$ holds, then also $P(n+1)$ holds:

$$0 + 1 + 2 + 3 + \ldots + n = n(n+1)\frac{1}{2}$$

Deductive and inductive logic, both run counter to the logic of this study, whereby the process has to move towards the hypothesis, and not away from it. It calls for abductive logic and the retroductive procedure. This will be shown in the following Section.

8.4.2   Abductive (Retroduction) Research Approach

Retroduction is the process of examining the hypotheses on probation, testing their ability to stand up to logical criteria, and to hold the data in order to either eliminate it, or to build an empirical generalisation (Rescher, 1978). Here, according to Peirce, we must accept criteria for checking the validity of the hypothesis. By this, he means the same criteria must be used when examining a hypothesis whether it is by a process of deductive derivation, hypothetical syllogism, disjunctive propositions, syllogism, and so on (Menzies, 1996; Santaella, 1997).

During the process of qualitative research or evaluation, the explanation is often a hypothesis. The hypothesis has to explain the facts, in the sense that it then makes it possible to derive the facts, logically, from the explanation. This is the essence of retroduction, distinguished from induction and deduction, which both work with abstract and generalised concepts. This is to say that the explanation, in itself, has no value without the facts from which it stems. Peirce would surely have agreed with Darwin (Kerlinger, 1986), who claimed that all observations must support or refute at least a single fact, if we wish to use them.

The process of retroduction demands a display of the findings that were collected in the field, and an explanation of these findings (these are hypotheses on probation, since they have not yet been checked), and the appearance of a logical connection between them. The process can be ongoing, moving from understanding to deeper understanding, and on to more complex claims (McKaughan, 2008; Santaella, 1997).

However, in terms of abduction, this technique is used to examine the logical structure relating to the facts, which inverts the process. We move from observed facts to general facts and not from the theory to the particular instance, which is why it is referred to as 'retroduction' (Peirce, 1955). The abductive research strategy is used within the interpretivist school of thought to produce scientific accounts of social life, by drawing on the concepts and meanings used by social actors and the activities in which they engage. Access to any social world is made possible by the accounts given by those people who inhabit it. These accounts contain the concepts that people use to structure their worlds - the meanings and interpretations, the motives and intentions, that people use in their everyday lives, and which direct their behaviours (Menzies, 1996; Santaella, 1997).

Abduction/Interpretivism acknowledges that human behaviour depends on how individuals interpret the conditions in which they find themselves, and accepts that it is essential to have a description of the social world provided by the respective world. It is the task of the social scientist to discover and describe this world, from an 'insider' perspective and not to impose subjective 'outsider' values. Some positions argue that research should go no further than to sift through diverse categories for, and 'pigeon-hole', the various constructs provided by the social actors within the study (Menzies, 1996; Santaella, 1997).

The Abductive/Interpretivist approach has been advocated either as the preferred approach for social sciences, or an adjunct to other strategies. The abductive research approach (Figure 77) starts with certain observations or findings revealed in the field, then raises questions about them, and attempts to answer these questions. In the next step, the validity of the hypothesis is tested and logical criteria are formulated. For the full scope of observation and findings, logical criteria have been formulated, and answers about the hypothesis have to be reached based on the procedure of probation and verification of this formulated logical criteria, thus building up an empirical generalisation, or, alternatively, disproving the hypothesis and starting again from the beginning (McKaughan, 2008; Menzies, 1996). The phases are shown in the following figure:

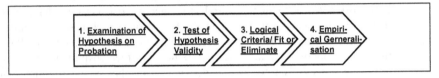

Figure 77: Phases of the abductive research approach

In logic-based abduction, explanation is given from a logical theory T representing a domain, and a set of observations O. Abduction is the process of deriving a set of explanations of O, according to T, and then selecting one of these explanations. For E to be an explanation of O, according to T, it has to satisfy two conditions (McKaughan, 2008; Menzies, 1996; Santaella, 1997):

■ O follows from E and T ;

■ E is consistent with T .

In formal logic, O and E are assumed to be sets of literals. The two conditions for E, being an explanation of O, according to theory T, are formalised as:

$$T \cup E \models O ;$$
$$T \cup E \text{ is consistent.}$$

Abductive validation, is the process of validating a given hypothesis, through abductive reasoning, and can also be called reasoning through successive approximation. According to this principle, an explanation is valid if it is the best possible explanation of a set of known data. The best possible explanation is often defined in terms of simplicity and elegance (e.g. Ockham's razor). Abductive validation is common practice in hypothesis formation in science; moreover, Peirce argues, it is a ubiquitous aspect of thought (McKaughan, 2008; Menzies, 1996; Santaella, 1997):

It was Peirce's own maxim that "facts cannot be explained by a hypothesis more extraordinary than those facts themselves; and of various hypotheses the least extraordinary must be adopted" (Peirce, 1955). After obtaining results from an inference procedure, we may be left with multiple, partially contradictory assumptions. Abductive validation is a method used for identifying the assumptions that will lead to your goal (Santaella, 1997).

This type of data processing consists of assembling or discovering, on the basis of an interpretation of collected data, a combination of features for which there is no appropriate explanation or rule in the score of knowledge that already exists (Blaxter *et al.*, 2001).

Within this process a set of logical rules must be discovered or developed with the aid of intellectual effort (Peirce, 1931-1935: Vol V, p.117). When something that appears unintelligible is discovered in the collected data, on the basis of a new rule, that the rule is then developed simultaneously, and it becomes clear. The logical form of this operation is that of abduction. The relationship of a typical new combination of features is a creative outcome that engenders a new idea. Abduction proceeds from a known result, to two rules and cases. It is therefore a cerebral process, an intellectual act, a mental leap, that brings things together one which had previously never associated, with the another. This is, according to Baxter *et al.* (2001), a cognitive logic of discovery.

8.5 Philosophical Position in Terms of the Research Design

The following Sections describe the philosophical position of research design. According to Orlikowski and Baroudi (1991), the philosophical debates around research can basically be separated into three categories on the underlined epistemology: positivism, interpretivism and critical.

Positivist researchers assume that an objective and social world exists independently of humans. It can be apprehended, characterised and measured. In the underlaying epistemology, positivist researchers work in a deductive manner to discover unilateral, causal relationships. There is, however, concern with the empirical testability of theories. Hypothesis, based on theory, are tested in the research for verification or falsification (Urquart, 2012).

Interpretive researchers have a presumption of social constructivism. This means that reality is a social construct and cannot be understood independently of the actors who make them a reality. Interpretive researchers study phenomena within their social setting. Constructs are generally derived from the field by in-depth examination of that field. Researchers aim to construct interpretations of practises and meanings (Urquhart, 2012). According to Brown *et al.* (2002), in qualitative research methodology the researchers are an integral part of the process whereas in quantitative research methodology they are detached from the variables of the process. From a qualitative perspective, researchers are viewed as instruments that data collection and analysis are conducted.

Critical researchers are under the impression that social reality is historically constituted and people have the ability to change their social and material circumstances. This in turn means, that their capacity to change is constrained by systems of social domination. Social reality is produced by humans, possessing objective realities that, then, dominate human experience. With respect to knowledge, the epistemological belief on critical perspective is that knowledge is grounded in social and historical practices. There can be no theory-independent collection, and interpretation of evidence, to conclusively prove or disprove a theory. Because of the commitment to a process view of phenomena, critical studies tend to be longitudinal (Urquhart, 2012).

9 Appendix B – Participants Correspondence

9.1 Cover Letter/Email to Participants of the Interviews

<u>Anschreiben/Email</u>

InterviewpartnerIn
Organisation/Firma
Rolle

Datum

Anfrage für ein Interview

Liebe potenzielle Interviewpartnerin, lieber potenzielle Interviewpartner,

ich bin ein PhD-Student der Leeds Metropolitan University, Faculty of Arts, Environments and Technology, unter der Betreuung von Professor Colin Pattionson und Professor Reinhold Behringer. Mein Forschungsprojekt besitzt das Ziel Service-Delivery-Plattformen und deren Anforderungen aus Benutzerorientierter Sicht in Bezug auf ICT-Systeme zu untersuchen. Die Forschungsmethodologie in diesem Projekt ist Grounded Theory Methodology (GTM).

Derzeit befinde ich mich in der Phase erfahrene Personen aus dem Europäischen Forschungsprojekt SPICE in Bezug auf Ihre Erfahrungen mit Service-Delivery-Plattformen zu befragen, um die Beziehung zwischen Design Aspekten und individuellen Sichtweisen im Bezug auf Herausforderungen im Servie-Delivery-Plattformen Umfeld zu verstehen und zu erfassen. In diesem Zusammenhang würde ich mich freuen wenn Sie mir mit Ihren Erfahrungen für ein Interview zur Verfügung stehen könnten?

Das Interview wir maximal 45 Minuten dauern und ich würde mich zeitlich sowie auch von der Lokation her nach Ihrer Verfügbarkeit richten und bereit halten. Anbei übermittle ich Ihnen drei Dokumente: 1. Geheimhaltungsvereinbarung, 2. Grundsätzliche Informationen zum Forschungsprojekt sowie 2. Einen Interviewleitfaden, nachdem das Interview ablaufen würde.

Ich bitte Sie mir kurz per Email mitzuteilen, ob und in welchem Zeitraum Sie für ein Interview zur Verfügung stehen könnten. Weiters möchte ich Sie bitten, mir Ihre telefonische Erreichbarkeit mitzuteilen. Ich würde Sie dann gerne kontaktieren wollen um einen Termin zu vereinbaren.

Sollten Sie Fragen haben, so stehe ich jederzeit gerne per Email oder telefonisch für weitere Informationen zur Verfügung. Ich bedanke mich vorab und freue mich auf Ihre Antwort und ein mögliches Interview.

Vielen Dank!

Mit freundlichen Grüßen,

Martin Bergaus
martin.bergaus@gmx.at
+43(676)9176049

9.2   Pledge of Confidentiality

The research interviewer, a student at Leeds Metropolitan University, assures respondents that data will be kept completely confidential. Please read the statement carefully and sign at the bottom to indicate that you have understood and pledge to uphold the policy of confidentiality.

STATEMENT OF PROFESSIONAL ETHICS

All individuals who have access to the respondent data, collected by the interviewer from the Leeds Metropolitan University, are expected to understand that their professional use of the data is directed and regulated by the following statements of policy.

SURVEY OBLIGATIONS

The Leeds Metropolitan University undertakes a study only after it has been evaluated in terms of its importance to society and its contribution to scholarly knowledge. It does not conduct studies which are, in its opinion, trivial, of limited importance, or which would involve collecting information that could be obtained more easily by other means. It does not undertake secret research or conduct studies for the sole benefit of one individual, company, or organisation. The University is a community of institutes whose findings are available to everyone. Every effort is made to disseminate research results, as widely as possible through books, journals and magazine articles, news releases, papers presented at professional meetings, and in the classroom.

Confidentiality is a matter of primary concern to the University. All study procedures are reviewed in order to ensure that individual respondents are protected at each stage of research. While it is the University's policy to disseminate research results, the utmost care is taken to ensure that no data is released that would permit any respondent to be identified. All information which links a specific respondent to a particular interview is separated from the interview and put into special secure files, as soon as the interview is received and logged in at the University. The interviews themselves are identified only by numbers.

SPECIAL RESEARCH INTERVIEWER OBLIGATIONS

The only acceptable role for the research interviewer is that of a professional researcher. To depart from this role may introduce bias and compromise research objectives. In no circumstance is the research interviewer to attempt to counsel a respondent, sell any goods or services to a respondent, or enter into anything other than a professional relationship with a respondent. If asked for help by a respondent, research interviewers must limit themselves to providing the names of regular recognised agencies, and are to do this only when such information or help, is specifically requested by the respondent. By the same token, no research interviewer should ask for advice or counseling from a respondent, or in any way exploit the research situation for personal advantage.

OBLIGATIONS OF UNIVERSITY EMPLOYEES AND OTHERS

The explicit respondent protection procedures observed by the University will be undermined if Leeds Metropolitan University employees and others do not maintain professional ethical standards of confidentiality, regarding what they learn from or about respondents. All information obtained during the course of the research which concerns respondents, their families, or the organisations they represent, is privileged information, whether it relates to the interview itself or is extraneous information learned by research interviewers during the course of their work. Leeds Metropolitan University employees and others are obliged to respect, as highly confidential, all observed information.

Location, Date   Signature

9.3   General Background Information

Die forschenden Interviewer, Studenten an der Leeds Metropolitan University und der Donau-Universität Krems, sagen den Interviewpartner zu, daß ihre Daten komplett vertraulich behandelt werden. Bitte lesen Sie dieses Informationsblatt, das Ihnen Hintergrundinformationen zu den Projekten liefert.

ETHISCHE ERKLÄRUNG

Alle Individuen, die in Kontakt mit den Antwortdaten, die die Interviewer gesammelt haben, kommen, versichern, daß all ihre Aktivitäten von den hier getroffenen Festlegungen geleitet werden und sie sich diesen verpflichtet fühlen.

UMFRAGEVERPFLICHTUNGEN

Die inkludierten Universitäten lassen eine Studie nur dann durchführen, wenn sie aufgrund ihrer Wichtigkeit für die Gesellschaft und ihre Bedeutung für die Wissensgenerierung evaluiert wurden. Es werden keine Studien durchgeführt, die ihrer Bedeutung nach trivial oder von geringer Wichtigkeit sind oder die die Sammlung von Datenmaterial beinhalten, das auf anderem Wege leichter zu erhalten wäre. Es werden keine geheimen oder der Öffentlichkeit unzugänglichen Forschungen durchgeführt, die allein zum Wohl einzelner Individuen, Firmen oder Organisationen wären. Die Universitäten verstehen sich als Teil einer Gemeinschaft von Instituten, deren Ergebnisse jedermann zugänglich sind. Es wird alles unternommen, damit die Forschungsresultate so breit wie möglich gestreut werden, durch Bücher, Journal- und Magazinartikel, Veröffentlichungen auf Tagungen und Konferenzen, und durch Lehre in den Klassenzimmern.

Die Individualrechte jeder einzelnen Person sind für die Universitäten von höchster Bedeutung. Alle Studienprozeduren werden dahingehend geprüft, daß die individuellen Rechte der Interviewpartner während des gesamten Forschungsprozesses geschützt werden. In gleichem Maße, wie die Forschungsergebnisse gestreut werden, wird höchste Sorgfalt darauf verwandt sicherzustellen, daß keine Daten veröffentlicht werden, die es erlauben würden, Rückschlüsse auf einzelne Personen zu ziehen oder diese zu identifizieren. Jedwede Information, die eine Verknüpfung zwischen einem Interviewpartner und einem speziellen Interview zulassen würde, wird von dem Interview getrennt und in speziellen, gesicherten Dateien abgelegt, sobald das Interview an der Universität eingegangen ist. Die Interviews selbst werden nur durch Nummer kenntlich gemacht.

SPEZIELLE VERPFLICHTUNGEN DER FORSCHENDEN INTERVIEWER

Die einzig zulässige Rolle des forschenden Interviewers ist die eines professionellen Forschers. Sich von dieser Roll zu entfernen würde Ungenauigkeiten nach sich ziehen und den Forschungszielen widersprechen. Es ist dem forschenden Interviewer ausdrücklich untersagt, einem Interviewpartner zu beraten, einem Interviewpartner irgendwelche Dinge zu verkaufen oder irgendeine Geschäftsbeziehung mit einem Interviewpartner einzugehen. Bittet ein Interviewpartner den Interviewer um Hilfe, so ist diese darauf zu beschränken, ihn mit den Namen von regulären, anerkannten Agenturen zu versorgen, und dies auch nur, wenn der Interviewpartner dies ausdrücklich verlangt. Ebenso darf der Interviewer den Interviewpartner niemals um Rat oder Beratung fragen oder in sonsteiner Weise persönlichen Nutzen aus dem Forschungsvorhaben ziehen wollen.

VERPFLICHTUNGEN DER UNIVERSITÄTSANGESTELLTEN UND ANDERER

Die von der Universität strikt überwachten Prozeduren zum Schutz der Interviewpartner würden unterlaufen werden, wenn sich die Universitätsangestellten oder andere Personen nicht an die ethischen Standards bezüglich der Geheimhaltung über alle Dinge, die sie von oder über die Interviewpartner erfahren, halten würden. Jedwede Information, die während des Forschungsvorhabens erhalten wird und die die Interviewpartner, deren Familien oder die Organisationen, denen diese angehören, betrifft, ist schützenswert, unabhängig davon, ob sie das Interview selbst betrifft oder ob es sich um eine Information handelt, die darüber hinausgeht. Die Universitätsangestellten und andere sind daher dazu verpflichtet, alle erlangten Informationen absolut vertraulich zu behandeln.

9.4   Interview Guideline

INTERVIEWLEITFADEN
ZU DEN INTERVIEWS MIT DEN SPICE-EXPERTEN

Als SPICE-Experten werden in dieser Studie im Wesentlichen 3 unterschiedliche Gruppen betrachtet (Benutzer und Entwickler von Service Delivery Plattformen sowie auch Architektur-Experten in Bezug auch Service Delivery Plattformen und im Speziellen in Bezug auf SPICE), für welche dieser Interviewleitfaden als Basis zu Abwicklung eines Interviews herangezogen wird.

SPICE-Experte: ....

Einstieg in das Interview:

- Vorstellung der Personen
- Hinweis auf Anonymisierung der Daten und keine direkte Auswertung des jeweiligen einzelnen Interviews.
- Darstellung der Ausgangssituation und kurze Bekanntgabe von Hintergrundinformationen – „Anytime, Anywhere, Anyplace" Paradigma zu „Anynetwork at any Device" Paradigma stellt heutzutage hohe Anforderungen an Netzwerkinfrastruktur und Endgeräte. Die Einbeziehung der neuesten Mobilfunktechnologien und des Internet zeigen, dass eine Auslagerung von Netzwerkintelligenz und ebenso von den Endgeräten weg auf eine Art Plattform, welche durchaus Internet-basierend betrieben werden kann viele neue Möglichkeiten bietet.

- Ziel der durchgeführten Interviews ist es, aus den rückgemeldeten Informationen Rückschlüsse auf allgemeine sowie auch technische Anforderungen an eine Service Delivery Plattform abzuleiten, um daraus in weiterer Folge Empfehlungen für den verbesserten Nutzen beim Einsatz derartiger Technologien in der Schienenverkehrstelematik zu entwickeln. Als Übersicht seien folgende Grafiken dargestellt:

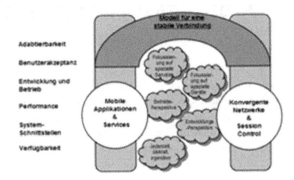

Identifiziertes Problem
Überblick

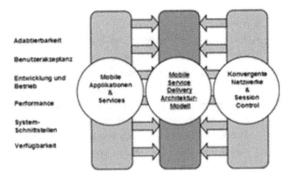

Vorgeschlagenes Lösungskonzept
Überblick

leeds metropolitan university

Fragen zu der Netzwerkinfrastruktur und zu den Zugangsmöglichkeiten:
Interoperabilität we auch Mobilität ist heute sehr stark geprägt durch die
Basisnetzwerkinfrastruktur und den Zugangsnetzen sowie der Ausbaugrad der
Basisnfrastruktur. Die Erarbeitung von Anforderungen an eine
Kommunikationsinfrastruktur der Zukunft wird dabei von 3 Hauptzielen geprägt: Der
Zugang zur Netzinfrastruktur muss zur Vernetzung möglichst aller gesellschaftlichen
Gruppen möglich sein. Der Betrieb der Netzwerkinfrastruktur muss einfach und
kostengünstig möglich sein. Die Auslagerung von Netzwerkintelligenz auf eine SDP
ist hierbei ein ganz wichtiger Faktor für die Kosten.

- **Zugang zur Netzinfrastruktur**
    - Welche Möglichkeiten von und zu Zugängen kennen Sie und sehen Sie
      für ein derartig vorgeschlagenes Szenario?
    - Sollen alle Bürger Zugang zu öffentlichen Netzen bekommen? Wenn ja,
      wie könnte dies realisiert werden?
    - Wie sehen Sie hier die Anbindungsmöglichkeit von privaten
      Subnetzen? Welches Modell könnten Sie sich hier vorstellen?
    - Sollen öffentliche Netzzugänge z.B. in Schulen und Bibliotheken bei
      zukünftigen Netzen möglich werden? Wenn ja, wie könnte man das
      umsetzen?
    - Gleichwertige Netzzugänge in Stadt und Land? Wenn ja, wie könnte
      man das umsetzen?
    - Wie stehen Sie zu dem Thema Netzzugänge müssen heute bei der
      Arbeit, zu Hause verfügbar sein, da man als Benutzer heute immer
      erreichbar sein sollte?
    - Welche Basisdienste einer Netzwerkinfrastruktur sind für Sie als
      Benutzer/Entwickler unbedingt erforderlich? Bitte begründen Sie Ihre
      Aussagen!

- Betrieb der Netzinfrastruktur
  o Ist eine hohe Netzzuverlässigkeit und –Verfügbarkeit aus Ihrer Sicht für das „Any Network on any Device" Szenario erforderlich? Bitte begründen Sie Ihre Aussagen!
  o Wie sehen Sie die künftigen Entwicklungen der NGNs und konvergenten Netzwerke?
  o Ist eine Einbindung der bestehenden Infrastruktur notwendig? Warum?
  o Wie schätzen Sie den zukünftigen Energieverbrauch für den Betrieb einer Netzwerkinfrastruktur ein?
  o Geringe Umweltbelastung in der Herstellung, Betrieb und Entsorgung?
  o Gibt es regulatorische Anforderungen die berücksichtigt werden müssen?
  o Was gibt es an Kernfeatures zu erfüllen um die Basisinfrastruktur auch für zukünftige Dienste (Allgegenwärtige Dienste – Ubiquitous Services) auszulegen?

- Kosten für Netzzugänge
  o Mit welchen Kosten ist für zukünftige Netzzugänge im Rahmen des „Any Network on any Device Szenarios" zu rechnen?
  o Sehen Sie einen Weg indem man Netzzugänge kostengünstiger gestalten kann?
  o Wie würden Sie den Umgang mit den Systemkosten bei Neuinstallation von Teilnetzen einschätzen? Werden sich diese verhältnismäßig erhöhen oder erniedrigen im Vergleich zu den heute bestehenden Netzen?
  o Wie würden Sie den Umgang mit den Inbetriebnahmekosten bei Neuinstallation von Teilnetzen einschätzen? Werden sich diese verhältnismäßig erhöhen oder erniedrigen im Vergleich zu den heute bestehenden Netzen?

- Gibt es aus Ihrer Sicht einen wesentlichen Aspekt der in Verbindung mit Netzwerken und Zugangsnetzen weiters berücksichtig werden müsste um ein derartiges Szenario abzubilden?

Fragen zur Dienste-Entwicklungs- und -Bereitstellungs-Plattform:

Service Delivery Plattformen scheinen aus heutiger Sicht die Zukunft zu sein um eine breite Palette an mobilen und interoperablen Diensten, welche auf einer offenen Plattform, rasch und ohne aufwendige Konfigurationen bereitgestellt werden können um eine möglichst große Erreichbarkeit für Benutzer unabhängig von deren Endgeräten bzw. die vorhandenen Zugangsnetze zu ermöglichen. Die Erarbeitung von Anforderungen an eine derartige Plattform wird dabei von 5 Hauptzielen geprägt: Der Zugang zur SDP muss Standardisierte Schnittstellen zu den Kernnetzen bereitstellen bzw. Schnittstellen für einen hohen Abdeckungsgrad im Endgerätebereich bereitstellen. Dienste müssen einfach und schnell ohne die Plattform außer Betrieb nehmen zu müssen bereitgestellt bzw. entwickelt werden können. Benutzerfreundlichkeit ist ein muss und Schutzmechanismen und Privatsphäreeinstellungen für den jeweiligen Benutzer sind ebenso hoch angeschrieben. Die Kosten für die Einführung bzw. Instandhaltung einer SDP ist von zentraler Bedeutung.

- Standardisierung und Schnittstellen
  o Welche Möglichkeiten für eine einheitlich, standardisierte Software-Architektur zur Entwicklung, Bereitstellung und Integration von Diensten kennen Sie und würden für ein derartiges Zukunftsszenario empfehlen?
  o Wie wird sich das Thema Mobilität auf Standardisierung und Bereitstellung von Standardschnittstellen auswirken?
  o Förderung von Produktivität und Automatisierung?
  o Welche Einflussfaktoren oder -Bereiche sehen Sie für eine Interoperabilität bezüglich Netzwerken bzw. Endgeräten?
  o Einfacher Zugriff auf Netzwerkfunktionen wie IMS und SIP als Basisdienste der SDP?
- Bereitstellung und Entwicklung von Diensten im Betrieb
  o Welche Vorteile sehen Sie durch eine schnelle und einfache Möglichkeit zur Entwicklung und Bereitstellung von Diensten?
  o Welche Art und Kategorien von Diensten sollen auf der SDP bereitgestellt   werden?

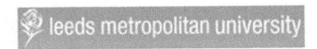

- o Welche QoS Parameter sehen Sie als notwendig an um Dienste mit einer hohen Güteklasse anbieten zu können?
- o Verschiedenste Dienste (z.B. Basisdienste – Netzwerk, Standardschnittstellen, Positionsbestimmungsdienste Datenübertragungsdienste, etc.)
- o In welcher Form sollte die Plattform die Bereitstellung von Diensten und Engeräte unterstützen?
- o Wie könnte man eine Trennung von operativer Dienstbereitstellung und Service-Komposition/Diensteentwicklung auf derselben Plattform bereitstellen und diese dann zusammenführen?
- o Welche Möglichkeiten sehen Sie im operativen Betrieb einer SDP in einfacher Form eine Erweiterung der Service-Landschaft abzubilden?
- o Eigene Dienste für spezielle Benutzergruppen? (z.B. Dienste-Entwickler)
- o Geringer Aufwand und Ressourcenverbrauch bei der Entwicklung?
- o Bereitstellung einer personalisierten und offenen Plattform?
- Benutzerfreundlichkeit
  - o Benutzerfreundlichkeit und praktisches Arbeiten mit der SDP?
  - o Welche SW wird zur Implementierung heutiger SDPs eingesetzt und wie gestaltet sich deren Bedienbarkeit?
  - o Multisprachen-Fähigkeit?
- Schutzmechanismen und Privatsphäre
  - o Welche Sicherheits- und Datenschutz-Mechanismen sollten aus Ihrer Sicht eingesetzt werden?
  - o Wie kann ein Schutz der Privatsphäre für jeden einzelnen Benutzer umgesetzt werden?
  - o Schutz vor Gewalt Rassismus und Pornografie?
- Kosten für SDP
  - o Mit welchen Kosten ist für eine SDP im Rahmen des „Any Network on any Device Szenarios" zu rechnen?
  - o Sehen Sie einen Weg indem man das Angebot verschiedenster Dienste – und –gruppen Instanzijerungen gestalten könnte?

o Wie würden Sie den Umgang mit den Betriebskosten bei einer SDP einschätzen? Werden sich diese verhältnismäßig erhöhen oder erniedrigen im Vergleich zu beispielsweise heute bestehenden unterschiedlichsten Portalen welche bereits Dienste für mobile Endbenutzer anbieten?

o Wie würden Sie den Umgang mit den Systemkosten bei Neuinstallation einer SDP einschätzen? Werden sich diese verhältnismäßig erhöhen oder erniedrigen im Vergleich zu den heutigen Dienste-Portalen?

o Wie würden Sie den Umgang mit den Inbetriebnahmekosten bei Neuinstallation einer SDP einschätzen? Werden sich diese verhältnismäßig erhöhen oder erniedrigen im Vergleich zu den heutigen Dienste-Portalen?

o Mit welchen Kosten ist für Einführung neuer und zusätzlicher Dienste zu rechnen?

o Risikokosten für Standardisierung im Rahmen der Einführung einer SDP?

• Gibt es aus Ihrer Sicht einen wesentlichen Aspekt der wir in Verbindung mit einer SDP berücksichtig werden müsste um ein derartiges Szenario abzubilden?

Fragen zu Anwendungen und Diensten aus der Benutzer-zentrierten Sicht:
Die Benutzer-zentrierte Sicht ist für ein derartiges Vorhaben standardisierte Plattformen für Dienste, welchen diverseste Anwendungen auf Endgeräten unterstützen bzw. bedienen können sollen, eine wesentliche Sichtweise im mobilen und allgegenwärtigen Computing. Wichtig ist aus Benutzer-zentrierter Sich Anforderungen für die SDP zu identifizieren und zu sammeln. Die Erarbeitung dieser Anforderungen wird dabei von 3 Hauptzielen geprägt: Die Endgeräte müssen einfach auf die SDP zugreifen und Daten kontextbewusst austauschen können. Die Benutzerfreundlichkeit der Endgeräte ist im Bezug auf die Interaktion mit den Diensten, welche auf der SDP bereitgestellt werden ein ganz wichtiger Punkt. Da die Auslagerung von Clientintelligenz auf die SDP notwendig wird ist hier auch der Kostenaspekt hierfür von zentraler Bedeutung.

- <u>Endgeräte</u>
  - o Welche Kategorien von Endgeräten sehen Sie für zukünftige allgegenwärtige breitbandige Anwendungen im Rahmen des „Any Network on any Device" Szenarios?
  - o Welche Aspekte muss ein mobiles Endgerät unbedingt aufweisen um Multimediaanwendungen zu unterstützen um diese Anwendungen auch effizient einsetzen zu können?
  - o Wie werden sich die Endgeräte bezüglich des Energieverbrauches im Betrieb in Zukunft verhalten müssen?
  - o Geringe Umweltbelastung in der Herstellung, Betrieb und Entsorgung?
  - o Rechnen Sie mit einer Zunahme der Mobilität der einzelnen Benutzer in den nächsten Jahren? Wenn ja, wie wird sich das auf die Endgeräte auswirken?
  - o Welche Einflussfaktoren sehen Sie um sicherzustellen, dass die Möglichkeit des Austausches von Informationen und Daten möglichst effizient ausgeschöpft werden kann?
  - o Umgang mit einer stetig anwachsenden Anzahl von Endgeräten und Anwendungen?
  - o Standardisierte Dienste und Schnittstellen?
- <u>Benutzerfreundlichkeit</u>
  - o Praktisches Arbeiten in Verbindung mit der SDP/auf der SDP vom mobilen Endgerät?
  - o Eingesetzte SW und Bedienbarkeit dieser?
  - o Multisprachen-Fähigkeit?
  - o Wie kann sich die Benutzerinteraktion zwischen mobilen Endgerät und der SDP gestalten und wie kann sichergestellt werden, dass kontextbewusste Informationen dem jeweiligen Benutzer bereitgestellt werden?
  - o Informationsdienste, welche durch Benutzer personalisiert werden können?
  - o Allgegenwärtige, mobile Kontext-bezogene Informationsdienste?
  - o Schutzmechanismen (Sicherheit und Datenschutz)?

leeds metropolitan university

- <u>Kosten für Endgeräte</u>
  - o Wie kann man künftig sicherstellen, dass kostengünstige Endgeräte für alle Benutzergruppen bereitgestellt werden? Warum?
  - o Wie kann man künftig sicherstellen, dass kostenfrei/-günstig auf Informationen und Wissen zugegriffen werden kann?
- Gibt es aus Ihrer Sicht einen wesentlichen Aspekt der in Verbindung mit der Endgerätevielfalt und dem stetig wachsenden Kontextbewusstsein berücksichtig werden müsste um ein derartiges Szenario abzubilden?

Fragen zum Abschluss:

- Welches Gesamturteil würden Sie für die Einführung einer SDP wie z.B. SPICE geben?
- Wie würden Sie das Aufwand-Nutzen-Verhältnis einer SDP wie SPICE einschätzen?
- Was ist aus Ihrer Sicht die richtige SW zur Abbildung einer SDP?
- ...

- Alter der interviewten Person?
- Position der interviewten Person?
- Studienabschluss der interviewten Person?
- Wieviele Jahre im Unternehmen?

10 Appendix C – Empirical and Literature-Based Data

10.1 Example of Transcribed and Colour-Coded Interview

An example of a completed transcribed and colour-coded interview is shown here, the interview with participant p11_u in German, the original language in which the interviews were done. All other transcribed and colour-coded interviews are available on DVD.

Interview 01 (p11_u)

Fragen zu der Netzwerkinfrastruktur und zu den Zugangsmöglichkeiten:

F1: Welche Möglichkeiten von Infrastrukturen und zu Zugängen kennen Sie und sehen Sie für ein derartig vorgeschlagenes Szenario?

A1:

F2: Sollen alle Bürger Zugang zu öffentlichen Netzen bekommen? Wenn ja, wie könnte dies realisiert werden?

A2: Ja, ich finde schon. Desto mehr Benutzer, desto stärker wird die Nachfrage an Anwendungen und das hilft wiederum den Betreibern ihre Investitionskosten zu decken und sie werden deshalb noch mehr in Infrastruktur und Services investieren, weil sie sich dadurch klarerweise einen Geschäftszuwachs erwarten. Es gibt viele Möglichkeiten von Zugriffen, zwei davon sehe ich als realistisch an: 1. Telefonnetzwerke mit entsprechendem Engagement um z.B. Multimedia Applikationen streamen zu können. Dazu gilt es sicherzustellen, das eine UMTS/HSPA Infrastruktur oder LTE flächendecken zumindest in Ballungszentren zur Verfügung steht. Die W-LAN und Wi-Fi Technologie kann bei eine großflächigen Abdeckung z.B. in Städten wie Wien, Graz, usw. einen kostengünstigen Einstiegspunkt bieten. Wenn die Betreiber derartiger Netze flächendecken und diese gratis anbieten könnten wäre eine sehr gute Voraussetzung geschaffen.

F3: Wie sehen Sie hier die Anbindungsmöglichkeit von privaten Subnetzen? Welches Modell könnten Sie sich hier vorstellen?

A3: Das selbe, allerdings mit einem entsprechenden Identifikations- und Abrechnungssystem dahinter. Ist aber eine sehr aufwendige Infrastruktur und mit hohen Kosten für eine reale Implementierung verbunden. Dies wiederspricht dem Punkt der ganzheitlichen Bereitstellung ein wenig, da Betreiber hier mit sehr hohen Kosten konfrontiert sind und zumeist nur einen bestimmten Teil von Benutzern ansprechen.

F4: Sollen öffentliche Netzzugänge z.B. in Schulen und Bibliotheken bei zukünftigen Netzen möglich werden? Wenn ja, wie könnte man das umsetzen?

A4: Definitiv Ja, wie zuvor schon angesprochen. Kostenlose Zugangspunkte wie heute in Schulen, Bibliotheken usw. bereits längst üblich auf größere Flächen ausweiten. Beispiel USA: Manche Städte sind dort längst komplett WLAN vernetzt und es zahlt niemand für den Zugang zum Internet.

F5: Gleichwertige Netzzugänge in Stadt und Land? Wenn ja, wie könnte man das umsetzen?

A5:

F6: Wie stehen Sie zu dem Thema Netzzugänge müssen heute bei der Arbeit, zu Hause verfügbar sein, da man als Benutzer heute immer erreichbar sein sollte?

A6: Internet ist privat wie auch für die Arbeit unabdingbar. Deshalb ist eine Erreichbarkeit des Benutzers sowieso immer gegeben. Die Frage die sich aber stellt ist, ob es wirklich sein muss jederzeit erreichbar zu sein. Ich persönlich empfinde dies als eine sehr subjektiv zu beantwortende Frage und mein selbst, dass ich mir damit mein Arbeits- wie auch Privatleben sehr gut einteilen und auch steuern kann. Allerdings möchte ich zum Beispiel gar nicht immer erreichbar sein.

F7: Welche Basisdienste einer Netzwerkinfrastruktur sind für Sie als Benutzer/Entwickler unbedingt erforderlich? Bitte begründen Sie Ihre Aussagen!

A7: Ich als Benutzer sehe die Notwendigkeit für Dienste wie Handover innerhalb von Netzwerken um zuverlässige Verbindungen **sicherzustellen;** Netzübergreifendes Roaming zwischen unterschiedlichen Netzwerken diversester Operator; Dienste zur Sicherstellung der Sicherheit in Netzwerken; intelligente Routingmechanismen; Identifikation eines Benutzers im Netzwerk.

F8: Ist eine hohe Netzzuverlässigkeit und –Verfügbarkeit aus Ihrer Sicht für das "Any Network on any Device" Szenario erforderlich? Bitte begründen Sie Ihre Aussagen!

A8: Ja, weil die Benutzer heute beruflich wie auch privat einen permanenten Zugang zum Internet haben wollen. Der Grund liegt darin, dass das Internet heute Medium für alle möglichen Arten von Anwendungen für beruflichen und privaten Gebrauch bereitstellt und somit der Zugang zum Internet gegeben sein muss.

F9: Wie sehen Sie die künftigen Entwicklungen der NGNs und konvergenten Netzwerke?

A9:

F10: Ist eine Einbindung der bestehenden Infrastruktur notwendig? Warum?

A10: Aus meiner Sicht definitiv ja. Weil die Betreiber in der Vergangenheit sehr viele Investitionen getätigt haben und die Infrastrukturen für solche Netze hoch komplex, stark automatisiert sind und die einzelnen Systeme aufeinander aufbauen. Das ist im übrigen auch der Grund warum immer noch GSM Basisinstallationen bei einzelnen Betreibern im Einsatz sind. Neusysteme wie UMTS sind hier natürlich kompatibel – ich glaube man sagt abwärtskompatibel! Aus meiner Sicht ist es heute unbedingt notwendig, dass bei neuen konzeptionellen Ideen im IT Umfeld immer auch die Einbindung bestehender Systeme berücksichtigt werden muss. Der Grund liegt darin, dass ein Betreiber bewehrte ältere System nicht unbedingt gleich in vollem Umfange tauschen möchte. Das ist eine Frage der Kosten.

F11: Wie schätzen Sie den zukünftigen Energieverbrauch für den Betrieb einer Netzwerkinfrastruktur ein?

A11:

F12: Geringe Umweltbelastung in der Herstellung, Betrieb und Entsorgung?

A12:

F13: Gibt es regulatorische Anforderungen die berücksichtigt werden müssen?

A13: Ich glaube ja, bin hier aber nicht der Experte für regulatorische Themen.

F14: Was gibt es an Kernfeatures zu erfüllen um die Basisinfrastruktur auch für zukünftige Dienste (Allgegenwärtige Dienste – Ubiquitous Services) auszulegen?

A14: Da sind zunächst einmal die technischen Voraussetzungen für die Mobilität zu treffen. Dazu müssen die unterschiedlichen Netzwerktechnologien sowohl im Umfeld von Mobilfunkbetreibern, wie auch bei Applikations- und Service-Providern bereitgestellt werden. Das sollte mit einer verbesserten Flächendeckung passieren. Weiters sehe ich im Internetzeitalter das Medium Internet immer stärker im Rampenlicht für Services und Anwendungen. D.h. das Internet muss verstärkt mobil bereitgestellt werden – damit meine ich, dass nicht nur Netzzugänge, genügend hohe Bandbreiten sondern auch konzentrierte Plattformen wie Portale für Benutzer bereitgestellt werden, welche die Vielfalt an explodierenden Anwendungen für Benutzer besser verwaltbar und kontrollierbar gestalten. Dabei wird hier die zentrale Frage zu stellen sein: Wie können Applikations und Serviceprovider ihren Kunden Anwendungen rasch, in großer Vielfalt und flexibel bereitstellen. Der dritte für mich wesentliche Punkt wird sein, wie gut es gelingen kann und wird den Wildwuchs am Endgeräte Markt auf der einen Seite seitens der Anbieter zu supporten und auf der anderen Seite Standard-Technologien und Schnittstellen bereitzustellen um die Anwendungsentwicklungen für diese Endgeräte professioneller zu gestalten.

F15: Mit welchen Kosten ist für zukünftige Netzzugänge im Rahmen des "Any Network on any Device Szenarios" zu rechnen?

A15: Die Kosten müssen in jedem Fall zurückgehen, da trotz hoher Investitionskosten für die Betreiber eine direkte Weiterverrechnung an die Kunden aus meiner Sicht damit bestraft werden würde, dass die Weiterentwicklung der Systeme und Technologien nur bedingt angenommen werden. Kunden sind nur bedingt bereit für mobile Internetzugänge höhere Kosten auf sich zu nehmen.

F16: Sehen Sie einen Weg indem man Netzzugänge kostengünstiger gestalten kann?

A16: Ja, Betreiber müssen versuchen die breite Massen an Kunden zu gewinnen und diese an sich zu binden, was heute in Österreich mit den verschieden guten Vertragsangeboten aufgrund des starken Wettbewerbes im Operator-Umfeld bereits passiert. Kunden also binden und über neue value-added Services oder verkaufen.

F17: Wie würden Sie den Umgang mit den Systemkosten bei Neuinstallation von Teilnetzen einschätzen? Werden sich diese verhältnismäßig erhöhen oder erniedrigen im Vergleich zu den heute bestehenden Netzen?

A17: Solange sich die Technologie nicht verändert sondern weiterhin optimiert wird, ich erinnere nur GSM → GPRS → UMTS → HSPA werden sich die Investitionskosten in Grenzen halten, da nur nachgerüstet wurde, die Basisinfrastruktur sich aber nicht verändert hat. Mit eine komplett neuen Technologie wie LTE, welches bereits diskutiert wird. Diese Technologie verwendet neue Funkfrequenzen und scheint zu der alten Technologie und den Systemen nicht kompatibel zu sein, müssen hohe Investitionkosten getätigt werden, da die Komponenten des Mobilfunksystems ausgetauscht werden müssen. In diesem Falle stehen hohe Investitionskosten an. Die hohen Wartungskosten beider genannten Systeme werden weiterhin hoch bleiben. Deshalb meine ich, dass die Kosten für die Betreiber um die Systeme zu betreiben nicht großartig günstiger werden können, aber durch hohe Anzahl von Kunden in Verbindung mit neuen, flexiblen und einer Vielfalt an Diensten die Erhaltungskosten für Netzwerke zum Einen gedeckt werden können und zum Anderen Operators trotzdem heute und in Zukunft gut verdienen werden können.

F18: Wie würden Sie den Umgang mit den Inbetriebnahme kosten bei Neuinstallation von Teilnetzen einschätzen? Werden sich diese verhältnismäßig erhöhen oder erniedrigen im Vergleich zu den heute bestehenden Netzen?

A18: Hatte ich gerade eben schon kurz beschrieben. Ich glaube dass eine Neuinstallation von z.B. LTE hohe Investitions- und auch Transferkosten verursachen wird.

F19: Gibt es aus Ihrer Sicht einen wesentlichen Aspekt der in Verbindung mit Netzwerken und Zugangsnetzen weiters berücksichtig werden müsste um ein derartiges Szenario abzubilden?

A19:

Fragen zur Dienste-Entwicklungs- und –Bereitstellungs-Plattform:

F20: Welche Möglichkeiten für eine einheitlich, standardisierte Software-Architektur zur Entwicklung, Bereitstellung und Integration von Diensten kennen Sie und würden für ein derartiges Zukunftsszenario empfehlen?

A20: Ein web-basierendes Portal auf welchem man fertige und auch neu entwickelte Applikationen und Services bereitstellen und Kunden anbieten kann ist eine solche Möglichkeit. Diese Service-Delivery-Plattformen beherbergen ganze Gruppen unterschiedlichster Dienste und Anwendungen und machen es dem Bereitsteller wie auch dem potenziellen Kunden einfach diese zu benutzen.

F21: Wie wird sich das Thema Mobilität auf Standardisierung und Bereitstellung von Standardschnittstellen auswirken?

A21: Standardisierung steht heute hoch im Kurs, da aufgrund der stetig reduzierten Kosten und IT Budgets der Betrieb von Systemen immer günstiger werden muss und oft auch hochspezialisiertes Personal im Unternehmen nicht mehr zur Verfügung steht. Standardlösungen helfen den IT Managern im wesentlich die Kosten besser zu kontrollieren und das Risiko im Betrieb zu minimieren, da die Wahrscheinlichkeit viel höher ist hier fachkundiges Personal im eigenen Hause aber auch extern verfügbar zu haben. Standardschnittstellen sind auch in der mobilen Welt aufgrund dessen aber auch aufgrund der technischen Verfügbarkeit notwendig.

F22: Förderung von Produktivität und Automatisierung?

A22: Automatisierung von einfachen sich immer wiederholenden Prozessen ist für eine breite Anwendungsbasis aus meiner Sicht absolut sinnvoll.

F23: Welche Einflussfaktoren oder –Bereiche sehen Sie für eine Interoperabilität bezüglich Netzwerken bzw. Endgeräten?

A23: Ich denke der wichtigste Einflussfaktor ist, dass ein Endbenutzer seine oder ihre Anwendungen oder Services unabhängig von seiner/ihrer im Moment befindlichen aktuellen Position benutzen möchte. Eine stabile und zuverlässige Unterstützung aller gängigen Netzwerke und Endgeräte ist notwendig.

F24: Einfacher Zugriff auf Netzwerkfunktionen wie IMS und SIP als Basisdienste der SDP?

A24: IMS und SIP sind nach meinem Verständnis Basisarchitekturen für echte Mobilität und Breitbandtechnologien, welche die mobile Übertragung von Multimedia-Applikationen supporten. Damit SDPs einen echten Mehrwert bieten können, müssen sie im Stande sein die IT und die Mobilkommunikations-Welten zu verbinden und dies funktioniert nur wenn derartige Technologien wie IMS und SIP hier auch berücksichtigt werden. In einem Benutzerszenario muss es egal sein ob Wi-Max oder 3G Technologie bzw. welches Endgerät der Benutzer verwendet um seine Anwendungen auszuführen.

F25: Welche Vorteile sehen Sie durch eine schnelle und einfache Möglichkeit zur Entwicklung und Bereitstellung von Diensten?

A25: Ich sehe hier viele Vorteile: Benutzer können auf fertige Diensten und Services Zugreifen und diese zu ihren eigenen machen wie es heute ja auch im Prinzip mit den Appstores schon machbar ist. Weiters können einzelne Services mit anderen oder auch eigen entwickelten also neuer Service-Verbund mit erweiterter Funktionalität provisioniert werden. Dies bringt vielfache Möglichkeiten für Endanwender. Wenn Entwickler auch Zugang auf die SDP haben können sie entwickelte Dienste sofort weiteren Benutzern bereitstellen und diese können genutzt werden. Ich sehe hier ein großes Potenzial an Möglichkeiten.

F26: Welche Art und Kategorien von Diensten sollen auf der SDP bereitgestellt werden?

A26: Aus meiner Sicht sollten Dienste jeglicher Kategorien bereitgestellte werden, da diese eine große Anzahl an potenziellen Benutzern adressieren. Lassen Sie mich einige Beispiele nennen: Das sind zum einen sehr System-nahe Services wie zum Beispiel ein Service zur automatischen Positionsbestimmung wie Cell-ID oder aGPS. Und zum anderen Dienste welche einen anwendungstechnischen Charakter verfolgen wie zum Beispiel eine Anwendung zur Erfassung von Reisespesen oder welche Visitenkarten einscannen und Kundendaten bearbeiten kann.

F27: Welche QoS Parameter sehen Sie als notwendig an um Dienste mit einer hohen Güteklasse anbieten zu können?

A27: Ich bin kein technischer Experte für QoS, aber zwei wesentliche Parameter möchte ich im Zusammenhang mit IP Datenübertragung hier an dieser Stelle in jedem Falle nennen: Die Latenzzeit ist ein wichtiger Parameter - dies ist die Zeit die die Verzögerung der Ende-zu-Ende Übertragung ausweist.

Weiters die Paketverlustrate, welche die Wahrscheinlichkeit, dass einzelne IP-Pakete bei der Übertragung verloren gehen, darstellt. Ah, da fällt mir noch die Durchsatz rate ein, welche die pro Zeiteinheit im Mittel übertragene Datenmenge darstellt.

F28: Verschiedenste Dienste (z.B. Basisdienste – Netzwerk, Standardschnittstellen, Positionsbestimmungsdienste Datenübertragungsdienste, etc.)

A28: Basis-Dienste: 2G, 3G, 4G, WLAN. Wi-Max, Bluetooth, API, HTML, HTTP und HTTPS, XML, Location-based Services: Cell-ID und aGPS bzw. Indoor WLAN-Lokalisierung. SMS, MMS, Email, etc.

F29: In welcher Form sollte die Plattform die Bereitstellung von Diensten und Endgeräte unterstützen?

A29: Eine SDP sollte die Bereitstellung von Diensten in der Form unterstützen, dass Standarddienste und Anwendungen sowie Spezialanwendungen (nach dem Apps Vorbild) bereitgestellt werden und zusätzlich die Option bestehen muss, dass Entwickler ihre Dienste auf der Plattform anbieten und bereitstellen können sollen, ohne das Downtimes berücksichtigt werden muss. Die Endbenutzer sollen also derartige Dienste sofort verwenden und provisionieren können. Also eine Möglichkeit des durchgängigen Angebotes an bestehenden und neu verfügbaren Diensten ohne den Betrieb einer SDP stören zu müssen.

F30: Wie könnte man eine Trennung von operativer Dienstbereitstellung und Service-Komposition/Diensteentwicklung auf derselben Plattform bereitstellen und diese dann zusammenführen?

A30:

F31: Welche Möglichkeiten sehen Sie im operativen Betrieb einer SDP in einfacher Form eine Erweiterung der Service-Landschaft abzubilden?

A31:

F32: Eigene Dienste für spezielle Benutzergruppen? (z.B. Dienste-Entwickler)

A32: Ja, klar macht es Sinn Dienste Benutzergruppenspezifisch zu adressieren. Allerdings meine ich, dass sich Operators hier nicht einschränken sollten. Es macht durchaus Sinn Dienste oder auch ganze Dienste-Gruppen zu bündeln und diese bestimmten Endbenutzer-Gruppen wie z. B. Entwicklern bereitzustellen.

F33: Geringer Aufwand und Ressourcenverbrauch bei der Entwicklung?

A33: Der geringe Aufwand und Ressourcenverbrauch müsste aus meiner Sicht vor allem beim Testen berücksichtigt werden. Die Vielfalt an Plattformen und Testgeräten und das was eine derartige Applikation kosten darf, damit sie bei einer breiten Masse an Benutzern angenommen wird, muss im Verhältnis stehen. Ebenso Kosten für eine Endgeräte-Testlandschaft. Ich erinnere nur an das zuvor schon angesprochene Szenario mit den Apps.

F34: Bereitstellung einer personalisierten und offenen Plattform?

A34: Ich glaube das Thema Sicherheit ist in diesem Kontext ganz wichtig zu betrachten ist. Endbenutzer möchten ihre Zugänge und natürlich auch ihre Daten schützen und diese nach entsprechenden Sicherheitsmechanismen auf der SDP aufbewahrt wissen. Deshalb sind sowohl Zugang (Authentifizierung) wie auch das Speichern nach entsprechenden Sicherheitsrichtlinien notwendig.

F35: Benutzerfreundlichkeit und praktisches Arbeiten mit der SDP?

A35: Die Benutzerfreundlichkeit wird ein ganz entscheidendes Kriterium für die Bedienung einer SDP und somit für Ihre Akzeptanz bei den Kunden sein. Die besten Systeme scheitern oft daran, dass sie zu kompliziert zu handhaben sind. Eine einfache Navigation mit wenigen Maus-Klicken und eine einfache Verständlichkeit für potenzielle Benutzer ist im Zuge einer praktischen Arbeit mit einer SDP notwendig. Der Endbenutzer muss sich in ganz kurzer Zeit zurechtfinden und navigieren können. Zugriff auf Dienste und eigene abgespeicherte Informationen und Daten sollte einfach durchführbar sein.

F36: Welche SW wird zur Implementierung heutiger SDPs eingesetzt und wie gestaltet sich deren Bedienbarkeit?

A36:

F37: Multisprachen-Fähigkeit?

A37: Multisprachenfähigkeit undbedingt ja, da man eine derartige Plattform natürlich länderübergreifend und international zum Einsatz bringen wird.

F38: Welche Sicherheits- und Datenschutz-Mechanismen sollten aus Ihrer Sicht eingesetzte werden?

A38: 2-Faktor Authentifizierung zur Anmeldung mit Passwort und Pin oder Pin und Token um zwei Beispiele zu nennen ist unbedingt notwendig, um den Zugriff von nichtberechtigten Dritten Personen abzuwehren und möglichst auszuschließen. Weiters gilt es im Zuge des jeweiligen Landesspezifischen Datenschutzgesetzes entsprechende Mechanismen vorzusehen, welche den potenziellen Zugriff von unberechtigten Personen erschwert.

F39: Wie kann ein Schutz der Privatsphäre für jeden einzelnen Benutzer umgesetzt werden?

A39:

F40: Schutz vor Gewalt Rassismus und Pornografie?

A40:

F41: Mit welchen Kosten ist für eine SDP im Rahmen des "Any Network on any Device Szenarios" zu rechnen?

A41: Diese Frage ist schwierig zu beantworten, da es immer von den entsprechenden Anforderungen und den potenziell möglich zu betrachtenden Endbenutzerkreis abhängig ist. Um eine SDP mit IMS Funktionalität bereitzustellen und einer potenziellen Anzahl von 100.000 Benutzern wird man schon mit ca. € 1Mio. Investitionskosten und ca. € 200-300k Betriebskosten pro Jahr rechnen müssen.

F42: Sehen Sie einen Weg indem man das Angebot verschiedenster Dienste – und -gruppen kostengünstiger gestalten könnte?

A42: Desto mehr Benutzer und Dienste bzw. Applikationen desto günstiger der Betrieb und desto höher die Margin für den Betreiber.

F43: Wie würden Sie den Umgang mit den Betriebskosten bei einer SDP einschätzen? Werden sich diese verhältnismäßig erhöhen oder erniedrigen im Vergleich zu beispielsweise heute bestehenden unterschiedlichsten Portalen welche bereits Dienste für mobile Endbenutzer anbieten?

A43: Aus meiner Sicht mit dem Anstieg an Services und Benutzern abnehmen.

F44: Wie würden Sie den Umgang mit den Systemkosten bei Neuinstallation einer SDP einschätzen? Werden sich diese verhältnismäßig erhöhen oder erniedrigen im Vergleich zu den heutigen Dienste-Portalen?

A44: Neuinstallation bleibt Neuinstallation und wird heutzutage gerade im Zeitalter der Einführung von LTE eher teurer werden.

F45: Wie würden Sie den Umgang mit den Inbetriebnahmekosten bei Neuinstallation einer SDP einschätzen? Werden sich diese verhältnismäßig erhöhen oder erniedrigen im Vergleich zu den heutigen Dienste-Portalen?

A45: Selbiges gilt hier für die Inbetriebnahme-Kosten.

F46: Mit welchen Kosten ist für Einführung neuer und zusätzlicher Dienste zu rechnen?

A46: Diese nehmen proportional mit der Anzahl an Benutzern ab.

F47: Risikokosten für Standardisierung im Rahmen der Einführung einer SDP?

A47: Ich sehe keine Kosten für Risiken im Rahmen der Einführung von Standardtechnologien.

F48: Gibt es aus Ihrer Sicht einen wesentlichen Aspekt den wir in Verbindung mit einer SDP berücksichtigen müssten um ein derartiges Szenario abzubilden?

A48:

Fragen zu Anwendungen und Diensten aus der Benutzer-zentrierten Sicht:

F49: Welche Kategorien von Endgeräten sehen Sie für zukünftige allgegenwärtige breitbandige Anwendungen im Rahmen des "Any Network on any Device" Szenarios?

A49: Ich glaube das es weiterhin Handies, Smartphone, Tablets, Laptops und PCs geben wird. All diese Geräte müssen dem Aspekt der Mobilität Genüge tun und neben den entsprechenden technischen Voraussetzungen auch das Verhalten der Benutzer berücksichtigen. Lassen Sie mich ein Beispiel geben. Technische Voraussetzungen sind glaube ich ziemlich klar um das oben genannte Szenario abzubilden: Dazu bedarf es der Integration von IMS und SIP. Benutzerverhalten lehnt sich sehr stark an die Analyse von einzelnen Testfällen unterschiedlicher Benutzer an um dann daraus ableiten zu können, dass entweder mehr Fokus auf dem Themenbereich Benutzer Management und Verhalten gerichtet werden muss und somit Rückschlüsse auf die Bedienung der Endgeräte geschlossen werden kann.

F50: Welche Aspekte muss ein mobiles Endgerät unbedingt aufweisen um Multimediaanwendungen zu unterstützen um diese Anwendungen auch effizient einsetzen zu können?

A50: Ein mobiles Endgerät muss Breitbandübertragungstechnologie (ab 3G sowie auch Wi-Max) kompatibel sein und diese Technologie bereitstellen. Weiters ist ein Farb-Multimedia-Display mit hoher Auflösung notwendig. Context-

Aware Content muss via Internet-Browser (Internet oder web-based Applikation) zur Verfügung stehen.

F51: Wie werden sich die Endgeräte bezüglich des Energieverbrauches im Betrieb in Zukunft verhalten müssen?

A51: Durch immer mehr Leistung am Smartphone und kleineren Baugrößen wird es schwierig bei sich nicht verändernder Energie-Basistechnologie das selbe aus einem Akku rauszuholen. Alternative Energiequellen wie Solarzellen oder Fotovolthaik sind noch nicht in der Lage ähnliche Ergebnisse bereitzustellen.

F52: Geringe Umweltbelastung in der Herstellung, Betrieb und Entsorgung?

A52:

F53: Rechnen Sie mit einer Zunahme der Mobilität der einzelnen Benutzer in den nächsten Jahren? Wenn ja, wie wird sich das auf die Endgeräte auswirken?

A53: Ja, es werden noch mehr Endgeräte gekauft und benutzt werden.

F54: Welche Einflussfaktoren sehen Sie um sicherzustellen, dass die Möglichkeit des Austausches von Informationen und Daten möglichst effizient ausgeschöpft werden kann?

A54: Mobilität, Verschmelzung der beiden Welten IT und Kommunikationstechnologien, Immer größer werdende Anzahl an Internet und web-Plattform Benutzern, Servicekreativität bei den Entwicklern. Druck an neuen Diensten und Anwendungen kommt von Benutzern selbst.

F55: Umgang mit einer stetig anwachsenden Anzahl von Endgeräten und Anwendungen?

A55: Ich meine dass hier Standardtechnologien und Schnittstellen immer wichtiger werden.

F56: Standardisierte Dienste und Schnittstellen?

A56:

F57: Praktisches Arbeiten in Verbindung mit der SDP/auf der SDP vom mobilen Endgerät?

A57:

F58: Eingesetzte SW und Bedienbarkeit dieser?

A58:

F59: Multisprachen-Fähigkeit?

A59:

F60: Wie kann sich die Benutzerinteraktion zwischen mobilen Endgerät und der SDP gestalten und wie kann sichergestellt werden, dass kontextbewusste Informationen dem jeweiligen Benutzer bereitgestellt werden?

A60:

F61: Informationsdienste, welche durch Benutzer personalisiert werden können?

A61: Jeder Endbenutzer muss selbstverständlich in der Lage sein seine Dienste die er/sie verwendet zu personalisieren und das eigene Portfolio an gewünschten Diensten abzubilden und bereitzustellen.

F62: Allgegenwärtige, mobile Kontext-bezogene Informationsdienste?

A62: Sind im Zuge der Vielfältigkeit an Endgeräten undbeding notwendig. Ebenso ist es notwendig Informationen sogar Benutzerspezifisch bereitzustellen. Fachleute für Medizin werden sich für andere Inhalte als Journalisten interessieren. Auch hier könnte man bereits gruppenspezifischen Kontext bereitstellen.

F63: Schutzmechanismen (Sicherheit und Datenschutz)?

A63:

F64: Wie kann man künftig sicherstellen, dass kostengünstige Endgeräte für alle Benutzergruppen bereitgestellt werden? Warum?

A64: Der Druck am Endgerätemarkt bleibt weiterhin groß und treibt die Preise nach unten. Der Wettbewerb der Betreiber wird auch größer, weil es künftig durch das Outsourcing und Service-Provider Geschäft immer mehr Anbieter geben wird, die ihre Kunden durch entsprechende Maßnahmen länger binden werden wollen. Eine entsprechende Vertragslaufzeit für eine Service-Delivery-Plattform mit entsprechend leistungsfähigen Services dahinter ist durchwegs mit der Bereitstellung eines entsprechenden Endgerätes für Endkunden denkbar. So wie das derzeitige Modell der Mobilfunkprovider in Österreich zum Beispiel

F65: Wie kann man künftig sicherstellen, dass kostenfrei/-günstig auf Informationen und Wissen zugegriffen werden kann?

A65:

F66: Gibt es aus Ihrer Sicht einen wesentlichen Aspekt der in Verbindung mit der Endgerätevielfalt und dem stetig wachsenden Kontextbewusstsein berücksichtig werden müsste um ein derartiges Szenario abzubilden?

A66:

Fragen zum Abschluss:

F67: Welches Gesamturteil würden Sie für die Einführung einer SDP wie z.B. SPICE geben?

A67: Ich meine dass eine SDP wie SPICE einen großen Mehrwert für einen potenziellen Web-Plattform-Benutzer bringen würde, weil er/sie die Möglichkeit besitzt jederzeit "any network on any device" auf Dienste und Anwendungen sowie eigene Daten zugreifen und diese verwenden zu können.

F68:: Wie würden Sie das Aufwand-Nutzen-Verhältnis einer SDP wie SPICE einschätzen?

A68:

Herzlichen Dank für das Interview.

10.2 Fact Finding Tool Result

Figure 78 shows three excerpts of the Fact Finding Tool with the colour-coded text passages related to the interview participants (p11_u, p12_d, p13_u and p14_d) and the final categories (shown for "Applicability"; "Interoperability" and "Mobility"). The whole FFT for all interviews and categories are available on DVD.

Category: Applicability
Sub-Category: Wide Field of Services
Sub-Category: Context Awareness

Interview 01 (p11_u)
F2: Sollen alle Bürger Zugang zu öffentlichen Netzen bekommen? Wenn ja, wie könnte dies realisiert werden?

A2: Ja, ich finde schon. Desto mehr Benutzer, desto stärker wird die Nachfrage an Anwendungen und das hilft wiederum den Betreibern ihre Investitionskosten zu decken, sie werden deshalb noch mehr in Infrastruktur und Services investieren, weil sie sich dadurch klarerweise einen Geschäftszuwachs erwarten. Es gibt viele Möglichkeiten von Zugriffen, zwei davon sehe ich als realistisch an: 1. Telefonnetzwerke mit entsprechendem Empowerment um z.B. Multimedia Applications streamen zu können. Dazu gibt es sicherzustellen, das eine UMTS/HSPA Infrastruktur oder LTE flächendecken zumindest in Ballungszentren zur Verfügung stellt. Die W-LAN und Wi-Fi Technologie kann bei eine großflächigen Abdeckung z.B. in Städten wie Wien, Graz, usw. einen kostengünstigen

Interview 02 (p12_d)
F55: Umgang mit einer stetig anwachsenden Anzahl von Endgeräten und Anwendungen?

A55: Die stetig anwachsende Anzahl an Endgeräten kann man heute als Anbieter durch die zunehmende Standardisierung und den damit verbundenen Einsatz von Standard-Schnittstellen gut kontrollieren. Die permanent und immer schnellere Zuwachsrate an Angeboten für neue Anwendungen wird man im eigenen Interesse als Anbieter von Services und Applikationen bis zu einem gewissen Grad unterstützen müssen, da eine Vielfalt an Möglichkeiten von Applikationen für unterschiedlichste Anforderungen unterschiedlichste Kundenbereiche anspricht. Ein gutes Beispiel hierfür sind Apps. Die Entwicklung von Apps am iPhone oder auch für Android impliziert das Testen auf vielen unterschiedlichen Testendgeräten, was mit großem Aufwand und Kosten verbunden ist, wobei die Anwendung selbst um einen kleinen

Interview 03 (p13_u)
F65: Wie kann man künftig sicherstellen, dass kostenfrei/kostengünstig auf Informationen und Wissen zugegriffen werden kann?

A65: Da Netzwerk- aber auch Service und Applikationsprovider viel in den Aufbau ihrer Infrastrukturen investiert haben und auch der Betrieb bzw die Wartung dieser Systeme operativ eine menge Geld kostet, ist es sehr wichtig hier über die Masse an potenziellen Kunden zu verkaufen. Deshalb ist sowohl von der Netzwerk- wie auch Endgeräte-Seite her sicherzustellen, dass die Anschaffungs- wie auch Betriebskosten gering bleiben, sodass letztendlich auch die Kosten für den Endbenutzer überschaubar bleiben. Eine breite Palette an Diensten und Anwendungen sichert eine breite Streuung über unterschiedlichste Kundensegmente. Die Vielfalt an Möglichkeiten und eine rasche Umsetzung bei den Kunden durch das Erkennen eines Mehrwertes sichern den Erfolg einer SDP zumindest istd as meine

Interview 04 (p14_d)
F29: In welcher Form sollte die Plattform die Bereitstellung von Diensten und Endgeräten unterstützen?

A29: Ein wichtiger Punkt ist sich zu überlegen wie Anwendungs- und Serviceprovider ihren Kunden Anwendungen Dienste und Applikationen rasch und in einem großem Umfang flexibel bereitstellen können. Das heutige Problem mit dem Wildwuchs an Endgeraten auf dem Markt ist, dass kaum ein Anwender seine Anwendungen auf allen Plattformen geschweige denn auf allen Endgeräten anbieten und bereitstellen kann. Sie können sich also vorstellen, dass ein Versionswechsel noch schwieriger zu handhaben wird auf Grund der Vielfalt an Unterstützungs-Notwendigkeiten. Um so wichtiger wird das Thema Service-Bereitstellung. Desto schneller ein Anbieter hier in Zukunft aggieren wird können, desto stärker wird er die Nase vorne haben können.

Category: Interoperability

Sub-Category: Compatibility to ICT-Systems, Interfaces & Components

Sub-Category: Compatibility to ICT-Standards

Sub-Category: Infrastructure Reusability

Sub-Category: Cost Effectiveness

Interview 01 (p11_u)

F10: Ist eine Einbindung der bestehenden Infrastruktur notwendig? Warum?

A10: Aus meiner Sicht definitiv ja. Weil die Betreiber in der Vergangenheit sehr viele Investitionen getätigt haben und die ... Das ist im übrigen auch der Grund warum immer noch ... – ich glaube man sagt abwärtskompatibel? Aus meiner Sicht ist es heute unbedingt notwendig, dass ...

Interview 02 (p12_d)

F56: Standardisierte Dienste und Schnittstellen?

A56: Entwickler müssen sicherstellen, dass entwickelte ... eingesetzt um Benutzern in Abhängigkeit von der aktuellen Lokation Informationen bereitzustellen. Weiters wird bei aktuellen Entwicklungen im Handy Umfeld z. B. der ... da nach dem Einschalten sehr lange für eine erste Positionsbestimmung benötigt. Ich glaube dass sowohl bei der ...

Cell-ID zu ungenau ist (100-150m) und GPS

Interview 03 (p13_u)

F29: In welcher Form sollte die Plattform die Bereitstellung von Diensten und Endgeräten unterstützen?

A29: Um Dienste über eine SDP Benutzern mit ihren mobilen Endgeräten bereitzustellen, ist es notwendig diese auf der SDP möglichst einfach handhabar bereitzustellen, da viele Anwendungen nicht dadurch scheitern, dass sie keinen etwas keinen Nutzen bringen, sondern, dass sie unübersichtlich und schwierige zu verstehen und zu handhaben sind. Dies ist mit ...

Beispiel mit einer ...

Interview 04 (p14_d)

F29: In welcher Form sollte die Plattform die Bereitstellung von Diensten und Endgeräten unterstützen?

A29: Ich denke Benutzer müssen in der Lage es sein Zurff auf ihre ... ... was natürlich eine Frage des Kapitals ist. Aber damit alleine ist es noch nicht abgetan. Weiters ist es notwendig ... Dies kann zum ...

Category: Mobility

Sub-Category: Availability

Sub-Category: Stability & Session Control

Sub-Category: Always on

Sub-Category: Any Network on any Device

Interview 01 (p11_u)

F6: Wie stehen Sie zu dem Thema Netzzugänge müssen heute bei der Arbeit, zu Hause verfügbar sein, da man als Benutzer heute erreichbar sein sollte?

A6: Internet ist privat wie auch für die Arbeit unabdingbar. Deshalb ist eine ... Ich persönlich empfinde dies als eine sehr subjektiv zu beantwortende Frage und mein selbst, dass ich wie mir damit mein Arbeits- wie auch Privatleben sehr gut entteilen und auch steuern kann eine

Interview 02 (p12_d)

F14: Was gibt es an Kernfeatures zu erfüllen um zukünftige Dienste - ubiquitäre Services) auszulegen?

A14: Die Benutzer die SDPs verwenden können ihre Services personalisieren und sie Wichtig dabei ist, dass die Dabei spielen und einer und d.h. technische ... Die ...

Interview 03 (p13_u)

F2: Sollen alle Bürger Zugang zu öffentlichen Netzen bekommen? Wenn ja, wie könnte dies realisiert werden?

A2: Ja, für mich ist es nur ein Mehrwert wenn ich mein ... Dazu benötige ich den Zugang zum Internet. Eine Realisation ist aus meiner Sicht ganz einfach mit ... Ich denke das ...

Interview 04 (p14_d)

F21: Wie wird sich das Thema Mobilität auf Standardisierung und Bereitstellung von Standardschnittstellen auswirken?

A21: Meiner Meinung nach ist die Integration der Standardtechnologien IMS und SIP der wichtigste Treiber dafür Endbenutzern die Möglichkeit zu offenerten ihre

Figure 78: Excerpts of the Fact Finding tool for participants p11_u, p12_d, p13_u and p14_d and the colour-coded text of the interviews

10.3   Literature-Based Criteria Catalogue

The following illustrations presents some excerpts regarding the literature-based criteria catalogue. Figure 79 presents an excerpt of the detailed criteria catalogue in bullet point form with a reference to the original literature.

Design Aspects for Service Delivery Platforms (SPICE)

General Aspects

- Provide an easy and simple way to create and roll out innovative services to reduce development time and introduction of costs and risks
- Provide a unified and seamless way to deliver services over heterogeneous execution platforms, network and terminal
- Enrich the service landscape, through an overlay structure supporting the users and offering a personalized user experience anytime, anyplace
- Create a trusted and open platform that will simplify the use of services and devices through personalisation and customisation
- Enrich current service platform functionality with content management and distribution, features and intelligent service-controlled context-information processing
- Open-up to new business models and value chains
- Enable Pan-European service provisioning
- Promote the uptake of innovative IT software technologies in a telecommunications grade service platform environment **[Advanced Beyond 3G service delivery environment: the SPICE service platform design principles]**
- Redefine the role of Telcommunication companies - from access to service provider regarding blurring roles and enabling new business models
- Hide complexity and heterogeneity and taking benefit of existing variety of services, networks and devices
- Make services intelligent and easier to use (Assist users)
- Inter-domain aspects - service provisioning, inter-working - Pan European service delivery platform
- Provide services timely - accelerate creation and delivery of services (fast service creation; reduce time-to-market for new services)
- Open platform capabilities to 3rd parties
- Support multi-vendor, multi-technology middleware platforms **[SPICE Overview and Architecture - Presentation]**
- Identity Provisioning - allow the user's home platform operator (or their trusted identity provider) to assert their identity to service components or 3rd party service providers, while preserving their pseudonymity or anonymity
- Charging and Billing - allow users to easily pay for connectivity, services and goods while allowing the operators to take a small premium from each service
- Improved service provisioning (e.g., through push technologies, search engines, or context aware service offering)
- Personalization and adaptation to specific situations, thus making mobile and converged services easier to use
- Media and content management (e.g., end user generated content, protected media)
- Service roaming - allow the user to access services from the home platform, and/or matching services from the visited platform

- Autonomous systems
- Support for new mobility modes: user, network and session mobility
- Semantic Web Services based middleware automatic service composition and processes on the top of the Semantic Web Services middleware **[Mobile Service Platforms Cluster - White Paper - Mobile Service Platforms – Architecture]**
- Time to market for new services developments is too long due to a lack of suitable service creation environment and to a vertical design approach
- Integration and deployment cost are too high due to the inherent complexity and heterogeneity of service execution environments
- Service provisioning involves more and more parties - Telco, content/service providers, third party networks and service providers, and even end-users - increasing the complexity of the environment in which services must live
- Users own many different communication devices and are surrounded by many access technologies but they usually cannot handle the complexity of accessing their services via several of these devices. In these cases, they look to the access and service providers for help
- Continuity of service from fixed to mobile access and seamless roaming of services across operators and network is far from being a reality **[Advanced Beyond 3G service delivery environment: the SPICE service platform design principles]**
- The concept of contextually aware environment for the user aiming at presenting the right information to the right users, at the right time and in the right place
- The heterogeneous network must thus have sufficient knowledge with respect to users and devices that exist within it, their interests and capabilities, and the tasks and activities that are being undertaken
- The system must be able to identify where, and under what context each user is engaged with the current task
- Context awareness includes the concept of user position knowledge that may be utilized in the provision of Location Based Services (LBS) [3]. As an example, we may mention network operators pushing custom advertising and other information to their subscribers based on their current location or profile **[Designing a service platform for B3G environments]**
- Service Creation Environment: A set of development and hosting tools for third-party service developers
- Profile/Identity Management: This is a component that manages general user data and user preferences for various services and user preferences for multiple user situations
- Service Provisioning/Service Brokerage: The broker represents the reference point for end-users to retrieve, subscribe and use Services and Service Components
- Charging & Billing: Charging and billing components are essential when considering service architecture development **[An Advertisement-based Platform Business Model for Mobile Operators]**
- Re-using existing service enablers in a fast and easy way
- Opening the networks for 3rd parties which can faster adapt to markets need when creating new services, business models, and value chains

- Unifying charging and billing, allowing users to easily pay for connectivity, services and other goods while allowing the operators to take a small premium from each service
- Simplified service provisioning and service discovery, thus making the life of the end-user easier
- Personalization and situation adaptation, which makes mobile and converged services easier to use and allowing new revenue models e.g. targeted advertisement
- Mediation providers supporting creation of service bundles from different players in the market **[SPICE: Evolving IMS to Next Generation Service Platforms]**

Special Aspects

- Service Lifecycle Management
  - Hiding the heterogeneous service execution platforms
  - Managing the personal communication sphere (devices,groups, networks)
  - Creating autonomous systems
  - Context/knowledge management
  - Automatic service composition
  - End-user/3rd party service development environments
  - Service Roaming **[Mobile Service Platforms Cluster White Paper Service Lifecycle Management]**
- User-centric Approach
  - The platform provider reduces development expenses while fulfilling customers' expectations. In the process, it obtains some profit from the use of its own services and a percentage of the profit from services created by end-users
  - End-users can create their own personalized services that fit their needs better
  - Users are allowed to share their services within a community, the most interesting ones tend to get advertised at a minimum cost through mechanisms such as the Viral Marketing
  - Users are allowed to recommend services, a set of high value services will flourish and succeed from among the great pool of services that may arise in a user-centric platform **[A USER-CENTRIC SERVICE CREATION APPROACH FOR NEXT GENERATION NETWORKS]**
- Context and Knowledge Management
  - Identification of the use and representation of information using Ontologies and other methods
  - Identification of relevant context information for each project : description/modelling
  - The uses of context such as adapting services, networks
  - Context Gathering, Interpretation, Synthesis and Reasoning
  - Context Publication and Discovery Profiles (Group / User / Service) : Negotiation , Management, Description **[Mobile Service Platforms Cluster White Paper Context and Knowledge Management]**
- Context Aquisition
  - Acquisition of information of visual character (primarily due to the complexity of its acquisition) - information which is acquired by humans via their senses of taste and smell, and human emotions and mood

(acquiring and utilizing context information of previously unexplored types has a potential to bring innovative services)

- o Context acquisition from a physical perspective include addressing distribution, heterogeneity and scalability challenges (Sensors are distributed over various (heterogeneous) mobile and fixed devices; Sensors are distributed over various administrative domains, e.g., home and office environment; In a real world context-aware system, many sensors are deployed, and a growing number of services are expected to utilize the produced sensor information generating an increased information flow) **[Context Acquisition, Representation and Employment in Mobile Service Platforms]**

- Charging and Billing
  - o Charging in a context where business models and roles envolved Ò Providing flexible charging schemes
  - o Charging in a context of several administrative domains Ò Identifying the applicable tariff and payment methods
  - o Charging of any types of services Ò Supporting several charging models : online and offline
  - o Charging of composite services Ò Providing means to correlate information **[SPICE: Charging and Billing - Presentation]**
- Adaption of Services
  - o Dynamic adaptation: the service should be dynamically adapted depending on the user context. Moreover, changes in the context should be followed by a re-evaluation and re-adaptation of the service
  - o Input/output adaptation: the adaptation mechanisms should apply to both the output and input models of the service. The service should be rendered in the most appropriate modality and the rendering component available to the end-user. Moreover, the end-user should b able to interact with the service using the most natural modality and using the most appropriate interaction component available to the end-user
  - o Non-obtrusive adaptation: the adaptation process should be the as unobtrusive as possible, thus limiting the impact on the end-user experience. The motto is: "the service follows and adapts to the user". Nevertheless, for usability reasons, the adaptation should not be completely automatic and the end-user should be able to approve/disapprove the adaptation decisions **[Mobile Service Platforms Cluster White Paper Service Adaptation over Heterogeneous Infrastructures]**

Relies on IMS as enabling technologies (Service Delivery Platform Architecture linking to IMS and embedding a knowledge layer)
Enhanced with semantics and knowledge management
Component-based middleware layer ensuring the inter-working of distributed servic components
Advanced semantically-enhanced service creation and composition tools
Definition and Setup of a distributed Service Execution Environment with different execution engines
Content management and delivery framework integrated in the SDP
Definition of a multi-faceted mobile service ontology, used throughout the project
Distributed Communication Sphere Management System, comprising

Figure 79: Excerpt of a detailed criteria catalogue in bullet point form

To present the general and detailed criteria catalogue in the end stage, the researcher chose also a representation form of Mind Maps. The following figures summarised the general as well as the detailed criteria catalogue for this research. Figure 80 represents the Mind Map representation form of a general criteria catalogue.

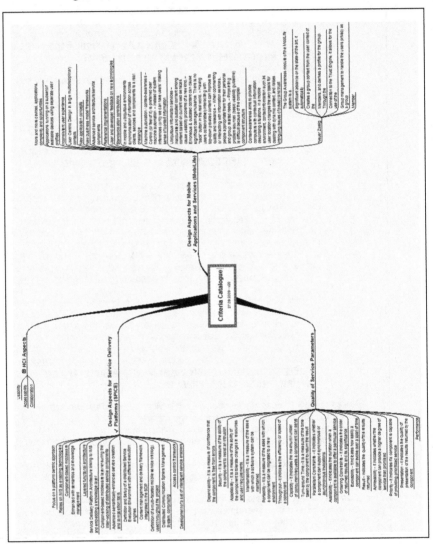

Figure 80: Excerpt of a criteria catalogue in mind map form

Figure 81 and Figure 82 were analysed by the CIT techniques as well as the interview guideline to structure due to the complex aspects of SDPs, so that the language focused on as many incidents and occurrences as possible. In this way, the author laid down the basis for a later analysis of the interviews, in order to maximise relevant content from the topics. Both figures represent the Mind Map form of a general CIT-analysed criteria catalogue.

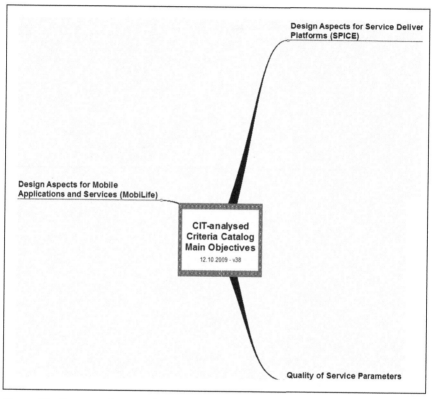

Figure 81: Excerpt of a general CIT-analysed criteria catalogue in mind map form (main objectives)

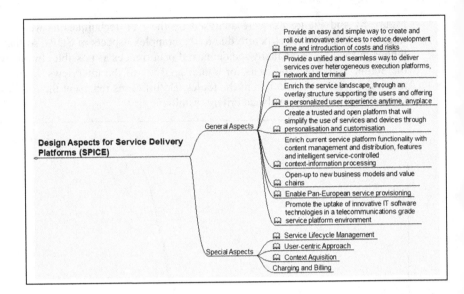

Quality of Service Parameters

- Dependability - It is a measure of confidence that the component is free from errors
- Security - It is a measure of the ability of the component to resist an intrusion
- Adaptability - It is a measure of the ability of the component to tolerate changes in resources and user requirements
- Maintainability - It is a measure of the ease with which a software system can be maintained
- Portability - It is a measure of the ease with which a component can be migrated to a new environment
- Throughput - It indicates the efficiency or speed of a component
- Capacity - It indicates the maximum number of concurrent requests a component can serve
- Turn-around Time - It is a measure of the time taken by the component to return the result
- Parallelism Constraints - It indicates whether a component can support synchronous or asynchronous invocations
- Availability - It indicates the duration when a component is available to offer a particular service
- Ordering Constraints - It indicates the order of returned results and its significance
- Evolvability - It indicates how easily a component can evolve over a span of time
- Result - Indicates the quality of the results returned
- Achievability - It indicates whether the component can provide a higher degree of service than promised
- Priority - It indicates if a component is capable of providing prioritized service
- Presentation - It indicates the quality of presentation of the results returned by the component
- Performance

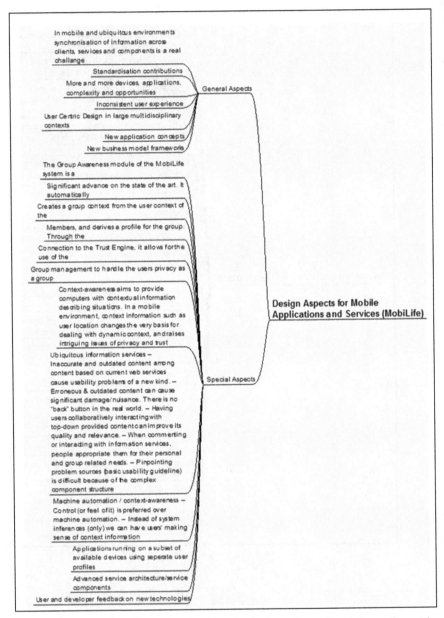

Figure 82: Excerpt of a general CIT-analysed criteria catalogue in mind map form (objectives from second hierarchy)

The following Figure 83 and Figure 84 represent the Mind Map form of a detailed CIT-analysed criteria catalogue:

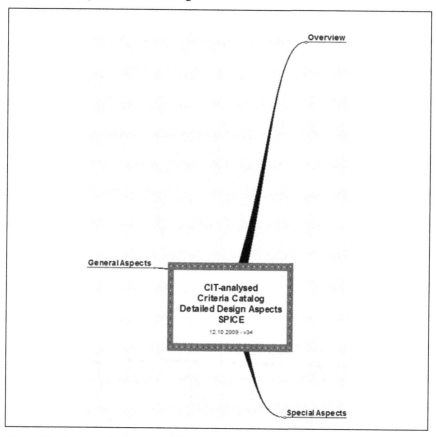

Figure 83: Excerpt of a detailed CIT-analysed criteria catalogue in mind map form (main objectives)

The following Figure 84 represents the Mind Map form of a detailed CIT-analysed criteria catalogue:

Overview

Relies on IMS as enabling technologies (Service Delivery Platform Architecture linking to IMS and embedding a knowledge layer)

Enhanced with semantics and knowledge management

Component-based middleware layer ensuring the inter-working of distributed service components

Advanced semantically-enhanced service creation and composition tools

Definition and Setup of a distributed Service Execution Environment with different execution engines

Content management and delivery framework integrated in the SDP

Definition of a multi-faceted mobile service ontology, used throughout the project

Distributed Communication Sphere Management System, comprising

Access control framework

Development of a set of Intelligent service enablers

General Aspects

- Charging and Billing - allow users to easily pay for connectivity, services and goods while allowing the operators to take a small premium from each service

- Improved service provisioning (e.g., through push technologies, search engines, or context aware service offering)

- Personalization and adaptation to specific situations, thus making mobile and converged services easier to use

- Media and content management (e.g., end user generated content, protected media)

- Service roaming - allow the user to access services from the home platform, and/or matching services from the visited platform

- Support for new mobility modes: user, network and session mobility

- Autonomous systems

- Semantic Web Services based middleware automatic service composition and processes on the top of the Semantic Web Services middleware

- Time to market for new services developments is too long due to a lack of suitable service creation environment and to a vertical design approach

- Integration and deployment cost are too high due to the inherent complexity and heterogeneity of service execution environments

- Service provisioning involves more and more parties - Telco, content/service providers, third party networks and service providers, and even end-users - increasing the complexity of the environment in which services must live

- Users own many different communication devices and are surrounded by many access technologies but they usually cannot handle the complexity of accessing their services via several of these devices. In these cases, they look to the access and service providers for help

- Continuity of service from fixed to mobile access and seamless roaming of services across operators and network is far from being a reality

- The concept of contextually aware environment for the user aiming at presenting the right information to the right users, at the right time and in the right place

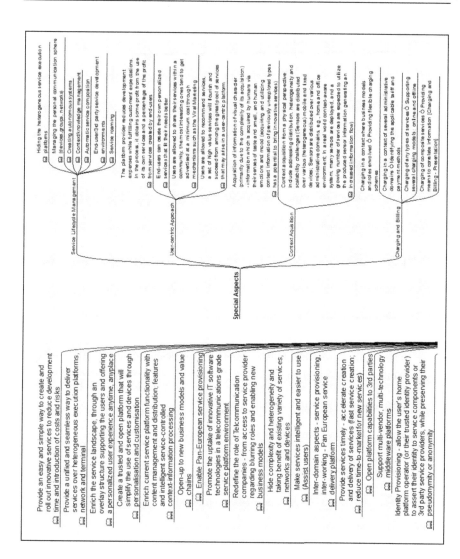

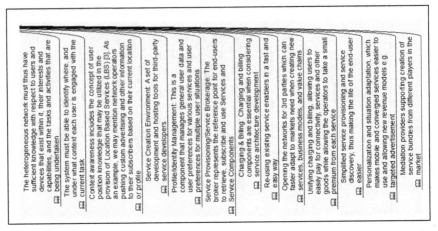

Figure 84: Excerpt of a detailed CIT-analysed criteria catalogue in mind map form (objectives from second hierarchy)

10.4 List of Mind Maps

The following both tables presents an overview about all Mind Maps created within this research study. Table 37 presents an overview about the Mind Maps that are also presented as general results or sub-results in this PhD thesis (see the third column "Illustrated in section ...").

Table 37: List of Mind Maps generated and presented in this thesis

Mind Maps generated and presented in the study	Description	Illustrated in section
Functional requirements of an ICT system of the future	Final result representation of the study; *result of the Mapping Process (comparison and validation of empirical and literature-based data) seen from a generic level*	Paragraph 5.5.1.2, Figure 52
General requirements on an ICT infrastructure	Sub-result of the Mapping Process	Section 4.4.1, Figure 30
Grouping and structuring result – Requirements for the service creation and provisioning platform	Sub-result of the Mapping Process	Section 4.4.2, Figure 34
Functional requirements of an SDP for an ICT system of the future as a result of the Mapping Process seen from a meta level	Final result representation of the study; *result of the Mapping Process (comparison and validation of empirical and literature-based data) seen from a meta level*	Paragraph 5.5.1.3, Figure 53
Requirements for an ICT infrastructure of the future	Sub-result of the Mapping Process	Section 4.4.1, Figure 31
Requirements for the creation, provision and execution platform	Sub-result of the Mapping Process	Section 4.4.1, Figure 32
Requirements on the services and mobile applications from a user-centered perspective	Sub-result of the Mapping Process	Section 4.4.1, Figure 33

Table 38 below presents other Mind Maps as part of intermediate data the Mapping generated and related to the study. These intermediate data are shown in the original language created, in German.

Table 38: List of Mind Maps generated as intermediate data within the study (presented in the original language created, in German)

Mind Maps generated as intermediate results in this study	Description	Illustrated in section
Anforderungen and die Dienste und mobilen Anwendungen aus der Benutzer-zentrierten Sicht	Intermediate result of the literature-based Mapping Process	see Section 10.5
Anforderungen an die Dienstentwicklung und –bereitstellung	Intermediate result of the literature-based Mapping Process	see Section 10.5
Allgemeine Anforderungen an eine ICT-Infrastruktur	Intermediate result of the literature-based Mapping Process	see Section 10.5
Anforderungen an die ICT-Infrastruktur aus Sicht der unterschiedlichen Zielgruppen – Nutzer; Betreiber/Kunden; Systemhersteller (Teil 1 und 2)	Intermediate result of the literature-based Mapping Process	see Section 10.5
Anforderungen an die ICT-Infrastruktur aus Sicht des technischen und wirtschaftlichen Umfeldes (Teil 1 und 2)	Intermediate result of the literature-based Mapping Process	see Section 10.5
Allgemeine Anforderungen an eine ICT-Infrastruktur der Zukunft	Intermediate result of the literature-based Mapping Process	see Section 10.5
Anforderungen an die Servicearchitektur für eine Dienste-Entwicklungs und –Bereitstellungsplattform	Intermediate result of the literature-based Mapping Process	see Section 10.5
Funktionale Anforderungen an die Dienstentwicklungs- und -bereitstellungs Plattform für ein ICT-System der Zukunft	Intermediate result of the literature-based Mapping Process	see Section 10.5
Allgemeine funktionale Anforderungen ein ICT-System der Zukunft	Intermediate result of the literature-based Mapping Process	see Section 10.5
Generelle Anforderungen an die Kommunikationsinfrastruktur in der ICT	Intermediate result of the literature-based Mapping Process	see Section 10.5
Logische Anforderungen an die Dienstentwicklungs- und –bereitstellungsplattform für ein ICT-System der Zukunft	Intermediate result of the literature-based Mapping Process	see Section 10.5

10.5 Examples of Generated Mind Maps (Intermediate data)

The following examples of generated Mind Maps are created within this study as intermediate results and these are presented in German (see Table 38).

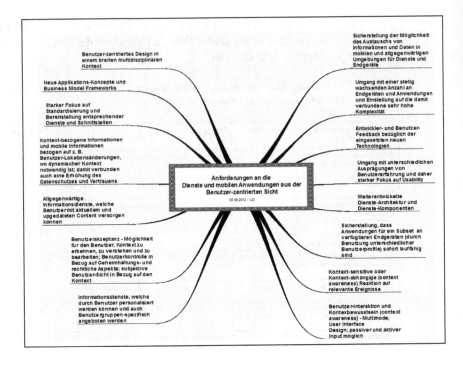

Benutzer-zentriertes Design in einem breiten multidisziplinären Kontext

Neue Applikations-Konzepte und Business Model Frameworks

Starker Fokus auf Standardisierung und Bereitstellung entsprechender Dienste und Schnittstellen

Kontext-bezogene Informationen und mobile Informationen bezogen auf z. B. Benutzer-Lokationsänderungen, wo dynamischer Kontext notwendig ist; damit verbunden auch eine Erhöhung des Datenschutzes und Vertrauens

Allgegenwärtige Informationsdienste, welche Benutzer mit aktuellem und upgedateten Content versorgen können

Benutzerakzeptanz - Möglichkeit für den Benutzer, Kontext zu erkennen, zu verstehen und zu bearbeiten; Benutzerkontrolle in Bezug auf Geheimhaltungs- und rechtliche Aspekte; subjektive Benutzer-Sicht in Bezug auf den Kontext

Informationsdienste, welche durch Benutzer personalisiert werden können und auch Benutzergruppen-spezifisch angeboten werden

Anforderungen an die Dienste und mobilen Anwendungen aus der Benutzer-zentrierten Sicht
05.09.2012 - v20

Sicherstellung der Möglichkeit des Austauschs von Informationen und Daten in mobilen und allgegenwärtigen Umgebungen für Dienste und Endgeräte

Umgang mit einer stetig wachsenden Anzahl an Endgeräten und Anwendungen und Einstellung auf die damit verbundene sehr hohe Komplexität

Entwickler- und Benutzer-Feedback bezüglich der eingesetzten neuen Technologien

Umgang mit unterschiedlichen Ausprägungen von Benutzererfahrung und daher starker Fokus auf Usability

Weiterentwickelte Dienste-Architektur und Dienste-Komponenten

Sicherstellung, dass Anwendungen für ein Subset an verfügbaren Endgeräten (durch Benutzung unterschiedlicher Benutzerprofile) sofort lauffähig sind

Kontext-sensitive oder Kontext-abhängige (context awareness) Reaktion auf relevante Ereignisse

Benutzer-Interaktion und Kontexbewusstsein (context awareness) - Multimode; User Interface Design; passiver und aktiver Input möglich

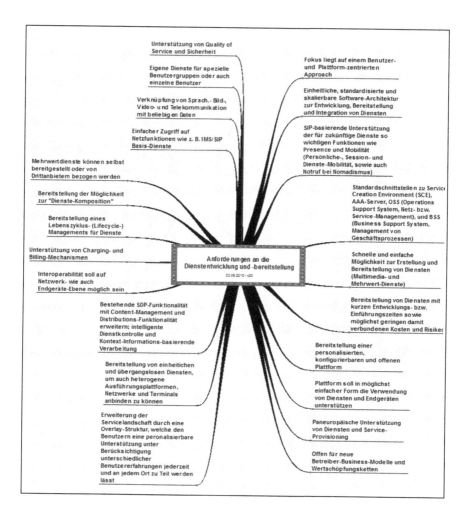

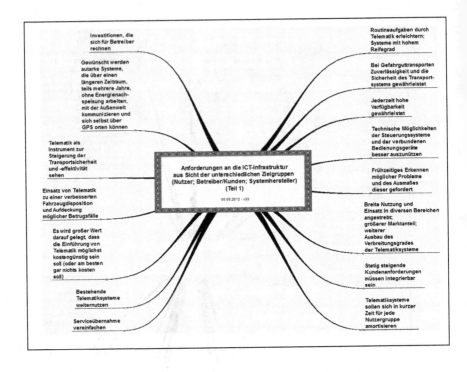

Investitionen, die
sich für Betreiber
rechnen

Gewünscht werden
autarke Systeme,
die über einen
längeren Zeitraum,
teils mehrere Jahre,
ohne Energienach-
speisung arbeiten,
mit der Außenwelt
kommunizieren und
sich selbst über
GPS orten können

Telematik als
Instrument zur
Steigerung der
Transportsicherheit
und -effektivität
sehen

Einsatz von Telematik
zu einer verbesserten
Fahrzeugdisposition
und Aufdeckung
möglicher Betrugsfälle

Es wird großer Wert
darauf gelegt, dass
die Einführung von
Telematik möglichst
kostengünstig sein
soll (oder am besten
gar nichts kosten
soll)

Bestehende
Telematiksysteme
weiternutzen

Serviceübernahme
vereinfachen

Anforderungen an die ICT-Infrastruktur
aus Sicht der unterschiedlichen Zielgruppen
(Nutzer; Betreiber/Kunden; Systemhersteller)
(Teil 1)

06.09.2012 - v33

Routineaufgaben durch
Telematik erleichtern;
Systeme mit hohem
Reifegrad

Bei Gefahrguttransporten
Zuverlässigkeit und die
Sicherheit des Transport-
systems gewährleistet

Jederzeit hohe
Verfügbarkeit
gewährleistet

Technische Möglichkeiten
der Steuerungssysteme
und der verbundenen
Bedienungsgeräte
besser auszunützen

Frühzeitiges Erkennen
möglicher Probleme
und des Ausmaßes
dieser gefordert

Breite Nutzung und
Einsatz in diversen Bereichen
angestrebt;
größerer Marktanteil;
weiterer
Ausbau des
Verbreitungsgrades
der Telematiksysteme

Stetig steigende
Kundenanforderungen
müssen integrierbar
sein

Telematiksysteme
sollen sich in kurzer
Zeit für jede
Nutzergruppe
amortisieren

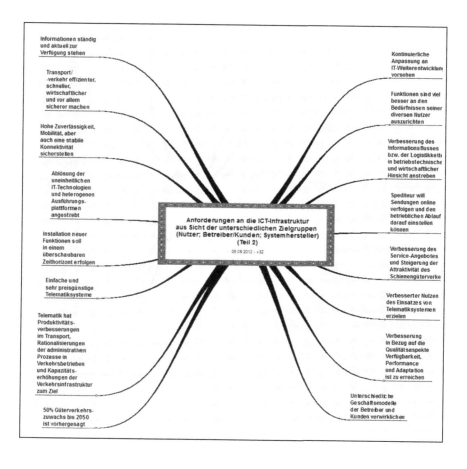

Informationen ständig und aktuell zur Verfügung stehen

Transport/-verkehr effizienter, schneller, wirtschaftlicher und vor allem sicherer machen

Hohe Zuverlässigkeit, Mobilität, aber auch eine stabile Konnektivität sicherstellen

Ablösung der uneinheitlichen IT-Technologien und heterogenen Ausführungsplattformen angestrebt

Installation neuer Funktionen soll in einem überschaubaren Zeithorizont erfolgen

Einfache und sehr preisgünstige Telematiksysteme

Telematik hat Produktivitätsverbesserungen im Transport, Rationalisierungen der administrativen Prozesse in Verkehrsbetrieben und Kapazitätserhöhungen der Verkehrsinfrastruktur zum Ziel

50% Güterverkehrszuwachs bis 2050 ist vorhergesagt

Anforderungen an die ICT-Infrastruktur aus Sicht der unterschiedlichen Zielgruppen (Nutzer; Betreiber/Kunden; Systemhersteller) (Teil 2)
06.09.2012 - v.32

Kontinuierliche Anpassung an IT-Weiterentwicklun vorsehen

Funktionen sind viel besser an den Bedürfnissen seiner diversen Nutzer auszurichten

Verbesserung des Informationsflusses bzw. der Logistikkett in betriebstechnische und wirtschaftlicher Hinsicht anstreben

Spediteur will Sendungen online verfolgen und den betrieblichen Ablauf darauf einstellen können

Verbesserung des Service-Angebotes und Steigerung der Attraktivität des Schienengüterverke

Verbesserter Nutzen des Einsatzes von Telematiksystemen erzielen

Verbesserung in Bezug auf die Qualitätsaspekte Verfügbarkeit, Performance und Adaptation ist zu erreichen

Unterschiedliche Geschäftsmodelle der Betreiber und Kunden verwirklichen

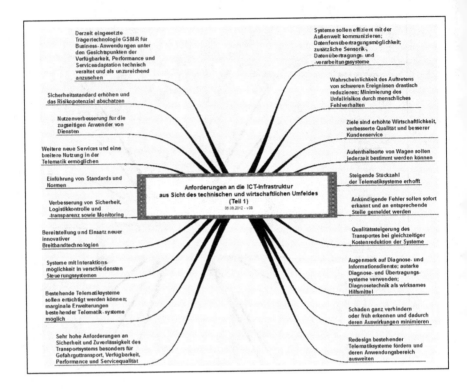

Derzeit eingesetzte Trägertechnologie GSM-R für Business-Anwendungen unter den Gesichtspunkten der Verfügbarkeit, Performance und Serviceadaptation technisch veraltet und als unzureichend anzusehen

Sicherheitsstandard erhöhen und das Risikopotenzial abschatzen

Nutzenverbesserung für die zugseitigen Anwender von Diensten

Weitere neue Services und eine breitere Nutzung in der Telematik ermöglichen

Einführung von Standards und Normen

Verbesserung von Sicherheit, Logistikkontrolle und -transparenz sowie Monitoring

Bereitstellung und Einsatz neuer innovativer Breitbandtechnologien

Systeme mit Interaktionsmöglichkeit in verschiedensten Steuerungssystemen

Bestehende Telematiksysteme sollen ertüchtigt werden können; marginale Erweiterungen bestehender Telematik-systeme möglich

Sehr hohe Anforderungen an Sicherheit und Zuverlässigkeit des Transportsystems besonders für Gefahrguttransport, Verfügbarkeit, Performance und Servicequalität

Systeme sollen effizient mit der Außenwelt kommunizieren; Datenfernübertragungsmöglichkeit; zusätzliche Sensorik-, Datenübertragungs- und -verarbeitungssysteme

Wahrscheinlichkeit des Auftretens von schweren Ereignissen drastisch reduzieren; Minimierung des Unfallrisikos durch menschliches Fehlverhalten

Ziele sind erhöhte Wirtschaftlichkeit, verbesserte Qualität und besserer Kundenservice

Aufenthaltsorte von Wagen sollen jederzeit bestimmt werden können

Steigende Stückzahl der Telematiksysteme erhofft

Ankündigende Fehler sollen sofort erkannt und an entsprechende Stelle gemeldet werden

Qualitätssteigerung des Transportes bei gleichzeitiger Kostenreduktion der Systeme

Augenmerk auf Diagnose- und Informationsdienste; autarke Diagnose- und Übertragungssysteme verwenden; Diagnosetechnik als wirksames Hilfsmittel

Schaden ganz verhindern oder früh erkennen und dadurch deren Auswirkungen minimieren

Redesign bestehender Telematiksysteme fördern und deren Anwendungsbereich ausweiten

Anforderungen an die ICT-Infrastruktur aus Sicht des technischen und wirtschaftlichen Umfeldes (Teil 1)
06.09.2012 - v38

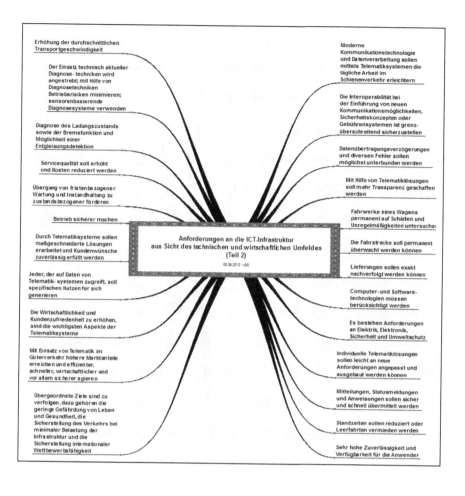

Erhöhung der durchschnittlichen Transportgeschwindigkeit

Der Einsatz technisch aktueller Diagnose- techniken wird angestrebt; mit Hilfe von Diagnosetechniken

Betriebsrisiken minimieren; sensorenbasierende Diagnosesysteme verwenden

Diagnose des Ladungszustands sowie der Bremsfunktion und Möglichkeit einer Entgleisungsdetektion

Servicequalität soll erhöht und Kosten reduziert werden

Übergang von fristenbezogener Wartung und Instandhaltung zu zustandsbezogener fördern

Betrieb sicherer machen

Durch Telematiksysteme sollen maßgeschneiderte Lösungen erarbeitet und Kundenwünsche zuverlässig erfüllt werden

Jeder, der auf Daten von Telematik- systeme zugreift, soll spezifischen Nutzen für sich generieren

Die Wirtschaftlichkeit und Kundenzufriedenheit zu erhöhen, sind die wichtigsten Aspekte der Telematiksysteme

Mit Einsatz von Telematik im Güterverkehr höhere Marktanteile erreichen und effizienter, schneller, wirtschaftlicher und vor allem sicherer agieren

Übergeordnete Ziele sind zu verfolgen, dazu gehören die geringe Gefährdung von Leben und Gesundheit, die Sicherstellung des Verkehrs bei minimaler Belastung der Infrastruktur und die Sicherstellung internationaler Wettbewerbsfähigkeit

Anforderungen an die ICT-Infrastruktur aus Sicht des technischen und wirtschaftlichen Umfeldes (Teil 2)
05.09.2012 - v06

Moderne Kommunikationstechnologie und Datenverarbeitung sollen mittels Telematiksystemen die tägliche Arbeit im Schienenverkehr erleichtern

Die Interoperabilität bei der Einführung von neuen Kommunikationsmöglichkeiten, Sicherheitskonzepten oder Gebührensystemen ist grenzüberschreitend sicherzustellen

Datenübertragungsverzögerungen und diversen Fehler sollen möglichst unterbunden werden

Mit Hilfe von Telematiklösungen soll mehr Transparenz geschaffen werden

Fahrwerke eines Wagens permanent auf Schäden und Unregelmäßigkeiten untersuchen

Die Fahrstrecke soll permanent überwacht werden können

Lieferungen sollen exakt nachverfolgt werden können

Computer- und Softwaretechnologien müssen berücksichtigt werden

Es bestehen Anforderungen an Elektrik, Elektronik, Sicherheit und Umweltschutz

Individuelle Telematiklösungen sollen leicht an neue Anforderungen angepasst und ausgebaut werden können

Mitteilungen, Statusmeldungen und Anweisungen sollen sicher und schnell übermittelt werden

Standzeiten sollen reduziert oder Leerfahrten vermieden werden

Sehr hohe Zuverlässigkeit und Verfügbarkeit für die Anwender

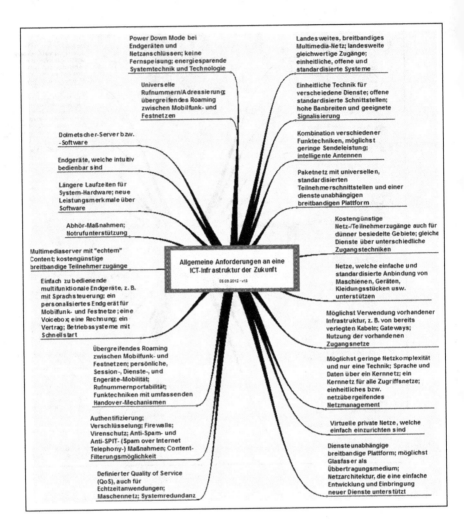

Power Down Mode bei
Endgeräten und
Netzanschlüssen; keine
Fernspeisung; energiesparende
Systemtechnik und Technologie

Landesweites, breitbandiges
Multimedia-Netz; landesweite
gleichwertige Zugänge;
einheitliche, offene und
standardisierte Systeme

Universelle
Rufnummern/Adressierung;
übergreifendes Roaming
zwischen Mobilfunk- und
Festnetzen

Einheitliche Technik für
verschiedene Dienste; offene
standardisierte Schnittstellen;
hohe Banbreiten und geeignete
Signalisierung

Dolmetscher-Server bzw.
-Software

Kombination verschiedener
Funktechniken, möglichst
geringe Sendeleistung;
intelligente Antennen

Endgeräte, welche intuitiv
bedienbar sind

Längere Laufzeiten für
System-Hardware; neue
Leistungsmerkmale über
Software

Paketnetz mit universellen,
standardisierten
Teilnehmerschnittstellen und einer
diensteunabhängigen
breitbandigen Plattform

Abhör-Maßnahmen;
Notrufunterstützung

Multimediaserver mit "echtem"
Content; kostengünstige
breitbandige Teilnehmerzugänge

Kostengünstige
Netz-/Teilnehmerzugänge auch für
dünner besiedelte Gebiete; gleiche
Dienste über unterschiedliche
Zugangstechniken

Einfach zu bedienende
multifunktionale Endgeräte, z. B.
mit Sprachsteuerung; ein
personalisiertes Endgerät für
Mobilfunk- und Festnetze; eine
Voicebox; eine Rechnung; ein
Vertrag; Betriebssysteme mit
Schnellstart

**Allgemeine Anforderungen an eine
ICT-Infrastruktur der Zukunft**
05.09.2012 - v15

Netze, welche einfache und
standardisierte Anbindung von
Maschinen, Geräten,
Kleidungsstücken usw.
unterstützen

Möglichst Verwendung vorhandener
Infrastruktur, z. B. von bereits
verlegten Kabeln; Gateways;
Nutzung der vorhandenen
Zugangsnetze

Übergreifendes Roaming
zwischen Mobilfunk- und
Festnetzen; persönliche,
Session-, Dienste-, und
Engeräte-Mobilität;
Rufnummernportabilität;
Funktechniken mit umfassenden
Handover-Mechanismen

Möglichst geringe Netzkomplexität
und nur eine Technik; Sprache und
Daten über ein Kernnetz; ein
Kernnetz für alle Zugriffsnetze;
einheitliches bzw.
netzübergreifendes
Netzmanagement

Authentifizierung;
Verschlüsselung; Firewalls;
Virenschutz; Anti-Spam- und
Anti-SPIT- (Spam over Internet
Telephony-) Maßnahmen; Content-
Filterungsmöglichkeit

Virtuelle private Netze, welche
einfach einzurichten sind

Definierter Quality of Service
(QoS), auch für
Echtzeitanwendungen;
Maschennetz; Systemredundanz

Diensteunabhängige
breitbandige Plattform; möglichst
Glasfaser als
Übertragungsmedium;
Netzarchitektur, die eine einfache
Entwicklung und Einbringung
neuer Dienste unterstützt

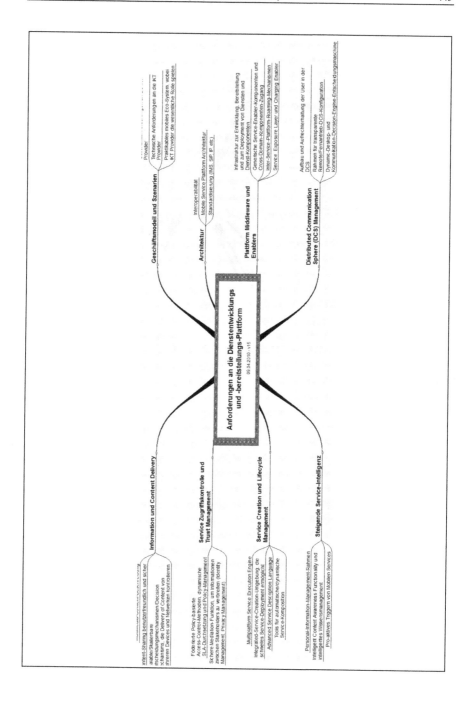

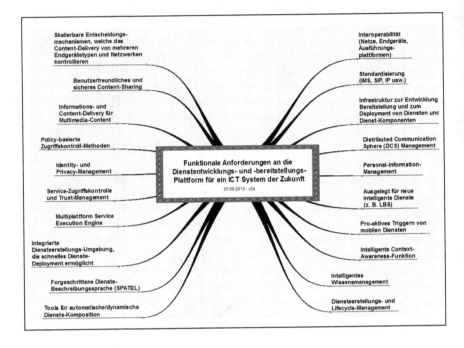

Skalierbare Entscheidungs-
mechanismen, welche das
Content-Delivery von mehreren
Endgerätetypen und Netzwerken
kontrollieren

Benutzerfreundliches und
sicheres Content-Sharing

Informations- und
Content-Delivery für
Multimedia-Content

Policy-basierte
Zugriffskontroll-Methoden

Identity- und
Privacy-Management

Service-Zugriffskontrolle
und Trust-Management

Multiplattform Service
Execution Engine

Integrierte
Diensteerstellungs-Umgebung,
die schnelles Dienste-
Deployment ermöglicht

Forgeschrittene Dienste-
Beschreibungssprache (SPATEL)

Tools für automatische/dynamische
Dienste-Komposition

Interoperabilität
(Netze, Endgeräte,
Ausführungs-
plattformen)

Standardisierung
(IMS, SIP, IP usw.)

Infrastruktur zur Entwicklung
Bereitstellung und zum
Deployment von Diensten und
Dienst-Komponenten

Distributed Communication
Sphere (DCS) Management

Personal-Information-
Management

Ausgelegt für neue
intelligente Dienste
(z. B. LBS)

Pro-aktives Triggern von
mobilen Diensten

Intelligente Context-
Awareness-Funktion

Intelligentes
Wissensmanagement

Diensteerstellungs- und
Lifecycle-Management

Funktionale Anforderungen an die
Dienstentwicklungs- und -bereitstellungs-
Plattform für ein ICT System der Zukunft

05.09.2012 · v24

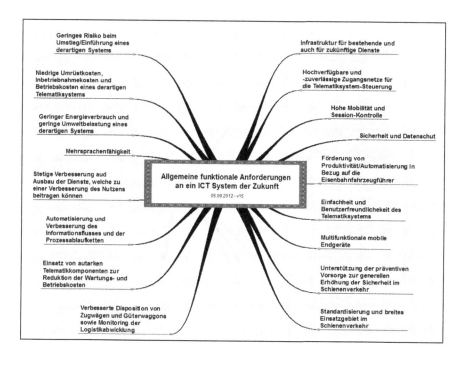

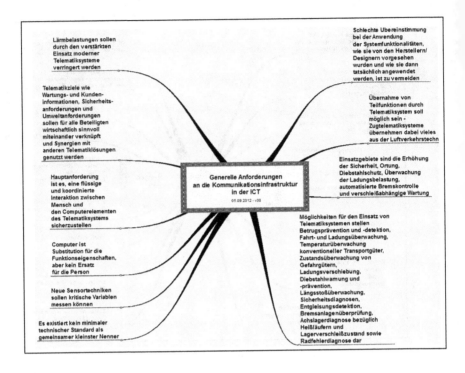

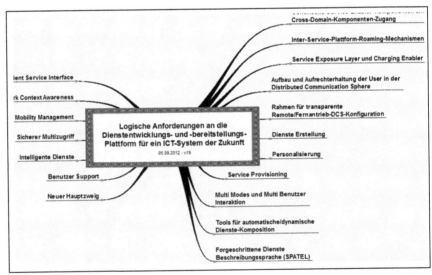

10.6 Consolidated Codes

Consolidated Codes from the Pilot Interviews

Mobility	Simple to Use	Data Protection	Compatibility	Relationship User - End-Device and SDP	Relationship User - Network and SDP	Relationship SDP and ICT system
being mobile anywhere and anytime (four/four)	easy to handle and use (three/four)	gaining access to own data and services (two/four)	integrating existing environments (three/four)	web-based SDP must support a broad range of enddevices	different connections to standard network technologies is a must (WWAN, WLAN, Wimax, Bluetooth)	SDP as standard gatway for ICT service-related user interation
access to resources independent of actual location (three/four)	supporting different types of enddevices (two/four)	Protection of user data and information (two/four)	enddevice compatability and broad range of different devices (two/four)	support in displaying different contents independently of display sizes	mechanism for controling the cheapest network connection at the actual point of location of the user	standard technologies and interfaces are a must for SDPs
supporting standardised wireless technologies (two/four)	generating trust and giving the enduser the feeling of dealing with a reliable working device	personalise the portal with the own used services (one/four)	use of different network types (one/four)	mobility and session stability is a must for enddevices and networks	automatic interaction with user, regarding connection possibilities within the networks	web and IP based mechanism for linking an ICT system with an SDP
being always connected with the ICT equipment (one/four)	web-based platfrom (one/four)	being under surveillance (one/four)	Minor costs for integrating existing environments (one/four)	personalised access to SDP and provided services anytime and anyplace	IMS and SIP as IP-based standard technolgies for SDPs	very important to address the challenges for users in SDPs as gateways to ICT systems
having access to important data files at all times (one/four)	litte count of interactions to use the wanted service or application (one/four)			group and personalise own service package		SDPs as standard communication technology for ICT systems

Consolidated Codes from the Second Interview Phase

Mobility	Simple and Friendly to Use	Wide Filed of Services	Cost-Effectiveness	Data Security and Protection	Infrastructure Compatibility	Relationship User / End-Device	Relationship End-Device / SDP	Relationship User / Network	Relationship Network / SDP	Relationship SDP / ICT System
being mobile anywhere and anytime (seven/seven)	easy to handle and use (five/seven)	ICT services should be available in a broad range, on a service provider SDP (three/seven)	has to be affordable for everyone (three/seven)	gain access to own data and services (four/seven)	integrate existing environments (five/seven)	mobility and Session stability is a must for enddevices and networks	web-based SDP must support a broad range of enddevices	users want to have high performance and available access to their services and applications	different connections to standard network technologies is a must (WWAN, WLAN, Wimax, Bluetooth)	SDP as standard gatway for ICT service-related user interation
access to resources at any network on any device (five/seven)	support different types of enddevices (five/seven)	provided services should be combined with others (two/seven)	services have to be affordable for a broad range of users (two/seven)	protect users' data and information (three/seven)	enddevice compatability and broad range of different devices (five/seven)	personalised access to SDP and provided services anytime and anyplace	support in displaying different contents independent of display sizes	mechanism to control the cheapest network connection at the actual location of the user	automatic interaction with user regarding the connection possibilities of the networks	standard technologies and interfaces are a must for SDPs
being cost efficient by using network ressources (three/seven)	content has to be dynamic for different types of enddevices and displays (four/seven)	services should be developed on standard technologies and offered for a broad range of use (two/seven)	automatic network switching mechanism has to be controlled in a cost efficient way for the users (two/seven)	offer reliable access to own services (two/seven)	use of different network types (three/seven)	group and personalise own service package		users want to have their own selection possibility for selecting a performant or cost effective network connection	IMS and SIP as IP-based standard technologies for SDPs	web and IP based mechanisms to link an ICT system with an SDP
support WWAN and WLAN, WiMAX technologies (two/seven)	litte count of interactions to use the wanted service or application (two/seven)	SDPs will bring increasing benefit for service and application providers, in delivering a broad range of services to users (one/seven)		personalise the portal with own services (one/seven)	minor cost for integrating existing environments (two/seven)					very important in addressing the challenges for users in SDPs as gatway to ICT systems
user's decision to switch to another network resource (two/seven)	support of a broad range of smartphones (one/seven)			being under surveilliance (one/seven)	standard technologies and components have to be used (one/seven)					#NAME?
having stable and reliable connections at anyplace (one/seven)										

Consolidated Codes from the Third Interview Phase

Simple to Use	Mobility	Wide Range of Services	Cost-Control	Data Security and Protection	Infrastructure Compatibility	Relationship User / End- Device	Relationship User / SDP	Relationship User / Network	Relationship Network / SDP	Relationship End-Device / SDP
simple to use (four/four)	being mobile on any network on any device and anytime (three/four)	provides many different services (two/four)	managable costs for everyone (three/four)	protected access to data and resources (four/four)	integrate existing environments (three/four)	mobility and Session stability is a must for enddevices and networks	easy to handle and administrate	performance and high available access to services and applications	different connections to standard network technologies is a must (WWAN, WLAN, Wimax, Bluetooth)	SDP as standard gatway for ICT service-related user interation
user acceptance (two/four)	session control and stable when user is moving (two/four)	service development and creation (two/four)	affordable for a wide field of users (two/four)	reliable access to user accounts (two/four)	compatible enddevices (two/four)	personalised access to SDP and provided services anytime and anyplace	a wide range of enddevices must be supported by the SDP	mechanism to control network connection at the actual location, from a cost and a quality service point of view	automatic interaction with user regarding connection possibilities of the networks	standard technologies and interfaces is a must for SDPs
user friendly (two/four)	support of mobile technologies (two/four)	services must be deployable (one/four)	good development of network coverage (two/four)	personalise own account (one/four)	integration of different network types (three/seven)	group and personalise own service packages	mobile technology standards must be supported by SDP and enddevices	users need possibility to select network type by themselves	IMS and SIP as IP-based standard technolgies for SDPs	web and IP based mechanism to link an ICT system with an SDP
interaction controlled by the user (two/four)	high available network access and reliable connections (one/four)	easy to operate, deploy and develop with no or very little downtimes (one/four)	offer own created service groups also for other users (one/four)	surveillance and data security (one/four)		confidence in integrating more and more enddevices in daily working and leisure activities	confidence to store user data in cloud-based infrastructure SDP	different standard network types with broadband capacity		very important to address challenges for users in SDPs as gatway to ICT systems
SDP easy to administrate and personalisable (one/four)	stable broadband connection while moving (one/four)					use applications and services reliable	confidence to use services from application and services providers			SDPs as standard communication technology for ICT systems
support of a wide range of enddevices(one/fo ur)							ability to support user needs with technologies and trust building activities			

11 Appendix D – DVD with Data Sources and Raw Data

11.1 Table of Contents

The following table of contents points out the document structure of the data sources and rough data related to this study and consolidates all data and materials which were relevant for this investigation:

- Colour-coded Interviews
- Conferences
- Criteria Catalogue
- Data Collection
- Fact Finding Tool
- Graphics
- Literature Research
- Methodology
- Mind Maps
- Peer-reviewed Papers
- Progress Documentation

Printed in the United States
By Bookmasters